Inside Newark

RIVERGATE REGIONALS

Rivergate Regionals is a collection of books published by Rutgers University Press focusing on New Jersey and the surrounding area. Since its founding in 1936, Rutgers University Press has been devoted to serving the people of New Jersey and this collection solidifies that tradition. The books in the Rivergate Regionals Collection explore history, politics, nature and the environment, recreation, sports, health and medicine, and the arts. By incorporating the collection within the larger Rutgers University Press editorial program, the Rivergate Regionals Collection enhances our commitment to publishing the best books about our great state and the surrounding region.

Inside Newark

Decline, Rebellion, and the
Search for Transformation

ROBERT CURVIN

RUTGERS UNIVERSITY PRESS

New Brunswick, New Jersey and London

Library of Congress Cataloging-in-Publication Data
Curvin, Robert.
Inside Newark : decline, rebellion, and the search for
transformation / Robert Curvin.
pages cm. — (Rivergate regionals collection)
Includes bibliographical references and index.
ISBN 978-0-8135-6571-2 (hardback)
ISBN 978-0-8135-6572-9 (e-book)
1. Newark (N.J.)—Politics and government. 2. Political culture—
New Jersey—Newark. 3. Urban renewal—New Jersey—Newark.
4. Newark (N.J.)—Social conditions. 5. Newark (N.J.)—
Economic conditions.   I. Title.
F144.N657C87 2014
320.09749'32—dc23   2013037741

A British Cataloging-in-Publication record for this book is
available from the British Library.

Visit our website: http://rutgerspress.rutgers.edu

Manufactured in the United States of America

In memory of Professor Duane Lockard, whose teaching and ideas are very much a part of this book.

Contents

Preface and Acknowledgments

At first, I was going to write a memoir about my life in Newark. A memoir would invariably have to be about me and it would be hard to give the many people I have worked with, and some who have done much more than I, sufficient attention. I then wondered if I should write a dispassionate, scholarly work on the city's politics. I decided that I could not do that either, for I could not avoid mentioning the movements, campaigns, and organizations that I have been involved with. I could not pretend that I was looking from the outside in. So this book is a hybrid of sorts, a mix of scholarly data sources and my personal experiences and reflections.

Including one's personal stories in a work that needs to be fair and grounded in fact is no easy feat. I, as author, have opinions and biases about some of the matters and individuals that I am obligated to write about. I have belonged to a long list of nonprofits in the city and I have contributed money and advice to political candidates. Some of the individuals I write about have been close friends, or in a few cases, former students. I have done several things in my effort to achieve a balanced account, including referring to historical records and archives of events I witnessed. For example, although I was the director of the Black and Puerto Rican Convention in 1969, I returned to many of the original records of that event as well as the excellent reporting of the convention by local newspapers. Secondly, I have talked with well over one hundred people about the events that I discuss over six decades of city life. For many of the interviews, I used a video camera, giving me a unique resource with some of the key figures in Newark's contemporary history. I also had one of the best local sounding boards a researcher can ever find: Richard

Cammarieri, who works for the New Community Corporation and is a dedicated soldier for every good cause in the city. During the early stages of writing this book, he read every chapter and returned with heaps of comments and criticisms. We did not always agree, but he often forced me to rethink or reappraise a statement, a comment, or a conclusion. In some cases, he pointed me to information or data of which I was not aware.

Many others also helped in reviewing the manuscript and offered helpful suggestions. Roland Anglin read several of the early chapters and a few of the later ones as well. Leonard Lieberman, a special friend of more than forty years, rendered timely critiques. Norman Glickman provided editorial advice on the first two chapters and was a terrific partner in our graduate seminar on postindustrial cities. Dan O'Flaherty, whose knowledge of the economic history of Newark and its financial challenges is unsurpassed, was generous with his time and insights. Thanks to Lisa Keller for her suggestions and encouragement. Clement A. Price would occasionally ask, "Bob, did you see this, or that?" Usually it was a gem I needed to know about. Nancy Zak made files of valuable data available to me. David Levering Lewis gave me several important suggestions and was a vital source of encouragement. Richard Roper shared his thoughts on the history and politics of the city. Special thanks to Kenneth T. Jackson and his nudge to tighten up the prose. Thanks also to Kendal Whitlock, Dennis Wygmans, and Frank Curvin, all of whom read parts of the manuscript. And special thanks to Joan Waring who gave me the first push: "Bob, when are you going to write your story?"

I am deeply indebted to all the staff at the Charles F. Cummings New Jersey Information Center at the Newark Public Library. The librarians there are simply superb and clearly have been left with some of that Charles Cummings devotion to Newark, and the countless researchers who are there every day. I would also like to thank Robert Morasco, Newark's city clerk, and his staff for providing me with access to the city archives. Special thanks to those city employees who granted me interviews or were helpful in making information available. Timothy Brown was a very careful and effective videographer. Beth Cohen, a Princeton student, spent a summer helping me to understand the East Ward. Nicholas Brown provided valuable assistance drafting charts and graphs. Tim Crist, president of the Newark History Society, and Warren Grover, the society's vice president, were supportive and always encouraging. They have made the telling and learning of the city's history an enriching community endeavor. Although the list is far too long to mention, I want to thank all of the people who gave videotaped interviews.

I owe a special thanks to James Hughes, dean of the Bloustein School of Planning and Public Policy at Rutgers University, who invited me to hang out following my retirement from philanthropy because I thought I might want to write a book. It was a critical step in the development of this project and gave me the opportunity to converse with Roland Anglin, Norman Glickman, Sanford Jaffe, Kathe Newman, Linda Stomato, Carl Van Horn, Cliff Zukin, and Dean Hughes as well, and to meet and interact with Bloustein students, all of which added to my learning. Many thanks go to Don Sutton for his advice. Adi Hovav was a terrific first editor. Many thanks to Marlie Wasserman and all of the staff at Rutgers University Press. Marlie saw possibilities in a pretty rough draft and provided the guidance to complete this project.

Last, but surely not least, thanks to my wife, Patricia. I could not have done this without her support, encouragement, and advice. She was there whenever I needed an outside eye for some of the more complicated passages. She has tolerated—usually with good spirit— the mounds of files and papers in the house.

While this has been a work of many hands, I alone am responsible for every error, every mistake, and every judgment and misjudgment in this book. Over the years, I have spent many hours in conversation with the residents of Newark as well as with the many people who have important roles in the city but do not live within its borders. I have also attended many public and governmental meetings regarding issues of large and small import. I am aware that fairness and objectivity, as in life, can be a challenge whether writing about an adversary or a friend. I have tried my best to be forthright and fair to all. There are indeed many risks and complications in writing from the inside. However, there are also opportunities and possibilities for capturing a richer, more complex, and more powerful story. As best as I could, I have tried to achieve that in an effort to provide the kind of learning that might help Newark and urban dwellers elsewhere move their places forward.

Inside Newark

Introduction

A Newarker Examines His City

ON THE EVENING of July 12, 1967, I was in my kitchen with my wife and four year old son, Frank. It was about 9:00 P.M., and we were having a cup of tea with our guest, Connie Brown, who had come to Newark to work with Students for a Democratic Society (SDS). The phone rang. The woman on the line told me with great excitement that a man had been beaten at the Fourth Precinct police station in Newark's Central Ward and I should get there right away. I left immediately. When I arrived at the precinct about fifteen minutes later, a large crowd had already assembled. I discovered that a black cab driver, who I later learned was a man named John Smith, had been dragged into the precinct by his legs, with his body bouncing along the pavement. Some observers thought he was dead. For everyone on the scene, the anger was intense. One could sense the fury in the air.

The crowd seemed to grow by the second. I decided to go into the police station and learn exactly what had happened. When I went to the desk, an officer told me a man had been arrested, that he was in a cell, and that he could not tell me anything more. Just at that moment, Police Inspector Kenneth Melchior arrived. Melchior, who recognized me from my civil rights activity, spoke to the officer at the desk and then asked that I accompany him to the cell. At the cell, I saw a man in great pain. He complained that he had been beaten. He said that he had bruises on his head and severe pains in his side and stomach. Melchior said that an ambulance was on the way.

Melchior and I then went to the lobby of the precinct, where other community leaders had gathered. The crowd had now swelled to several hundred. The police asked a select group of community leaders, including myself, to tell the crowd to disperse and go home, that the prisoner was on his way to the hospital. That did not seem like a feasible option to the group of about seven people, which included Tim Still, a revered leader of public housing tenants, and Oliver Lofton, the director of the Legal Services Program. I was asked to go out and speak to the crowd. I mounted a car that was parked in front of the building and told the crowd that the prisoner was alive, that this was another example of police mistreatment of a black citizen, but that we should not respond with violence. We could not win or accomplish anything that way. I urged the crowd to organize a peaceful march to City Hall where we would let the mayor and city officials know that we would not accept this kind of treatment anymore.

Suddenly rocks began to fly over my head, aimed at the police. The police retreated into the precinct house, as did I. As the police were donning their riot gear, we pleaded with them to allow us to make another try at calming the crowd and organizing a peaceful demonstration. We went back outside and I mounted the car with a bullhorn provided by the police. Perhaps one-fourth of the crowd responded to my request and began to line up for a march, but before I could dismount the car, a hail of rocks and Molotov cocktails rained through the air, aimed at the police and the building right behind me. The burning gasoline slid down the façade of the building. With nightsticks flailing, the police then charged toward the crowd, and one of the worst riots in American history began. For Newark, perched along the Passaic River and founded in 1666 by Puritans from Connecticut, those five days in July 1967 would deeply change city life and politics.

Newark, with all of its troubles, is a many-sided story, full of good life, bad life, fun times, painful times, opportunity, and many of the remnants and legacies of an old American industrial city as well as the intimations of a postindustrial city. Newark speaks volumes regarding the plight of America's urban places and the enduring effects of poverty, disadvantage, and race. And I am an elder of the Newark story.

I was born in Newark and spent my childhood in the adjacent

town of Belleville, a section populated mainly by Italian immigrants. I had my first formal job as a teenager operating an elevator in Bamberger's department store and attended college at Rutgers University in Newark. I have lived in Newark since I returned from military service in the 1950s, interrupted only by four years in Princeton attending graduate school. I raised my children in the city and was a leader in the Newark protest movement for racial justice in the 1960s. I was also part of the cadre that worked for Kenneth A. Gibson's drive to become the first black mayor of Newark. So I am the guy who gets the Newark questions at a party in New York or on a plane ride to Washington. Were you there during the riots? Do you know Cory Booker? Do you think he will be president some day?

It isn't ever really possible to have a complete and satisfactory conversation about this sometimes wild and rambunctious city, which nonetheless has made me and my family love it. How, for example, do you explain mayor-council relations and the horse trading at City Hall in a casual exchange? How do you paint the variety and vast differences among the city's ethnic and racial neighborhoods? How do you describe the pathos of Newark's poverty, the down-and-out families, the crime, the bold and brutal reminders of racial injustice and segregation? How do you tell someone over the boom of airplane engines that Newark is also a vibrant and hopeful city, driven by gritty determination? Although Newark is in many ways a unique city, it is also a representative case of American urban life, a metaphor for both the resiliency and excitement of the urban journey as well as the truth about urban hardship. While Newark is by no means the only city that is home to large numbers of people who are economically at the bottom of the ladder, it is rare to find another city in the United States with such a high proportion of poor people.

For several decades, Newark has been undergoing a slow but steady recovery from the decline that began just prior to World War II and reached a peak shortly after the civil disturbances in 1967. Newark today is old, tired, and decrepit, but it is rebuilding. In downtown Newark, there is the world-class New Jersey Performing Arts Center, as well as the Newark Museum, which ranks among the best of its peers in the nation. A few large law firms remain in the city, and there has been a spate of new commercial enterprises. Recent major developments include the Prudential Center, home to the New Jersey

Devils, a National Hockey League franchise, and a venue for con-
certs, circuses, and college basketball games. Since 1970, there has
been extensive growth among the area's five colleges and universities,
bringing 40,000 commuting and residential students into the city
each day. Newark's seaport and airport, both under the management
of the Port Authority of New York and New Jersey, are major employers and contributors to the local economy. While Newark's neighborhoods lag behind downtown renewal projects, they have not been
neglected, at least not physically. Almost every poor residential area
of the city is dotted with handsome new brick-front homes, replacing the traditional wood-frame housing from the beginning of the
last century.

Still, there are graphic signs of a decayed and abandoned city,
often in close proximity to the shining new developments. Empty,
crumbling structures and the barren lots that have marred the
cityscape for decades remain. If you were to stand on Broad Street at
Military Park, just west of the dazzling performing arts complex, and
look southward along the city's commercial spine, you would see the
darkened windows of a huge abandoned department store building,
beckoning for change. The crime rate began falling in 1999, but crime
remains a serious social and political concern that has worsened
with the effects of the recent economic downturn. Joblessness generally continues to be a major challenge. Most significant, there are
only a handful of schools in which pupils are meeting state standards
in language arts and mathematics. As some law firms move into the
city, others leave. Day by day, the old, poor, and struggling Newark
challenges the new, recovering Newark in defining the city's image,
quality of life, and future.

Most of us have a primal attachment to the place of our rearing.
Other than religion and family relations, one is hard-pressed to
find a more frequently discussed subject in the conduct of human
affairs. Although places cannot physically hold our memories, they
can help us to recall the warmth of good times as well as the less
pleasant memories that shape our lives. The passion that went into
writing this book stems from the inseparability of my life and attachment to Newark, not to mention the trauma of witnessing a historic
rebellion. I do not expect most readers to share this passion or experience as I attempt to chronicle the political and economic events

that undergird Newark's decline and its recent struggle to reinvent itself. Newark is a story of the struggle to transform a postindustrial American city and all that implies. These are themes that have been examined many times, especially in the field of urban studies. Nevertheless, I introduce personal observations as well as the observations and experiences of those who were closely involved with city life and politics. My aim is to use my access and knowledge of the community, its leaders, and the city's political culture to illuminate the nexus of ethnic succession and urban decline. In doing so, I also address the limitations of racial and ethnic politics in Newark, which came to represent a new urban reality. As a result of the departure of the white ethnic groups, the city's black and Latino population became the majority and captured the key political offices. The opening of the political system was supposed to come with group benefits—or so argued the democratic theorists. But unlike other ethnic groups, political power for blacks and Latinos did not readily translate into group benefits in Newark.

The politics of decline offers only a partial explanation. The leaders of postindustrial Newark made choices, and many, if not most, chose the least common denominator—simply trading for a job or position with little or no regard for the social concerns or conditions of the poorer citizens of the city. Indeed, Newark has a long history of patronage embedded in almost every aspect of city politics. Many American cities, not just Newark, struggle to escape this conundrum. Ultimately, the extremes of democracy have to be balanced with efforts to build a civic culture that is not overly reliant on electoral politics. At the risk of generalizing, Newark's civic culture is not strong. Although there are a few examples of what ordinary citizens can do to protect the interests of neighborhoods and common citizens, overall, Newark's civic culture is too often overwhelmed by the strength of extreme electoral politics.

Mayor Cory A. Booker articulated a vision rare for any urban community and certainly rare for Newark. "We in Newark, in this city, are going to lead the nation in the transformation of urban communities," he frequently promised. Did he deliver? Can there be rejuvenation in Newark with benefits flowing to residents, leading to a better quality of life in the city? Can there be meaningful reform of education? Can new leaders address the growing cadre of jobless young black and Latino men, surely one of the most important challenges of all, with more effectiveness than their predecessors? As I attempt to examine the extent to which Newark can reach for such a future, I rely on its recent history; an examination of its social systems and politics; its relationship to the regional, state, and national environment; and the stories and voices of the many people who have been a part of Newark's journey over the last half century.

⟨1⟩

About Newark

ONE OF THE NATION'S oldest cities, Newark was founded in 1666 by a faction of Congregationalists who ventured south from New Haven, Connecticut, to establish a church and community that they fervently hoped would continue their religious and social values. The adult settlers were all born in England, but they also considered themselves New Englanders. They were deeply committed to the Bible and "sought to establish a community where church and civil state were in close alliance."[1] Why these settlers, about three hundred strong, left New Haven had as much to do with political events in England as it did with circumstances in New Haven. The New England families had sided with the forces that had executed King Charles I and had thus interrupted the monarchy. They were at peace with the times and their autonomous church-centered governing system; membership in the church and land holding were requirements for voting rights—that is, for men only. However, when the monarchy was restored with the return of Charles II, their world took a disastrous turn. Soon an edict came from England that the New Haven colonies were to be merged with the state of Connecticut. Life would surely be different. New Haven churches restricted the vote to members, while Connecticut churches did not. New Haven churches also restricted the sacrament of baptism to church members and their infant children. In contrast, many Connecticut churches allowed for the baptism of grandchildren of church members even if their parents had not become members of the church. Those in New Haven would no longer be able to live by their own rules and conception of a godly life, and so they left for what was to become Newark, a place on the

"Passaick" River, carefully explored and purchased from the Native Americans by a delegation led by Robert Treat.[2]

In an essay presented to the Newark History Society, Tim Crist offered an illuminating reflection on the motivation of the settlers and how the patterns of their lives provide an important backdrop for understanding the relationship of Newark to many of its adjacent communities. Crist, a trustee of the Newark Public Library and the president of the Newark History Society, points out that unlike the settlers of New York, the founders of Newark did not come to establish a trading post or to build vast estates that could be worked by slaves and indentured servants. They aimed simply to worship God and build a common life together. They shared the New England view that when a town got too big and there was no more land to distribute within easy distance of the church, it was time to move to the next area with land and establish a new church and a new town government. As a result of this New England tradition of church-centered community, Newark shrank while surrounding towns expanded. Crist further explains, "Today, Newark is comprised of only twenty-five square miles, but the city has historical ties to all the surrounding towns. . . . Newark's current lack of scale and lack of space, which clearly limits so many choices, can be traced to its founders and their puritan ideals of church and community."[3]

Located a mere fifteen miles from New York City, Newark developed rather quickly and became a leading industrial center during the late 1800s. Excellent geographical and natural features for water and eventually rail transportation helped drive development. By the beginning of the twentieth century, Newark was one of the leading manufacturing cities in the nation. It was of course a beneficiary of the Industrial Revolution in Europe, as immigrants from that continent frequently brought their skill and entrepreneurship to America to tap new markets. Newark was a popular destination for immigrants from all over Europe, especially Germany, England, Ireland, and Italy.

The names and brands that originated in Newark give a measure of the city's role in industry: Dr. Edward Weston of Weston Electrical Dynamo; Wiss, maker of scissors and shears; shoe manufacturers Johnston and Murphy; John Wesley Hyatt, the inventor of celluloid; the Schickhaus meat producers; Mrs. Wagner's pies; Breyer's ice cream; George and William Clark, who produced thread; and Carrier engineering. The most concentrated area of industry is known as the Ironbound, where paint and chemicals as well as metalwork and crafts were produced. (The Ironbound district acquires its name from the fact that its geography has been shaped by the numerous rail lines—Pennsylvania, Jersey Central, and B & O—that once ran through Newark.) Other areas of the city had a variety of small and large enterprises, such as an electrical products plant in the Third Ward; a Tiffany jewelry factory at the northern end of the city; beer factories with the labels of Krueger, Ballantine, and Pabst in several areas; bread, food, and candy makers that often gave off such sweet scents that it was possible to close one's eyes and identify the neighborhood through which you were passing. The odors of the factories where leather goods were made, or tanneries, were notorious for their smell.

Like urban places throughout the Northeast and Midwest, Newark has lost much of its manufacturing base to cheap labor in the Sunbelt or abroad. The loss has had a devastating impact on Newark's economy. Like Boston, Detroit, and Baltimore, the city is disadvantaged by the well-known list of ills common to urban America. Crime severely tarnishes its reputation and is a major hurdle in convincing businesses to come to Newark. The education of children, many of them from poverty-stricken families, remains a topic of conflict and controversy. In 2011, the graduation rate from the city's public high schools was just above 50 percent, and many students who graduate are still unprepared for the job market.[4] And Newark, like many postindustrial cities, is heavily dependent on subsidies from the state and federal governments to meet the service needs of its residents.

The most striking feature has been the decrease in population over the last six decades. In 1950, the population totaled 434,000; in 2000, it dropped to a low of 272,500. According to the 2010 census, the city's population is now 277,000. While over half of the population is black and Newark has had black mayoral leadership since 1970, the demographics are shifting as well: the black majority will likely be closer to parity in several decades with the Latino population, which currently numbers about 93,000 (33.8 percent). Twenty-eight percent of the city's population lives below the poverty line, and the median household income is $35,659, compared to a state median of

$69,811. Only 25.3 percent of Newark families own their own homes, one of the lowest rates for any city in the nation, and a mere 60 percent of the adult population over twenty-five years old has a high school diploma.[5]

Since its founding, Newark has undergone many transformations, with each era leaving behind its own indelible mark. The 1967 disturbances surely worsened the city's plight, but it did not mark the onset of Newark's troubles. While the postriot period saw a burst of disinvestment, the signs of exodus and decline began to appear in the 1930s, when the entrepreneurial and business leadership packed up and headed for the suburbs. In her study of Newark schools, the prominent urban education scholar Jean Anyon wrote: "In the thirties, a decline in economic resources led to a decline in city services and in the maintenance of the infrastructure. Lack of resources had a dampening effect on education as well. . . . The bias against cities in the state's reliance on local property taxes to fund education became apparent in this decade, as dwindling 'ratables' led to impoverishment of the city government and no meaningful state or federal support existed."[6] The mansions on High Street, with their views of the New York skyline, had housed some of the wealthiest and most powerful families in America. They were, however, on small lots. Suburbia offered copious acreage at low prices. The *Newarker*, the Chamber of Commerce of Newark magazine, would lament as early as 1925 that "no one lives in Newark anymore, but instead in the city's suburbs."[7] Times were very hard during the Great Depression, particularly in industrial Newark where many manufacturing plants slowed to a halt. The boom of the World War II years inspired false hopes that the city would regain economic prominence. It was not to be.

A Tour of the City

More than a century ago, the various areas that make up the city of Newark were given names based on an historical, structural, or demographic feature. Thus were named neighborhoods such as Weequahic, Ivy Hill, Ironbound, Clinton Hill, Roseville, or Doodletown. Since the adoption of mayor-council government and ward elections

Source: City of Newark

⟨ FIGURE 1.1 ⟩

Map of Newark Neighborhoods

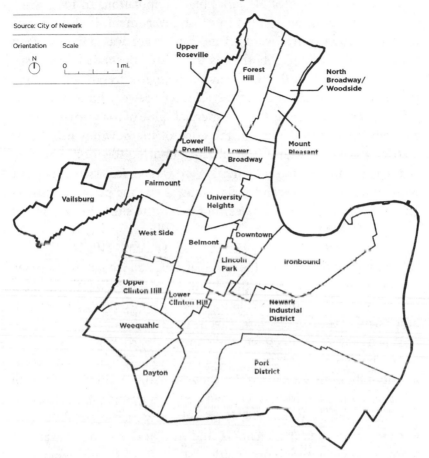

Source: Shifting/Forward 2025, City of Newark Master Plan Re-examination Report, February 2009, 2:28

in 1954, city residents are defined by the neighborhoods and wards in which they live. There are five wards in Newark, and dozens of neighborhoods. Elections for the city council are based both on wards and four at-large positions while nine advisory school board positions are filled through at-large elections. (Since 1954, the wards have been redrawn at least twice, thus moving some neighborhoods to different wards. For example, the Roseville neighborhood is now in the West Ward; previously it was in the North Ward.)

The Central Ward is where the entrepreneurial foundations of the Jewish community were built. Later, the Central Ward would be home to the largest portion of Newark's black population. In 1953, when the charter change altered the form of government, it also allowed for the creation of five wards. The Third Ward was one of at least three heavily black neighborhoods that were consolidated to create the Central Ward. In the war years of the 1940s, the manufacturing plants of General Electric and the Krueger Brewery hummed in the area. Springfield Avenue, the commercial spine of the ward, still runs through the community from the edge of the downtown business district of the city westward to the neighboring town of Irvington. In the 1940s and 1950s, the Central Ward was a lively, swinging place with numerous taverns and social clubs. It was the place of business and worship for Jewish families, and it was the stomping ground of Prohibition kingpin Abner "Longie" Zwillman, perhaps Newark's first national celebrity. It was also the site of an emerging black political strength and produced the first black elected leadership in Essex County in the 1940s and in the city in 1954. For Newark's blacks, it was an area well known for its poverty, its run-down housing, and other symbols of second-class citizenship.

When Jewish families left the Central Ward beginning in the 1920s, they migrated to the city's South Ward and established a community rich in religious traditions, culture, and politics. The Jewish community of Newark has left many enduring imprints on the city. The South Ward's Weequahic High School, which opened in 1929, was one of the area's best schools, and many of its students went on to four-year colleges and universities, producing a second generation of professionals in law, medicine, and science, including the literary giant Philip Roth. The ward is also home to Beth Israel Medical Center, a world-class institution founded over one hundred years ago. Leaders of "The Beth," now owned by a private network of health facilities, fought the impulse to leave Newark during the city's hardest times. The South Ward has two distinct sections: Clinton Hill, which is on the ward's northern side, and the Weequahic area. Prior to the major and destructive bifurcation of the area in the early 1960s by a large highway (Interstate 78), the neighborhoods were more coherent. Today, most of the ward is inhabited by blacks and Latinos. The Clinton Hill area is severely decayed and has high rates of poverty.

The Weequahic area is largely black, but economically diverse. Many of the city's black civic and political leaders occupy the well-kept single-family homes in this section of the ward.

While the Central Ward was a mostly Jewish community in the early twentieth century, the North Ward was the home of the majority of Italian immigrant families. The Italians, who came to Newark mostly from Naples, Sicily, and points in southern Italy, formed a tightly knit community around the Catholic parishes that dotted the area, which included family-owned shops and businesses that later grew into major enterprises in trucking, construction, crafts such as shoe making and tailoring, and services. Italian American elected officials who won offices in the 1940s, such as Mayor Ralph Villani, often lived in the North Ward. This ward was also the bailiwick of Mafia leader Richie "The Boot" Boiardo and his successor son, Tony Boy. The North Ward today has but a small share of the Italian Americans who lived there in the 1950s through the 1970s; most of that community headed to the suburbs and New Jersey Shore communities. Today, North Ward residents are largely Latino, though there are smaller groups of whites and blacks. Steve Adubato Sr., whose family came to the United States in the late nineteenth century, continues to live in the North Ward, although his children joined the exodus to the suburbs. Adubato is one of New Jersey's most powerful political leaders, and the North Ward is his political base. He operates his North Ward Center, which includes a network of social services and a charter school, from an old mansion on Mount Prospect Avenue. The North Ward is also home to Branch Brook Park, a four-hundred-acre park that now boasts the largest collection of blossoming cherry trees in the United States.

The West Ward was once the home of predominantly Irish and Italian civil servants, including firemen and police officers. Today, the largest group in the area is African American, followed by Haitian immigrants, although a large private housing development adjacent to Ivy Hill Park is home to immigrants from almost every corner of the world. The West Ward is also home to the largest Ukrainian Catholic church in the United States. In 2000, when the city's wards were last redrawn, the West Ward gained parts of the old North Ward such as the Roseville section and the area next to an entrance to Branch Brook Park. However, the redrawing carved out the famous Roman

Catholic Basilica of the Sacred Heart to ensure that it remained in the North Ward. South Orange Avenue traverses through the Central Ward, into and through the West Ward, continuing into adjacent South Orange.

The East Ward was home to a very diverse population that included Irish, Italian, and Polish immigrants, African Americans, and Portuguese. Today the population is dominated by Portuguese and Brazilian immigrants. The East Ward is generally divided into three distinct areas—Ironbound, Dayton South, and the downtown central business district east of Broad Street. The East Ward in particular also has a rich history of protest and social action, beginning with antinoise campaigns in the 1930s aimed at the growing air traffic over its neighborhoods. In more recent years, Ironbound activists fought against the toxic dumping and resultant pollution from the large and numerous chemical and paint factories in the area. Unfortunately, much of the area along the once vital river and the river itself have been despoiled by the spillage of dioxin, which was manufactured in the area.[8] Ironbound community groups have also led efforts to protect Riverbank Park, which is located on the northern edge of the ward and abuts the Passaic River. With the airport, the strong industrial and shipping businesses, and a very entrepreneurial Portuguese and Brazilian community, the East Ward remains the most economically vibrant area of the city. The East Ward's Portuguese and Brazilian restaurants and food shops are patronized by people from throughout the region, and on any weekend evening, Ferry Street, the commercial spine, is likely to be crowded with foot traffic. For more than a century, the Ironbound has been the home to most of the key manufacturers in the city. The Ironbound Manufacturing Association has for years been a fulcrum of business and political power.

City Politics and the Region

Newarkers live in two political worlds: the nonpartisan city and the partisan County of Essex, which includes twenty other municipalities. The nearby towns of East Orange, Irvington, and Orange have a large percentage of poor people much like Newark, while towns such as Millburn–Short Hills rank among the wealthiest communities in the nation. When Newark's population was 434,000 in 1950, it represented over 50 percent of the county's total. Now the population of Newark represents about 35 percent of the county's total population, which was 765,000 in 2010. City political leaders often enter politics through the activities of the county Democratic or Republican organizations, either as district leaders or as party functionaries. Although Newark city elections are nonpartisan, the partisan elections for district leader at the neighborhood level are very important, for district leaders select the ward chairmen for the party. It is the ward chair who can tap into the patronage system of the city and the county: he or she often identifies new emerging political activists, has control of the Election Day apparatus in the ward, and is likely to be in touch with residents/voters in the community. To build a local political machine, one has to have major influence and control over district leaders. In years past, the county control has passed from Protestants to Germans to a coalition of Irish and Jews. In the past decade however, the Newark-based political machine made up mainly of Italian Americans (led by Steve Adubato Sr. and county executive Joe DiVencenzo), blacks, and Latinos has controlled the county Democratic political apparatus.

Most employees in Newark's private and public sector jobs live outside the city, somewhere in Essex County, or in more distant suburban communities. In 2000, according to a report of the Newark Alliance, an organization sponsored by local business leaders to promote development, just 24.6 percent of the 147,000 jobs located in Newark were held by city residents while about 21 percent were held by Essex County residents.[9] That means that more than half of Newark's jobs were being held by people who did not live in Essex County, let alone Newark. That is one reason why Newark has such a hard time sustaining commercial activity after dark. Some residents of the more affluent areas of the county such as South Orange, Millburn–Short Hills, and Glen Ridge have little to do with Newark. They are loath to share or consolidate services with Newark, which might cut costs for the cities and suburbs. Some suburban residents fear the city because of the frequent incidents of crime. In 2008, several suburban high schools canceled scheduled football games with Newark schools after a rash of shootings in Newark.[10] Many suburban residents consider the cities to be responsible for their high property taxes, which is partly true, particularly since the New Jersey Supreme Court ordered the state to equalize funding for poor school districts (see chapter 9). Most of the commercial activities that once were within the city of Newark are now available at shopping malls in Livingston, Short Hills, and elsewhere. Federal, state, and county offices are located in Newark, but that doesn't bring many people to the city. However, there are reasons people travel to or through Newark. The Newark Museum, the New Jersey Performing Arts Center (NJPAC), and the Prudential Center, which is both a major entertainment venue and the home of the New Jersey Devil's hockey team, bring many suburban residents to the city. And suburbanites heading to far-off places are likely to use Newark Liberty Airport or Penn Station in downtown Newark. The city's governmental and civic institutions are staffed and governed by a combination of city residents and suburban dwellers, and many suburban residents grew up in Newark or lived, worked, or attended college in Newark. Some remain deeply involved in Newark's cultural and political worlds.

Why Newark Struggles

It is always risky to suggest this or that issue explains the dynamics of a community. Nonetheless, several issues help explain Newark's predicament, its decline, and its ongoing struggles. The powerful legacy of housing and mortgage policies; the historic and continuing impact of racism, poverty, and economic disadvantage; the culture of corruption in the city and state; the political fragmentation of decision making; and the city's small size have all contributed to Newark today. Again, it would be imprudent to distill Newark's problems down to one simple thing. Newark's challenges are a prism of what plagues contemporary urban areas around the nation. A look back explains the complexity and depth of today's Newark.

HOUSING POLICY

The discriminatory antiurban and antiblack national housing policies established by the Home Owners Loan Corporation in the

1930s, and later by its successor, the Federal Housing Administration (FHA), made a deep and perhaps indelible imprint in the social makeup of urban and suburban America. The FHA, created to stimulate the housing and construction industries by offering mortgage insurance to homebuyers, promulgated a list of restrictive regulations that essentially prohibited mortgage opportunities when buying a home within the boundaries of certain cities, leading to what is called redlining. The FHA rules also made it impossible for blacks to acquire bank mortgages for home buying anywhere. The message to white residents was to get out of urban communities if you wanted to own a home, which would likely cost less than a rental in the city. When federal appraisers looked at Newark in 1939, for example, not a single neighborhood was worthy of an "A" rating, the rating generally required for getting mortgage insurance for a bank loan.[11] Neither the tree-lined streets in the city's stable Jewish enclave in the South Ward nor the larger colonial homes that lined Roseville Avenue in the North Ward qualified. Blacks were locked into the city, and the cities of America bore the disadvantages of race and place. Federal policy set the terms for national and local banks to provide access to capital, and private real estate agencies followed suit. The National Association of Real Estate Boards once had a "code of ethics" that listed a long series of undesirable persons (bootleggers, prostitutes, gangsters) who should never be accommodated in the purchase of housing in a "good" neighborhood because they would be detrimental to property values. To emphasize the boundaries set by the code, a 1943 NAREB brochure included in the list of prohibited parties to a property sale was "a colored man of means who was giving his children a college education and thought they were entitled to live among whites."[12]

The implications of denying mortgages to an entire group have had far-reaching negative consequences. While the aim was to forestall integration of white neighborhoods, the result kept blacks in separate communities and denied them the housing choices available to everyone else. Almost one hundred years after the end of slavery, blacks were denied full economic citizenship, and the result was the same in other major cities in the East and the Midwest. In her book *Family Properties*, Beryl Satter of Rutgers University documents in illuminating detail the human toll on black families in Chicago, who were grossly exploited by speculators. Satter explains how blacks who wanted to own their own homes and had the financial means to do so could not get bank mortgages. They were sold properties under an arrangement called contract sales, which allowed them to buy from a seller without financing by a bank. Contract sales often meant paying as much as two or three times the price of a property that had been purchased by a speculator only weeks or months before. Moreover, if the black buyer missed a single payment, the seller could reclaim the property and sell it again—which happened often. In Satter's view, blacks were not only discriminated against by the mortgage industry but cheated out of their savings wealth, the kind of wealth that white families were able to build by having access to fair mortgages and open housing markets.[13]

In a much earlier analysis of the financing and ownership of slum housing in Newark, George Sternlieb suggested that low-cash housing transactions (such as contract sales) have a "built in inflationary element." In his 1966 analysis, Sternlieb contended that "the question of race is actually subordinate to economic risk, though undoubtedly significant racial prejudice still exists among lenders."[14] However, by 1966, the Essex County suburbs had opened up to blacks to a degree. In the 1950s, white neighborhoods in the Central Ward, the Clinton Hill section of the South Ward, and parts of Weequahic were "block-busted" by speculators, who used scare tactics to frighten white homeowners. White homeowners were led to believe that a black family moving into their neighborhood would quickly depreciate the value of their property, and thus many sold in panic, or sold directly to a black family at a higher than market price. The transactions were often similar to the arrangements that Satter documents in Chicago, where speculators could turn around a property for a 50 to 75 percent profit in two to three months.[15]

By the year 2000, Newark was among the most segregated cities in the nation, ranking high on the list with Detroit, Philadelphia, Chicago, Buffalo, and Boston.[16] The impact of segregation, partly facilitated by the exclusion of black people from the home mortgage market, cannot be underestimated, and the social and financial damage it has inflicted on society at large is immense. Mortgage exclusion and redlining not only denied blacks the opportunity to accumulate wealth, but also created multiple disadvantages in the

FRIED CHICKEN AND A BEAUTIFUL HOUSE

Those who lived in Newark in the 1950s and 1960s fondly remember Mrs. Amelia Stewart, one of the city's first successful black entrepreneurs. Mrs. Stewart could fry the best chicken you have ever tasted. Seeing an opportunity at the all-night gambling houses that thrived in the Third Ward, she would show up with pots of food. She had no bank, so she stashed her money in the corner of a clothes closet. When she had enough for a down payment, she found a beautiful home in the South Ward on Baldwin Avenue. She made a deal with the owner to pay off the cost on a monthly basis. No bank, no lawyer—just a handshake. Mrs. Stewart's home-based business eventually grew to several outstanding restaurants, first in the Central Ward and then in the South Ward. John Stewart, her son, who operated his own restaurant for over twenty-five years in the East Ward, recalls that as a child, each month his mother would give him a sum of money in an envelope to take to the seller of their house, who lived in Maplewood. "My mother would record each payment in a little book she kept," John said. "And I walked to the man's house and back every time!"

—conversation with John Stewart

areas of education, employment, health, and criminal justice. Racism reinforced by government housing policies helped produce the social and economic disparities we see in today's urban ghettos. Most white and black Americans are completely unaware of our government's complicity in creating the racially segregated inner city; many Americans, white and black, believe that the ghetto is the sole responsibility of the people who live there.

Beginning in the 1940s, Newark city officials were forced to address the need for housing and services for the influx of newcomers while at the same time paying deference to the values of the political machine. Between 1941 and 1962, more than 13,000 units of public housing, more per capita than any city in the country and most built with inferior design and construction, were spread throughout the city. Three of the massive high-rise projects were in the Central Ward, within an area of three square miles. The public housing system was thoroughly politicized under the direction of Louis Danzig, who became executive director of the Newark Housing Authority in 1949. During his tenure, which lasted into the late 1960s, Danzig built the authority into a political powerhouse. The Newark Housing Authority's dual role in public housing and redevelopment made it the most potent bureaucracy in city government. Danzig was not the powerful implementer that the famous Robert Moses of New York was, but he was a close second. He built his power by carefully nurturing strong ties to key local leaders as well as those at the state and federal levels. According to federal housing law, cities could choose whether or not to build public housing. Cities like Detroit yielded to white community pressures against public housing and built only a few projects. Newark took all it could get. Without question, new housing was needed for the rising numbers of the city's poor. And for poor black families to obtain an apartment in a newly constructed public housing project was a considerable step up, a significant improvement in the quality of life. Indeed, the attractiveness of public housing for blacks often persuaded families living outside the city to move to Newark.

Regrettably, the quality of the construction was not good. As a result, Newark became one of the worst cities in the nation in the management and upkeep of its public housing stock. And for most places, particularly Newark, the practice of putting hundreds of the poorest families into a community with limited amenities and services was disastrous. City leaders mainly saw opportunities for hefty construction and supply contracts to be used as patronage. An official of the city's human rights commission concluded that public housing in the Central Ward helped to create "one of the most volatile ghettos anywhere on the Eastern seaboard."[17]

The federal public housing programs provided shelter for low-income families who would not have had the means to compete for decent housing in the commercial real estate market. And in many cities, governments established strong local housing agencies to manage the units. Through the 1940s and 1950s, public housing in Newark worked, and many of the older black families living in Newark today remember fondly the safety, cleanliness, and security of places like Baxter Terrace (1941), Pennington Court (1940), and Hayes Homes (1954). Until the regime of Hugh J. Addonizio, who was mayor of Newark from 1962 to 1970, public housing was well managed and orderly. The Addonizio machine in collaboration with Danzig made the city's housing programs serve the interests of the political machine. Upkeep and management were secondary to doling out jobs and contracts. Eventually public housing in Newark became a dismal and costly failure

In Chicago, Baltimore, St. Louis, and numerous other cities where management faltered, public housing became a major source of patronage, and the buildings became reservoirs of crime and social problems. In too many cities, public housing produced vertical slums. The general failure of high-rise public housing was most dramatically illustrated in 1972 when a photograph of the demolition of the massive Pruitt-Igoe public housing projects in St. Louis appeared on the front pages of newspapers across the county.[18] Since 1979 most of Newark's public housing projects built in that period have been similarly demolished.

RACISM AND ECONOMIC DISADVANTAGE

Racism, poverty, and economic disadvantage profoundly shape life and politics in Newark. The historic maltreatment of blacks is undeniable, but with the legal affirmation of the equal rights of blacks and the passage of laws barring racial discrimination, the overt and brutal treatment of blacks has faded. As Michael Katz writes, inequality in America no longer grows out of the massive and mutually reinforcing legal and extralegal public and private system of racial expression. "It is a subtler matter, proceeding through a series of screens that filter African Americans into more or less promising statuses, progressively dividing them along lines full of implications for their economic futures."[19]

With the election of an African American president of the United States, can one still make the claim that race is a critical factor in the allocation of essential needs such as housing, jobs, education, and health care? Are we not in a postracial period where the playing fields are level and the need no longer exists for special protections or efforts to ensure equal treatment for blacks? Certainly not. The legacy of racism has left the playing field tilted in many respects. There are continued and current acts of mistreatment, sometimes unconsciously applied, that serve to remind us that in the eyes of some individuals and institutions, blacks are still second-class citizens. Racial disadvantages created by the historic treatment of blacks in the city and region have served to diminish the power and resources available to blacks to support their families and neighborhoods, which results in a diminished voice in the political arena. While racial exclusion and subjugation were harsh and overt in the South, the practice of Jim Crow was more nuanced and subtle in the North. For example, Newark could not prevent blacks from taking civil service exams, but if they qualified and had to be hired, they were often dismissed at the end of their probationary period. In the school system, minorities often passed the written exam, but were disqualified in the highly subjective oral exam. In employment and housing, the system of exclusion worked quite efficiently despite laws prohibiting discrimination; personnel managers smiled and acted civilly and then marked "not qualified" on the application. While the many protests and changes in law made a significant difference in the manner in which people of color are treated, undoubtedly a "racial order" has remained in America's cities. As Thomas Sugrue has written, "Urban inequality is the result of the mapping of understanding of racial differences onto the geography of a city—and the power of racial difference to create racial hierarchies that shaped housing patterns, workplace practices, private investment, and the public policies that reinforced them."[20] Institutional disadvantages remain as well as systems of prejudice are often veiled and thus harder to reveal. "The story of America and race is hardly resolved and progress is not inexorable," wrote Frank Rich in the *New York Times*. "Even in the new century, we still take steps backward and forward in bewildering alteration."[21]

Sometimes it is hard to see forward steps, particularly in the deeply impoverished neighborhoods of the Central, South, and West Wards, where men and women are without work. Poverty in Newark is pervasive, concentrated, and highly visible. The homeless, who often are also mentally ill, wander the streets and loiter in the public institutions such as the Newark Public Library, Washington Park, Military Park, and Penn Station, the city's core transportation hub. Most of the poor, however, are out-of-work members of black and Latino families, with a substantial representation of young unmarried women with children. Many are receiving welfare, and crowd the free clinics and hospital emergency rooms for health care. The hard truth is that many of the poor lack the skills and training necessary to have a secure place in a twenty-first-century workforce. How to get the urban poor into more productive lives is a challenge of the highest order. The poor are often isolated, unfairly treated, and consequently alienated; many are often caught in a frustrating cycle of poverty and joblessness. But being poor does not necessarily mean that one is inclined to commit criminal acts. In fact, the poor people who engage in crime are a relatively small percentage of the poor population. Nonetheless, it is a reality in the inner cities of America where poverty is concentrated that for some, particularly young black and Latino males with limited skills and education, crime is a way of life.[22] Other behavioral consequences of poverty combined with poor education and the acute absence of resources are apathy, failure to participate in civic life, and a sense of alienation that can lead to self-destructive behavior.

Poor families command a sizable subsidy for everything from daily maintenance to health care and administration of the criminal justice system. For example, support for policing is the second largest item (education is first, although the major portion of the school budget—72 percent in 2010—is provided by the state) in the city's expenditure budget. The children of the poor are much more likely to be unprepared for the rigors of classroom learning and thus require special attention if they are to be given a chance to acquire the skills and learning needed for today's world. Poor children and their families also often have complicated health problems, exacerbated by limited access to quality health care. The poor and socioeconomically disadvantaged are also more likely to be exploited by commercial forces, as they have been in the subprime mortgage business. They generally have weaker voices in policy debates, and low rates of voting and political participation. Although many of the political debates in the spheres of local government are over issues that directly affect the lives and prospects of poor people, the people most affected are only heard as a result of extraordinary efforts at mobilization by community organizers.

Cities with large numbers of poor people are often starved for financial resources, and they thus give huge concessions to attract commercial activity. In the development game, Newark and the state grant major tax breaks, often in addition to other subsidies, to induce businesses and firms to locate or expand their facilities in the city. In winning financial support from the state, the city has to yield control over its spending. At times, the city has been so eager to win new projects and expand its business and tax base that it has been exploited by hustlers proposing unrealistic or even bizarre schemes.[23] In 1986, a developer named Harry Grant persuaded the Newark city government to provide him land and tax abatements to build the tallest building in the world in downtown Newark. To demonstrate his commitment to the project, Grant paid for the painting and restoration of the golden dome on top of City Hall, a project that was clearly overdue. Grant had a site cleared for his project on Broad Street on land formerly occupied by a terminal for the Central Railroad, two blocks from City Hall. Aside from the lunacy of the idea in the first place, Grant became a celebrity in the city and received considerable media attention throughout the country. It soon became clear that nothing was being done to erect the structure. When appeals were made by City Hall to get the project under way, Grant had workers repave the sidewalks near the site in the middle of the night. As the delays, stalling, and bizarreness continued, it was finally realized that Grant was an odd character with no real ability to follow through on his promise. In 1991, he filed for bankruptcy protection.

CORRUPTION

A long-standing and deeply embedded culture of illegality in the state, and particularly in Newark, stifles efforts to improve the performance of government as well as brighten the city's image. Since the change in the form of government and with the exception of Mayor Leo Carlin's administration (1954–1962), in every administration there has been an indictment of wrongdoing by public officials and revelations of underworld and gangster activity. The pattern of deals with underworld figures, entrepreneurs, and developers who are willing to pay officeholders for contracts, and people showering political candidates with lavish campaign contributions in exchange for favors or jobs, never seems to fade away. It is hard to predict who will provide the next example of cheating and bribery, but periodically some city official or bureaucrat is charged with acting illegally. All three mayors serving the city from 1962 to the election of Cory Booker in 2006 have been in trouble with the law, although Kenneth Gibson did not create the kind of suspect government that characterized the administrations of Hugh Addonizio (1962–1970) and Sharpe James (1986–2006). Several councilmen, a police director, Mayor Addonizio, and Mayor James and his chief of staff were imprisoned for corruption. A deputy mayor for Booker was convicted of extortion and sentenced to one year in jail. Although Mayor Booker was not charged with violating the law, he acumulated milllions of dollars through speaking engagements, participation in a social media venture that cost him nothing and netted him several million dollars, and lucrative fees from his former law firm while serving as mayor. Mayor Gibson was indicted for providing a no-show job to a former councilman but was exonerated after a lengthy trial. In another matter, he escaped indictment when he was investigated for having a Swiss bank account. There was a time when the Essex County prosecutor would convene a grand jury to review the operations and administration of Newark city government, particularly the behavior of elected officials. However, county prosecutors have apparently abandoned the role of overseeing the behavior of local government since the state senators who represent Newark in the state legislature, by tradition, have the power to approve or disapprove the appointment of county prosecutors.[24] James held the position of mayor and senator, which gave him the power to veto the appointment of any county prosecutor.

By all indications, there is still a vibrant criminal underworld operating in and around Newark. From the 1930s through the 1950s, the city witnessed the emergence of mob figures Longie Zwillman in the old Third Ward and Richie "The Boot" Boiardo in the North Ward. Those organizations withered with the death of their leaders and multiple prosecutions of those who lived. In the 1960s, the Campisi family, located in the West Ward, operated one of the most violent and destructive criminal organizations in the history of the state. The Campisi mob ran gambling operations and mastered the art of holdups and break-ins to acquire cash. They were as ruthless in real life as the mob portrayed in *The Godfather*. When the leadership thought it necessary to kill a rival or an associate to protect the interest of the "family," it was carried out efficiently by underlings. When Addonizio was running for the mayoralty in 1970 against Kenneth Gibson, the Campisi family gave a party in their restaurant to support Addonizio. The guest speaker was Newark's police director, Dominick Spina. Eventually, the Campisi gangster activities came to an end in 1972 when gang member Ira Pecznick cooperated with authorities. Peznick spent fourteen months spilling out the details of the Campisi operation to state police and lawyers, which led to the indictment and prosecution of the gang leadership.[25] Peznick co-authored a book, *To Drop a Dime*, about his mob career. When the book was released in 1976, almost all of the copies were immediately purchased. An official at the Newark Public Library contends that they cannot keep a copy in the building for more than a few days. They immediately disappear. (Anyone who wants his own copy will probably be disappointed unless he has a few extra hundred dollars to spend on it.)

Through the years, there have been occasional arrests and charges brought against people who are considered to be members of various underworld gangs. Often these gangs are regional in nature and have associations with well-known Mafia families in New York or Philadelphia. Sports betting has always been one of the major enterprises of the mob, and for those who wish to engage in that activity, it is always possible to get a "slip" during football season, or find a bookie to bet on a horse race. The legalization of the lottery and the development of legalized gambling in Atlantic City put a dent in the underworld gambling market, but it has not eliminated it. The numbers rackets are deeply institutionalized in some poor communities, where the winning percentages are higher. And for most winners, there is no tax.

Newark has also seen the growth of black-led underworld organizations that distribute illegal drugs through underlings in the streets. The Newark regional drug trade was led by Wayne "Akbar" Pray for nearly twenty years until he was sentenced to a life term in federal prison in 1989. According to a New Jersey State Commission of Investigation (SCI) report, Pray's group had about three hundred members and associates. Former Newark police director Claude Coleman explained the difficulty in investigating a kingpin like Pray: "For some years . . . [Pray] was considered to be one of the so-called untouchables, because he never came close to the [narcotics]. He was leading the life of wealth and influence. . . . I think everyone knew that he was involved in drug dealing. . . . Nonetheless, he had not been . . . brought to justice, so to speak." Coleman, who is now a retired superior court judge, said that it was only with the help of the U.S. Attorney's Office and the FBI that the evidence could be developed to end Pray's reign. According to testimony by law enforcement officials, Pray's organizations continued to operate at a much lower level after he was imprisoned. The SCI report added, "Reliable sources have indicated that Pray has maintained his customers and contacts and is still overseeing his drug transactions."[26]

In 2011, federal prosecutors charged fifteen New Jersey residents, including an alleged member of the Genovese organized crime family, with racketeering. At the time of the announcement, U.S. Attorney Paul Fishman said, "Organized crime still has a grip on the New Jersey waterfront." An FBI representative said that "organized crime continues to operate through corruption, extortion, racketeering and violence." Much evidence indicates that Newark continues to be an important home base for organized crime, although a significant part of the criminal apparatus has been decentralized.[27]

While Newark is a major league player in venality, the same might be said for the entire state of New Jersey "The old political machines have proved extremely durable," observed political scientist Brigid Harrison. "It's like the Mafia," she added. "If you take out one family, the other family takes up more authority."[28] Over the years, voters in New Jersey have become accustomed to reading of the countless ways elected officials and their cronies use official power for private gain. In 1981, the SCI issued a report of a two-year examination of the operations of the New Jersey Housing Finance Agency (HFA). The investigators found the agency rife with payoffs, bribes, and kickbacks. Contractors inflated their bills to pay the kickbacks to HFA officials; the HFA approved the inflated bills and simply added the excess charges to the amount it borrowed from private investors through the sale of tax-exempt bonds. Officials of the U.S. Department of Housing and Urban Development agreed to give the developer enough rent subsidy to repay the inflated HFA loan, so the HFA could pay its bondholders. The rent subsidies were of course the public's money. The SCI documented cases in which

HFA officers doctored or destroyed official records, failed to report expensive gifts or bribes from developers or consultants, attempted to mislead the SCI in sworn testimony, covered up evidence of wrongdoing by powerful developers, and took jobs the SCI characterized as "post-employment conflicts of interest." The investigation was initiated when the *Trenton Times* published a series revealing the suspect activities at the "$1 billion state housing bank."[29]

In recent years, several officials in various parts of the state have been indicted and convicted of bribery, extortion, or other forms of corruption. In 2009, the FBI arrested forty people, including elected city officials from Jersey City and Hoboken as well as a member of the state legislature, for taking bribes from an FBI informant named Solomon Dwek, who posed as a developer. Dwek had fallen into trouble with the law himself, and agreed to assist the authorities round up a few of the weak and potentially corrupt. The bait was an envelope with as much as $5,000 in cash, and all the target had to promise was assistance in the development process. Dwek, who had been caught attempting to defraud a bank, was wired to record the conversations. The pickings were easy, and included a mayor of Hoboken who had won an election and had not yet been sworn into office.[30]

When Newark Mayor Hugh J. Addonizio fought to have the New Jersey College of Medicine and Dentistry built in his city, political observers suspected that the mayor was smacking his lips at the prospect of payoffs from construction and vendor contracts. No one imagined that lawlessness would emanate from white suburban professionals at the institution. However, with the help of a whistle-blower, federal officials found that medical school administrators bilked the federal government through Medicare out of unjustified payments for treatment of the elderly. Contrary to law and professional ethics, doctors were paid hefty sums simply to recruit patients. Wayne Bryant, an influential state senator for South Jersey, had a low-show paid position at one of the units of the medical school in return for delivering state grants to the school. Bryant was convicted and sent to jail. Lobbyists for corporations and major institutions in the state dole out perks and gifts to legislators as the price for action on favored legislation. A highly placed political official said, "You can make anything happen in New Jersey, if you have enough money."

In the annals of New Jersey corruption, it is hard to match the episode involving David Friedland, a former state senator from Hudson County who was convicted of racketeering charges in 1980. Friedland was indicted in October 1979 with his father Jacob for their role in accepting $360,000 in bribes to arrange a $4 million loan from the pension of Teamsters Local 701, based in North Brunswick. The loan went to companies controlled by Barry S. Marlin, an attorney who had been convicted of swindling $43 million in several unrelated schemes. On April 11, 1980, Friedland and his father were convicted by a jury for taking kickbacks, income tax evasion, and obstruction of justice for asking a witness to lie to a grand jury. A few years later he reached an agreement with the United States Attorney's office in Newark. He was able to avoid prison in exchange for his assistance in recording incriminating conversations with his former associates. While in the federal witness protection program, he took a job with a mortgage firm. While there, he and his superior (also a former New Jersey legislator) made additional efforts to defraud the same pension fund. While Friedland was awaiting sentencing in 1985, the U.S. Coast Guard received a report from a boat in the waters off the Grand Bahamas that Friedland had disappeared while scuba diving. His body was not found, and a warrant was issued for his arrest. Friedland went on the run, using fake passports and identification papers. During his fugitive life, he had been traced to Africa, France, Italy, Hong Kong, and Singapore. Two years after his disappearance, he was arrested by officials in the Maldives and returned to the United States. Friedland was sentenced to fifteen years in prison. He shortened his time to nine years by once again striking a deal with prosecutors to share information about illicit drug dealing he had heard from other prisoners.[31]

Legislators often resist supporting the city, knowing that they would not gain any points with their suburban constituents. Despite the fact that the suburbs are not immune to corruption, the reputation of wrongdoing provides the rationale for suburbanites to argue that the city does not use its resources wisely, and is therefore undeserving. Moreover, when government officials abuse the system for their own material gain, or for the gain of their friends, they diminish the potential of efforts to improve conditions for their constituents. It is at times perplexing that anyone could believe that they

could get away without notice after committing blatant acts of bribery and wrongdoing. Corruption always seems to rear its head, and
ultimately displaces positive visions.

FRAGMENTATION

Local, municipal, and state governments have long developed an
array of local agencies, special districts, suburban townships, regional authorities, and county, state and national bodies, each with
some fragment of power. And New Jersey is probably one of the most
fragmented states in the nation, with 566 local jurisdictions and close
to 600 school districts, and an array of other autonomous and semi-
autonomous agencies and entities. How to get this vast and complicated system of power to work to solve the problems of cities is one
of the greatest challenges of urban life.

Newark is the largest city in New Jersey and home to some of the
largest and most powerful businesses in the state, including the behe-
moth Prudential Financial, Public Service Electric and Gas, and the
New Jersey operations of Verizon. One might think that this would
help to empower Newark, but the city's ability to determine the outcome of so many things critical to its health is severely limited. For
example, the city is dependent on federal funds and state subsidies
to support its housing programs, as well as other efforts in the areas
of health, education, welfare, job training and placement, and the
environment. State revenues are at times vitally important, but the
tradeoff for funds is often more state involvement in local decision
making. This means that at times the state can dictate the rules of
the road. As such, the Newark Public School District has been under
state control for eighteen years (with little improvement) and the city
is dependent on state monies for over 70 percent of its school district
budget. In a state where 566 local jurisdictions cherish home rule,
urban districts are highly dependent on the whims of suburban voters, who have much more influence in the state legislature.

In 2009 and again in 2011, Newark was forced to borrow from the
state in order to balance the city's budget. In 2011, the state loaned
Newark $32 million and required that Newark sign a memorandum
of understanding (MOU) granting state control over virtually all

financial decisions. In effect, the MOU placed Newark under state supervision, as is true for at least five other urban centers in the state. In the case of Newark, the New Jersey Division of Local Finances also included in the MOU a request that Newark show a "good faith effort" to establish a municipal utilities authority to run its water and sewer systems. The actions of the director of the state agency showed that the city was expected to implement a municipal utility authority if it was to receive further monetary assistance. It did not matter to the state (or to Mayor Booker, I might add) that there was overwhelming opposition among the residents of the city to establishing a municipal utility authority.[32]

SMALL CITY, BIG DREAMS

Newark is hampered by its small size and tight geography. It covers a mere 24.8 square miles, and a very large portion of that is marshland or occupied by the huge Newark Liberty International Airport. Only about 17 square miles are habitable, and a good share of that houses tax-exempt public and nonprofit institutions, including churches, further shrinking the city's tax base. By comparison, Oakland, California, with a population of 401,000, encompasses 78.2 square miles; Miami, with a population of 400,000, is 35.68 square miles; and Minneapolis, with a population of 377,392, is 58.4 square miles. As urban historian Kenneth Jackson has pointed out, Newark simply failed to annex its outlying suburbs the way cities like Philadelphia, Dallas, and Chicago did. Newark leaders once eyed nearby East Orange, Vailsburg, Harrison, Kearny, and Belleville, but among them, Vailsburg was the only one annexed, in 1904. Even in the northern part of the city adjacent to Branch Brook Park, where many of the commercial and industrial leaders of the city lived during Newark's golden years, homes were built on lots of about one acre, which is quite small in comparison to the large estatelike residences for which they left. Unlike Baltimore, Cleveland, and Chicago, the options for working- and middle-class families to purchase an aspirational larger home within the city continue to be severely limited. In addition, there are few options for the growth and expansion of light commerce and industry. While it may seem odd to highlight size as a critical issue

for the health and development of a city, the limitations imposed by
Newark's diminutive footprint help account for a small middle class
and the virtual absence of corporate as well as civic leadership living
in the city. The talent needed to run and manage the city's government and its civic institutions simply does not exist within Newark.
This is often a source of public tension, as grandstanding elected officials make unrealistic calls for residency rules.

In reality, so-called outsiders have always been an important part
of Newark's civic community, for better or worse. For example, over
the years the city has been targeted by romantic ideologues like Tom
Hayden, who led a cadre of youthful college students to Newark to
organize the poor and join an imagined "revolutionary trajectory."
And then there was the self-proclaimed military leader Colonel Hassan, a convicted rogue, who visited Newark to test fanciful ideas for
social change. Colonel Hassan ranks as one of the most intriguing
and destructive visitors to Newark. He arrived just prior to the 1967
disorders with a band of about five young followers, all clad in khaki
uniforms. He and his recruits stood at attention at public meetings
and marched around as though they were real soldiers. At every
community gathering, Hassan and his followers attempted to pro-
voke local activists to take more aggressive actions. Years later, it was
revealed in the *Washington Post* that Hassan had an extensive criminal record and had been working as an informant for government
intelligence agencies.

Others have stayed and have made outstanding contributions
that will be remembered in history. Such individuals include the
early inventors and entrepreneurs who account for a major part of
Newark's industrial history. Today there are social entrepreneurs
such as Gloria Buck, the founder of Newark's Black Film Festival;
scholars such as history professor Dr. Clement Price of Rutgers University; Gustav Heningburg, the founding executive of the Newark
Urban Coalition; and Nancy Zak, who came to Newark to teach in
a community school. Nonetheless, Newark's talent shortages resem-
ble those of developing nations where local people who are lucky
enough to get an education often leave for greener pastures. Most
significant, however, in a geographically small city like Newark, the
tax base is also small. With limited space for single-family homes
owned by occupants, and lacking the concentration of business and

corporate wealth of Manhattan or Dallas, there are severe financial limits that in turn create greater dependence on subsidies from other levels of government.

What Can Be Changed?

Some of the issues that make Newark struggle are historic givens, such as the boundaries of the city, which could be changed although it is highly unlikely they will be. Others, such as the segregation of blacks in the inner city as a result of federal housing policies and the subsidization of the suburbs by the construction of a commuters' highway system, a tax deduction for home ownership, and gasoline subsidies, have left institutionalized structural and social issues that are not likely to be altered for years to come, if ever. All combine and overlap to create very high hurdles for any effort to upgrade urban life, particularly for the poor. Such challenges create a constant and often distracting battle for resources, usually won by those who have a disproportionate influence in the region's political system. There is, however, major economic strength in the region that could work to the city's advantage. Newark is neighbor to New York City, still the wealthiest city in the world, with the most advanced and globally integrated economic, transportation, and communications systems. Newark also sits in the center of one of the richest areas of the world, and itself has some of the most highly valued assets imaginable. For example, Newark is located adjacent to one of the nation's most active seaports and one of the East Coast's busiest airports. But can those assets work for everyone, including the poor?

It is not that nothing can be done. On the contrary, major changes in programs and policies can provide new opportunities to those who are left out. First, however, there must be a vision of change, a belief that change is possible and that leadership has a responsibility to work for economic and social improvement for all groups, particularly those at the bottom of the ladder. Secondly, there must be integrity and effective efforts to curtail the tendencies of some to see government as a source of personal enrichment through graft, bribery, or wrongdoing. Thirdly, government must be effectively managed for change; good things do not happen if the bureaucracies do not set standards for performance and do not have systems in place to measure and hold accountable those who are in charge. And in any city, to be effective, to be able to effectively gain power and influence through local neighborhood elections, to make the vision real, leadership has to have a clear understanding of the political environment and must be politically competent. Fashioning a winning coalition for the top office opens possibilities for change, but it is only the beginning.

───〈2〉───

Winds of Change

FRED MEANS LIVED with his grandmother in Pacolet, South Carolina, during the 1930s and 1940s. There was not much work there for African Americans except perhaps for farming. When his grandmother died, Means's parents sold the house and "became a part of that great migration of Negroes from the segregated South to a place of hope in the North seeking a better life." Eventually ending up in Newark, Means recalls the frigid northeastern winters: "The cold weather was a shock to a kid who never knew snow."[1]

Following World War II, large numbers of poor blacks, along with the Means family, headed north to find jobs and new lives. Between 1940 and 1950, there was a net migration of just over 1.2 million blacks from the South; between 1950 and 1960, that number reached 1.4 million. By 1960, the nation's black population, which was 73 percent rural in 1910, had become 73 percent urban, thrusting upon urban governments demands for jobs, housing, and health services, increasing decentralization and accelerating decline.[2] At the same time, a major exodus of whites and industrial corporations from urban areas such as Newark was just beginning. For Newark, the change was cataclysmic. This change of place and home for southern blacks caused the transformation of Newark's population from primarily European stock in 1940 to more than 50 percent black by 1970. Only two other cities—Washington, DC, and Gary, Indiana— changed more rapidly. The transition precipitated a series of social, economic, and political changes that helped to place Newark at the center of what was then called "the urban crisis."[3]

In the census of 1950, Newark's black population had grown to

17 percent of a total population of 434,000; by 1960, the percentage had doubled to 34 percent, with another 5 percent Hispanic. In 1960, whites outnumbered blacks by two to one. By 1970, the white population became a minority at just 36.6 percent, while the black population rose to 54.3 percent. The Hispanic population, almost entirely Puerto Rican at that time, made up the remaining 9 percent. During the 1960s, over one-quarter of the city's census tracts went from white to black majorities. The flight of whites, facilitated by easy access to mortgages and a building boom in the suburbs induced by federal policy, added up to a net out-migration of 106,500 (or the departure of four of every ten whites) living in the city in 1960. Blacks were prohibited from participating in the exodus by both the lack of access to mortgage money and racial discrimination.[4]

The Third Ward, formerly a Jewish enclave, had by 1940 become a decaying and crime-ridden ghetto housing most of the city's black population in dilapidated, wood-frame cold-water flats. Their concentration was facilitated by the Newark Housing Authority (NHA), which, after 1939, began constructing massive public housing projects in the Third Ward. Several developments, all closely located, created a large government-sponsored ghetto where apartments were assigned on the basis of race: Felix Fuld Court, built in 1941, housed 276 black and 32 white families; the Reverend William P. Hayes Homes, built in 1954 and enlarged in 1962, housed 1,390 black families compared to 41 white families; and Stella Windsor Wright Homes, erected in 1959, housed 1,172 black families and just 14 white families. Poverty, vice, and exploitation were widespread. The 1942 city tuberculosis rate was 255 per 100,000, with the major share of cases occurring in the central parts of the city.[5] In 1946, novelist Curtis Lucas painted a grim picture of the area, referred to as "the Hill":

> It is a slum area and blighted. There people hang out on the street corners; there women and children stand in doorways of tumbling, roach-infested houses, and there pimps stand in front of the taverns that line the street, talking shop. The characters on the Hill are as varied as they come; strong men and weaklings, frustrated wrecks, religious-minded folks, and vicious fellows. Beautiful young girls, and old hags; fortunate, well-kept women, and debased hustlers.[6]

In earlier years, blacks were more scattered throughout most wards, but several factors forced them to the Hill. Antagonism toward blacks had increased following World War I and reached its peak during the Depression as competition sharpened for the decreasing number of jobs. Housing for blacks became increasingly scarce in outlying areas of the city as landlords grew resistant to blacks.

Nonetheless, in the face of the NHA's slum clearance programs, the Central Ward became a neighborhood of movers. Those who lived within the core area found themselves in a state of perpetual motion as block after block was deemed blighted and cleared for renewal projects. According to Harold Kaplan, the city's ambitious redevelopment program had condemned sixty blocks in the Central Ward, designated a large area of land in the Clinton Hill section for light industry, and reserved more than sixty blocks for expansion of Rutgers University and the Newark College of Engineering.[7] By 1950, some 28,000 blacks, over one-third of the city's total, had jammed into the Third Ward.[8] The large-scale uprooting decreased the black community's political strength and potential for participation, yet at the same time, the concentration of blacks in the Third Ward created a bloc of potential voters and thus laid the foundation for broader participation in politics.

Life in the Third Ward

Amid the adverse environment of the Third Ward, there existed an active and vigorous social life. An extensive network of after-hours spots, social clubs, fraternal organizations, and churches made physical discomfort secondary for many who enjoyed the kinship of living among their own people and institutions. Indeed, some institutions, particularly churches, were patronized by blacks residing outside the city. By 1947, the Metropolitan Baptist Church on Prince Street boasted 4,500 members, the "largest congregation in the state." Metropolitan Baptist offered a home and missionary relief program for church members as well as an opportunity to invest in the Metropolitan Realty and Investment Association. Saint James African Methodist Episcopal Church waged an aggressive campaign against the spread of tuberculosis.[9]

The black community was not without its advocates, who represented a range of views and approaches as to how the community
should advance its interests. The local affiliates of the National Association for the Advancement of Colored People (NAACP) and the
National Urban League (known as the Essex County Urban League)
were the most widely respected and had the largest memberships.

The Newark NAACP, founded in 1914, spent most of its energies
during the 1940s and 1950s in efforts to remove barriers against the
employment of black teachers and administrators. Applicants for
teaching posts had to take a written test and an oral examination.
There was an established pattern in which black applicants who
passed the written test would then fail the subjective oral examination. The Newark NAACP's style and approach to issues was deeply
influenced by the attitude and philosophy of the chair of its local
board of directors, Grace Baxter Fenderson. Fenderson was one
of the founders of the Newark NAACP, and she also served on the
national board of the organization for many years. She was also the
daughter of one of Newark's historic black pioneers, James Baxter,
who served as principal of the city's first "colored" school. A wise and
shrewd strategist, she was the kingmaker and chief coordinator of the
activities of the NAACP branch through the 1940s and 1950s. Within
the branch, her support was essential in order to win the organization's presidency. During the 1950s, Harry Hazelwood, Theodore Pettigrew, and Carlton B. Norris, a Newark police detective, served as
presidents of the branch, with Fenderson's blessing.

Hazelwood was a native of Newark, attended Newark schools, and
was the first African American to earn a law degree from Cornell
University. He passed the bar exam and opened a private practice in
downtown Newark, since it was highly unlikely that any white law
firm would offer a position to a black person. Hazelwood was one
of the most highly respected citizens of New Jersey and a man of
extraordinary talent.[10] Theodore Pettigrew was an employee of the
U.S. Postal Service, where he won promotion to a supervisory position. He was the first African American to be appointed to serve on
the board of governors of the NHA.[11] Carlton B. Norris was a very
unusual candidate to head a local civil rights organization. He joined
the Newark Police Department in 1930. Many members of the black
community did not consider him a friend; he was assigned to cases

and matters involving black citizens, and had a reputation for hastily using his billy club on offenders.[12] When he was nominated to hold the top position in the Newark branch of the NAACP, several younger members protested. However, with Fenderson's support, there was not much of an argument.

Each of the presidents pursued Fenderson's gradualist, cooperative policies. The group did indeed prod city officials for more opportunities for blacks, but ever so cautiously and politely. The NAACP leadership was staunchly middle class, and many of its principal spokesmen had attained a degree of respectability afforded few others. Its leaders worked quietly behind the scenes, cooperating with whites rather than opposing or publicly criticizing them, or at least accepting a gradual pace of change. To put it another way, if changes were to be made, they had to occur at a pace set by the white establishment. Demonstrations and public protests were not in the arsenal of the Newark NAACP.

During this period, the Essex County Urban League sought increased jobs and improved social services for the black community. In addition, James Pawley, who became the agency's director in 1956, worked to gain fair employment opportunities within the welfare agencies, especially those serving the black community. The league depended on its good relations with businessmen to make jobs available, and large downtown corporations were a major source of financial support.

Thus, for reasons of orientation and expediency, both the NAACP and the Urban League tended to avoid open controversy.[13] In a few other cities around the nation, NAACP chapters were quite outspoken, and indeed, in the same period, the Philadelphia branch of the NAACP was considered militant.

Other groups openly disagreed with the conservative views of the established middle-class civic leaders. A few ministers were quite vocal, and the Baptist Ministers Conference regularly criticized the slow rate of progress for the city's blacks. The most vocal voices often came from a group of loosely affiliated radical activists in various left-wing organizations such as the New Jersey Civil Rights Congress, the Negro Labor Council, and some of the more socially conscious unions. Principal among them was Larry "Clarence" Coggins, who headed his own group, called the Negro Labor Vanguard, and neighborhood leaders such as Timothy Still, a resident of the Hayes housing project who became a spokesman for public housing tenants.

Far more influential than the churches, the NAACP, the Urban League, and some black ministers were the representatives of the entrenched ethnic political system that determined which economic and political aims of blacks were met and which were denied. The immigrant machines, as the historian Richard Hofstadter has noted, "operated on a political style which stressed personal obligation, and placed strong personal loyalties above allegiance to abstract codes of law or morals."[14] It was the kind of politics that allowed special interests, graft, and corruption to become common to Newark's political culture. By the late 1930s, much of the city's old civic leadership was leaving for the suburbs. As historian Stanley Winters observed:

> The type of politician that then began to dominate city hall was a self-made man, usually from the lower-middle class, closely identified with a specific ethnic, religious, or political group, and tending to speak for special interests rather than general welfare. They included dedicated men, but some maintained dubious links with racketeers; others engaged in financial and real estate deals that raised suspicions of misuse of public office, if the many indictments and occasional convictions are reliable clues.[15]

ZWILLMAN AND MOB POLITICS

The person who truly reigned over the economic and political life of the Third Ward was the white bootleg entrepreneur Abner "Longie" Zwillman, who headed the most profitable and toughest underworld dynasty on the East Coast. Zwillman, born and raised in the Third Ward, quit school in the eighth grade to support his family following the death of his father. He began his career as a peddler. Tall and strong, he became the muscle for bootleggers, which led to his partnership in the so-called Reinfeld syndicate, a group of illegal alcohol traders who operated on two small islands off the coast of Canada.[16]

Zwillman's millions in rum-running money, it was widely believed, helped finance several state gubernatorial campaigns in return for the "right to name, or at least approve, the new attorney general."[17] It was also widely suspected, although never proven, that Zwillman's influence and cash helped John V. Kenny control the mayor's office in Jersey City. Voluminous FBI surveillance and investigation files on Zwillman are now available on the FBI's Freedom of Information web page. The files may represent exaggerations of informers and other criminals covering their own backs, but even so they reveal that Zwillman was engaged in extensive commercial investments and economic activity. The files also confirm his prominence in mob circles and indicate that he ranked among the most powerful underworld figures in the nation. It is interesting that FBI officials in Washington labeled the records pertaining to mobsters such as Zwillman, Meyer Lansky, and Richie Boiardo as the "hoodlum files."

Zwillman had an incalculable power over Newark city government. Politicians like Meyer Ellenstein, a dentist turned lawyer and politician, was reputedly a beneficiary of Zwillman's largesse for his successful campaigns for the city commission in the 1930s. Ellenstein served as mayor from 1933 to 1941 and returned to the commission from 1946 to 1953. A close associate of Zwillman, William J. Egan, a city commissioner in the 1930s, gained important positions in several businesses with heavy Zwillman investments. According to one old-time Newarker, Zwillman's influence was so extensive that he could determine assignments in the police department.[18] In 1951, when the U.S. Senate Crime Committee held hearings on organized crime in New Jersey, testimony revealed that the city's corporation counsel was also an agent for a Zwillman-owned trucking firm. The *Newark Evening News* once commented, "Zwillman's bootleg liquor is purchased in Canada, shipped to the Jersey Shore, carried by barges to Port Newark and there loaded on trucks. The trucks are escorted into the city by Zwillman's motorcycle policemen."[19]

Early Third Ward politics was controlled by Zwillman's money, political ties, and muscle, all of which he used freely. In the presidential election of November 1932, the Eleventh District of the Third Ward gave all the Republican candidates just eight votes, and Herbert Hoover none, while almost every Democrat received 587 votes. The "stuffed ballots," as the press labeled them, were impounded and brought to city hall. Several indictments against a number of Zwillman's associates followed an investigation of the "unusual display of democratic consensus."[20] However, just before the men were to face trial, all evidence disappeared and no one was convicted. City

officials would not say how the evidence disappeared. The Zwillman
FBI files offer the following report on the episode:

> On November 15, 1932, the poll books of the First, Third, Fourth, and
> Fifth Wards of the City of Newark were stolen from the Office of the
> Commissioner of Registration. Ballots from the boxes of the First,
> Third and Sixth Wards, City of Newark, were stolen from the City
> Clerk. A confidential informant, whose information is believed to
> be reliable, stated that preceding the theft, William Egan, City Com-
> missioner and Director of Public Safety; Charles Gillen, another
> Newark City Commissioner; Peter J. O'Toole, City Clerk; and Abner
> Zwillman met at the Riviera Hotel and planned this theft. Zwillman
> was reported to have furnished the men for the job.[21]

Throughout the 1930s and 1940s, black democratic political leaders were aligned with politicians supported by the Zwillman forces.
Prosper Brewer, who became the first black to head the Third Ward
Republican Committee, stayed clear of the mob, but by the time
Brewer gained his position, Republican strength in the ward had
diminished. Charles Matthews, who became the ward's first black
Democratic chairman, boasted that he owed his ascendancy in politics to the Zwillman organization. He recalled that the mobster was
like a father to him: "The night I was elected, Zwillman sent a lawyer
up to the headquarters to write my acceptance speech. Later Zwillman told me to meet him in New York where he bought me two suits
and twelve shirts. He said to me, 'When you're a leader, you've got
to look like a leader.'"[22] Toussaint Ware, a former black Republican
ward leader, described how "free liquor, free money, and easy morals
always had important roles in Third Ward politics." Under Zwillman,
Ware wrote, corruption reigned at the polls; the dead, the infirm,
and those who never ventured near the polls voted. People could not
complain because of the collusion between the "organization" and
the police. Ware admitted that he had participated in the illegality
he wrote about. In 1941, he traded his county committee vote for a
promise that a gambling place in the ward would be reopened.[23]

The key to Zwillman's influence rested on the political and economic system he had created with the fruits of his earnings during Prohibition. His system had extensive reach and the capacity

to inflict real harm to people who opposed him. His investments in railroads, manufacturing, and commerce provided jobs to underlings and family members, and the coalition he shaped of Jews, Italians, and blacks provided instruments of power in all realms of Third Ward life. Wielding money and influence, Zwillman worked the system, especially in the interest of people who showed up at the polls. Calvin West, who grew up in the Third Ward and, in 1966, became the first black to be elected in a citywide election, recalled how Zwillman's organization delivered turkeys and food baskets to black households for Thanksgiving and Christmas holidays.[24] The legends of Zwillman's influence have clearly been stretched over time and history. Among those stories that still live are tales about a soup kitchen for the poor Zwillman supported in Military Park; an occasion when Zwillman went to police headquarters and had several black men released who had been charged with attacking a police officer; and the extraordinary act of generosity when he bought a building housing a black social club because the building had been bought by a soda company that planned to evict the club. These acts of benevolence clearly polished the mobster's reputation, but they also helped to protect his power and his distribution system for liquor and the policy rackets. Sometimes it was difficult to distinguish where the lines of politics and mob activity began and ended, but there was a clear relationship between the two. Many blacks, recipients of the food baskets or an occasional job referral to a factory, saw only the charity and concern of Zwillman. Matthews, who became one of the leading black politicians of the 1950s and 1960s, said, "Zwillman left the politics to me, and I left the corruption to him."[25]

These activities and associations strengthened a milieu congenial to vice and wrongdoing that had existed from the early days of the century. Political leaders, both black and white, developed biases and obligations that grew out of such relationships, based on bribes, extortion, and violence. Criminal figures like Zwillman established not only an economic and political system, but also a network of values and rules about politics that affected governments throughout northern New Jersey, and to some extent, throughout the state. Since Prohibition, almost all Newark political leaders have lived in this milieu and have been influenced by it; payoffs, extortion, campaign money for favors (pay to play) are all part of the game. Questionable associations never end. Surely, every Newark political official does not engage in corruption. However, there have been few periods in which investigators have not discovered an alleged violation of the law by some official accepting personal gain for official actions.

The ties between the black community and the mob persisted because the underworld provided a source of livelihood for some members of the black community, which in some ways surpassed the meager opportunities afforded blacks in the licit structure. Matthews gave this assessment of the impact of the racketeers: "They provided more jobs for blacks than city government could provide. They had various plants and contractors that they controlled. They put blacks in the brewery, an aeronautics factory, or other companies. Blacks were nonentities in the day, and [mobsters] were the only ones who gave them some kind of opportunity."[26]

The system of underworld values lasted long after the individual gang leaders fell from power. In the mid-1950s, the federal government launched an intensive assault on organized crime in New Jersey, resulting in Zwillman's imprisonment for tax evasion. In 1959, he committed suicide, according to the official version, although to this day there is speculation that he was killed in a ward struggle over control of his empire. Leadership of Newark's profitable rackets passed to Richie "The Boot" Boiardo and Gerald Catena, Zwillman associates in several business enterprises then entrenched in the North Ward. An Italian underworld thus came to play a major role in city politics and exerted considerable influence in the Third Ward. The political structure proved readily adaptive to the impending change in ethnic hegemony when several black leaders joined forces in the early 1950s with Ralph Villani, the principal Italian politician in the city. From that time on and through the mid-1960s there was a kinship between Italian political figures and the leading black politicians of the Third Ward.

GAINING GROUND:
BLACK POLITICS IN NEWARK

The rising black vote brought new opportunities and posed new challenges to the political structures that ruled Newark and Essex County. Ordinarily, the Italian city machine and the Irish county politicians who dominated the twenty municipalities, towns, and boroughs outside of Newark maintained an easy tradeoff in patronage and support. In matters affecting the black community, however, the Irish and Italians were united in opposing anything more than a token distribution of benefits. The black vote, however, had become important following Franklin's D. Roosevelt's victory in 1932 and the establishment of the New Deal coalition of working-class people and minorities. The shift in loyalty of black voters to the Democratic Party and the demographic changes in Essex municipalities forced the recruitment of blacks as district leaders. Harry Van Dyke became the first black Democratic district leader in the mid-1930s, and Matthews emerged as a district leader shortly thereafter. It became clear that black voters could be pivotal in close countywide or congressional elections.[27]

The Republican Party unsuccessfully tried to counter these changes by placing more blacks on county slates. Black Republican assemblymen were elected in 1933 and 1937, at a time when Republican support in the black community showed its first signs of waning, especially in the latter part of the decade. By 1945, most Democratic district leaders in the Third Ward were black, and as the black vote soared in the city along with the concomitant exodus of Jewish families to the South Ward and white ethnic families to the suburbs, the strength of the county Democratic Party grew to a point where it threatened Republican control. The role of the black vote in undermining Republican dominance was critically important, as evidenced in 1948, when Democrat Hugh J. Addonizio won a seat in the Eleventh Congressional District by narrowly beating GOP Congressman Frank L. Sundstrom, 52,633 votes to 50,920. The Third Ward, which had given Sundstrom a 400-vote edge in the previous election, gave Addonizio a plurality of 4,175 to 1,582, a difference larger than his margin of victory.[28]

In county races, rising black voter strength gave blacks a larger role. In 1947, Republican James A. Curtis, a lawyer who had served as president of the Newark NAACP, won a place on the Republican slate for the state assembly and was swept into office with a Republican landslide. Curtis was returned to Trenton in 1949, an election in which two black candidates, Charles Matthews and Arthur Chapin, lost on the Democratic slate. Edward T. Bowser Sr., a suburban black

Republican, won an assembly seat in 1951, while Monte Irvin, the former New York Giants outfielder and a resident of Orange, had a place on the Democratic assembly ticket that year and received 1,720 votes in the Third Ward, more than any other Democrat.[29] In 1957 Madeline Williams in East Orange won an assembly seat as a Democrat in 1957, as Fenderson had in Newark. At the end of the decade, Herbert Tate, a black lawyer who had served on the United States Embassy staff in Pakistan and was prominent in civil rights activities, won a Republican seat in the assembly. The county competition produced black representation in the state legislature, although their small numbers meant they could serve mainly as voices of conscience. Also, the increase in black city district leaders, especially in the Third Ward, gave blacks a voice in county affairs. Again, this was a limited measure of influence, not only because there was a small number of black leaders but also because county chairmen ran their business with an iron hand, and no group could do anything about it.

Despite breakthroughs in county politics, there was only token progress for blacks in the city. Shortly after World War II, the most blatant Jim Crow practices in public accommodations ended. The Elmwood Theater in East Orange curtailed the practice of segregating blacks on one side of the movie house. In 1950, the Far Eastern Restaurant, a downtown Chinese establishment, served its first black customers, Charles Matthews and Larrie Stalks, who had led an earlier protest at the restaurant.[30] Stalks, then a young and ardent voice for black participation in politics, had also become a close associate of Congressman Addonizio. In 1947, the Reverend William P. Hayes became the chairman of the board of commissioners of the NHA, the most important position held by any black person in Newark. William R. Jackson, also black, served on the board of education in the mid-1940s and was succeeded by Herbert H. Tate and Mary Burch, who had established an organization called the Leaguers to mentor young blacks. By 1952, George Jones was appointed manager of the Felix Fuld Court housing project, and a small number of functionaries held jobs at City Hall.

Yet in the larger picture, Newark blacks had hardly dented the all-white structures, and in a few vital areas, they lost ground. While the city economy slumped, racial discrimination remained pervasive in government and private business. Between 1950 and 1960, the city suffered a net loss of 250 manufacturers, and a drop from 47 to 34.7 percent in the proportion of manufacturing jobs in the total workforce.[31] The 1950 U.S. Census figures for the Newark Standard Metropolitan Statistical Area (SMSA) reflect with fair accuracy the employment limits for blacks in Newark. Approximately one-third the percentage of black males as compared to white males worked in finance, insurance, and real estate, while over three times the proportion of blacks compared to whites labored in personal-service jobs. Only one quarter of black women were in manufacturing as opposed to 40 percent of white women. In general, a much higher percentage of blacks worked in private household and laborer categories that offered low status and pay. The 1950 census also indicated that in Newark, where the median family income of $2,961 was already $500 below the median for the SMSA, black families earned an average of $750 less than white families.[32]

Frequent accounts of police brutality, massive housing code violations, discrimination in the city hospital, and fires in wood-frame tenements appeared in the *New Jersey Afro-American*, a subsidiary of the Baltimore-based *Afro-American*. In 1953, the Newark police had a total of 1,000 officers, 27 of whom were black patrolmen. Five were promoted to detective in 1955. In 1953, only 120 black elementary school teachers and 1 full-time secondary school teacher—out of a total teaching corps of 2,900—held appointments in the entire city school system. It took more than a decade of struggle before the first black physician, Dr. Mae McCarroll, was appointed to the Newark City Hospital in 1946. Not until 1951 did the hospital take on the first black intern, and a year later, hire its first black ambulance driver.[33] A 1952 conference of black Baptist ministers, which demanded the appointment of a black magistrate, was told by then mayor Ralph Villani, "The bench presently reflects certain representations which I do not deem it advisable for the welfare and contentment of other large segments of our people to change at this time."[34] Translation: Appointing a black magistrate would upset a lot of white residents. Only after a public rebuke from the NAACP did Villani name a black attorney, Roger Yancey, as assistant corporation counsel and hire a black secretary in the mayor's office.[35]

Black demands for more jobs, better housing, racially mixed schools, equal treatment in the administration of justice, and entry into the political arena brought only grudging concessions. In 1949, the New Jersey legislature passed the Freeman Bill, which enabled state and local governments to establish human relations agencies, but with virtually no enforcement powers. The city's fledging agency, the Newark Intergroup Relations Committee, formed a year later. It helped to limit the most blatant forms of racial discrimination but hardly changed the covert decision making that ignored black rights, despite the frequent lip service officials gave blacks in addressing their complaints. In 1952, for instance, the NHA announced, "Henceforth all public housing apartments are to be allocated on the basis of need, regardless of race and color."[36] A decade later, the U.S. Civil Rights Commission found occupancy in three housing projects to be more than 90 percent white and in four others more than 90 percent black, a pattern of segregation resulting from "racial discrimination in the assignment of public housing" that had continued with the full knowledge of the NHA's leadership.[37]

In 1949, the Newark Board of Education quietly initiated the practice of allowing white students to transfer from mostly black schools in the central city to schools at the periphery of the city, which remained predominantly white. By 1951, just over 3,000 white pupils attended schools outside their neighborhoods. When this practice came to the public's attention, it created the interesting paradox in which black parents, who favored integration, argued for a neighborhood school policy and white parents, who sought to have their children escape what they perceived to be inferior schools, called for open transfers. The conflict was decided in favor of white parents after several hundred demonstrated at a board of education meeting. The practice continued, and in 1953, some 300 white students were transferred out of Avon Avenue School, located at the border of the Central and South Wards.[38] Ironically, when the NAACP in 1961 asked the board of education to institute a transfer program to curtail patterns of racial segregation that were spreading throughout the system, the board agreed to a very limited plan, which was too little and much too late to make a difference in the growing racial segregation of Newark public schools.

The People Had Enough

By the early 1950s, growing black resentment against the continued dominance of white politicians, whose constituency was dwindling in the city, converged with feelings of disappointment among businesspeople, labor organizations, and many civic groups concerned about the local government's inability to halt rising taxes and mismanagement at City Hall. Much of the criticism focused on the city commission, the governing body of the city. The commission form of government had been installed in Newark in 1917 as an effort to stem ethnic divisions and corruption. However, by the early 1930s, the five-member body had become dominated by the city's various ethnic groups, as each demanded representation by an "ethnic leader" on the body. After each election, the commissioners selected one of their number to become mayor and parceled out the various city departments to themselves like medieval fiefdoms. Thus, the commissioners had administrative power as well as their collective legislative powers. In the absence of cohesive party partisanship, each commissioner built his or her own machine on the patronage resources of a department. Blacks, having no representative on the commission, were largely left out of the spoils. Because the black vote was concentrated in the Third Ward, and since commissioners were elected in at-large contests, a black could never attain a seat on the commission. The *New Jersey Afro-American*'s assessment of the commission was that it "kept colored citizens in Newark in the status of second-class citizenship ever since its inception." Commission government, said the paper, "was made for corrupt political machines and race baiters; it has been extremely difficult for Newark's 76,000 colored citizens to have a voice in municipal affairs for thirty years."[39]

In 1953, a reform movement led by representatives of labor, business, and professional groups emerged. Tired of the indictments and "administration by grand jury," they were determined to throw out the commission and "arrest the city's economic and social decline."[40] They formed an ad hoc study group to evaluate charter reform and other recommendations, including minority representation in government, as a means of improving the city's conditions. They produced a scathing review that pointed out that the commission form of government was shortchanging the people and had created an environment of mismanagement and wrongdoing. They accused the system of operating essentially as five separate governments with no consistent standards or accountability. The reformers said, "It's been Newark's shame that the only noticeable check on commission government has been a long series of grand jury presentments which, at best, could not get to the root of the trouble." They called for the establishment of a strong mayor-council government with the high expectations that the new government form would remove many of the bad aspects of Newark's government.[41]

The charter change report was considered by many observers and the local press to be a thoughtful and constructive evaluation of Newark's government. However, the group failed to include blacks or give blacks any significant role in the reform movement. When pressed for an explanation, reform leaders argued, "Their [blacks'] interests will be considered by the liberals in the movement," which included the prominent lawyer and civic leader Alan Lowenstein and Willard Heckel, dean of the Rutgers Law School.[42] The liberal reformers were courageous and forward-looking men, and it was clear that replacing the commission would benefit the black community. But the reformers were very much in the tradition of white liberalism at that time; while it was critical to do things to aid the advancement of blacks, encouraging the participation of blacks in such activity was not important. Black leaders had a different view, and the question of black involvement precipitated a split among the reformers. Eventually, several blacks were named consultants to the reform group.[43]

The squabble over black participation did not dampen the enthusiasm of black groups. Black leaders, particularly those associated with middle-class reform, lined up solidly behind the charter movement. The major concern was to create a system of ward elections. It was assumed the Third Ward would provide the core of one of the new wards to produce black elected representation. As a result, black voters strongly endorsed both the charter commission in 1953 and the commission's recommendation for a mayor-council form of government. The new charter, adopted in November 1953, established a strong mayor and nine-member city council, four of whom were to be elected at-large and one from each of the five wards.

A five-member election commission of city and council officials then drew boundaries outlining the wards. The commission's efforts

ALAN V. LOWENSTEIN AND THE SYSTEM'S REVENGE

In August 1953, Lowenstein, a partner at the law firm of Riker, Emery, and Danzig, was summoned to meet Horace K. Corbin, chairman of the board of Fidelity Union Trust Company, New Jersey's largest bank and the firm's biggest client. Corbin told Lowenstein that he should delay filing the charter commission report so that it could not come up on the November ballot. It was a gubernatorial election year and Corbin, who was supporting Republican candidate Paul Troast, thought it would be a bad idea for a bunch of Democrats in Newark to turn out for Robert Meyner. Lowenstein told Corbin that it was too late to delay the filing of the final commission report.

That October, Lowenstein was told by senior partner Irving Riker that, despite seventeen years with the firm, he would be removed at Horace Corbin's insistence. Riker explained that it was not his or the firm's fault, but that there was no other choice given that Fidelity Union Trust Company accounted for almost 90 percent of the firm's income.

The charter commission report was approved handily in the November election, but Lowenstein, at the age of forty, was out of a job. He turned misfortune into opportunity, however. Lowenstein began a private law practice in 1954, and eventually formed Lowenstein, Del Tufo, Callahan & Kean, which grew to over two hundred lawyers by 2001, with offices in several cities. Lowenstein never lost his concern for the city of Newark or its people. In 2002, he provided a substantial gift to establish the New Jersey Institute for Social Justice, which is located in downtown Newark. Lowenstein died in 2007. Today, the firm, now known as Lowenstein Sandler, has an active pro bono practice, which often engages in critical public policy issues.

---

stimulated wholesale lobbying on the part of every ethnic and political constituency to ensure that ward boundaries would guarantee the election of a member of the favored group. Under such pressures, the election commission initially proposed a Central Ward that included Third Ward territory and extended westward through predominantly white areas to the border of Irvington. It was a proposed ward so gerrymandered that the election of a black from an area so configured would have been impossible. A group of Third Ward black activists protested, including the public housing tenants advocate Timothy Still and Larry Coggins, the head of Negro Labor Vanguard, a splinter group of left-wing advocates that often held meetings calling for a socialist government. Still traveled to Washington, DC, to consult with U.S. Census officials concerning the accuracy of the population statistics the commission had relied on and learned that the city clerk had provided the commission with inaccurate data.[44] Still was able to confirm that the commission's plans, if approved, would not have enabled Third Ward blacks to elect their own representative, a promise the reform leaders had repeatedly made in efforts to gain black support. Irvine Turner, an emerging political leader, had strongly opposed the charter reform effort but upon learning that a favorably designed ward could result in his election to be the ward council representative, joined a lawsuit challenging the validity of the boundaries. The commission then revised its outlines for the Central Ward and carved out an area in which blacks made up a decisive majority. This was a major victory for the black community and provided the first opportunity to elect a black representative to city government.

Newark held its first election under the new charter in May 1954, and Leo Carlin, a member of the city commission and local labor leader, was elected mayor. Carlin's triumph was the result of both the strong backing of the reformers and the strength of organized labor in the city at that time. It also mattered that Carlin's résumé was impressive, and although he was the president of a teamsters union local, he was regarded as a straight and honest man. He had served as president of the board of education and served several terms as a commissioner, where he learned firsthand of the body's ineptitude. After his election, he immediately launched a wide range of improvements in government administration. Shortly thereafter, two of the city's major corporations, the Prudential and Mutual Benefit insurance companies, reversed plans to leave the city and announced that they would build new headquarters downtown.

There was much celebration from all quarters about the charter change and a "new beginning" for the city. But the economic prowess of the city was diminishing overnight. One of Carlin's first initiatives was to convene a meeting of major businesses in the city. Despite the Prudential and Mutual Benefit reversals that benefited Newark, the momentum of economic and commercial dispersal was overwhelming. To some extent, Carlin relied heavily on the NHA and encouraged the massive clearance program initiated by the NHA director, Louis Danzig. After his second-term victory, he hired a new police director from New York City who aggressively attempted to clean up the gambling and underworld operations. Carlin stood for honest management, which did not do much for his political standing in a city whose unofficial governance system was boldly corrupt.[45]

MAN OF THE PEOPLE

Irvine Turner, a Newark-born black newspaperman already known for his flamboyant personality and fiery rhetoric, was elected to the first Newark city council as representative of the Central Ward.[46] Ironically, Turner faced his greatest challenge from within the black community, particularly black middle-class civic leaders who looked down on Turner as uneducated and not ready for this pathbreaking leadership role.

Prior to the charter change, leaders of the NAACP, the Urban League, and other civic groups were the major political operatives in the black community. In city affairs they conferred more with the white political leaders than the emerging political activists in the inner city. What they lacked in official standing, they made up for in prestigious associations with organizations such as the NAACP, and they were proud of their education and social achievement. As a result, their pronouncements helped to shape the public view on matters of importance to the mass of black voters. They provided the most active support for the reform movement in the community. As indicated earlier, Turner aligned with the old guard to oppose charter change. Thus, after the wards were established, black civic leaders preferred a candidate of their own choosing to represent the new Central Ward.

To carry out their hope to designate a single black candidate to represent the Central Ward and another for the at-large race, the civic leaders established an organization called the Ad Hoc Voters Independent Council to screen candidates. The group included such established elites of the black community as Ted Pettigrew, then president of the NAACP; Grace Fenderson; Mary Burch, wife of a prominent black obstetrician and organizer of a highly popular youth development program; and others.[47] They looked into the educational background, administrative expertise, and policy-making experience of each candidate. They did not have Irvine Turner in mind. His educational qualifications were highly suspect, and, if he had any experience in "policy," it was not the kind they were thinking of.

On the other hand, Turner had strengths. Although he was not a Zwillman protégé, as Matthews admitted being, the local mobsters knew him as an eager hustler who was not reluctant to use their resources or influences. Indeed, one of Turner's former associates said that among members of the Jewish-controlled underworld, Turner was called a *landsman* (countryman). The racketeers were always ready to support a friendly politician. In addition, he had the support of the leftist activists from the Civil Rights Congress and the Negro Labor Council, both of which were considered disreputable by middle-class civic leaders. Turner's backers made a puzzling coalition of expediency, the radical left supporting a candidate in league with the mob. The criminal organizations had no sympathy for the views of the Left, and surely the radicals did not condone the mob's codes of behavior. For the Left, whose members apparently romanticized the whole arrangement, Turner symbolized the emerging black working class, and some members envisioned that a close, continuing relationship with Turner would provide an important voice for their views. Turner also had high regard for leaders of the Negro Vanguard, particularly Coggins, who was a highly intelligent political strategist and a bit of a hustler himself. Turner, most of all, wanted to win, and the racketeers and the Left were convenient to his goals.

The civic reformers were determined, however, to capture the major support of residents in the ward and win with a candidate of their choice. Thus, the Ad Hoc Voters Independent Council held a meeting to present its acknowledged preference, Roger Yancey, a Central Ward lawyer who had been an assistant corporation counsel for the city and had served as an assistant United States attorney. Turner and his supporters appeared at the meeting en masse. When a representative of the screening committee rose to announce that it would back Roger Yancey for the Central Ward position and NAACP President Harry Hazelwood for an at-large position, the

Turner forces literally disrupted the meeting and took it over. Most of the civic leaders, unaccustomed to this kind of chaotic democracy, walked out. The people who remained (led by Larry Coggins) then endorsed Turner as the choice for the Central Ward and Hazelwood to run for one of the at-large positions.

William Payne, who was an active member of the Youth Council of the NAACP at the time, recalls the Turner-Yancey battle and said he sided with the Turner forces "because Turner was seen as a fighter against the status quo and the establishment."[48] Yancey announced that he would run anyway and immediately received the endorsement of the NAACP leaders and other civic spokesmen. Hazelwood ran but refused to accept the support of the Turner forces for his at-large race. The *Afro-American* endorsed Yancey and criticized the associations Turner had with "organizations which are listed on the Attorney General's list."[49] A few weeks before the election, Yancey quit his campaign and literally disappeared, not to be seen until weeks after he was decisively beaten at the polls. According to Alan Lowenstein, the leader of the reform movement, "Several weeks after the election, Roger Yancey came to my office and said the he felt that he owed me an apology. He said that he had grown up as a poor kid and never had much money, but during the campaign, certain members of the mob offered him a lot of money to leave the race, and he took it."[50]

Turner beat his nearest competitor, a white candidate backed by the Italian organization, by nearly two to one. He won because he had behind him a coalition that was effective at the street level, whereas the middle-class civic leaders had few roots in the community, especially among the poor. Turner knew everyone. He could walk up to the guy hanging on the corner and call his name. The activists who supported Turner were seasoned organizers and turned out their supporters on Election Day. And in many important ways, Turner met the expectations of the activists. As an aspiring, ambitious politician, Turner could be militant; measured by his rhetoric, he was Newark's first Black Power political leader. He would frequently make racial appeals that offered nothing in the way of tangible rewards but fulfilled important psychological needs. When the League of Women voters held a debate for Central Ward candidates, Turner used the forum to call for a black police chief and a black mayor, while other candidates emphasized the need for improved services and better race relations. Coggins recalled, "We knew he was being ridiculous at the time, but the people loved it."[51]

With his victory, a common man with intriguing connections and one-time neighborhood hustler was transformed into one of the most important politicians in New Jersey. Prior to his election, Turner had held a trivial sinecure, with neither office nor phone, as a "home secretary" to Congressman Addonizio, and earlier, in 1943, he had been given a menial municipal job cleaning bathhouses in Commissioner Ralph Villani's Department of Sanitation. After his Central Ward victory, Turner controlled nearly all of the patronage afforded to blacks. In return for jobs, favors, or mere recognition, Turner delivered the support of black Central Ward voters to "deserving" office seekers. Politicians throughout the country and the state, when eager to gain black support, sought out his endorsement. His ability to deliver black ballots for at-large candidates or Democratic candidates running for county offices extended his contacts and influence. His support was frequently given in exchange for money, disguised as contributions for campaign materials or pay for Election Day workers.[52]

Much of Turner's popularity was the result of his frequent criticism of the white establishment in the 1950s. He denounced slumlords as "cheap, law-violating beasts that have the nerve to go overboard in their greed for money at the expense of poor citizens."[53] He had a way of convincing his followers that he would stand up to any official on their behalf. He was known to telephone white officials, scold them in the presence of his supporters, and then later call back to apologize, explaining, "You know I had to do that."[54] Other officials became so accustomed to his routine that eventually it was unnecessary for him to call back and explain his deception. This kind of behavior outraged the NAACP and Urban League leaders, who called him "an erratic unprincipled demagogue who appeals to the newly-arrived, uneducated Southern Negroes with his 'vote black' harangues but achieves little for Negroes in the long run."[55]

Turner built a large and loyal following, despite the fact that he did not get along with Mayor Carlin, who denied him patronage and favors. He had turned the Central Ward against Carlin in the 1954 election and did so again in the 1958 election, when it was the only ward that Carlin did not win. Turner relied more on his close ties to the NHA, where he could occasionally obtain jobs for his followers through NHA director Louis Danzig. He could also help supporters get apartments in public housing or encourage the NHA to delay eviction when a constituent's rent was in arrears. In addition, Turner's relationship with the NHA offered a business connection when he ventured into the real estate business in the 1950s. Thus, Turner frequently served as mediator between the NHA and black churches when the churches were forced to sell property to the NHA and relocate.[56] If a church got a good price with Turner's help, it provided important political mileage for the councilman. In return, Turner supported the NHA's massive slum clearance program in the black community and the construction of concentrated high-rise projects at a time when most middle-class black leaders were calling for low-rise units dispersed throughout the city. Turner often defended the authority and attempted to squelch any resistance to NHA policies. As Danzig put it, "Turner was a vote on the city council I could always count on."[57]

Turner demonstrated the classic "vested interest" that ethnic and racial leaders have always had in the concentration of their constituencies in the city wards. As has been written of other flamboyant leaders of black neighborhoods during that time, "Turner must be understood in terms of the massive pathology of the ghetto, where people seek a concrete hero."[58] It did not matter that Turner often fought sham battles. His public defiance against white politicians and institutions was enough to gain him the ardent support of his poorest constituents. Frequent criticism aimed at him by the black middle class and the press was to his advantage, for it proved to his followers that he, too, experienced the scorn and indifference that outsiders felt for black people, particularly the poor. Middle-class ridicule simply made him better known. Many blacks in the Central Ward gained considerable satisfaction from Turner's prominence, regardless of how it was achieved.[59] Through him there was recognition, the kind sought by all groups that seek to obtain greater security in relations with the larger society. It is well known that a notable achievement, conspicuous appointment, or reward given an ethnic group member gives a sense satisfaction to the entire group. For blacks it meant not only a mark of personal achievement but that a racial barrier had been surmounted.

Turner was not just a symbol. He often raised important issues for blacks in his early years on the city council, and his constant prodding of officials won limited gains. He would issue a constant flow of press releases, calling for opportunities for blacks in jobs, housing, and government, but rarely would he speak at council meetings where policy issues were discussed. When he broke his silence, his statements were usually moral preachments asking for harsher treatment for juvenile delinquents, the death penalty for heroin pushers, or long-term prison sentences for drug addicts. At the same time, he was careful never to reproach the behavior of potential supporters, as when he once condemned a police raid on two hotels in the Central Ward or when he suggested that unmarried couples should be allowed to register in the city's hotels as long as they intended to marry in the future. It was one instance in which Turner was clearly ahead of his time.[60] He often called for constructive changes. One of his first steps as Central Ward representative was to present a plan to Mayor Carlin for the integration of the police force, the appointment of a black municipal judge, and the organization of a recreation program for children at the Hayes Homes.[61] Turner's demand for a black magistrate became his favorite issue during the Carlin years, despite the fact that he had been silent when black ministers and others made the demand to Mayor Villani in the early 1950s.

Turner provided the vital link between the political system in Newark and poor black voters in the Central Ward. He worked closely with politicians like Villani and Addonizio, and figures like Danzig, and on their behalf, he served as boss of the Central Ward. These leaders took care of Turner, and Turner assured voter support or compliance for them. He helped to soothe, co-opt, or challenge any opposition to the white leaders to whom he was loyal. It was not that Turner avoided issues that would embarrass the political leaders or upset the status quo. Rather, after he had artfully preempted or taken over the issues raised by others, he made no effort to ensure they were discussed or acted upon. Similar to other well-known black politicians like Oscar DePriest in Chicago and Adam Clayton Powell Jr. in Harlem,[62] Turner found the militant style an effective way of gaining attention and strong support. Occasionally, benefits did flow to the Central Ward with the help of Turner's agitation.

Hope, But Clouds in View

Despite the struggles and defeats on many issues of great importance, the period following the Second World War was, after all, one of significant advances for blacks in Newark. State laws were passed that eliminated some of the most overt forms of bias in public accommodations, and there were gains in employment which had remained tightly closed. Public housing projects provided new housing for inner-city blacks. Barriers against the employment of black doctors at the city hospital were removed, blacks were named to the Newark Board of Education, and a black manager was appointed to run a public housing project. By the late 1950s the number of black teachers had climbed to over five hundred, while more than one hundred black patrolmen and one black municipal court judge had begun to make their impact on the criminal justice system.

Many of these gains were the result of the rising black vote and its impact on both county and city politics. The new victories were important, but they did not significantly improve the relationship of blacks to the political system. In the context of Newark politics and county politics, Turner was but one against many, and thus he was weak. The major reasons for his weakness were the reality that the black community was constrained by long-established barriers of discrimination, and the community lacked cohesion. In comparison to the white ethnic communities, blacks had fewer skills and resources necessary for political effectiveness. More important was the nature of the Newark political system, a collection of ethnic political congeries, most related in some way to the networks of organized crime or political alignments that were bent more on personal enrichment than on addressing mounting social problems. Added to this, Turner himself was a shady personality and prone to use public bravado, which was seldom followed by action. The victory of representation turned out to be more symbol than substance, and had little effect on the major social and economic issues that were becoming ever more prominent.

The early Turner years brought a kind of progress to Newark's black community, but the period was also filled with hardship and struggle that produced only meager rewards. Nonetheless, locally and nationally, it was a period of great change that fundamentally altered the dynamics of race relations as well as the economic futures of American cities. The period from the end of World War II to 1960 saw a greater mobilization of civil rights forces, major shifts in the demography of cities, a monumental U.S. Supreme Court decision striking down the doctrine of "separate but equal," the emergence of Dr. Martin Luther King Jr., and the election of President John F. Kennedy. Much of this change laid the groundwork for the movements, conflicts, battles, and violence that were to occur in the 1960s.

Near the end of the decade, two reports pointed toward what was to come. *Economic Development of the Greater Newark Area: Recent Trends and Prospects*, issued by the Business Executive Research Committee, a group that included business executives and members of the faculty at Rutgers University Business School, both outlined the economic changes that had taken place from 1947 to 1956 and projected similar areas of change up to 1975.[63] The report found that the core of the region—which included Newark, Elizabeth, and Jersey City—had lost 1 percent of its population from 1947 to 1956, while the surrounding areas, the contiguous suburban areas referred to in the report as "the ring," had gained 9 percent. Total employment in the core had declined slightly (less than 1 percent) while increasing 8 percent in the ring. The report took a surprisingly neutral view regarding the already apparent decline of the core areas. It said, "Although growth performance may afford a generally useful criterion for judging the condition of business organizations, and even of the national economy, there is considerable doubt as to its relevancy in appraising the state of affairs within metropolitan areas in America." The committee predicted that by 1975, population decline in the core areas would be about 6 percent, and employment would decrease by 10 percent; while the ring would grow by 12 percent in population and 5 percent in employment. To the committee, "part of the expansion of population and economic activity in suburban areas reflects growth which was generated in the older core communities. . . . It seems wide of the mark to regard [core decline] as a matter of unhealthy retrogression in the core and healthy progress in the ring. Such judgments tend to blur the real problems of metropolitan development, for which solutions are required in the Greater Newark Area (the larger region surrounding the city) and elsewhere in the United States."[64] It is very likely that the committee was swept by the optimism that prevailed about the new building and construction in Newark, and also saw the impending expansion of urban renewal as a remedy for the growing exodus. However, the committee manifested a common tendency to bury the hard problems and to ignore issues of race. Nowhere in the report was there mention of the reality that the opportunities in the ring, and the growing movement to the ring, could not be shared by the minority population. The report also failed to mention that the continuing decline of jobs and resources would accelerate.

In June 1959, the Mayor's Commission on Intergroup Relations published the results of an extensive two-year survey on racial and ethnic attitudes among Newark residents. The study leading up to the report had found wide disparity in the views of blacks and whites regarding the Newark school system. Blacks, particularly those residing in the Central Ward, complained of overcrowded schools. Weaker, less experienced teachers were being assigned to black neighborhood schools in large numbers and the teacher ranks in the Central Ward were staffed by a disproportionate number of substitutes. School officials consistently denied that the black schools were being treated differently and argued that overcrowding occurred in predominantly white schools as well. They also argued that many teachers refused to accept assignments in black neighborhoods, thus requiring the placement of higher numbers of inexperienced teachers and substitutes in those areas.[65]

The consistent denial of school officials regarding the unfair and discriminatory treatment toward blacks ignored the fact that school decision making was largely influenced by politics. The members of the school board at the time were mainly Jewish and Italian and catered to the interests of their own communities. Plainly, they were often directed by the political leaders who had facilitated their appointment to the school board.[66] The Newark branch of the NAACP surveyed the entire school system and found that schools of high white composition had smaller class sizes than schools in black areas, and that there were 128 double-session classrooms in black areas and only 14 in white areas. The NAACP report concluded:

> Almost without exception, there has been a deplorable shortage of text books available to elementary school children in districts with high Negro enrollment. . . . In schools with high Negro enrollments textbooks were either not available or outmoded and in such poor condition as to be virtually of no value as texts. While the supply situation has not been flawless in the primarily white enrollment school, there is a marked difference in the supply situation between high white enrollment schools and high Negro enrollment schools. In one reading class, no "reader" books were available for pupils and the teacher simply read to the students.[67]

There was also abundant evidence that the school board systematically denied black teacher applicants the opportunity to become certified and thus achieve benefits and long-term employment. The NAACP report found that only six blacks passed all portions of the exam for vice principal in the 1958–1959 period. The report went on to say, "However, their placement on the list was such that it was almost guaranteed that no Negro would be reached during the life of the list. On the other hand, white candidates with low written scores had been given very high oral scores, thus placing them above the Negro candidates on the list."[68]

To make matters worse, the schools became a major source of patronage for the neighborhood politicians. Carlin had virtually shut down the patronage system at City Hall, but he could not control school board politics. Administrators began to notice a decline in quality. Moreover, the influx of black students, many of them from families recently arrived from the South, challenged the cultural and professional aptitude of the teaching corps. The teachers' union complained of new pressures on their members as they now had to face students who had different cultural experiences and attitudes.

Some teachers adapted and excelled. Fred Means, whose story opened this chapter and who in later years became an important civil rights and education leader in Newark, recalls how his white Jewish teachers at Miller Street School took extra steps to teach him science and how to play chess. Walter Chambers, who in the 1960s became the first black executive hired by the telephone company, tells the moving story of his white teachers supporting him and helping him to find Lincoln University, from which he graduated and later became a member of the governing board. Former mayor Sharpe James, as an adolescent, became an aide to the gym teacher when his mother dropped him off each morning at Miller Street School before school opened.[69] But overall, many forces were pressing the schools downward. The battle over education in Newark, which began over issues of equity and representation, later evolved to issues of quality, readiness of students, competency of personnel, and results.

While the report of the Mayor's Commission on Intergroup Relations cautiously danced around many of the realities of discrimination and inequality, it found that blacks had much resentment over the discrimination black citizens experienced in the areas of employment and housing. Regarding police–community relations, the report warned, "Stories about police discrimination—physical abuse, unfair arrests, and, to a lesser extent, laxness in the protection of Negroes—are widespread, and have been heard by almost half of the Negro community. Belief in stories about the mistreatment of Negroes at the hands of the . . . police is so widespread among Negroes as to present a very real problem for the City of Newark. A thorough investigation to learn whether these charges have any foundation in fact is clearly called for."[70]

The events and developments of this period helped form the underlying forces and impulses that remain to this day as all-too-obvious aspects of Newark's political culture. But there is also herein a story of the vision, protest, and change that are part of the city's political and social fabric, with strong roots going back to the moderate but persistent challenges of the Newark branch of the NAACP, the Essex County Urban League, and others who contributed to efforts to advance the condition of black citizens, against considerable odds.

In the next chapter, a different city emerges—a struggling city, distinctly and profoundly altered by national as well as local winds of change. The efforts of Irish voters to hold on to power through Mayor Carlin come to a close as the Italian American community, bolstered by the support of blacks, successfully reasserted itself through former congressman Hugh J. Addonizio. A growing presence of African Americans and Puerto Ricans, many who came to Newark looking for jobs that were rapidly disappearing, was the basis of Newark's own version of the civil rights decade, a period of protests, marches, and sit-ins. The battles over justice at the street level, including demands for land for housing and an opportunity to share in the leadership and political life of the beleaguered city, heightened tensions to a boiling point. The city exploded. By the end of the 1960s, Newark's economic problems had worsened. The decade ended with a regime change, a passing of leadership to the black community, and a generation of new hopes and visions.

⟨ 3 ⟩

The Collapse of the Machine

Newark is the working laboratory of democracy. . . .
What we learn and develop here will be used in every
major community throughout the world.

Mayor Hugh J. Addonizio at a hearing before the
U.S. Commission on Civil Rights, 1962

As THE 1960s BEGAN, the civil rights movement, led by Dr. Martin Luther King Jr., was inspiring civil rights activities all over the nation. It was a movement with many disparate parts, and it was sometimes chaotic and disorganized. Nonetheless, it was powerful and based on the idea the time had come for the end of racial discrimination and equality and opportunity for all. With the election of John F. Kennedy to the presidency of the United States in 1960, not only did that movement gain a special legitimacy, but the social advances for which the movement advocated found a place on the national agenda. Newark's political and social life had its own peculiar features and dynamics, but the force of national events from Alabama to Mississippi to Georgia had much to do with what occurred at the local level.

In the 1950s, the general lack of public policy efforts to address growing postwar urban problems was encouraged by President Dwight D. Eisenhower's stagnant domestic leadership and the conservative climate his political party helped to create.[1] The election of

President John F. Kennedy brought progressive leadership to Washington. During the campaign, Kennedy pledged to eliminate housing discrimination "with a stroke of a pen" and to launch programs to combat poverty and injustice. Although President Kennedy took almost two years to inscribe that much anticipated "stroke of the pen," he did eventually, late in 1962, order federal housing authorities to cease discrimination connected with federal financing of private homes.[2] The executive order President Kennedy signed fell far short of what civil rights advocates expected. It excluded all existing housing and all new housing except that owned or financed directly by the federal government. The White House also attempted to limit the publicity about the order by "deliberately sandwiching" it between two major foreign policy announcements by President Kennedy. Yet civil rights leaders applauded the action, and Martin Luther King Jr. said it was a step that "carries the whole nation forward to the realization of the American dream."[3]

Where Eisenhower had been intractable and mainly subject to international pressures (as when he finally sent troops to Little Rock, Arkansas, to enforce the Supreme Court's decision integrating an all-white high school there), Kennedy was aware that he had received strong support from blacks in his election; more importantly, he was aware of the growing power of the black vote. Although there has been much debate about the degree to which the Kennedy administration repaid blacks for their support, it is clear that his election raised expectations among blacks and encouraged increased activity on behalf of black equality. There was much ambivalence and caution in the Kennedy White House concerning its support of civil rights goals. There is little doubt, however, that the leadership of the civil rights movement as well as the foot soldiers of the marches assumed that President Kennedy brought to Washington a fresh view of America's race issue. Nationally, the civil rights movement gained increasing momentum as countless local groups sprang up to support student sit-ins, Freedom Rides, mass demonstrations in the South, and new and bolder attacks on discrimination and racism in northern communities. Activists of various stripes would join in the effort to bring justice and opportunity to the minority citizens of Newark and help to dismantle an entrenched political machine.

Assessing Reform

By the beginning of the 1960s, the reform movement had made several important changes in the governance of the city. Mayor Carlin, who took office in 1954, prevailed over the demands of members of the city council that they share administrative responsibility with the mayor's office, and he cut short the kind of influence they held under the commission. The new mayor-council government gave assurances to some members of the business community that better government would protect the city's economic future. Shortly after the charter change was approved in 1953, Mutual Benefit Life Insurance Company announced that it would stay, and build, in Newark. Prudential Insurance Company announced it too would build a new development—a twenty-four-story edifice with two seven story wings. Businessmen, enthusiastic over the abolition of the commission, formed the Greater Newark Development Council and the Newark Economic Development Committee to enlist financial and political support for Newark enterprises and to attract new industry.[4] At the beginning of the new decade, it was in such corporate circles that the idea of a tax abatement program originated. In short, the program would provide major tax concessions to companies that chose to relocate to Newark or other urban areas of the state. Known as the Fox-Lance Act, it was signed into law by Governor Robert B. Meyner, a Democrat, in 1961.[5]

Reform was also afoot in the criminal justice system. Joseph F. Weldon, a high-ranking police officer from New York, was appointed to direct Newark's police department, which was considered to be poorly managed, ineffective, and corrupt.[6] Weldon shifted precinct captains who were allegedly taking graft to protect a syndicated gambling ring. He also reorganized the department and attempted to establish a sense of professionalism in the force. Aside from Weldon's efforts to rein in the police forces and the commitments from various entities to new building projects, the pace of disinvestment and decentralization quickened. Unfortunately, government and business leaders overrated the potential of the charter change. The popular view held that mayor-council government failed to halt declining social conditions or arrest the wrongdoing that had plagued the city for many years. Carlin was an unusually humble and modest man, and as an old unionist said, "he was squeaky clean."[7] But the suspicions about shady land deals and closed-door bargaining over contracts remained among several of the members of the council.

Moreover, the black community, largely crowded into the Central Ward, remained at the margins of civic and political activity. "Just about everything was white," recalled Bob Bender, who came to Newark to run the Essex County Chapter of Americans for Democratic Action (ADA) in 1961: "There were only a few blacks in transportation, the police and businesses. It was economic and geographic apartheid."[8] The unemployment rate at the start of the decade was 13 percent for blacks, twice the national average. The schools in minority areas were increasingly overcrowded. Mass clearance of huge parcels of land for public housing, new highways, and universities was extensive. And relocation programs were inadequate and so mismanaged that black inner-city residents as well as residents in the Italian American North Ward complained of abuse and mistreatment. Residents in white neighborhoods became angry at Carlin when blacks moved into their neighborhoods. Members of the Clinton Hill Neighborhood Council, a strong neighborhood civic organization that was dedicated to creating integrated neighborhoods, filed a legal challenge to the NHA's plan to put light industry in their area. In addition, a new highway, Interstate 78, would traverse the South Ward, providing a convenient commuter route for the growing suburban populations at the cost of hundreds of Newark homes. The view of most civic groups was that Mayor Carlin was responsible for the disruptive redevelopment plans, which was not totally inaccurate since he had stacked the governing board of the NHA with his union friends, who in turn faithfully backed NHA's plans.

Many residents also concluded that Carlin had become "co-opted by the downtown leaders" and lost contact with the people.[9] Carlin, an unusually reserved politician, was described by one observer as a "cold fish" who failed to attend social gatherings and community meetings, did not kiss babies, and did not shake enough hands.[10] In a city rich with ethnic traditions, such a failure could be politically fatal. The fact that he was Irish hurt him in many areas of ethnic-conscious Newark, except among his own group, which was rapidly leaving the city for the suburbs. What also contributed to this perception of Carlin was that he carried some of that hard edge you might expect in an erstwhile union type. Also, being a labor leader was no great plus among blacks.

Then, in the winter of 1961, Carlin had the worst of luck. While he and his family vacationed in Florida, the city was hit with a major snowstorm and the city's workers were not prepared for it. The snowplows took days to get to all the neighborhoods. It was all his opponents needed to prove he was not the strong manager reformers had promised. Also, since Carlin had served with the commissioners under the old rules before becoming mayor, it was hard to erase suspicions that he too had gone along with the venality of the old arrangement. Hence, there was some reluctance, even by the new council—and only a few of them had supported charter change—to believe that the politics of mayor-council government was really any different from the commission-style government that had been removed.

Further weakening the reform movement was the fact that its base in the city had almost totally vanished. Harold Kaplan, in his study of Newark's urban renewal program, notes that, "Throughout the 1940s, the city's corporate executives, lawyers, realtors, and educators fled Newark for suburban residence."[11] The exodus continued into the 1950s and would grow to include many working-class Irish American families, many of which were civil servants and teachers. A major share of the South Ward's Jews (who were among the most ardent supporters of reform) left for the suburban towns of Maplewood, South Orange, West Orange, and Livingston.

Moreover, according to Kaplan, "the reform movement in Newark was dominated by business and real estate interests . . . and as a result . . . had strong conservative overtones." The same forces that championed the progressive objectives of central planning, charter revision, and vigorous code enforcement also demanded economy in government, reduction in taxes, fewer public expenditures on social problems, and an end to public housing. In Kaplan's words, "In Newark the terms 'reform' and 'conservative' must be bracketed."[12] The major flaw in the reform effort, however, was that "the reformers sought to remedy a bad situation . . . by changing laws . . . and not the city's social and political character."[13] The deterioration and the pace of change were too rapid and extensive to be arrested by the mere centralization of government. The forces of decay and distrust were generated by indifference in city and suburb. Patterns of neglect and discrimination emanated from wide areas of private and public policies at all levels—federal, state, and local. High taxes, overcrowded and declining schools in black neighborhoods, crime, unemployment, and growing racial conflict seemed already beyond control. Not only were there no meaningful plans or strategies to address these issues, but waiting in the wings was a new cast of political leadership eager to make the city, once again, a machine-oriented town. In order for change in the city's constitutional structure to have maximum effect, as Stanley Winters pointed out, "the city needed committed elected officials, an enduring and involved support base, and especially a changed political culture for nourishment."[14]

Carlin versus Addonizio

When Congressman Hugh J. Addonizio challenged Carlin for the mayoralty in 1962, reform had already lost much of its glow. If there was a glow, it was in the impressive background of Addonizio, a six-term congressman who had supported every progressive and civil rights legislative proposal. Prior to his political career, he had enlisted in the army as a private and before his discharge, he was promoted to captain. He won the Bronze Star and eight campaign ribbons. A Fordham graduate who had been an outstanding pulling guard on his college football team, Addonizio had participated in the historic Normandy invasion and the Battle of the Bulge, which earned him a place in the Infantry Hall of Fame at Fort Benning, Georgia.[15] Addonizio had already locked up support from Central Ward Councilman Irvine Turner as well as many of the leaders of black social and political organizations. With Turner's help, Central Ward voters had played a pivotal role in sending Addonizio to Congress in the 1950s. Turner was rewarded for that contribution with a job—in reality, a sinecure with no office or phone—in Addonizio's home office. However, next to all the laudable points of Addonizio's résumé, rumors swirled around the city that nefarious underworld forces had lined up to support his campaign.

During one of the campaign debates, a member of the audience rose to ask Carlin if he had any concerns about his opponent's honesty and integrity. Carlin snatched the bait. He replied that, yes, voters should be aware of Addonizio's associations. He added, "Beware the Black Hand," hinting at underworld influence. Addonizio bolted from his seat and said to Carlin, "Are you accusing me of being tied to the Mafia? Are you making such accusations because I am an Italian American?" Carlin was mute and stunned. He would say no more, and the audience turned against him. From that point the crowd showed obvious support and sympathy for Addonizio, whom they thought had been unfairly accused. Paul Reilly, who was Addonizio's campaign manager and later served as deputy mayor, said of the "Black Hand" statement: "We pounced on it . . . it just riled up the Italians in Newark, the biggest voting bloc in the North Ward." Associates of Addonizio contend that the entire episode was set up by the Addonizio camp. Apparently, they knew Carlin had made similar accusations in private, and they correctly surmised that he would not back up his statement. Tom Giblin, a state assemblyman and long-time union leader, said, "I do think Carlin was set up. It gave Italian-Americans the [opportunity] to say, 'I was at the Battle of the Bulge; this is detrimental to my heritage.'"[16] It was not until years later, in 1969, that Addonizio was indicted for taking bribes. During his trial, FBI surveillance recordings disclosed his conversations and close association with underworld figures, who were heard in conversation deciding how they (the mob) would choose the police director if Addonizio was victorious in 1962.

Addonizio's campaign renewed the spirit of machine politics. To win black votes, he promised an end to police brutality and discrimination in the school system, and an end to split school sessions, which were the school board's answer to overcrowding. In addition, he pledged to hire more blacks at city jobs and said he would strengthen the Mayor's Commission on Human Rights.[17] In the South Ward, he vowed to limit the NHA's plans for mass clearance to make way for light industry and instead use the Meadowlands for such developments. To the North Ward Italians, he offered an end to Irish control over the bureaucracies. Unlike Carlin, his great strength was his ability to relate to all the different groups in the city. Steve Adubato Sr. recalled, "He was the first Italian to connect to the Irish. His wife was Irish. He lived in an Irish area. He got along with Italians, blacks, and the Irish."[18]

Congressman Addonizio beat Carlin in a landslide. Voters gave Carlin little credit for trying to improve the operation of government and for the eight years he had managed to keep city leadership free of scandal. Addonizio carried every ward in the city and beat Carlin two to one in the North and Central Wards. It was a decisive victory that resulted from his success in exploiting the reversals in ethnic dominance that made Italian Americans and blacks the city's two largest voting blocs. The victory spelled the end to any semblance of reform, a movement already stymied by sweeping changes in demography and economics during the previous decade. Although Addonizio brought back the politics of a previous era, he could not restore peace and stability, as social problems became more evident and civil rights advocates applied more pressure for change. He faced an entirely different political situation from what had prevailed in the 1950s.

Donald Malafronte, a former *Star-Ledger* reporter, was hired by Addonizio in 1964 to serve as the mayor's principal aide. While at the *Ledger*, Malafronte had written an article explaining the legislation that created the federal antipoverty program, and how the various programs would affect city governments. Shortly after the article appeared, Malafronte was invited to City Hall. He recalled that he was interviewed by one of the deputy mayors and immediately offered a job. "I made twice the salary I earned as a reporter, but I received two paychecks; one from the city and one from an assistant business administrator who managed a mysterious special fund. I did not know where the money came from, and I did not ask."[19] Concerning Addonizio's foibles, he said, "He simply had a gambling problem, and that led to other issues. He was not a bad person, and the stories that he left Congress to rip off the city are not true." Nonetheless, Malafronte recognized that the mayor's management was unusual. According to Malafronte, the department heads were essentially on their own, with no direction or leadership from the mayor's office. He recalled that he once suggested that the mayor's top officials get together to discuss plans for the city, and one of the mayor's close aides said, "A meeting? What would we do?"[20]

Sam Convissor, who left the Newark Chamber of Commerce to work for Addonizio shortly after his victory, recounted a trip he made to Washington with Mayor Addonizio to visit housing officials about programs in Newark. They flew to Washington the evening before the meeting, and the next morning Addonizio told him that he was not going to attend the meeting but was going to the racetrack instead. "You handle it," he told Convissor. When Robert Weaver, the secretary of the Department of Housing and Urban Development, walked into the meeting, he asked, "Where's Hughie?" Convissor replied that the mayor had other business to take care of. The secretary replied, "He's probably at the track."[21] Steve Adubato Sr., who was then a school teacher and just getting involved in North Ward politics, told me, "Addonizio was sick with the gambling habit. He was in major debt to the mob, and they controlled the city. If you wanted a job, you went to the mob, not to the mayor."[22]

Before long, Addonizio's administration would come face to face with local civil rights activists. While it was easy for Addonizio to be progressive in Congress, he was overwhelmed and resistant to the new demands for change that were put before him.

CORE Comes to Newark

In 1960, organizers from the Congress of Racial Equality (CORE), which had conducted Freedom Rides into the South, visited Newark to recruit volunteers to organize a local chapter.[23] Purely by coincidence, separate groups sprang up in East Orange and Newark. When both sought approval to represent CORE in the area, the national CORE office suggested that the two groups unite. The merger led to the formation of Newark-Essex CORE. At its peak years 1963 and 1964, Newark-Essex CORE had seventy-five to one hundred active members who attended meetings, worked on committees, or participated in demonstrations. In addition, the chapter had several hundred supporters. For some events, such as a march and rally against police brutality, the chapter could draw a crowd of close to one thousand.

From its beginning, it was a thoroughly racially integrated organization, although by consensus among its members, the leader of the group was always an African American. I served as the first chairman of Newark-Essex CORE and was succeeded by Raymond Proctor, who, like me, was a case worker at the Essex County Welfare Board. After Proctor, Fred Means, a Newark high school teacher, took the helm, followed by Walter Stevens. James Hooper, who was the first working-class leader of the group, was the last chair before the chapter dissolved. The chapter membership was based in Newark, but at least half of its members lived in the nearby suburbs of Maplewood, South Orange, West Orange, Montclair, and Nutley. And while CORE received support from several Christian churches in Newark and the suburbs, there was also strong Jewish representation. The churches and synagogues provided a good share of the funds that supported CORE's work. Some private attorneys and the legal committee of the American Jewish Congress provided volunteer legal assistance. The chapter always had volunteer lawyers to help in its battles with City Hall, particularly in efforts to address police abuse. Several members of the chapter, including myself, were social workers who in their professional roles dealt with poor families every day. However, unlike a welfare rights organization that was formed in alliance with the Newark Community Union Project (NCUP) and the local antipoverty program, Newark-Essex CORE did not attempt to mobilize poor neighborhoods. CORE's local membership was made up of working people—all volunteers who occasionally used their own money to support the activities of the group—plus a few students from nearby colleges and high schools.

Newark-Essex CORE's major activities were campaigns against employment and housing discrimination, police brutality and mistreatment of black members of the community, as well as discrimination practiced by recreational facilities such as swimming pools. (New Jersey had passed laws in 1948 against discrimination in employment and housing. However, the legislature decided to put the Office of Civil Rights in the Department of Education, thus interpreting the problem of fairness and rights as a matter of education.) From 1962 to 1964, Robert Bender, executive director of the Essex County Chapter of Americans for Democratic Action, headed a CORE employment committee of almost forty members, which divided into subgroups to investigate hiring and promotion practices at scores of employers in the area.[24]

In 1963, CORE joined a coalition of other civil rights groups to form the Newark Coordinating Council (NCC). The NCC was mainly the idea of a former assemblyman, George C. Richardson, who said at a meeting, "We need to bring all these groups that are fighting for the same thing under one umbrella."[25] The first major action of this amalgam was a demonstration protesting discrimination in the construction trades at a site in the North Ward of Newark. Specifically, the plan was to target the site where a new Barringer High School was being built. The Barringer demonstration would be the first display of mass civil disobedience in the city, and it signaled a profound shift in the tenor and tactics of civil rights activity in Newark and New Jersey.[26]

The Barringer action also began a protracted struggle between civil rights groups in the city and the construction trade unions, which were affiliated with the American Federation of Labor (AF of L). The Barringer construction site was a perfect target to attack the entrenched forces of inequality in education and employment. The school, located at the southern end of Branch Brook Park and in the shadows of the magnificent Sacred Heart Cathedral (later named the Cathedral Basilica of the Sacred Heart), was known as one of the stronger schools in a declining system. It had adopted several features of Jim Crow that were unusual for northern institutions. For example, although there were no signs and certainly no laws supporting such an arrangement, black students were expected to use a certain door for entering and leaving the school. The construction industry was a bastion of discrimination, although union leaders vehemently denied that the absence of blacks in the industry was in any way related to unfair rules and procedures. Although union workers were employed on sites throughout the city, only 4 percent of all Newark residents had jobs with the unions.[27]

On July 3, 1963, promptly at 6 A.M., about two hundred demonstrators arrived at the construction site. The group included members of CORE; a loose group of Richardson's followers called the New Frontier Democrats (a title borrowed from the Kennedy presidential campaign); members of the Essex County Chapter of Americans for Democratic Action; Rabbi Israel Dresner from Springfield, who years earlier had ventured to the South to march with the Reverend Martin Luther King Jr.; neighborhood activists from the South Ward; and a contingent of white far left–leaning suburbanites. Many in the group had spent the previous evening, late into the night, making posters for the picket line. The boldly printed signs said "Negroes Want to Build Too" and "Unions Discriminate." The picket line circled in front of the only entrance to the site. When the workers began to arrive, they huddled and watched from about twenty-five yards away. They stared, they were angry, they conferred, and then they marched toward the gate. As they approached the line, they pushed, shoved, and threw fists at the demonstrators. The police moved in and added to the turmoil as they dragged a few of the demonstrators and placed them under arrest. Rabbi Dresner was struck across the shoulder by a policeman's billy club.

Mayor Addonizio's first reaction was to order a halt to construction until the complaints of NCC could be investigated. At the same time, he denounced the organizers of the action, calling them "troublemakers attempting to stir up the community." A few days later, the mayor rescinded his stop-work order and named a Citizens Negotiating Committee (CNC) to negotiate with the unions over the civil rights grievances. School board members, city officials, and union and construction contractors met to discuss the NCC charges. Louis Vehling, the head of the Essex County Building Trade Unions, reacted angrily to the demonstration and particularly to the mayor's decision to stop work at the site. He called the mayor's order "illegal and made without any consultation with the unions." Addonizio sought to appease the union leadership by appointing several union officials to the Mayor's Commission on Human Rights.[28]

The NCC accomplished a major objective by forcing the problem of racially closed unions onto the public agenda. However, the mayor initially did not include any members of the NCC on the newly appointed CNC. The members of the committee were carefully selected to protect the administration and were likely expected to reach a settlement consistent with the inch-by-inch racial progress characteristic of Newark. Much to Addonizio's dismay, several of the handpicked members of the CNC expressed support for the NCC action and pressed the mayor to stand fast against the unions. James Pawley of the Essex County Urban League and Carlton Norris of the NAACP as well as the clergymen on the committee openly criticized the unions.

Addonizio then invited the Reverend John Collier, a member of CORE and the Ministers Alliance, to join the CNC. Soon after, the CNC was reorganized and the NCC gained increased representation. Bender, chair of CORE's employment committee, was also added to the CNC. The inclusion of more members of the CNC allowed for the NCC to push for stronger demands, and they called for at least 50 percent minority representation on all municipal construction jobs to make up for the imbalance that had existed for many decades. Vehling called the proposal "arbitrary, unrealistic, and unreasonable." He contended that the civil rights activists wanted the unions to abandon their meritocratic hiring standards and give apprenticeships to less qualified workers as compensation for past discrimination. Reverend Collier and others questioned the objectivity of union membership criteria and pointed out that most people were aware that the trade unions used their standards selectively, as a way to preserve jobs for family members and friends. Vehling and other union leaders had conceded this point in testimony before the U.S. Commission on Civil Rights.[29]

A breakthrough finally occurred in mid-August when the building trades agreed to devise a response to the CNC proposal if NCC stopped picketing. The civil rights groups saw this as an opening and began preparing young men to take advantage of the new opportunities. The NAACP Youth Council sent teams to Central Ward housing projects to encourage residents to fill out applications for construction jobs, and the Negro American Labor Council proposed to county high schools to create "on the job training programs." In early September, the NCC reached an agreement with the unions in which the city Youth Career Development Center and the State Employment Service would screen and refer potential craftspeople to the unions. The unions agreed to hire on a "nondiscriminatory basis." State officials would monitor the plan. The agreement assumed that there would be good faith by the unions in its implementation, but the unions stalled, rejected applicants, and often found reason to turn applicants away. By the end of the year, there may have been one or two minorities hired as apprentices on government-sponsored construction sites.

The NCC action at Barringer had little impact on the entrenched and exclusionary practices of the unions. Still, the campaign did begin a slow and painful process that laid the foundation for subsequent and more successful efforts. The shallow arguments by union leaders in defense of their practices became well known, which helped to convince the more conservative members of the black community to support efforts to change the union's hiring practices. Federal officials, also troubled by similar confrontations taking place in other cities, became more active in overseeing union apprenticeship programs. Most importantly, the Barringer demonstration shattered the moderate, go slow, accept-little-or-nothing as progress that had been the way of race relations in Newark for decades. As a result of the action, the downtown business leaders agreed to join a forum called the Business and Industrial Coordinating Committee (BICC) to address the fact that blacks and Puerto Ricans were systematically excluded from the city's private and public workforce.[30]

CORE subsequently staged direct action campaigns against the New Jersey Bell Telephone Company, Pabst Brewery, Sears and Roebuck, the Hoffman–La Roche pharmaceutical company located in Nutley, Western Electric in Kearny, and the Veterans Hospital in East Orange.[31] In most cases, investigations of discriminatory practices began with informants from within the companies reporting examples of unfairness or outright racism. For example, the negotiations began at Western Electric when black employees who had been hired as a result of Fair Employment Practices Executive Order in the 1940s remained in their entry positions while whites hired much later were regularly advanced or promoted above them. CORE activities were frequently reported in the local press and often gained the attention and support of other groups. The campaign against hiring practices at the New Jersey Bell Telephone Company became a case study of a civil rights organization and a major private corporation ultimately working together to improve employment opportunities for minorities.

Ringing Up the Phone Company

In the latter part of 1963, when CORE representatives first met with officials of the New Jersey Bell Telephone Company, a subsidiary of American Telephone and Telegraph (AT&T), the meeting did not go well. Bell executives contended that they were doing a good job in hiring minorities, but, they said, certain areas of the company had few or no minorities because it was difficult to find qualified people. Bell executives said that more than 50 percent of the people hired the previous year in the Newark area were minorities. Furthermore, they contended that the firm had signed up to participate in "Plans for Progress," an initiative begun under President Kennedy in 1963 to encourage large corporations to increase minority hiring.[32]

CORE's informants painted a very different picture of how the company looked from the inside. They told CORE that most of the minorities working in the company were female operators, one of the lowest-paying jobs in the business. They described a company with an all-white male leadership team and an almost total absence of minority men. There were five thousand men in the plant division, and only two hundred were minorities. Of over seven hundred linemen in the state, there was one person of color. With eight foremen in the Newark area, the minority count was zero. There were sixty instructors, and none were minorities.[33]

CORE advised the Bell executives that unless the company presented a concrete plan to integrate its workforce, the organization would take direct action. New Jersey Bell officials were not pleased at the threat of demonstrations. They then issued a public statement charging that CORE's "attacks" were unjustified since Bell was "playing a leading role in the hiring of minorities, and the company was meeting with CORE in good faith." The threat to "take action," they said, "would only disrupt the progress being made." Racial discrimination became nasty words in some important circles of the North, and no company, particularly one doing business with the public, wanted to be branded as discriminatory.[34]

Richard Proctor, who succeeded Bender as head of CORE's employment committee, said company representatives "offered nothing but a continuation of the tokenism which they have engaged in since they agreed to the president's Plans for Progress in 1963."[35] He accused the company of distorting its hiring record and asserted that of the two hundred people hired the previous year (1963), most were female operators. CORE was not at all impressed by the generalizations, unsupported by data that the Bell representatives provided. CORE leaders called for a demonstration, which was staged the following Saturday. Several dozen CORE activists went to Newark Airport, where they occupied telephone booths while holding signs calling for an end to unfair treatment of blacks and the hiring of minorities in jobs where there were few, if any. When the television news highlighted the protest at the airport, an urgent call went out immediately from the office of the president of AT&T in New York. According to a former vice president of operations at New Jersey Bell, the AT&T president ordered the president of New Jersey Bell to "get those people with those signs out of the airport." The Bell president explained that they were civil rights demonstrators over whom he had no control. The president of AT&T responded: "I said get them out of there."[36]

I was not accustomed to receiving calls from a vice president of the phone company. But that is what happened. The tone was cordial and easy. "We need to get together right away. Can we meet tomorrow?" Negotiations resumed the next day. New Jersey Bell was now willing to share specific information about its workforce and set clear objectives for recruiting and hiring minorities. The firm also did something it had never done before: it hired someone from outside directly into its management ranks. Walter Chambers, an African American staff member of the Newark Human Rights Commission, was recruited to become an executive at New Jersey Bell. Chambers became an important advisor to company leadership on civil rights and other matters. One of his first tasks was to establish a training program on civil rights for the firm's management employees.[37] The seminars were taken seriously by top officers of the company; they usually included both local and national civil rights leaders as speakers and panelists. Raymond Proctor, Fred Means, and I, who all served as chairs of Newark-Essex CORE, participated in several of the seminars. Bell executives were encouraged to ask any and all questions. At CORE's suggestion, the firm also financed the production of a documentary film aimed at minority high school students regarding the challenges and responsibilities involved in preparing for a job. For several years, the film was used at Bell installations throughout the country.

One of the executives who participated in the negotiations with CORE once said to me, "You know, New Jersey Bell is like a huge ship. It is difficult to get it to change course, and it takes time. However, when it does, it will move in a different direction."[38] Without question, New Jersey Bell Telephone Company changed course. As this case demonstrates, public protests, borrowed from the earlier tactics of the union movement, were an effective tool, particularly when used after well-publicized efforts to negotiate had failed.

Collaborating for Racial Progress

The Business and Industrial Coordinating Committee (BICC) was formed shortly after the Barringer High School demonstration, when the NCC announced that its next targets for direct action would be the downtown department stores and banks. The idea of a civil rights–business–labor partnership was the brainchild of several people, including Arnold Harris, the community relations secretary of the Jewish Community Council; Peter Schuyler, executive secretary of the Essex County Welfare Federation; and Derek Winans, a scion of the family that owned the Winans Paper and Twine Company. The coming together of these conflicting forces was a very new turn: to suddenly have representatives of Bamberger's, Fidelity Union Trust, Prudential, Public Service Electric and Gas, Western Electric, New Jersey Bell Telephone Company, and others sitting down on a bimonthly basis to discuss the demands of the most vocal civil rights groups was unprecedented. The meetings were often quite candid; the concerns of corporate leaders who worried about their businesses and the ability of new applicants to meet their standards were also on the agenda. Generally, business and civil rights leaders were hopeful about the effort. A CORE officer described the development as "a tremendous step in the right direction."[39]

In January 1964, after meeting for only six months, BICC employers sent 188 job orders to the Essex County Urban League, which responded with 187 black applicants. Only 32 were hired.[40] It was obvious from the beginning that some firms were reluctant to open up new areas of employment to blacks and Puerto Ricans, but they also felt they could ward off public criticism and demonstrations if they joined the BICC and attended its meetings. Convissor, who served as an aide to Mayor Addonizio at the time and represented City Hall at BICC meetings, said, "Businessmen apparently viewed the BICC originally as a kind of protective agency, and thought they would be immune from picket lines and boycotts if they joined."[41] That notion was quickly dispelled when CORE staged demonstrations against several BICC members. On the other hand, some of the business leaders met the issues head-on, made significant changes in their own companies, and worked very hard to convince other firms to do likewise.

FURIOUS FREEDOM FIGHTER

During the turbulent days of the 1960s, Derek Torrey Winans was Newark's tie to its long-gone Anglo-Saxon past. His father, James Dusenberry Winans, was a noted progressive political activist and owner of the C. G. Winans Company, a salt, paper, and twine manufacturer. His ancestors could be traced back to the founding of Newark, and his great-grandfather fought in the Civil War.

Derek was a lean, pipe-smoking Harvard graduate. He usually seemed to work on the periphery of various Newark groups, except for the Essex County Chapter of Americans for Democratic Action (ADA), of which he became president. Wherever he landed, he was passionate—indeed, furious—about racial injustice. During his tumultuous leadership of ADA, he turned the organization upside down, partly because it did not move far and fast enough on civil rights issues.

Derek discovered more comfort as advisor and strategist for other more engaged grassroots organizations. In 1963, after the burst of demonstrations over discrimination in the construction trades, Derek helped to shape the idea of a Business and Industrial Coordinating Council. When Tom Hayden and the SDS students came to Newark, he joined them. For some time, he worked on the staff of City Councilman Donald Tucker. Derek was also the founder of the Newark Community Project for People with AIDS. In the late 1970s, he began volunteering as a planner and grant writer for the International Youth Organization (IYO), a local community organization. Its leader was Caroline Wallace, who came to rely on Derek not only for his grant writing but also for his skill as a counselor for the young people the organization served. IYO, like many groups, occasionally ran out of money. Derek always faced periods of drought by showing up every day, without compensation, and helping to get IYO on its feet again.

Nonetheless, it was difficult for the BICC to live up to its promise. The civil rights groups discerned too much caution in the companies about taking in more nonwhites; the companies constantly complained about the lack of preparation (usually caused by poor schooling) of many of the applicants. Both sides were right to a degree. An assessment of hiring data from 1966 to 1967 of the larger member companies gave a fair picture of the extent to which blacks and Puerto Ricans were marginalized in the labor market of the city of Newark, six months after the gunfire and mayhem of 1967 had subsided. Data indicated that the five firms included in the assessment had a total of 24,318 employees. Of that number, 2,727 were nonwhite, which was 11.2 percent of the total. However, a total of 2,181 were in clerical, labor, and service jobs. Only 2.8 percent of the nonwhite employees were in managerial or official positions. These figures are probably more favorable to the firms than they deserved, for the nonwhite category would include Asians, and the category of officials and managers included supervisors of security, cleaning, or kitchen employees.[42]

Although the gains in jobs were modest, the BICC was an important example of collective action by leaders of business, government, and civic and labor organizations, all of the sectors necessary to create positive changes.

Politician and Freedom Fighter

It would be a serious omission to discuss the 1960s in Newark without giving special attention to George C. Richardson, a tough-minded, dynamic personality who became a cochairman of the BICC and was one of the outstanding fighters for racial justice of the era. Richardson, an African American born and raised in Newark, made it into the Democratic political machine, but he did not give up his voice, which was a tenet of machine politics.

In 1960, Richardson was working as a bartender and manager of Knobby's, a popular Central Ward tavern, where he also doubled as the organizer of Knobby's softball team. When team members wondered why they had no ballfields in their neighborhood and had to travel miles to find one, they appealed to city officials to build one in the area. Promises came to the group, but no ballfields. Richardson concluded that they could not get a field because they had no political power. He told the group they had to get involved in politics and would have to run people for district leader positions. Richardson then put together a slate, won several seats, and soon after, his group was invited to join forces with Eulis "Honey" Ward, who was also building a base of support by running district leaders. With their combined support, they were ready to take over the leadership of the ward from Dan Salvatore, who had become ward chair by consolidating his strength in the western area of the ward, still largely populated by Italians and Irish. At a subsequent Essex County Democratic Party meeting at a hotel in downtown Newark, Richardson and Ward decided to propose to Dennis Carey, the county Democratic chairman, that he add more blacks to countywide tickets. According to Richardson, Carey strongly rejected their plea and reminded them that it was he who decided when and how the various groups would be represented on election tickets. Carey had taken over the county Democratic Party in 1953 when it was firmly in the control of Republicans, who then held all nine freeholder seats. Carey, a shrewd old-line politician, with his crafty ethnic ticket balancing, now had the Democratic Party in control of the county. He had no patience for any dissent. Richardson and Ward were taking on a formidable foe.

When Carey rebuffed Ward and Richardson, Central Ward delegates began to shout back at Carey, and the meeting became very chaotic. A few scuffles broke out and a few chairs were turned over. "I went up to the podium," Richardson remembered, "and took the microphone out of Carey's hands. I urged him to recognize that the black community provided significant support for the party and had no representation in the legislature, and had little representation in the county." Carey abruptly ended the meeting and left.[43]

The next day, Carey called Ward and Richardson to a meeting. "He could not have been nicer," Richardson recalled. "He offered a drink from his stash of fine liquor that always decorated the top of a small table in his office. He told us he wanted Ward to become chairman of the Central Ward Democratic Party and said he would put me on the ticket for an assembly seat."[44] In 1961, Richardson was elected to the assembly to represent Essex County. The following year, he served as a cochair of Addonizio's mayoral campaign, since all the black political organizations were closely tied to the North Ward Italian organizations. When Addonizio was elected, Assemblyman Richardson became the city's insurance commissioner.

Shortly after Addonizio took office, CORE initiated a drive for a civilian police review board, and one day the mayor agreed to meet with a few CORE members to discuss the idea. When we (the CORE delegation) entered the mayor's office, there was the mayor, his corporation counsel, Norman Schiff, and Richardson, who the mayor obviously thought would impress the CORE delegates because he was black. As the discussion proceeded, and the mayor stated his opposition to a review board, much to the mayor's surprise and discomfort, and to our surprise as well, Richardson suddenly interrupted the mayor and said he agreed with CORE's arguments about the need for a police review board. He then said to the mayor, who was now speechless, "I know a lot of black people who have been beaten by the police." Following the meeting, which was a complete bust for CORE, we began picketing City Hall, and Richardson joined the CORE picket line. Political leaders abhor people who are independent and willing to openly defy the organization.

Richardson recalled: "The mayor called me to his office and said, 'George, you can't picket against me.' I said to him, 'I am not picketing against you; I am picketing against the police.' The mayor said, 'I'm the mayor. They are my police. That's me.'" Soon after, Richardson was fired. When his assembly term expired in 1963, he was dropped from the Essex County Democratic ticket, which prevented him from running for a second term. His independence cost him his job and his office. However, he became closely allied with CORE and other vocal civil rights groups.

In 1963, Richardson formed an insurgent political organization called the New Frontier Democrats—borrowing the title from the Kennedy campaign—to challenge the county Democratic ticket. "We were taking our cue from what was happening down South in the civil rights movement," said Richardson. "Imagine a northern city like Newark without a black anything: no black sales clerks, no black bus drivers. We needed something to confront that."[45]

It was clear that the New Frontier Democrats could not win a single position in a countywide race—not for the state senate, assembly, or county positions. Nonetheless, even a relatively small diversion of Democratic Party voters could put Democratic Party control in jeopardy. And that is exactly what happened. Richardson received 10,164 votes as a candidate for state senate, which was not decisive but cut deeply into the Democratic candidate's support. Republican Robert Sarcone won the senate seat by 16,000 votes. However, a smaller vote total for Richardson's running mates helped the Republicans wrest five assembly seats and two freeholder positions from the Democrats.[46] The Richardson insurgency led to Republican control of the assembly, a devastating blow to the Democratic Party and to Democratic governor Richard Hughes, whose legislative proposals would be stalled by the increased Republican strength in the assembly

The party leadership was livid, as were black Democrats Irvine Turner and Charles Matthews, who had briefly held the Central Ward Democratic Party chairmanship, and Honey Ward, who by now had split with Richardson. The black party faithful joined in issuing harsh criticisms of the dissident Richardson and gave a passionate defense of the leadership of Boss Carey. They labeled Richardson a "shill for the Republican Party," and Turner concluded that Richardson's 10,000-vote total was proof that his constituency was limited. Despite his success in disrupting the county Democratic machine, Richardson, in the long run, wanted in. Ever the idealist, he wanted to be accepted on terms to which the political machine was not accustomed. He continued to call for the establishment of a police review board. At the same time, he appealed to Governor Hughes to broker a peace with Carey and the local political leaders. As the party lined up its ticket for a 1964 race, Governor Hughes convened a gathering that included Addonizio, Carey, and Richardson. Hughes tried to persuade Carey to put Richardson back on the ticket. Carey would not budge.[47] But four blacks made it onto the Democratic ticket instead of the usual one or two. The Richardson protest strategy was paying off, although not in his favor. Nonetheless, in 1964, Richardson eventually withdrew his insurgent ticket and left the city to work for the National Democratic Party. It was part of a deal brokered by state party officials, which allowed Richardson to argue that the threat of the conservative Republican presidential candidate, Barry Goldwater, compelled him to forgo local politics and support Lyndon Johnson.[48]

In 1965, Richardson again fielded a slate of candidates under the banner of a new organization, this time called the United Freedom Democratic Party, borrowing the appellation of the Mississippi Freedom Democrats. Richardson described his slate as the first true rainbow coalition, for it had whites, blacks, and Puerto Ricans vying for state and county offices. It was indeed a multihued coalition of civil rights activists, neighborhood organizers, peace advocates, and several members who opposed the use of nuclear weapons. The slate did not have the same impact it had in the 1963 race, because it was a gubernatorial election year and a small rump party was insignificant because of the much larger turnout.[49] In 1966, Richardson persuaded Kenneth A. Gibson to run for mayor. Richardson challenged Turner for the council seat in the Central Ward, as Gibson entered the race for the big prize. Richardson, who was clearly the most visionary among the civil rights/opposition forces, felt that a race for mayor in 1966 would prepare the black community for a major effort in 1970 when the numbers of registered blacks would be sufficient, with Puerto Rican and modest white support, to win the office. Gibson would test the waters but Richardson himself planned to be the black community's candidate in 1970.

Richardson's best-laid plans did indeed go astray, and he never did get elected mayor. However, his voice and leadership were significant in the Newark drive for equality and significantly aided in the effort to dismantle the Italian-dominated political machine. He was also a strong supporter of CORE's direct action campaigns, and other CORE activists and I often worked for his insurgent tickets. Richardson went on to have a role—not a supportive one for his friend Kenneth Gibson—in the mobilization and politics leading up to the 1970 election.

Seeking a Revolutionary Trajectory

In early 1964, a group of Newark activists invited a group from Students for a Democratic Society (SDS) to Newark to help the Clinton Hill Neighborhood Council wage its ongoing battle with the city administration and the Newark Housing Authority (NHA). The NHA had major plans to bulldoze housing in the area and build light industry.[50] The SDS group was part of a national campaign to organize a social movement of poor and working-class people to create fundamental changes in American society under the auspices of the Economic Research and Action Project (ERAP). In the summer of 1964, the SDS contingent arrived, led by Tom Hayden, a founder and former president of SDS, and Carl Wittman, who served as the initial staff lead organizer. Hayden had been the principal architect of the plan to move SDS members off campuses and into poor communities.

Within a few months of their arrival, a deep schism developed between the youthful SDS members and the leadership of the Clinton Hill Neighborhood Council. The council, mainly white homeowners trying to prevent their community from being declared blighted, wanted the students to work on neighborhood improvement projects and to mobilize protests against the NHA and City Hall. The SDS members made clear they were not interested in working with people who had "something to protect" (meaning homeowners) and thus moved eastward to the Lower Clinton Hill neighborhood that was populated mainly by poor black families renting wood-frame flats. There they formed a new group called the Newark Community Union Project (NCUP), rented a home in the area, and proceeded to encourage tenants to fight for better conditions.[51]

When Hayden arrived in Newark with his group of about twelve SDS organizers, all were white except one. The students were later joined by two other blacks, Phil Hutchins, an African American from Cleveland, and Junius Williams, a Yale law student, who remained in Newark and later led the community fight against plans to build a medical school in the Central Ward. Despite a few failed attempts to proselytize neighborhood people, the young white visitors did some impressive organizing. Jesse Allen, an illiterate, unskilled laborer, was discovered by NCUP. Allen, who had an extraordinary ability to recall facts and figures, became a key organizer, and in 1974, he won a seat as the Central Ward representative on the city council. Terry Jefferson, Wyla McClain, and Betty Moss, all neighborhood women, were recruited by NCUP and helped to organize other poor women. The SDS organizers also tutored neighborhood women about their welfare rights. With the resources of the antipoverty program, the SDS troupe created the Bessie Smith Health Clinic in the neighborhood, named after a beloved fallen community leader (not the storied singer Bessie Smith); they virtually took over the governance of the local neighborhood antipoverty program, made it more effective and democratic, and made the government-financed office essentially an outpost of NCUP.[52]

In some cases, the local CORE chapter either supported or collaborated with NCUP organizers on actions in the Lower Clinton

Hill neighborhood (in one instance, I was arrested at an NCUP demonstration against a food market that systematically cheated neighborhood residents). NCUP, in turn, occasionally supported actions initiated by Newark-Essex CORE. Among most of the CORE members, there was considerable respect for the dedication and commitment the SDS students showed in working with the poor of the Lower Clinton Hill neighborhood. However, the outlook and visions of NCUP and CORE were fundamentally different. Hayden and his group fancied themselves as potential revolutionaries, in search of a "revolutionary trajectory" as Hayden had once put it; CORE simply sought to capture a piece of the pie for blacks and Puerto Ricans. In short, CORE wanted more jobs, better schools, better treatment by the police, and equal access to all neighborhoods in the state.[53]

The SDS organizers scared the hell out of Newark government leaders, especially the police. Dan Gerwin, in his Columbia University Ph.D. dissertation on NCUP, contends that the white members of the group spent a lot of time "looking forward to a riot."[54] Surely some of their newsletters and leafleting alarmed officials and seemed intended to incite. For example, in NCUP's newsletter of July 1966, in a passage entitled "Seeds of Riot," there is the following: "The Police are drilling. The State Troopers are ready. But what is being done about the community to improve it so that nobody will want to burn it down?"[55] At times, the NCUP members were threatened and harassed by the police, and the police tried to find ways to intimidate them. Malafronte, former aide to Addonizio, said that "we always had at least three or four informants in their group, so we knew everything they were doing."[56]

The NCUP-ers did not mind the attention; they often exaggerated their accomplishments. They had a very active publicity campaign that celebrated every sign of victory, no matter how small. A few of their members made a documentary film of their work. They also had meetings and staged actions for fund-raising purposes. Other filmmakers, even the noted documentarian Henry Hampton, treated footage from NCUP's promotional material as objective reporting. Newsletters advertised their meetings and celebrated bus rides and trips for children. The organized flows of information about the project were also augmented by Hayden's public speaking and writings in New Left journals. The "excitement" of the action in Newark reverberated throughout the white liberal/left establishment. The publicity reaped financial support. Hayden was also an important international peace advocate and, along with actress Jane Fonda, whom he later married, made trips to Vietnam and Paris where he conferred with North Vietnamese officials who were negotiating with American diplomats to bring an end to the Vietnam War.

In 1967, after the Newark rebellion, when, as Hayden said, "It was time for us to leave," NCUP could point to a few tiny victories. His parting salute to Newark was his polemic on the Newark outbreak, *Rebellion in Newark*. Hayden's grand vision of organizing the poor and building a coalition of blacks, whites, labor, and other progressive organizations never came to pass. For sure, there was no "revolutionary trajectory" to be found in Newark. For one of the organizers, the major achievement was a job working for the Newark Police Athletic League in a street playground. Steve Block, who spent several years in NCUP, said, "In truth, we got more out of the community than we gave."[57]

Despite the fact that the grand radical vision was not realized, the SDS and NCUP organizers could rightly claim that they helped to raise the decibel level and the tempo around race and poverty. Their presence contributed to the growing assault on the corrupt political machine headed by Addonizio.

The Machine's Demise

Increasing agitation by community groups created a hostile and unstable environment in which Addonizio's policies were constantly challenged. To remain effective and sustain control, an organization needs to anticipate and determine the nature and scope of demands made by outside forces. For the political machine, this is essential in order to maintain the distribution of resources according to the preferred status of the dominant group. In the dying days of the commission government, Mayor Ralph Villani was quite explicit about this need when asked to appoint a black magistrate. In essence, his response was that if he gave a judgeship to a black person, he would not have that position to give to a member of a more powerful group. By 1965, the demands of civil rights organizations, accompanied by a

change in norms in race relations, constituted a threat to the arrangements that had allowed Italian Americans to gain a vastly disproportionate share of the spoils of victory. As the machine scrambled
to protect itself, Councilman Turner became an outspoken critic of
CORE and all of the new civil rights forces. He said on one occasion, "They fan flames by mentioning short patience and violence . . .
where are we going with these inflammatory remarks? Violence, rash
words, or insulting remarks are not going to get my race any further
ahead than they have come." Turner explained his recipe for dealing
with anyone who would start violence in Newark: "Let them come
within peeping distance of my men (who will go so far as to destroy
for me) and I'll show you how to get rid of them, 'cause they will
give 'em a good old-time beating. That's what they need."[58] In an ear-
leir comment, Turner had urged all the splintered civil rights groups
to "throw in the towel" and join the NAACP, which was locked into
the Addonizio camp. According to Turner, "It is the only recognized
organization which has fought the battles for the Negro race down
through the century."[59]

It was not so easy for the political machine to find ways to commu-
nicate or counteract the community pressures. A crescendo of forces
demanding moves toward equality came crashing against increasing
criticism from whites in the city that blacks were now getting too
much. Addonizio, at first, did in fact make significant concessions
to the black community. During his first term in office (1962–1966),
he appointed several blacks to key spots in city government. Wilbur
Parker became the city budget director, Grace Malone the head of
the city welfare department, and Richardson secretary of the insurance fund. In addition, Harry Hazelwood and Theodore Pettigrew
were reappointed to positions they held during the Carlin administration as city magistrate and commissioner of the NHA respectively.
Jennie Lemon, a black woman, was made an administrative aide to
the mayor, and Larrie Stalks became executive secretary of the City
Planning Commission. Gladys Churchman and Harold Ashby, both
black, were appointed by the mayor to the school board, and Ashby
soon became board president. Alma Flagg became the first black
school principal, and her husband, Tom Flagg, was appointed director of the city's Neighborhood Youth Corps program. Addonizio also
appointed more blacks to the Human Rights Commission, ordered

the integration of police patrol cars, and saw to it that blacks were at least minimally integrated in the fire department and other city agencies. In addition, more than five hundred temporary jobs were added to the city payroll, supported by federal funds, thus avoiding the constraints of civil service regulations. Some of the jobs were dispensed through the patronage arm of Turner's organization. At the completion of his first term, Addonizio named James Threatt to head the Human Rights Commission. In accord with a campaign promise, Addonizio convinced the NHA to cut back boundaries on the Lower Clinton Hill (South Ward) renewal project, pacifying some of the opposition to redevelopment in that area.

These were highly important gestures to the black community and represented new levels of progress. Nonetheless, they were inadequate in both social and political terms. On the first score, such changes did not affect the basic needs of the black community. Secondly, they did not approach what civil rights forces deemed equitable treatment, and thus the appointments did not quiet growing criticism of the mayor's leadership. Moreover, the results were comparable to what had been found in other urban centers with large black populations. In short, blacks were underrepresented in the major policy-making positions. Where they did have representation, their actual power was limited. In contrast to what blacks had gained, the directors of the major city departments of police, public works, and health, four members of the board of education, the city's business administrator, the assistant business administrator, the tax assessor, the mayor's top administrative assistant, and the deputy executive director of the NHA were Italian Americans. All of the other top administrative posts were held by whites of other ethnic groups. In addition, the blacks appointed "had to be politicians first and blacks second."[60] They had to soft-pedal racial issues that were of most concern to blacks. Richardson's experience served as a stark lesson of the consequence of violating that code.

Despite continuing dissatisfaction in the black community, Addonizio maintained a clear majority of black voter support through his first term. His large margin of victory in 1962 was diminished in the 1966 race by the combined effect of Italian mayoral candidates Michael Bontempo and Nicholas Castellano as well as by the competition from Kenneth Gibson. Addonizio still won significant black support during the 1966 election through the support of Calvin West, who won an at-large seat on the council, thus becoming the second black member of the council and the first elected to a citywide position. West recalled approaching Addonizio prior to the 1966 election to seek the mayor's support. Addonizio, he said, explained that he could not support him because there were other candidates from the Italian American community he would have to back. However, he promised his support if West got into the run-off election. Ironically, West won on the first ballot, and it was Addonizio who was forced into a run-off. Addonizio then sought West's support in the run-off.[61]

Addonizio employed a variety of strategies to contend with the rising black opposition. He exploited the long-standing divisions in the black community, which kept civil rights forces divided and deeply suspicious of each other. At the time, the NAACP leadership, some of the ministers, and surely Councilman Irvine Turner resented the appearance of CORE on the political scene. Kenneth Clark, a sociologist, explains in his classic study of ghetto politics how the "constricted opportunities and the racially determined limits of the rewards available to the inner city black community" fuel the infighting and bickering so prevalent in the black community.[62] Despite the overwhelming burdens of ghetto life, the dire need for unity, and the advantages and benefits that could be gained from unity and cohesion, solidarity was nearly impossible. On one occasion during this period, I attended an NAACP general membership meeting, hoping to simply inform the NAACP about CORE campaigns in the community. When Larrie Stalks, then an aide to Mayor Addonizio and also an officer in the Newark Branch of the NAACP, saw me in the back of the room, she rose to her feet and asked the president, Carlton Norris, to ask me to leave the meeting. Norris promptly addressed me: "Bob, I have to ask that you leave."

Turner and Norris, and some of the church leaders as well, not only aimed to accommodate the leaders of the machine, but also sought to maintain the legitimacy of their own positions and continue to have access to the incumbent leaders to bargain for their own rewards. What often appeared to be simply selling out to the more vocal and impatient activists was, for the conservatives, protection of their own positions and organizations. Moreover, as one NAACP official boasted, "We believe we can do much more for the Negro masses than CORE: after all we have a pipeline to the city administration."[63] It was true that CORE had a very small membership in comparison to the NAACP and lacked any significant contacts with officials who could gain jobs or favors in government. It was also true that CORE did not aim to dispense jobs or favors but sought to protect the rights of minorities and encourage private and public institutions to hire in a fair manner.[64] With the turn of events in the 1960s, national concern about rights and justice placed unusual pressures on local officials. It was highly important for white political leaders to have contacts and supporters in the black community. The ward boss, like Turner, was a tradition; his presence as an agent for the machine was certain in any situation. But with new dissident black leaders emerging, the ethnic, or racial, boss was not enough to assure political leaders adequate influence among black voters. The support of local civil rights organizations could not only legitimize the administration's proposals regarding the black community but also serve to counterbalance the more aggressive and outspoken groups like CORE and the NCC. For example, a few black ministers lauded Addonizio's announcement that the city would submit police brutality complaints to the FBI, while CORE and other activist groups condemned the plan. (The ministers were later embarrassed when the FBI announced that it had not made any agreement regarding such a plan and that the FBI could not investigate local complaints.) Norris, president of the Newark NAACP when Addonizio took office, was a former Newark police officer and was appointed as a detective in the Essex County Sheriff's Office. He also held a paid appointment as a member of Newark's Board of Adjustment, the agency that ruled on applications for zoning changes. Norris's wife became secretary of the City Insurance Fund when George Richardson was fired. Stalks, vice president of the NAACP, was secretary of the Central Planning Board and Jennie Lemon, an aide to Addonizio, was on the executive board of the NAACP. Paradoxically, throughout the early 1960s, as protest throughout the nation attracted many new members to the NAACP, the Newark Branch was effectively co-opted by the administration, and thus became less active.

An *Afro-American* editorial charged, "The Newark NAACP under Norris has probably been the most non-militant organization in the country."[65] Other leaders became highly critical of the branch's close relationship to City Hall and its lack of action on public issues. In June 1963, several black community leaders sent a telegram to Norris asking that he resign because he and his wife held political appointments with the administration and could not avoid conflicts of interests.[66] That and other attacks on Norris led to an open split in the organization, and several NAACP board members signed a petition asking the national office to remove Norris from office. Norris died of a stomach ailment before the conflict with his critics was resolved. He was succeeded by the Reverend Boyd Cantrell, whom county officials promptly appointed to a chaplain's position in the sheriff's department.[67] Cantrell was no less dedicated to the city administration than his predecessor. In November 1964, a dissident group within the NAACP threatened Cantrell's leadership with an opposition slate for an upcoming election.

The election contest became so divisive that the NAACP national staff intervened and conducted a hearing on charges of unfair tactics that both the incumbent and insurgents leveled at each other. The hearings revealed that members of the Addonizio machine and the county Democratic Party helped to "physically" prevent insurgents from entering the NAACP office one evening to file new memberships. A union leader testified that he enrolled "close to 400" members of his union in the NAACP at the urging of Eulis Ward, Central Ward Democratic chairman, and was told by Ward that "payment of the dues would be taken care of" by someone else.[68] Turner announced his support for Cantrell and called the insurgents, some who had been NAACP members for decades, outsiders. Taxicabs carried posters supporting the Cantrell slate, an arrangement allegedly made by City Hall. One observer noted, "All the resources of the mayor's office including personnel, money, and influence, were thrown into this campaign in a desperate effort by Addonizio to keep control of the NAACP."[69] The Cantrell slate, which included numerous city and county public officials, won the election and assured the NAACP's continued support of the Addonizio administration. Unlike the situation in many other cities, where NAACP branches opposed the leadership of local governments, the Newark branch provided Addonizio his main support in the black community.

Some of the strategies employed by the Addonizio forces were more aggressive, such as labeling critics irresponsible, extremist, or disloyal to the United States. This was a widely used tactic that white authorities used when they wished the public to believe that people who attacked the pillars of segregation and discrimination "were unreasonable fanatics with whom one could not negotiate."[70] The police director, Dominick Spina, once summoned a Newark news reporter to his office to relay scurrilous rumors about the personal and family lives of CORE leaders.[71] Those who protested against the administration were subject to arrest or harassment for minor traffic violations. A white member of the NCC was visited by Newark police at his suburban home shortly after the Barringer demonstration because he owed penalties on several parking tickets. An *Afro-American* columnist reported that in the administration's efforts to stop a Central Ward CORE program "persons on welfare were intimidated . . . and residents in public housing were warned against civil rights activity." The writer concluded, "The police are more interested in following civil rights demonstrators than gamblers, dope addicts, and pushers."[72]

None of these methods were comparable to the vicious brutality and repression directed toward civil rights workers in the South. However, subtle forms of intimidation could bring fear and consequences similar to more blatant acts of violence and reprisal. Nevertheless, no tactic that Addonizio and the political leaders employed, from outright concessions to co-optation, to using conservative black leaders to protect him in conflict situations and protecting the retrograde leadership of the NAACP, to various forms of harassment and attempts at intimidation of civil rights activists and their supporters, was capable of stopping emerging forces, both local and national. Such forces would soon cause the relationship between Newark's Italian American political machine and the black community to collapse.

The War on Poverty

The federal government's antipoverty program brought extensive resources to the black community, further shrinking the political machine's control over jobs and favors. The requirement of "maximum feasible participation" in antipoverty legislation legitimized efforts to involve a wider range of the community, especially the poor, in new programs.[73] Addonizio initially supported the federal infusion of new resources to fight poverty, apparently thinking that many of the resulting jobs would be controlled by his organization. City Hall did gain a share of the jobs and controlled a few new programs, but Addonizio could not prevent some of his most outspoken enemies from gaining key positions and access to important resources.

The Newark program consisted of neighborhood boards in almost all parts of the city, emphasizing extensive involvement and participation of the poor in rule making and governance.[74] These boards functioned as service centers aimed at bringing groups together to solve problems. Although officials of the United Community Corporation (UCC), the umbrella governing organization of the Newark program, insisted that the group's goal was merely to improve services and publicly downplayed the program's importance to politics, the program encouraged the development of new anti–City Hall political leadership, improved coordination among black and Puerto Rican groups throughout the city, and allowed community activists to hone negotiating and organizing skills. With the aid of the federal antipoverty program, neighborhood forces working for a greater share of power and benefits for the black community reached a degree of independence that would have been impossible otherwise.[75]

Added to the emergence of new leadership, resources, and skills was a radicalization of protest in which activism underwent a shift from the go-slow, polite, never-fight-in-public, to the entry on the scene of a self-proclaimed colonel named Hassan Jeru Ahmed. Hassan was accompanied by a small band of about six other men who called themselves the Blackman's Volunteer Army of Liberation.[76] Also joining this loose and ideologically varied group of protestors was the black playwright Amiri Baraka (LeRoi Jones), who organized an all-male, highly disciplined nationalistic group called United Brothers, which formed the nucleus for a more politically oriented group called the Committee for a Unified Newark.[77] This succession of groups, along with the numerous neighborhood organizations arising from the activities of the antipoverty program, gave the black community a vigilant and aggressive political force (financed by federal funds) that challenged the legitimacy of Addonizio's regime. The new leadership no longer accepted the sycophantic black leaders who protected white officials. Kenneth A. Gibson's first run for the mayoralty in 1966, orchestrated by Richardson, made a surprisingly strong showing, giving further impetus to the movement for change.[78] Inspired by the knowledge that the population had become at least 50 percent black, political consciousness heightened. A large segment of the black community was no longer willing to accept token representation and symbolic recognition of black needs.

The Parker-Callaghan Battle

In early 1967, Arnold Hess, a former deputy mayor and longtime influence in Newark politics, announced plans to retire as secretary to the board of education. Addonizio quickly named James Callaghan, who had served on the city council since 1954 but had never completed high school, to replace Hess in the job, which paid about $25,000 a year at the time. The pay was not the prize of the job; rather, the secretary of the board of education handled all vendor contracts for the school board. This meant that the secretary wielded power over all of the board's most significant financial transactions. Wilbur Parker, the city budget director and the first black certified public accountant in New Jersey, was also a candidate for the position and received strong support from the black community. Board president Harold Ashby informed civil rights leaders that Addonizio insisted that the board appoint Callaghan. For several months in 1967, at every school board meeting, CORE and other groups, also backed by white community leaders from the South Ward, as well as church leaders, staged vehement protests that disrupted the conduct of board business. At the board of education meeting on June 28, 1967, when the appointment was to be made, civil rights activists occupied the seats of the board of education members while they adjourned to caucus on their deliberations. The meeting was terminated. Neither Callaghan nor Parker was appointed. Hess, after consulting with Addonizio, then withdrew his decision to retire. A year later, Parker was appointed secretary of the board of education, with the support of Mayor Addonizio.

The victory of the civil rights forces in halting the Callaghan appointment was the first instance in which the Addonizio machine could not prevail. While he maintained the support of the NAACP leadership, Irvine Turner, and Calvin West, the two black elected officials, support for challenges to the machine deepened and broadened throughout the black community via massive gatherings at the city council, board of education, and planning board meetings. The violence delivered the final blow to the long-standing alliance between Central Ward blacks and North Ward Italians, presaging the destruction of the already wounded Addonizio machine.

In 1962, Addonizio had captured the support of almost every community in Newark. In the final analysis, though, he was a dismal failure. He was not a force for the times; he was indifferent to the hopes of both his own constituents in the North and West Wards and the people throughout the city who had put him in the mayor's office. A small circle of blacks had his ear, and when pressures mounted he made faint gestures to do more. He was hobbled by his ties to mobsters and he was unprepared to respond to growing demands for opportunity and justice from ever-enlarging forces for social change in the city.

──── ⟨4⟩ ────

Rebellion and City Politics

*Just treat a Negro like a man. It is so easy, but the
white man will not stand for a black man being a man.
He's got to be a boy.*

—Newark African American businessman
testifying before the Governor's Select
Commission on Civil Disorders

THE VIOLENCE THAT occurred in Newark over a five-day period
in the summer of 1967 left twenty-six people dead, more than two
hundred seriously injured, and property damage of more than $10
million. It would be difficult to assess the real costs to the city, for
the disturbances further damaged the image and reputation of Newark, already known for its crime, corruption, and poor governmental management. From 1967 forward, almost every magazine article
about the city's economic, political, or social life began with a reference to the rebellion, often branding the city as a place of violence
and racial strife. In economic terms, the rebellion was nothing to cel-
ebrate, for it retarded revitalization for decades. Most analyses of the
Newark riot, or rebellion, as black and Puerto Rican residents chose
to call it, focus on the breakdown of law, the absence of social control,
and the violent behavior of local and state police and the National
Guardsmen. However, this historic outburst of disorder played a
major role in validating the grievances of community activists, and

then galvanizing and unifying the black and Puerto Rican communities. The rebellion of 1967 helped to make possible a black takeover of City Hall in 1970.[1]

A civil rights activist at the time, I experienced the rebellion firsthand. The experiences of city residents during those five days in July are unforgettable for many. And we would all learn soon that the impact of the rebellion would have an important impact on the city's political life, particularly the creation of the Governor's Select Commission on Civil Disorder and the negotiations between community representatives and government officials to determine the terms on which a new medical school to be built in the heart of Newark could qualify for federal support.

Rebellion or Riot?

Civil disturbances of the kind that occurred in Newark in 1967 are usually labeled "riots" or "civil disorders" in social science literature. As we know, the people who participate in civil disturbances vary in motivation and purpose. Some might aim to exploit the absence of control and join in the looting to get whatever they can. Others might be swept up in the moment, drawn into the frenzy of mob behavior. Still others might bear a message, a political message if you will, that calls for authorities to address long-standing grievances of inequality and mistreatment. So if we grant that there are multiple things going on, why have the residents of inner-city Newark chosen to call events of July, 1967 a rebellion?

Let us briefly note what this kind of violence is about. Extensive scholarship argues that urban violence has its roots in poverty. Nathan Wright, former director of community affairs at the Episcopal Diocese of Newark, reminds us that in *Utopia*, Thomas More wrote of the social, political, and economic basis for rioting during the reign of Henry VIII. Aristotle wrote in the same vein of social rebellions of his own day.[2] More recent scholarship has suggested that the relationship between poverty or oppression and violence can best be explained by what is called relative deprivation theory. More hypothesis than theory, relative deprivation holds that violence results from a perception of the discrepancy between what people believe they are rightfully entitled to and what they think they are capable of getting. The emphasis is on the perception of deprivation: how people perceive their relative position in terms of where they are in comparison to others, and where they expect to be. People may feel deprived, for example, even though an objective observer might not consider them to be in need. Conversely, the existence of what an observer judges to be abject poverty or "absolute deprivation" is not necessarily thought to be unjust or harmful by those who experience it.[3]

However, is there not enough constant deprivation to have violence all the time? When there has been violence in the inner city, the majority of residents do not participate, as was certainly the case in Newark. Why are some violent and not others? The answer to the last question is that most residents are not sufficiently alienated to risk breaking the law, so the overwhelming majority stays out of harm's way.[4] Regarding the larger question of why there is violence at a particular time, scholarship suggests that the onset of urban violence has two sequential parts. First there is the creation of the climate, simmering feelings of discontent widely shared by a substantial number of people. For example, Stanley Lieberson and Arnold M. Silverman wrote before the Newark disorders, "Riots are more likely to occur when social institutions function inadequately, or when grievances are not resolved, or cannot be resolved under the existing institutional arrangements."[5] Populations are then predisposed or prone to rebel; they are not simply neutral aggregates transformed into a violent mob by the agitation or charisma of individuals. The second factor is the role of social control agents, particularly police and law enforcement. Indeed, the immediate precipitant (like a police beating or shooting, or an accidental death perceived to be racial, as was the case in Crown Heights, Brooklyn, in 1981, or in Watts, Los Angeles, in 1992 when the brutal beating of Rodney King was shown around the world) "simply ignites prior community tensions revolving around basic institutional difficulties, and law enforcement loses the capacity to exercise control."[6] This interpretation seems to fit how things happened in Newark. Social institutions did not perform effectively, and social issues were suppressed or ignored for a long period of time. The beating of the cab driver was a match to the tinderbox created by neglect and inaction.

The foregoing helps to explain why most minority residents of

Newark chose to label the 1967 episode a rebellion. Aside from the common use of the word "riot" in literature and social science research, to the aggrieved community in Newark, a riot and a rebellion mean different things. As Henry Bienen wrote in *Violence and Social Change*, "To choose a theory is to choose a policy. If one chooses to emphasize the participants in violence and to see criminality pure and simple (and label the event a riot), calls for law enforcement are in order. If one chooses to focus on conditions (and use the term rebellion), it follows that massive attacks on the economic and social order are called for."[7] "Rebellion" then is first an expression of the street-level theory of the event, a plea for improvement of the conditions that led to the upheaval.

Whatever the label, "civic rebellions," as Nathan Wright wrote, "are a form of social insanity . . . they are basically the crazed behavior of men who sense that they are driven to distraction."[8] However, when one speaks of "crazed behavior," and being "driven to distraction," it is not just the inner-city residents to whom we refer. In the case of Newark and Detroit, the initial violence and looting—almost entirely against property—was followed by several days of indiscriminate violence by the police, state police officers, and the National Guard against citizens, homes, and businesses. In his analysis of the killings during the Newark and Detroit episodes, Albert Bergesen writes, "There seems to have been an increasing lack of organizational or normative control over the actions of officials, which suggests the presence of a 'police riot' in both cities."[9]

What Happened

By 1967, the patterns of decorum that earlier ruled race relations had already been shattered by the demands and demonstrations of a newly emerged cadre of civil rights and black power activists in the city. However, most officials and observers never expected that Newark was capable of the extreme violence that occurred. New Jersey historian John T. Cunningham argued that Newark was different and had done enough of the right things to avoid the kind of eruptions that were occurring in other cities. "Newark, through the summer of 1966, had not been rocked by the riots and disorder that had swept

other cities," wrote Cunningham in his volume commemorating
Newark's 300th anniversary. He continued,

> It certainly is not a matter of luck. For one thing, there long has been
> sincere dialogue between volunteer Negro and white leaders. City-
> appointed racially mixed commissions have worked hard at settling
> racial tensions before the point of explosion. Even before extreme
> racial imbalance began to hit the schools, educators had sought to
> make tolerance a part of school teachings. Church leaders, Negro
> and white, clergy and lay men and women, have worked together to
> reduce tension. The election of Irvine I. Turner to the city council
> in 1954 and his continued election throughout four campaigns have
> assured the Negro of a voice in city government. In 1966, another
> Negro, Calvin D. West, joined Turner on the council. Other forces
> have helped ease tensions. Business and industry have in recent
> years searched for Negro employees—belatedly in many cases—and
> employment opportunities for Negroes have been greatly broad-
> ened. There has been awareness by city administrators that new
> office buildings downtown do not solve sociological problems—and
> urban renewal housing has swept into the blighted slums, bringing
> a spirit of hope.[10]

Cunningham's words represented both the denial and the wishful
thinking of city leaders at the time: Newark had in fact become a
social volcano, ready to erupt. A long list of grievances by the black
community concerning education, housing, and employment opportunities were at the center of the almost weekly debates and conflicts,
often involving public demonstrations. Tensions between police and
minorities had reached a fever pitch. Federal authorities, under the
pressure of local mayors, were eviscerating the provisions in the antipoverty program that encouraged participation of the poor. A few
people had distributed leaflets during the summer of 1966 in Central
Ward high-rise public housing projects, the vertical ghettoes of urban
America, with instructions for making a Molotov cocktail, the home-
made incendiary device that requires merely a rag or sock inserted
into a bottle containing gasoline and then mixed with soap powder.

As I wrote in the introduction, at the onset of the conflict I had
made an attempt to calm the crowd and to organize the assembled

people into a peaceful march. When my effort proved futile and the warriors in the streets threw rocks and the police began swinging their nightsticks, I ran to my car and drove home, where Tom Hayden had arrived to pick up his girlfriend, Connie Brown. When I explained what had happened, Hayden was eager to go to the area of the precinct. So he and Connie, my wife, Patricia, and our four-year-old son, Frank, got into my car and headed toward the Central Ward. About halfway there we encountered a mob of looters who had apparently broken into liquor stores. The beer they could not drink, they hurled at cars and buildings. As we slowly moved through the area, one of the rampaging men yelled, "There's a white guy here," pointing to Tom Hayden who was sitting next to me in the front seat. A few of the group approached the car in a menacing way. We were terrified. I got out of the car and yelled at them, "Get back! My child is in this car and I am going to turn around and get the hell out of here." Amazingly, there was at least one humanitarian soul in the crowd who endorsed my plea and commanded, "Okay, everyone step back and let the man turn around." The group stepped away; I turned my Chevy Impala around and headed home. On the way, we listened to radio news reports that announced, "Violence has broken out at a police precinct and housing project in the Central Ward of Newark. It has already been declared a police emergency, and officials are attempting to prevent the violence from spreading to other areas of the city."

The next day I attended a meeting at the mayor's office with a group of other community activists, officials from the antipoverty program, and a group of black ministers. We were all contacted by telephone by Jim Threatt, the executive director of the Newark Human Rights Commission. As I walked into the mayor's office, Mayor Addonizio said he appreciated the effort I had made to forestall the violence. From that point forward, the meeting was a disaster. The mayor failed to recognize that anything serious had happened. He thought it was an isolated incident and the police and government should not overreact. It was true that the violence had not spread far beyond the precinct; it had not yet reached most other poor areas of the city. But the signs of further violence were clear. Molotov cocktails were in play. Youths were roaming the streets. It was a sweltering week with temperatures in the nineties. Reporters and television crews were rushing to the city. The gist of the mayor's control strategy was that a black police captain would be assigned to head the precinct and he would order an investigation into charges that the taxi driver had been beaten by the arresting officers. But while the mayor and black civic leaders were discussing ways to curtail the violence, members of the Newark Community Union Project as well as other community activists passed out leaflets calling for a demonstration that evening to protest police brutality. The leaflets read: "STOP POLICE BRUTALITY, Come out and join us at the mass rally, TONIGHT, 7:30 P.M. FOURTH PRECINCT." One news television vehicle arrived in the vicinity of the precinct at 4:30 P.M. Within an hour, there were five more television crews in the area, drawing a larger crowd of curious youths and adults. The demonstrators organized by NCUP arrived at around 6:00 P.M. James Threatt appeared at the demonstration and announced to the crowd that a black captain had been appointed to head the Fourth Precinct.[11] No one seemed impressed. Most people booed. The crowd swelled far beyond the numbers of the previous night. A woman left the picket line and, using a metal pipe, smashed a basement window of the precinct. The crowd threw rocks at the building and police again waded into the crowd. The violence spread northward a few blocks to Springfield Avenue and before long, young men were challenging the police and breaking into stores in the Central and South Wards.[12] The violence and disorder of the previous night spread and escalated to a much higher level.

The next morning I received another telephone call from Threatt. He told me that word was circulating around City Hall that the police had a list of people they hoped to "take care of" during the violence and that I was on the list. Commissioner Threatt suggested that I be careful in my travels through the city. I then went with my wife and son to my brother's home in Union, New Jersey. We remained until the end of the violence, which continued for five days. During the first two days, rioters roamed the streets in the Central and South Wards, breaking into stores and looting at will. On the third day of the violence, the mayor requested that the governor send in the state police and the National Guard. According to Donald Malafronte, the mayor was under heavy pressure from Governor Hughes to call for additional support. Governor Hughes had received several calls from Vice President Hubert Humphrey urging him to get things under control or Washington might have to send federal troops. Hughes sent 3,000 National Guardsmen and 500 state police officers into the city. Both forces joined the Newark police in patrolling the streets in what was supposed to be a combined effort to restore order. Instead the state police and guardsmen joined the local police in an orgy of violent, brutal retaliation against black citizens and businesses.[13]

In *Memoirs of a Newark Police Officer*, Anthony Carbo describes his experience during those violent days.[14] While the book is a running diatribe about police actions, most which involve Officer Carbo, it is nonetheless a stunning firsthand testimony of the disorganization and lack of discipline and training that characterized the department's actions during the disturbances. Carbo was a true blue officer who loved his work, probably too much. He spent a good part of his career as a member of the motorcycle unit, which was known for its tendency to rough people up. Carbo tells of the absence of any department plan or training to respond to the disorder. Patrol officers disobeyed command orders to stay at their posts and instead ventured into areas where they thought other officers were in danger or had had to abandon their cars. He also contends that a command order was given to the department for officers to bring their private shotguns to work during the disturbances, and many of them did so. When a van loaded with ammunition arrived in an area in which he worked, he loaded up the front seat of his car with as much as it could hold, never signing for the ammunition as protocol required. Thus, there was no accounting and no accountability for the massive firepower used against the community. Carbo admits to his enjoyment of violence, and writes that during the period of the riots, it was "legal" to shoot looters. It is likely that many officers worked with that belief as a result of the vague and contradictory statements issued by Newark Police Director Spina and Governor Hughes. Without being explicit, Spina said that officers should use force to curtail the looting and protect themselves. Governor Hughes, playing to the national press, said, "The line between the jungle and the law might as well be drawn here as any place in America."[15] Neither statement was a command to shoot looters, but in the absence of more precise directions and appropriate training, law enforcement was left to interpret the statements as they saw fit. For Officer Carbo, and probably for many others, it was a license to take aim to kill. For Carbo, the situation was no danger and tragedy, but fun and recreation. He wrote,

"We were ready to book off for the night and one of the old time superiors asked us, 'How was the duck hunting last night, fellers?' We responded: 'It went very well last night, sir.'"[16]

In the face of such chaos, disastrous results were unavoidable.[17] The state police and guardsmen had little, if any, knowledge of city life. Many of them were from suburban and rural towns throughout New Jersey and apparently harbored strong racial prejudices similar to those held by a segment of white Newark police officers. They also lacked a suitable communications and command system that would have enabled all forces to coordinate their actions. As a result, they were fearful and would react indiscriminately with gunfire at any noise or sign of movement. With fear fueled by rumors and suspicion, many came to suspect that there were black snipers shooting at them, although sniper fire occurred in only a few instances. Officer Carbo wrote that at times, Newark police fired torrents of bullets under automobiles "just in case someone was hiding behind a car."[18]

As in riotous situations in other cities, black store owners put signs in their windows indicating their ownership. Late into the third night of violence, hundreds of black-owned businesses with such signs in their windows were shot up. In the view of former mayoral aide Donald Malafronte, the assault on black businesses was definitely planned. Among the commanding officers of the state police, he said, there was strong feeling that it was unfair for black businesses to escape damage while white-owned businesses were being plundered. After all, in their view, it was the black community that had started the trouble in the first place. "It happened while the State Police held a press conference at 1:00 A.M., drawing all the reporters and news media to the armory in the North Ward where a command post had been established. No one was watching and the troopers went wild."[19]

By the fifth day, many of the city's civic leaders took to the streets to encourage young people to stay at home and out of harm's way. In the evening, Governor Hughes met with a group of civic leaders and ministers at the home of Oliver Lofton, the general counsel of the United Community Corporation, the city's antipoverty program. The community leaders urged the governor to remove the state police and National Guardsmen, an act that he pledged to consider. As the night wore on, an aide to the governor called me and advised me that the governor wanted to meet with me at the office of David

Satz, the United States attorney for New Jersey, in the Federal Building in downtown Newark. A state police vehicle arrived within minutes at my brother's home in Union, with four state police officers, two sitting in the back with rifles protruding through open windows. They carried me to Satz's office. Tom Hayden had also been summoned and delivered to the meeting. There was Governor Hughes, the director of the state police, Raymond Kelley, and Paul Ylvisaker, the state commissioner of community affairs, and U.S. Attorney Satz. The governor said he had invited Hayden and me to meet with him because he was told (by Ylvisaker) that we would tell him the truth. With his tie loosened at the neck, a rumpled shirt, and bleary eyes, it was clear that he was angry and frustrated. He began the meeting with an off-color remark about why looters were stealing mattresses. Hayden told him that the people who had been out in the streets were spent, and what was going on now was the uncontrolled violence of law enforcement forces, particularly the state police and the guardsmen. I concurred and conveyed to the governor reports I had heard of random shooting as well as looting by the Newark police, who were seen in several cases taking booty from patrol cars and putting it in their private automobiles near station houses. Tom and I pressed the point that the community violence was over and that the forces sent to the city to quell the disorder were now the problem. The governor responded that it would be very risky to remove the state police and the National Guard, and that if it did not work, he would be held responsible for the continuing violence, perhaps even the loss of more lives. At that point, Commissioner Ylvisaker said to Governor Hughes that he did not see any option other than to remove the state police and the National Guard. As Ylvisaker continued his plea, the governor said, "Okay, let's remove most of them and leave a small security contingent in the city. If it doesn't work, we can bring all the forces back in." Governor Hughes then thanked Hayden and me. He also gave each of us his personal card and said that we should use it if anyone tried to harm us, suggesting that he might have heard of the "hit list" rumored to have been created by some members of the Newark Police Department.

When the state police and National Guard were removed, the tragic and devastating episode was over. The loss of life and damage to stores, buildings, and homes was extensive. The control forces had used massive amounts of ammunition in the span of just a few days. The state police reported that they had expended a total of 350 rounds of .38 caliber, 1,168 of .45 caliber, 198 rounds of 00 buckshot, 1,187 rounds of .30 caliber, and 2 rounds of No. 9 birdshot. The National Guard reported that a total of 10,414 rounds were expended: 10,198 rounds of .30 caliber, 200 rounds of .30 caliber carbine, and 16 rounds of .45 caliber pistol. Newark police officials could not determine the number of rounds expended, since records were not kept during the chaos. Among the dead were twenty-four black civilians, one white fireman, and one white policeman. More than 95 percent of the 1,500 people arrested were black.[20] Law enforcement personnel had engaged in a deadly expression of white hatred, including the perverse irony of state police officers willfully damaging black-owned businesses, whose owners were the best example in the inner city of the hope of buying into the American dream.

With the rebellion, the negative reputation the city had acquired through the 1960s as a result of the increasing problems of poverty, crime, and corruption became more deeply burnished in the minds of outsiders, particularly for those in the suburbs and their representatives in the state legislature. City officials and police blamed the violence on outside agitators and civil rights advocates. Some blamed it on staff members of the antipoverty program and others saw it as a massive disturbance of lower-class city dwellers, the so-called riff-raff out of control. The disturbances represented a total breakdown of the political system. The city was controlled by an intransigent leadership that was virtually closed to the growing black population, which by then had become the largest group in the city. Many people among the community and civil rights activists had assumed that the recalcitrance of city leaders, the provocations against the black community by police officers, and the depth of the social despair would sooner or later explode, as had occurred in so many other places.

The local CORE chapter had done everything it could to prevent an outright explosion. It conducted workshops on nonviolence; volunteer marshals were assigned to help with crowd control at street rallies; a CORE cadre was left behind after street meetings ended to make sure that incidents did not erupt. But abuse by the police was common in spite of the growing complaints from citizens. The police department, by its sometimes blatantly aggressive behavior, seemed eager to start a disorder. Months before the disturbances, Newark police placed riot helmets and clubs in the back window of patrol cars. They were removed prior to the disturbances after complaints by local NAACP officials. A small number of police officers were frequently involved in alleged incidents of mistreatment, and their reputations and names became known in the black community. The pleas for the city to establish a civilian review board were rebuffed, and no adequate alternative was offered. A survey following the disturbance found that 32 percent of blacks in the city thought that the police performed poorly, compared to only 6 percent of whites who had such a view. Only 5 percent of blacks thought the Newark police were excellent, while 19 percent of whites considered the department excellent.[21] With the help of volunteer civil rights and civil liberties lawyers, a complaint was filed in 1965 in U.S. District Court asking that Newark Police Department be placed in receivership by the Justice Department.[22] The action was dismissed. The explosion came, the damage was extensive and costly, and the wounds and scars were deeply embedded in the images and reputation of Newark, perhaps forever. A once-vibrant city known for manufacturing goods and products for the nation, its jazz and verve, and yes, its dirty politics, became a metaphor for outbursts of anger, crime, and disorder.

The violence had a profound effect on the city's life and politics. The black community became decidedly more militant; new leadership, more nationalistic and aggressive, emerged. Willie Wright, of the Afro American Association, and Amiri Baraka, the Black Nationalist poet and playwright, became principal leaders in the black community. The ideology of racial separation became so pervasive that few whites could continue participating in the black community. Most of the white NCUP organizers, including Hayden, left the city. A new and unprecedented sense of unity emerged in which the NAACP, now under the helm of Sallie Carroll, an Essex County police officer, and the Essex County Urban League joined more militant groups in criticizing City Hall. Carroll disconnected the Newark NAACP branch from City Hall. The NAACP maintained its moderate approach but became less about politics and more committed to the advancement of the black community.

Whereas blacks saw the eruption as the result of City Hall's neglect and the racism of white society, many whites, particularly those in the suburbs, saw the violence as lawlessness and a direct threat to their safety. Some white families in Newark feared for their lives and left their homes to stay with relatives in the suburbs during the five days of disturbances. A white self-styled vigilante, Anthony Imperiale, formed the North Ward Citizens Committee and announced his intention to keep peace in Newark with guns and a tank if necessary. In 1968, Imperiale and Anthony Giuliano, a Newark policeman, were elected to the Newark City Council in a special election, with massive support from white voters. On the same day, Alabama's segregationist governor, George Wallace, who was running as an independent for president, received over 4,000 North Ward votes, nearly 15 percent of the votes cast in the ward. At Essex Catholic High School in the North Ward, whose nearly 3,000 students were drawn from the white ethnic families of Newark and Essex County, George Wallace won a straw poll contest for president of the United States. Meetings of the city council and board of education became battlegrounds. Whites, fired up by Imperiale, persuaded the city council to approve the purchase of police dogs. A subsequent meeting was stormed by members of the black community, and the council, fearing renewed violence, reversed the decision.

Out of this overheated urban cauldron of racial anger and passion, three crucial things happened to move blacks closer to political control of the city. First, Governor Hughes appointed a commission of distinguished citizens to investigate the causes of the disturbances and make recommendations for improvement in the conditions that led to the disturbances. Second, federal authorities informed state officials that financial support for the medical school would not be available unless state and local officials reached agreement on the terms of the medical school with community groups. Finally, the black and Puerto Rican communities coalesced in anticipation of the 1970 city-wide elections.

The Governor's Select Commission on Civil Disorder

On August 8, 1967, Governor Richard Hughes announced the formation of the Governor's Select Commission on Civil Disorder "to examine the causes, and incidents, which have afflicted New Jersey." Robert D. Lilley, president and chief executive officer of the New Jersey Bell Telephone Company, would head the commission, which would become known as the Lilley Commission. Raymond A. Brown, a prominent African American attorney, became vice-chair. The group also included two former New Jersey governors, Alfred E. Driscoll and Robert B. Meyner; Bishop John J. Dougherty of the Catholic Archdiocese; and Bishop Prince A. Taylor of the United Metodist Church. The commission included lawyers John J. Gibbons and Oliver Lofton, the black attorney who served as director of the Newark Legal Services Corporation and had provided legal counsel to John Smith, the cab driver whose beating by police changed Newark's history.[23]

"It is important that the people of New Jersey be given a full, impartial report on the events in Newark and other communities in our State. It is necessary that the causes of these disorders . . . be fully and objectively explored. But it is most important that the Commission, in its maturity and wisdom . . . point the way to the remedies which must be adopted by New Jersey, and by the nation to immunize our society from a repetition of these disasters," Governor Hughes said in his charge to the body.[24]

Sanford Jaffe, a former federal prosecutor, served as executive director of the commission. Jaffe, a brilliant lawyer and manager, assembled a staff of social scientists, lawyers, and street-wise investigators. He proceeded to gather a mountain of information regarding the underlying causes as perceived by hundreds of citizens. The inquiry followed a model similar to that of a grand jury, where the building blocks of information based on facts, details, and credible stories from many different points of view and angles lead to a strong, powerful conclusion.[25]

Jaffe said that in the first weeks of the inquiry, he was concerned that the commission would be divided when it came time to present its report and recommendations. Former New Jersey governor Alfred E. Driscoll had been instrumental in establishing the state police in New Jersey and was not pleased that police authorities were the target of so much criticism by witnesses. However, as a black merchant whose business had been shot up by the state police was describing his losses as a result of the attack, Governor

Driscoll, who appeared to be agitated by the discussion, interrupted and said he would like to ask the witness a question. According to Jaffe, Governor Driscoll said to the witness: "Tell me, what do you want? What is it that you people want?" The witness, soft-spoken but resolute, responded: "Just treat the Negro like a man. It is easy, but the white man will not stand for a black man being a man. He's got to be a boy."[26] As Jaffe tells the story, Driscoll seemed moved. He got up from his chair, walked over to a telephone, called his secretary, and told her to get Attorney General Arthur Sills on the phone. Governor Driscoll said to Sills: "You have got to come here and testify to this commission. You and the state police have a real problem."[27] Jaffe said from that point forward, the commission was united. Although it was a profoundly important moment, what changed the attitude of some members of the commission was the process of education that allowed powerful leaders of business and government to hear first-hand the agony of life among people in the inner cities of New Jersey.

The final commission report was voluminous, a nearly foot-high mass of paper. The commission did not shy away from politically controversial subjects. Several sections of the report were devoted to the Addonizio administration's shortcomings. The relationships and disputes between the city administrators and the black community received close scrutiny. The report critically reviewed inadequacies in the performances of city agencies, condemned the city admin-istration for displaying insensitivity to the black community, and concluded that "distrust, resentment, and bitterness" characterized police–community relations in Newark. A second politically contro-versial area was the behavior of law enforcement officers and agen-cies during the July 1967 disorders. Police forces, the commission noted, had expended ammunition in amounts "out of proportion to the mission assigned to them." It strongly condemned the conduct of the state police and National Guard for firing into black-owned stores "with no possible justification."[28] Indeed, the Newark police department had been a sore point with the city's blacks for a long time. A survey conducted by the commission revealed that 49 per-cent of blacks in Newark believed the police were too brutal and 80 percent believed that blacks' complaints to the police did not receive the same attention as complaints from whites.

The commission concluded that the members of NCUP had used

poor judgment in organizing a demonstration the night after the initial incident. However, it said, the riots were not planned or part of a conspiracy, and the causes were deeply rooted in the social, political, and economic fabric of the city and state. It called the situation a matter of crisis and urged appropriate action. Of its ninety-nine recommendations, only twenty-six were implemented; in most cases, those addressed were minor matters. After members of the commission threatened to publicly call attention to the lack of action, Governor Hughes asked the Republican-controlled legislature to enact a special appropriation of $126 million to finance actions recommended by the commission. After a long debate, the legislature approved an appropriation of $83 million but required that the money be distributed to all localities, which would have aided already affluent towns at the expense of the urban areas with the most severe problems. The governor vetoed it, and nothing further was enacted.[29]

Ultimately the commission's recommendations were subjected to the usual political debates between opposing political interests. Recommendations that required increased spending became entangled in a battle between the Democratic governor and the Republican state legislature. Other recommendations were engulfed in turf conflicts between municipal and state executives. Mayor Addonizio was ambivalent about the commission report; he praised some aspects but was willing to implement only seven of thirty-three recommendations directly pertaining to Newark He quickly supported those recommendations whose costs would fall to the state.[30] The commission's attention to official corruption in Newark resulted in one of the most significant by-products of the investigation. Although corruption had little to do with the direct causes of the civil disorders and was peripheral to the thinking of the commission, the matter of corruption stimulated more action than any other part of the report. The report noted "a widespread belief that Newark government is corrupt," and one of its ninety-nine recommendations called for a special grand jury to investigate allegations of corruption. According to Donald Malafronte, the statement on corruption was bound to capture the attention of the press. He said, "I think some people on the Commission wanted to play down corruption, but that damn [former governor] Meyner had to have it in there . . . and it got all the headlines."[31] Jaffe said that the issue could not be ignored, and he had to find a way to put it in the report recognizing that the commission was not a legal investigative body and had no direct evidence to support the numerous claims of witnesses. So, he recalled, "we simply said there is 'a pervasive feeling of corruption.' That was enough to get the attention of legal authorities."[32]

In response to the report's artful insinuation of wrongdoing, local newspapers published stories that caught up with the common knowledge among residents. Illegal gambling houses flourished all over the city and the police ignored them. The heightened attention forced the city administration to act—if only for a short while. Police Director Spina established a special gambling squad under the leadership of Deputy Chief John Redden, an experienced, highly decorated officer who was considered by members of the department to be the agency's best example of professionalism. The gambling squad stepped up enforcement and conducted several raids on gambling houses. Suddenly, Spina dismantled the gambling squad. The Essex County prosecutor then impaneled a special grand jury that indicted Spina for allowing the gambling houses to operate. Spina then offered to resign. However, Mayor Addononizio refused to accept his resignation and strongly defended his police director. Spina was later acquitted; the state could not prove that he was aware of the hundred or so gambling places that were listed in the indictment, which the rest of the world seemed to know about.

The county grand jury continued a sweeping investigation of the mayor's office and the council. In a period of nineteen months, it heard 228 witnesses and developed more than 5,000 pages of testimony. The inquiry was eventually turned over to federal authorities who, according to the county prosecutor, John Lordi, could better protect witnesses.[33] Three federal grand juries were impaneled to conduct a sweeping inquiry of corruption in Newark and other areas of the state. Among those indicted for falsifying tax information of reputed Mafia organization members were a high-ranking Internal Revenue Service official and several employees of the agency. A second grand jury indicted fifty-five people alleged to be members of the Mafia for conspiring to operate an interstate lottery or numbers racket. The investigation of official corruption in Newark concentrated on bribery, kickbacks, and extortion. Mayor Addonizio, Chief Municipal Judge James Del Mauro, and numerous other Newark officials refused to testify and only reluctantly supplied the grand jury with subpoenaed information. The chief justice of the New Jersey Supreme Court suspended Judge Del Mauro for invoking the Fifth Amendment when asked by the grand jury about discrepancies in his income tax returns. Judge Del Mauro then resigned from the municipal court. Mayor Addonizio's refusal to testify before the grand jury prompted demands for his removal by business leaders, civic organizations, and the local press. Phillip W. Gordon resigned as Newark's corporation counsel after admitting to the grand jury that he had accepted cash payments from a businessman.[34] On December 17, 1969, a federal grand jury indicted Addonizio and nine incumbent or former city officials on sixty-four counts of extortion, conspiracy, and income tax evasion dating back to January 1, 1965. Five persons not elected to or holding public office were also indicted, including Anthony "Tony Boy" Boiardo, son of Richie "The Boot" Boiardo, who reputedly held a high position in the Mafia.[35]

The legal pursuit of the corruptors and the corrupted produced a healthy cleansing of the political establishment. However, there would be no indictments of those responsible for killings during the rebellion. An Essex County grand jury investigated the twenty-six deaths, taking testimony from more than one hundred witnesses and issuing a twenty-seven-page presentment two months after the Governor's Commission released its report. The grand jury commended state and local police for acting with "courage and restraint." It found no evidence to justify charges against police officers or guardsmen. Most of the witnesses were law enforcement personnel and their views were substantially represented in the final presentment. The grand jury virtually eliminated the possibility that state and local police would be held accountable for the deaths, let alone any of the damage that had occurred. Rather than placing responsibility on law enforcement, the grand jury report stated that "the responsibility for the loss of life and property that is the inevitable product of rioting and mass lawlessness . . . rests squarely upon the shoulders of those who, for whatever purpose, incite and participate in riots and the flouting of law and order in complete disregard of the rights and well-being of the vast majority of our citizens."[36] From these words, one can reasonably conclude that the jury shared the deep resentment and anger toward the rebellion that existed in the larger public.

Thus, the "rioters" were really responsible for the deaths, not the law enforcement agents who fired the weapons that killed the victims. By the grand jury's logic, the rights of the victims had been forfeited. The jury would not indict police officers for their loss of discipline, even though some individuals were clearly identified as responsible for wanton killings. The essence of the jury's statement was that the rules of law and justice did not apply in this case and the police and agents of the law did in fact have a license to kill.

The Governor's Commission did an exceptional job. Their efforts resulted in a two-hundred-page document titled *Report for Action*, one of the most complete documents ever produced to investigate civil disorders at the state level. Every critical issue facing the city of Newark was forthrightly addressed by the commissioners, including public safety, housing, education, employment, and the inherent problems of an urban jurisdiction without sufficient wealth to support the service needs of an increasingly poor population. Nonetheless, the ultimate response to disorder and its underlying causes of racism, poverty, and political indifference had to be left in the hands of a fragmented, suburb-dominated political system that, unlike Governor Driscoll, was never moved by or educated to the plight of the minority poor of the inner city of Newark or elsewhere.

The Conflicts and Consequences of Urban Renewal: The Medical School Hearings

In 1963, writer James Baldwin spoke with the famed psychologist Dr. Kenneth Clark in an interview for public television in the wake of their meeting with Attorney General Robert Kennedy. During the conversation, he spoke with Clark about urban renewal projects:

> A boy last week, he was sixteen, in San Francisco, told me on television—thank god we got him to talk—maybe somebody thought to listen. He said, "I've got no country. I've got no flag." Now, he's only 16 years old, and I couldn't say, "you do." I don't have any evidence to prove that he does. They were tearing down his house, because San Francisco is engaging—as most Northern cities now are engaged—in something called urban renewal, which means

moving the Negroes out. It means Negro removal, that is what it means. The federal government is an accomplice to this fact.[37]

Through the 1950s and 1960s, local urban governments eagerly implemented a federal program that had been created in 1949 during the administration of President Harry Truman. The legislation was intended to provide housing for poor families and returning veterans; it also included an urban renewal program that was touted as a major weapon for rebuilding declining cities. The record of urban renewal programs is mixed; however, the experience of poor communities has been disruption and displacement. The urban renewal program in Newark, under the direction of executive director Louis Danzig and the Newark Housing Authority (NHA), initiated redevelopment plans in almost every black area of the city, always rationalized by what was called slum clearance. Indeed, public housing was built, and in the North Ward, three major market-rate residential high-rise towers were constructed, designed by the prominent architect Ludwig Mies van der Rohe. Overall, however, the program, often operating in secrecy and reeking with politics at every turn, became more a threat than a promise for black residents.

The NHA was created in 1938 under the terms of the United States Public Housing Act of 1937 and the New Jersey Local Housing Authorities Act of 1938. Like housing authorities across the country, it was an independent public corporation responsible for the construction and management of low-rent housing projects. It was governed by a locally appointed board of housing authority commissioners and was sustained by federal subsidy, the rent from its projects, and federally guaranteed housing authority bonds. Even before passage of the 1949 Housing Act, which established the federal government's first urban redevelopment program, Danzig, who served as executive director of NHA from 1948 to 1969, had his legal staff prepare an ordinance making NHA the city's official redevelopment agency.

A genuine Newark story, Danzig arrived in New Jersey as an immigrant from Lithuania in 1911 at the age of three. He lived in the North Ward as a child, attended Newark public schools, and graduated from Central High School. Danzig earned a law degree at New Jersey Law School and later took evening courses at Columbia and New York University. He had closely watched the city's German and

Irish immigrant leadership in the 1930s and 1940s shape land and housing decisions, well before the largesse of federal programs became available. He saw early on that Washington was building a large role in local housing policy, and he prepared himself to get in on the ground floor.

According to Harold Kaplan, author of *Urban Renewal Politics in Newark*, the Newark urban renewal system was a "relatively small closed circle." NHA success, Kaplan wrote, was the result of "the permissive character of the local environment." Indeed, the NHA had its way about things since civic leaders had only a peripheral role in redevelopment policies and opposing groups, especially blacks, who were most affected by slum clearance and other NHA programs, were virtually powerless.[38] Danzig was both king and kingmaker: he was at the center of a coalition of business, labor, and the local press pushing hard for large slum clearance projects. "Rather than confront ongoing deindustrialization, middle-class suburbanization, in-migration of poor southern African Americans, and pervasive racism head on," as one observer noted, "these upper-class civic leaders pinpointed intensifying and spreading slum conditions around downtown as the source of the city's problems—instead of the result of them. The plans for the medical school fell dead in the center of their thinking and vision for the future of the city."[39]

It was not surprising that urban renewal became the central focus of civil rights and neighborhood groups in the Central Ward over plans to build a sprawling new medical school on 150 acres, right in the heart of the city's most densely populated black community. Seton Hall University had operated a small medical school in Jersey City since the early 1950s. By 1966, however, the university's good intentions to be a leader in medical education were fraught with both political entanglements and unbearable financial costs. So the state announced that it would take over the small medical college and build a large medical center with a wide range of medical research facilities. State and school authorities initially planned to build the new school in Madison, New Jersey, a wealthy suburb about twenty-five miles west of Newark. Madison had a black and Hispanic population of less than 5 percent at the time. There has been much speculation as to why Mayor Addonizio immediately launched an all-out effort to put the medical complex in Newark. Surely a large medical institution in the heart of the city would provide medical services to residents as well as new business activity and jobs. However, some suspected the mayor's stronger motive was the potential influence he would have in parceling out contracts. In addition, it was well known that Addonizio had visions of becoming governor. A medical school built in the city would demonstrate competence and leadership. On the other hand, a suspected hidden agenda was that a huge project requiring the dislocation of thousands of black Central Ward residents would diminish the voting power of blacks, assuring white control of the city for years to come.

Leaders in the black community were in favor of a medical school being built in Newark but were firmly opposed to yielding such a large amount of land. In the designated area, a middle-aged black woman named Louise Epperson, who ran a hairdressing shop in her home, formed the Committee Against Negro and Puerto Rican Removal to oppose the plans. In a way, Epperson became the spirit of community opposition to the project. She was deeply proud of her modest, well-kept home with pretty flower boxes hanging from the first-floor windows. When the medical school plans were announced, she was fearful about her future and not at all reluctant to express her concerns, particularly to city and state officials. Epperson was not slick or learned; she was blunt and passionate and carried herself in a way that made people listen to her and respect her. Community leaders admired her. The medical school hearings provided a perfect forum for her to ensure that her concerns were heard. She was a powerful example of the human impact of slum clearance and an equally powerful example of the grassroots ability to fight the injustice of slum clearance.

As news of the project circulated, opposition grew. The local chapter of CORE issued public statements criticizing the pledge of land; along with many others, Assemblyman George Richardson and his Freedom Democratic Party publicly opposed the granting of the land. Junius Williams, a Yale Law School graduate who had come to Newark to participate in the SDS project in the South Ward, became the principal organizer and leader of the protest against the medical school plans. By 1966, Williams had left the SDS project because, he said, in the era of Black Power, he no longer felt comfortable working with the young white outsiders of SDS in a black community.

He formed his own organization called the Newark Area Planning Association (NAPA). Williams, though only twenty-two years old at the time, was a gifted organizer. He, more than anyone else, brought together key factions in the community and was able to attract dozens of professional volunteers in land use planning, law, medical facilities construction, and the development and management of health services. Most important, with the support of Gustav Heningburg, who was now heading the newly formed Greater Newark Urban coalition, Williams was able to persuade the NAACP Legal Defense Fund to provide legal advice and counsel to the protest effort. Soon after the rebellion, NAPA, with the aid of the Legal Defense Fund attorneys, filed a complaint with the federal government against the project as a prelude to going to court.

Despite resistance from the community, the state and city authorities pushed ahead. Before the public became generally aware of the medical school plan, Mayor Addonizio had told a state legislative committee that a medical school belonged in Newark and could serve as the centerpiece of the city's revitalization. He promised that the state could have all the land it needed, 150 acres or more. He also assured state officials that the land would be sold at bargain basement prices. In December 1966, Newark signed an agreement granting the state two parcels of land totaling 57 acres with a pledge to deliver to the state an additional 100 acres when needed, ignoring the fact that under federal law the city had to meet certain requirements, which included a blight declaration and a relocation plan for displaced residents and businesses. Danzig had already submitted clearance and building plans to Washington well before hearings on the project were under way. The public discourse and meetings at City Hall concerning the medical school became raucous and bitter, often with community residents stomping their feet and demanding a revision of the project.

Prior to the disturbances in July 1967, the self-styled colonel Hassan Jeru Ahmed appeared in the city with his handful of followers calling themselves the Blackman's Volunteer Army of Liberation. Hassan and his cohorts wore khaki armylike uniforms and marched around as though they were under strict discipline. At first glance, they looked like true warriors who were taking the struggle to another level; in time, however, they showed signs of fanaticism and plain

A ONE-MAN MOVEMENT

Gustav Heningburg was a rarity for many reasons, not the least of which was his moniker, a thoroughly German label assigned to a black man born and raised in Alabama. Gus, as we knew him, had established a very successful career as a public relations strategist and fund-raiser for organizations like the United Negro College Fund and the Legal Defense Fund. In 1968, during Newark's period of extreme duress, Don McNaughton, the chief executive officer of Prudential, led a trio of prominent Newarkers in a nonstop all-out recruitment drive to convince Gus to head a yet-to-be-established Greater Newark Urban Coalition. After some intensive coaxing, Gus agreed to build and run the organization. His first office was in Prudential's executive suite, a few doors down from McNaughton's office.

Gus's work deeply affected people far below the executive suite. Gus was a tremendous advocate and fighter for those who had been left out. He knew how to plan, organize, and manage. My sense is that Gus always knew that he only needed to ask, and hundreds of activists would show up in a minute to march beside him and support his goals. An expert cajoler, Gus had a talent for implementing change even without a demonstration. When Newark community activists bargained for construction jobs in the building of the medical school, Gus organized the programs and negotiated with the unions and contractors to implement the agreements. When students occupied Conklin Hall at Rutgers University in Newark, demanding that black and Latino students be given more access to the nearby campus, it was Gus who helped to shape a minority recruitment plan that became known as the Equal Opportunity Fund. Gus, by himself, forced the Port Authority of New York and New Jersey to open opportunities for minority businessmen to share in the wealth of the airport business. The black-owned duty-free shop and bookstore at Newark Liberty Airport are both the result of Gus's work.

craziness. When they appeared at a public hearing on the medical school before the City of Newark Planning Board in May 1967, they displayed aggression and violence that, until then, was unknown to Newark. Colonel Hassan approached the lectern at the front of the room. Instead of stopping at the podium, he reached over and took a large map of the designated area and hurled it toward the planning board members, who sat on a dais. He then seized the stenographer's machine, ripped the recording tape, and threw the machine to the floor. Hassan was immediately apprehended by police and escorted out of the hearing; curiously, he was not arrested and was not charged with any crime. His bold action foreshadowed the violence that was to erupt at the Fourth Precinct just a few weeks later. Years later it was revealed in a *Washington Post* article that Hassan, who lived in the Washington area, had a long arrest record and had been in the employ of federal intelligence agencies.

The July rebellion changed the thinking of authorities, particularly officials in Washington who were key in providing resources for the medical school project. In January 1968, a letter signed by Robert Wood, undersecretary of Housing and Urban Development, and Wilbur Cohen, undersecretary of Health, Education, and Welfare, advised Governor Hughes that requirements for community participation of the Model Cities Act had to be met if the medical school project, which was slated to receive $35 million in federal funds, was to be approved. In effect, the letter directed school officials and the NHA to yield to community demands for a much smaller site. The letter further spelled out seven areas relating to the building of the institution that had to be satisfactorily addressed in discussions between community groups and state authorities. The areas included the size of the site; relocation plans for displaced residents; job opportunities for minorities in construction of the institution; health and education services that the new hospital would provide; jobs for residents in the institution; special efforts to recruit minorities for medical training; and an upgrade of Martland, the city hospital that served Newark's poor.

Governor Hughes then announced that community groups could negotiate with city, state, and federal officials on the terms of the project in accord with the mandate laid out in the Wood-Cohen letter. Several months of negotiation followed with Junius Williams, Louise Epperson, Harry Wheeler, and Duke Moore leading a team of community representatives sitting on one side of the table, advised by a group of experts in planning, law, and health. On the other side of the table sat state, federal, and local officials, including Danzig and the president of the medical school, Dr. Robert Cadmus. The negotiations were facilitated by the state chancellor of higher education, Ralph Dungan. For the first time, Danzig had to face questions about his decision making, reveal the names of developers to whom he had committed parcels of land, and openly discuss how he planned to relocate the thousands of people and businesses in the area. His comments were frequently vague and evasive as he attempted to limit the amount of information available to the community. The negotiations were not only a public discussion about urban renewal; they also represented a new and profound shift in the way redevelopment took place.

While the community had a negotiating team of people who had been meeting and planning the resistance to the medical school plans, the announcement of formal negotiations brought out others, including some from the Addonizio machine who challenged the right of the negotiating team to represent the community. There was clearly tension between the negotiating team and representatives of the medical school as well as tension between community representatives and city and NHA officials. Dungan ably managed the deliberations, and Epperson was a special force in the proceedings as well. When two black ministers attempted to interject their personal concerns into the discussions, she rose and said, "To the two good reverends, I am the person who started the crying and belly whining about the medical school coming to Newark . . . rang doorbells, stood in front of churches, gave out literature. . . . I think you should have taken part in it and you didn't, and you can't speak now because you don't know what you're talking about. We been fighting . . . and not one of you came out and said one word about it. You sit and listen and take back to your community and then stand shoulder-to-shoulder and fight for it."[40] Community representatives made it clear they wanted the medical school in Newark, but not at the price of 150 acres of land. They had little trust in city officials generally and little trust in Danzig specifically. Danzig would not be pinned down about his and the NHA's plans to allocate parcels of land for development. He was particularly vague about the NHA's capacity to rehouse the more than 22,000 residents who would be displaced.

The medical school conflict was about much more than land. More fundamentally, it was a conflict that has been played out in poor and minority communities repeatedly. The establishment wants to build highways, universities, or new industries; if poor and minority people are in the way, their communities are at risk. The first step is to claim that the community is "blighted," which in brief means that it is costly in terms of service needs and lacks the capacity to produce taxes and thus income to the government. It is a taker, not a giver. The area in the Central Ward that was designated for the medical school had more than its share of low-income families; it was nonetheless a strong and stable working-class community. In response to claims by medical school officials that the institution would immediately improve health services for the Newark community, Junius Williams reminded them that "it is a fallacy to assume that because a teaching hospital comes and takes over the municipal facilities, that automatically health care for the community will improve."[41] Dr. Cadmus, however, was insistent. Not only did he make promises that hospital management would be improved, as would relations with the neighborhood, he also promised collaborative efforts to develop *and fund* programs to address the city's health needs. In addition, he said the institution would establish a first-class teaching hospital that would handle referred medical cases from throughout the state.

There were major divisions between, on the one hand, objectives of the medical and dental school as a teaching institution with the mission of training professional and nonprofessional personnel, and on the other hand, a community with some of the most severe problems of health and disease in urban America demanding to know how the city's gift of its land would be leveraged into an improved environment for Newark residents. Nonetheless, the negotiations, deftly guided by Dungan and held together on the community side by Williams with the inspiration of Epperson, resulted in several important agreements regarding the future medical school. First, it was agreed that the medical school would be limited to no more than 57.8 acres. Second, the agreement would provide more than 60 additional acres of land for nonprofit groups to build new housing. The municipal hospital would be upgraded, and the state pledged $2.5 million to help get that project started. In addition, the agreement called for a review council to ensure that minority contractors receive a fair share of opportunities. Special efforts would be made to recruit minorities for apprenticeships and journeyman jobs in the construction of the medical school and special programs would be created to recruit black and Latino students for medical and dental training. The agreement also called for community representatives to work with the Department of Community and Preventive Medicine to improve relations and health services for the community.

The medical school agreements represented a monumental victory for the minority community; for the first time, the bulldozing power of the Newark Housing Authority had been turned back. It was now time for the community to reach for larger things, including the power to lead and manage the city through elected office.

⟨5⟩

Political Mobilization in Black Newark

NEWARK IS A NONPARTISAN CITY for which local elections bear no political party designation, and factions and groups go at it largely according to their ethnic/racial, neighborhood, and family ties. So for a minority candidate to win at the game, the numbers have to be favorable and special efforts have to be made to rally black and Hispanic voters, who generally do not turn out in high numbers for local elections.[1] Into the 1970s, the black and Puerto Rican communities in Newark mobilized to stir their followers in a drive to capture city hall.

The 1967 civil disorders were devastating for the city, but if there were any positives to grow out of the tragedy, it was that the rebellion led to a deep and broad unification of forces within the minority community, a coming together that had not occurred before in the city's recent history. Indeed, if the 1967 disorders had not happened, it is unlikely that the black and Puerto Rican communities would have coalesced in such a swift and almost complete way. But during the rebellion, the forces of law—local police, state police, and members of the state National Guard—perpetrated such violence against members of those communities, it became clear that the only answer was greater political power, which would ultimately lead to the control of city government. Sally Carroll, president of the local NAACP, which for years had defended the Addonizio administration, publicly condemned the actions of the Newark police, state police, and National Guard. Fred Waring, a history professor who was active in George Richardson's political movement, thought that the rebellion "moved up the timetable for black power in Newark by at least four years" and imposed unity as well as organization on the minority community.[2]

Still, unity is just a beginning. If the grander mission was to be realized, strategy, organization, and leadership were required. There were two people who would play leading roles in preparing for the election in 1970: Kenneth A. Gibson, the expected candidate for the mayoralty, and LeRoi Jones, known then as Imamu Amiri Baraka, who had returned to Newark from his cultural and artistic sojourns in Greenwich Village, Harlem, and other parts of the world.

Gibson Tests the Waters

Gibson had had just a taste of politics. After some arm twisting by his friend George Richardson, the maverick Central Ward politician and former assemblyman, he ran for mayor in 1966.[3] Gibson readily conceded that Richardson "was good at getting people to do things for him."[4] Richardson viewed the 1966 race as an opportunity to raise the consciousness of the black community, as a chance to demonstrate that there was black leadership ready to assume the responsibilities of leadership in high office. "Gibson was the perfect candidate for the time," he said. Gibson was "a black resident of the Central Ward who had completed college, an engineer, and active in the community."[5] It was widely assumed, by Gibson as well as others, that Richardson would be the candidate for mayor in 1970 when the prospects for a black victory would be more possible. "Kenny" was, in effect, Richardson's stalking horse.

If the 1966 campaign served to politicize the black community, it did that and more for Gibson. It was a ragged, rather chaotic campaign that started at the last moment and had a mere $2,000 in financial support, a paltry sum even for a dry run. Nevertheless, Gibson shocked the city when he garnered 16,000 votes. He was expected to receive only about one-third of that number. His votes forced a runoff between the two top vote getters, Hugh J. Addonizio and Leo P. Carlin, who was attempting a comeback. In the course of the campaign, workers observed that Gibson seemed astonished by the attention and activity around him. While riding through the city in the early days of the effort, he said to a friend, "the people know who I am."[6] He discovered that the aspiration for black political power had touched many people in Newark, much as it had in black communities throughout the nation. With a poorly funded organization of about twenty-five volunteers, he had gained considerable support and had excited black residents. Gibson came to realize that he was capable of doing all the things that politicians do—shaking hands, giving speeches, articulating a program to improve the city, and making promises he had no idea of how to fulfill. A Gibson constituency emerged; citizens summoned him for advice; the press now accorded him attention no other black leaders in Newark enjoyed. Gibson went from stalking horse to a man who could do it for himself. Although Gibson lost the 1966 bid for mayor, the experience in conjunction with the 1967 rebellion inspired him to plan for a mayoralty race in 1970.

Amiri Baraka: The Poet Politician

LeRoi Jones, aka Amiri Baraka, has defied convention in art and in politics. He has also defied the old adage that "you can't go home again." In 1966, Baraka did just that—he returned to Newark, the town of his birth and early schooling, to establish a Black Nationalist cultural/political organization to advance the aims of black community development and ascendancy to political power.[7] By the time he returned to Newark at the age of about thirty-two, Baraka was already a world-renowned personality whose poetry and writings had won a lengthy and impressive list of honors. His fame was rarely equaled in Newark, except for the genius of Newark natives Sarah Vaughn and James Moody. Baraka has been compared to the likes of Ralph Ellison, Norman Mailer, Toni Morrison, and Thomas Pynchon; to some critics he resides in the creative company of Langston Hughes, Richard Wright, and James Baldwin. So for Baraka to return to Newark to lead efforts to mobilize the black community was a game changer.

Baraka acquired use of a large empty building on High Street (now Martin Luther King Boulevard). The building was owned by the Newark Housing Authority. Within its walls, he and his followers created a vibrant, dynamic organization. They provided programs for education and training in black history, culture, and politics, as well as self-defense. His main organization was the United Brothers, and there was also an amalgam of groups called Committee for a Unified Newark (CFUN), all of which were under Baraka's leadership. His followers were required to show special deference and obedience to Baraka, and to live under a rigid discipline. For instance, in order to enter the building, one had to say, "All Praises to Imamu Baraka." Baraka returned to Newark at a time when sentiments concerning black pride were at a peak, and the push for political power was beginning to gain traction. Baraka was a big draw for many community activists and leaders, many of whom readily joined his organization.

In 1968, a special election was called to replace two vacancies on the city council. Baraka saw this as an opportunity to advance the Black Power agenda. Thus, he organized a convention that was not only black but built around the nationalist themes and practices of CFUN. At committee headquarters, aides answered the phone in Swahili, and dashiki-clad ushers strutted in militaristic style during the conclave, making many of the people who participated complain about the rigid and martial atmosphere. What is more, the candidates backed by the convention never won broad support. They were soundly defeated.

Kenneth Gibson, who had become a member of Baraka's organization, was worried that Baraka would attempt to run another convention for the 1970 mayoral election. As noted earlier, Gibson was gearing up to run for mayor that year. It was early 1969 and Gibson expressed his concern to me that a Baraka-led convention would divide and alienate many members of his base of support.

Gibson and I were friends. In addition to working together at the local CORE chapter and the United Community Corporation, I was a volunteer in his 1966 campaign. He invited me to join his early team, which met occasionally at my home in the South Ward on Sunday mornings for breakfast and political talk.[8] Gibson then asked me to organize a committee to sponsor a political convention. I consented and soon after wrote a memorandum that was distributed to a select group of black leaders, including Baraka, proposing a black convention. The memorandum spelled out the objectives of a convention, how it could serve to narrow the field of candidates from the minority community, how it could lead to a more effective support system for the candidates endorsed by the gathering, how it would give community representatives an opportunity to discuss the city's problems and possible solutions, and, lastly, how a convention could establish a degree of accountability of those selected. A specific goal was to create a cadre of campaign workers and fundraisers to support the entire slate. The memorandum also made clear that the nationalistic and militaristic approaches used in the earlier convention of 1968 would not be allowed in the gathering leading up to 1970. It warned against making the convention an effort to proselytize; the goal was to help put together a system to win and people of all views and ideologies were needed. In the final paragraph of the memorandum, I wrote, "Unity is very difficult to achieve since individual and group interests never completely disappear; however, one should be consistently reminded of the state of our city; dirt in the streets, horrible schools, mass corruption at city hall, an effort to give away the city's water resources, and an urban renewal program that is a black removal program. These are the things that must drive us to set aside petty differences and past rivalries. We owe that much to ourselves and the future children of Newark."[9] Baraka did not object to the content of the memorandum, although some points directly criticized his strong emphasis on Black Nationalism. He seemed clearly about winning.

The Black and Puerto Rican Convention of 1969

At the first meeting held to establish a convention-planning committee, there was unanimous agreement to invite leaders of the Puerto Rican community to join the effort. I was elected to serve as chairman of the planning committee and executive director of the convention. John Bugg, a deputy to Baraka, served as deputy chairman of the group; Ruth McClain, associate director of the Urban Coalition, headed a credentials committee; and James Pawley, executive director of the local Urban League, served as treasurer. Since the Urban League was heavily dependent on corporate contributions, Pawley's participation meant that the corporate leadership was not opposed to the convention. Hilda Hidalgo, a leading Puerto Rican activist, joined the group, as did Jennie Diaz, the leader of a Puerto Rican student association at Rutgers University, and Ramon Rivera, who had organized a Young Lords group in the North Ward. Most of the members of the planning committee were not members of Baraka's organization and there was a consensus that the convention had to be open to all organized groups. It was an extraordinary demonstration of unity to have such a wide range of opinion and positions in the minority community working together.

When the Black and Puerto Rican Convention was publicly announced, the idea was attacked by Addonizio supporters as well as by Harry Wheeler and George Richardson; Richardson was now back in the assembly and still hoping that he might someday be mayor. Wheeler had served as chair of Baraka's convention in 1968 and charged that the new convention would be "stacked for Gibson." The Addonizio supporters called the convention idea racist and said it did not represent the majority of the community. It was an example, they charged, of the exclusionary way blacks would manage the city. Richardson's public criticisms were similar; he added that the convention would further polarize the city's voters and drive away potential white support. It was clear, however, that Richardson's main concern, like Wheeler's, was that the convention was heavily tilted toward Gibson. Ultimately, Richardson feared that he would have very little chance of winning the endorsement of the participants.[10]

In that respect, he was right. Most of the convention's leaders, as well as the overwhelming majority of representatives from community organizations, had expressed their allegiance to Gibson, partly because of his surprisingly strong run in 1966, his continued leadership in the city as a principal player in the antipoverty program, and as a leader of the Business and Industrial Coordinating Committee (BICC). I was solidly in the Gibson camp. Richardson's and Wheeler's criticisms were eventually beaten back by a groundswell of white and black support for the convention, since many people feared that a divided black community would allow Addonizio to win the election. The majority of black and Puerto Rican civic and neighborhood organizations lined up behind the effort.

Baraka and his troops played several critical roles in the operation of the convention and subsequent support activities. First, he

made sure that a good number of his CFUN members attended planning meetings and helped to mount campaign posters and signs on
telephone poles. Baraka's celebrity and his contacts among national
political leaders and entertainers helped the convention develop a
high-profile list of speakers for the meeting. And then Baraka began
to take actions that would lead people to believe that he had organized the convention. He organized a separate support group called
the New Ark Fund, which publicly claimed ownership of the convention and established a separate fund-raising campaign with the same
objectives as the Black and Puerto Rican Convention Committee. In
the minds of some, particularly outsiders, the convention was perceived to be under Baraka's direction and Baraka's New Ark Fund
had been set up by the convention.

The convention opened on the night of Friday, November 14, 1969,
at a public school that was rented for the weekend. Of the 332 people
who registered as delegates, 229 were from community-based organizations. More than 2,700 people attended as guests; most were residents of Newark but some came from other cities throughout the
region.[11] The keynote address was delivered by Raymond Brown, the
defense attorney who had served as vice chairman of the Governor's
Select Commission on Civil Disorder. Brown warned delegates that
they had to forge a broad coalition that included white voters if they
wanted to win. Other speakers included Richard Hatcher, the first
black mayor of Gary, Indiana; Julian Bond, the civil rights activist
and Georgia state representative; and Shirley Chisholm, congresswoman from Brooklyn, New York. On Saturday, November 15, the
delegates and guests participated in workshops and drafted a twelve-
page platform, which was ratified by the entire assemblage. The candidates for city council seats spoke to the group and, as it turned out,
Kenneth Gibson was the only candidate for mayor to participate in
the convention. Gibson addressed the convention on Sunday and, on
late Sunday afternoon, delegates cast their votes.[12]

Although Gibson's selection was a foregone conclusion before the
convention began, his endorsement by the body brought cheers and
signs of great enthusiasm. Seven candidates were selected to run
for council seats: Dennis Westbrooks for the Central Ward; Sharpe
James for the South Ward; Alvin Oliver for the East Ward; and the
four at-large candidates—Earl Harris, Ted Pinckney, Donald Tucker,

and Ramon Aneses (who was selected by a caucus of Puerto Rican delegates and unanimously endorsed by the convention). With the energy of the convention spurring them forward, the candidates began their campaigns.

The 1970 Mayoral Campaign

The campaign of 1970 manifested the upheavals that had reshaped Newark since the 1950s, including the changes in demography that now gave blacks a majority, the racial polarization and antagonism that had helped to precipitate the rebellion, and the venality of city officials that had led to federal indictments. Mayor Addonizio and his cohorts faced voters and a jury at the same time. Race was the most important factor; history and the realities of urban life made it so. For the incumbent mayor, who was already in deep trouble, ultimately, it was the only thing he could run on. Earlier campaigns for the election of black mayors in other cities had displayed racial conflict, regardless of the qualifications or ideology of opponents. The move toward race as the major issue was not always precipitated by the white opponent. In 1967 in Cleveland, Carl Stokes, the black candidate, apparently used race to stir his constituency when he said, "The only reason I might lose is because of my color." Stokes went on to win the election. In Gary, Indiana, where Richard Hatcher was elected the city's black mayor in 1967, "[T]he tension in the city became so great that the Governor, fearing violence on election night, called up 4,000 National Guardsmen."[13] As the only candidate for citywide office who lived in the Central Ward, Gibson had a degree of credibility in his community that George Richardson, Gibson's patron turned competitor, had lost. Though a racial moderate, Gibson's appeal covered a broad spectrum of the city's voters. He had joined Baraka's organization, was a member of the local chapter of CORE, and as cochairman of the BICC, he worked closely with many downtown businesspeople and labor leaders. He could win the support of diverse groups in the black community because the neutrality of his "good government" position did not place him squarely in either camp. His simple brand of reform had given him a great deal of flexibility, which enabled him to campaign for the support of the Black and Puerto

Rican Convention without damaging his appeal for "government in the public interest," which meant voters of every race and ethnicity.

Nonetheless, the excitement of the campaign veiled underlying differences that would surface in the future. The most significant was that the Gibson campaign was a merger of starkly different ideological positions. It was really two separate campaign organizations, both theoretically aiming for the same result. The campaign headed by Baraka was based on the ideas and vision of Black Nationalism, while the other campaign was headed by a white professional from New York who was hired to serve as campaign manager for the "official" campaign, which was open to everybody.[14] Politically, it was a wise response to the fact the Baraka and his troops viewed the campaign as a vehicle for moving the Black Power movement forward. And the people who worked in the "official" campaign were composed of a mixture of blacks, browns, and whites; city people and suburbanites; church and synagogue members; leftists and peace advocates; some county political machine operatives; and a few corporate officials, all of whom would have nothing to do with Baraka's organization. Eulis "Honey" Ward, Democratic chairman of the Central Ward, was also in the Gibson camp, as was Clarence Coggins, the left-leaning activist who had engineered Irvine Turner's election to the city council in 1954.[15] Many young black women showed up at campaign functions wearing the Gibson colors of black and gold and came to be known as the "Gibson Girls." It was more a social movement than an organization. The logistics of the two operations were an organizational nightmare: two staffs, two campaign funds, and two uncoordinated schedules.

GIBSON THE REFORMER

Gibson's appeal to blacks was that he would show concern for the multitude of problems they had experienced at the hands of Addonizio's machine-dominated government. Gibson's wider public appeal, however, was "the prospect for better execution of government functions." In Gibson's own tempered words, "I really think that all the issues revolve around how municipal services have been provided or have not been provided, and how they should be provided by the next administration."[16]

MAYOR LINDSAY AND THE BLACK VOTE

Support and encouragement came from many quarters far and near. The staff of New York mayor John Lindsay called one day to invite Kenneth Gibson and his advisors to a meeting at Lindsay's office. Lindsay was a very popular mayor who had walked the streets of black neighborhoods during periods of conflict and had served on the presidential commission appointed by President Lyndon Johnson, known as the Kerner Commission, to study the riots. There was much speculation that Mayor Lindsay had plans for a run for the presidency. In any event, Gibson and a few of his campaign aides, including myself, trekked to New York and sat with key Lindsay aides, who made extraordinary promises that they would send people to Newark on Election Day to help get the vote out in black districts.

When we returned, I told Eulis Ward about the meeting and his response was unforgettable: "Shit!" he exclaimed. "What can Lindsay's people tell you about running Newark? Now if you went to Chicago and met with Richard Daley's people, you would be doing something." Ward was definitely old school, a product of the county's Democratic machine. His tough view of politics was an asset to a campaign populated mainly by civil rights and Black Power idealists. And by the way, the Lindsay people never showed up on Election Day.

Gibson occasionally hit at corruption: "Newark cannot tolerate absentee employees and half-baked performances. We have a big job to do. Corruption and carousing at the taxpayers' expense must cease."[17] Nevertheless, it was a calculated campaign strategy to avoid direct attacks on Addonizio for wrongdoing because such attacks were not necessary. Addonizio's trial was approaching and the media carried daily stories concerning the indictments. Most damaging to the mayor were the revelations of FBI surveillance tapes that caught mobsters as early as the 1962 campaign discussing how they would choose Newark's police director. FBI tapes also caught mobsters instructing Addonizio to establish a centralized payoff system to make sure things did not get out of hand. Such soundings gave special resonance to Gibson's promises to "sweep city hall clean," and that his first act in office would be to have police director Dominick Spina "clean out his locker."[18]

Despite widespread cynicism about Newark city government at the time, the extent of corruption uncovered by Addonizio's trial during the runoff campaign was probably most shocking to Newarkers. An informal survey taken immediately after the indictments were made public revealed a geographical pattern to citizen opinions of Addonizio. In the Vailsburg section of the West Ward, the mayor's home area, most people spoke in his defense. Predictably, the consensus among blacks in the South and Central Wards was strongly critical of the man who now was attacking the black community. However, in the North Ward, many Italian Americans expressed a surprisingly angry and vitriolic reaction to Mayor Addonizio. The assessment of the *Newark Evening News* was that "the political futures of Anthony Imperiale and Kenneth Gibson were enhanced. The indictments had given blacks an opportunity to win." While some kind of coalition with whites was needed, the indictments had clearly strengthened those interested in political reform.[19]

The third element of Gibson's reform campaign was his assertion that he was not "a traditional politician." Charging that Addonizio was the candidate of the bosses, Gibson promised to end machine politics and restore a more democratic government to the people of Newark. In this way, Gibson's campaign, at least on the surface, fulfilled all three conditions political scientists have attached to reform politics: efficient government and services, attacks against corruption, and a neutral, open approach to government. However, the strength of his appeal was based on more than reform issues. His personality was a perfect alternative to the high-pitched emotional rhetoric that usually characterized campaigns for office. Gibson's reaction to the indictments handed down against Mayor Addonizio was typical. "The after effects of shock should be a calm, reasonable approach to the problem. Some of the things I pointed out in 1966 are just coming to light."[20] Gibson's campaign style is best described by L. H. Whittemore in his book *Together*: "If elected, he was going to pick up the garbage, get rid of the Police Director and be an honest person. And beyond these three firm resolutions there was no 'magic formula' for Newark, no promise other than a sense of decency, possible harmony, a strong business sense, a stand against the Mafia, a spirit of renewed determination to accomplish what might, in the end, prove impossible."[21]

TWO PRIMARIES MAKE ONE ELECTION

As the election approached, Donald Malafronte, administrative assistant to Mayor Addonizio, described the May 12 primary election: "What you really have is two primaries, a black primary and a white primary. You know one black and one white will get into the run-off, and the run-off situation guarantees black unity and white unity behind the winners."[22] It became increasingly evident that Gibson had established himself as the only viable black candidate. George Richardson received little attention in the press, and several of his associates joined the Gibson campaign. Black political aspirations were no longer threatened by the prospect of a divided black community.

The emphasis of black leaders at this point was centered on efforts to mobilize the community to achieve the highest possible turnout on Election Day. After a year-long registration drive, Baraka coordinated a parade of national celebrities who came to Newark to endorse Gibson. Gibson walked the streets with Harry Belafonte, Dick Gregory, Dustin Hoffman, Ossie Davis, and Stevie Wonder. Each day he attended scores of house parties to reach potential voters. Harry Belafonte read a message of encouragement from Coretta Scott King. He told hundreds of Gibson supporters at a rally at City Hall, "I'm here because I don't want to see another black child lying bloody in the street here in Newark." He then shouted, "Ken Gibson is the property of black people around the world. His destiny is our destiny."[23] Massive canvassing and leafleting covered almost every black neighborhood. College students, most recruited by Baraka's organization, journeyed to Newark to ring doorbells. Suburbanites held parties to raise money.[24]

The grassroots efforts were rewarded on May 12 when Gibson led the field of seven candidates, winning over 40 percent of the vote.[25] Addonizio came in a distant second with 20 percent. Anthony Imperiale, who early in the campaign looked as though he might beat Addonizio, was third. George Richardson, the only other black candidate (Harry Wheeler withdrew three days before the election), garnered a mere 2,000 votes. Blacks were also encouraged by the fact that all four at-large candidates endorsed by the Black and Puerto Rican Convention made it into the runoff. Dennis Westbrooks in the Central Ward and Sharpe James also made it into the runoff. Concerning the mayoral contest, it was, as Malafronte said, just a primary.

THE PROMINENCE OF RACE

Despite Gibson's strong showing in the May vote, victory in the June 16 race against Addonizio was by no means assured. Malafronte professed to be encouraged by the results: "What Gibson has to remember is that 37,000 voted for him, mostly blacks, and that 45,000 people, mostly whites, voted against him."[26] Malafronte's calculus was a hint of the soon-to-be-adopted Addonizio strategy. In his campaign for the May election, Addonizio had attempted to stake out the middle ground, depicting himself as the moderate who was being challenged by extremists such as Gibson and Imperiale on both sides. For example, Mayor Addonizio told a group of supporters: "I believe the main issue is whether we can keep Newark together and on the move, and whether we will choose men who represent the politics of repression and division or who represent the politics of progress and peace. I feel I tend to represent a feeling of moderation and a feeling of integration."[27]

There was no feeling of moderation in evidence during the runoff, however, as Mayor Addonizio abandoned efforts to appeal to black voters. Two factors prompted his shift to a racial campaign. First, the mayor's extortion trial began on June 3. Thus he was required to be at federal court in Trenton during every weekday of the campaign. Not only did this limit his campaigning, but as the prosecution developed its case during the last two weeks of the campaign, it generated a flood of the kind of publicity no candidate would ever want. Second, the implications of the primary election were clear to his strategists. Imperiale's strong showing indicated broad anti-Addonizio sentiment among white voters. Almost 25,000 whites had voted for white candidates other than the current mayor, demonstrating that many would vote for him only reluctantly, if at all.

A racial strategy had worked for Mayor Sam Yorty of Los Angeles after a primary campaign in 1969 in which Tom Bradley, a black candidate, had led Yorty handily, but then lost white support after

Yorty strategists polarized the electorate over race.[28] Thus, the desperate Addonizio opened his runoff campaign with the assertion that Gibson was part of a "raw and violent . . . conspiracy to turn this city over to LeRoi Jones and his extremist followers."[29] The mayor told white audiences, "You all know what is involved here. Everything you hold sacred—your homes, families, and your jobs. We cannot let the leaders of race hatred take control of our city. You all know what I am talking about."[30] Tape recordings of Baraka reciting poetry that accused whites of bestiality were played for white groups. Leaflets showing a group of armed black students occupying a college building at Cornell University were mailed to white voters. Police Director Spina traveled the city telling voters that the election had boiled down to an issue of "black versus white."[31] Perhaps the most inflammatory piece of literature was a leaflet that had a picture of Baraka and a series of vile, antiwhite statements he allegedly had made, but were likely excerpted from his fictional writings. At the bottom of the leaflet was a picture of Gibson with the words "I think Leroi Jones has some good ideas" flowing from his mouth. Addonizio's strategy of polarization served to move Gibson further to the center. Since it was believed a segment of the white vote was needed, Gibson extended his campaign more deeply into white areas.

On June 16, Gibson soundly defeated Mayor Addonizio by a vote of 55,097 to 43,086.[32] He won overwhelmingly in the Central and South Wards, where the turnout surpassed all previous municipal election efforts, and Addonizio received a combined total of 2,000 votes. Furthermore, Gibson did unexpectedly well in the West Ward, where defeated primary candidate John Caulfield, who had served as Addonizio's director of the city's fire department, endorsed Gibson. An election board official alleged a "distinct pattern of voting fraud" in the North Ward; nevertheless, Gibson managed to win over one-third of the votes in the ward.[33] Steven Adubato, who was a community leader in the North Ward and active in the Democratic Party, had pledged to support Gibson in the runoff election. Gibson, however, contends that Adubato never fulfilled his pledge.[34] Nonetheless, the fact that Adubato did not endorse Addonizio might have helped the Gibson candidacy.

Gibson's running mates did not fare as well. In the at-large race for the city council, "Community Choice" candidates generally ran 13,000 votes behind Gibson. Finishing fourth among the at-large candidates was Earl Harris, the only black to be elected in the at-large race. Sharpe James won in the South Ward and Dennis Westbrooks beat out the ailing Irvine Turner in the Central Ward. For James and Westbrooks, it was the first try at elective office. Calvin West, who had won an at-large seat in 1966 on the Addonizio slate and had been indicted along with the mayor, was defeated.[35]

Every indicted candidate lost in the June 16 election. It seems safe to assume that in the voting booth, for a significant margin of voters, racial fears could not win over the costs and damages of corruption. The support system and publicity placed behind the convention's choices also helped to make a difference. Notables and celebrities, mostly recruited by Baraka, poured into the city. The convention-planning committee leaders worked for the team and raised money. The convention committee purchased billboards for Gibson as well as for the councilman-at-large nominees.

While the convention showed its worth, there were also down-sides to the contradictory interests that made up the campaign. Baraka played a major role in mobilizing the black community, but he also used the convention to promote his reputation as a king-maker. He told a crowd during the campaign leading up to the runoff that following a Gibson victory, there would be a movement, appar-ently led by him, to take over fifteen major cities on the East Coast. He expected Gibson to administer the city from a Black Nationalist perspective. Along with the severe problems of a decayed city, Gib-son had to contend with the polarizing politics of his erstwhile ally, who, according to Gibson, was eager to get as much media attention as Gibson himself.[36]

A CLOSER LOOK AT THE VOTE

Newark's population in 1970 was 62 percent nonwhite, 10 percent of which included the Latino population of the city. The *Newark News* estimated that of the 130,000 registered voters, 63,000 were black and 5,000 were Hispanic.[37] While these statistics may have under-estimated the black vote, they demonstrated that in electoral terms, blacks were still not overwhelmingly in the majority. Furthermore, there were indications that Gibson may not have had the undivided support of Newark's Latino community. Ramon Aneses, the Puerto Rican candidate for city council, did not run well in Puerto Rican neighborhoods.[38] Also, to bring home the victory, Gibson needed at least minimal white support.

In the Italian American North Ward, Gibson gained 3,200 votes between the primary and the runoff, winning more than one-third of the votes cast there on June 16. Addonizio supporters were also disappointed by the white turnout. The mayor's strategists had hoped to win the support of at least 25,000 of the 34,513 voters registered in the North Ward.[39] However, the 76 percent turnout in that area was not any higher than in the city's other wards despite the intense scare campaign carried out by the Addonizio camp. The 26,000 voters who did go to the polls in the North Ward gave the mayor only 19,000 votes. It was obvious that many prospective Addonizio supporters chose to stay home on Election Day.

Addonizio had troubles with the white vote in the East and West Wards as well. The at-large candidates on his ticket received higher margins in these neighborhoods than he did. While Gibson failed to carry any of Caulfield's districts in the runoff, the effect of the endorsement was evident in Gibson's increased totals in these areas. In one all-white West Ward district, Gibson received 345 out of the 700 votes cast. Gibson lost the West Ward as a whole by only 1,500 votes. Gibson's unexpected strength in many white neighborhoods can be explained by the findings of a Quayle poll that found that prior to the primary, some 6 percent of whites who favored Imperiale had Gibson as their second choice.[40] The depth of white disillusionment with Addonizio was also indicated by the small but significant number of voters (3,000) who went to the polls, but did not cast ballots in the mayoral contest.[41]

The evidence strongly suggests that if whites who voted for Gibson did not provide the margin of victory, those who stayed home probably did. The election was a reform victory as well as a black and Latino victory, although it may have been so by default. It was surely not the first election to have been won, in part, because of those who failed to vote.

Time to Celebrate

Election night ended with Gibson supporters dancing in the streets of downtown Newark. The campaign had been tough and hard fought, with numerous incidents of vandalism and violence. On election night, bitter Addonizio supporters lashed out in rage at newsmen by smashing their cameras and blackening eyes.[42] Addonizio's eight-year reign over Newark politics had come to an end. The scene was all the more tragic to the losers because an Italian American mayor of Newark had brought shame and disrespect to their community. For black Newark, it was a new day.

Mamie Bridgeforth, who had worked a frightening day at the polls in the North Ward amid angry and hostile whites, recalls the night of victory as a truly unforgettable moment. "I was at Symphony Hall where everyone had gathered to hear the returns. The place was packed so I sat on the floor. Suddenly someone shouted, 'We won! We won!' Everybody then went outside and it looked like most of Newark had come downtown. People got off of passing busses to join the crowd. There was dancing and singing. A Hispanic man was standing next to me with a child on his shoulders. When Gibson appeared to speak, he said to the child, 'That's him. That's him.'"[43]

Gibson was calm and thanked everyone for their support. He promised to pull the city together and told the crowd, "When you leave here, do not leave any paper on the ground; it is now my responsibility to clean the city." Thus, Newark had its first black mayor, and one who not only pledged to be responsible for cleaning the city but also for dealing with the high expectations of his black constituency. He would face major challenges in running a city that had lost much of its economic base and many of its middle-class citizens. One of the most complicated challenges would be to manage the divergent ideological currents at the base of his constituency. Could he be a good politician and leader for all the people of Newark, still a place of considerable ethnic and racial diversity, and keep Baraka in the fold?

‹6›

The Arrival of Black Power

ON JUNE 16, 1970, Kenneth A. Gibson was sworn in as mayor on the steps of Newark's city hall, becoming the first black mayor of a large northeastern city. Three years had passed since the rebellion, but Gibson was facing a city that was still reeling.[1] Signs of decay and disinvestment were ubiquitous. The poverty rate was 22 percent; around 7.1 percent of the population was unemployed. Burned-out houses scarred inner-city blocks, and abandoned vehicles dotted the streets. The city's black and Hispanic poor were tightly packed into the most decayed areas of the city.[2] Conflict between races was almost routine. Many of the institutions of government were severely outmoded. Mayor Addonizio had padded the city's payroll, creating a substantial budget deficit. The city council was still dominated by the old guard—six Italian Americans, five of whom had endorsed Addonizio. The three black councilmen would soon demonstrate that they had no intention of agreeing with Gibson on every issue.

Inauguration day gave the new mayor a taste of what his life would be like. About one hour prior to the swearing-in ceremony, he was informed that the city council was in session and that all of the white members, joined by the black Central Ward representative, Dennis Westbrooks, had rejected Gibson's appointment of the highly respected senior officer John Redden as police director. Redden was known for his toughness and integrity. He had for years been a bright spot of professionalism in a dismal and badly tainted force. The white council members did not want the department to have Redden's brand of leadership, and Westbrooks made it clear he would not support any white person for the police director's job. Gibson promptly went to the council conference room and told the council members that if they did not approve Redden, he would announce to the thousands of people outside, including media from all over the world, that the city council had chosen to continue to have a corrupt police department. They squirmed and grimaced, but most changed their votes. Redden was approved by a vote of 7–2; Westbrooks provided one of the opposing votes.

Gibson the Nonpolitician

Although Gibson had lots of experience in the nonprofit world, he was a neophyte at politics. Unlike Richard Hatcher in Gary, Indiana, and Carl Stokes in Cleveland, Ohio, who both had considerable political experience and had held public office before rising to mayor, Gibson's preparation for the mayoralty had been scant.[3] Carl Stokes, who came to Newark in 1966 to support Gibson, wrote in his biography, "I tried to give Gibson some basic lessons in the principles of organizing, but there was just nothing in his background to prepare him for it. He is personally not built for the business."[4] Still, his 1966 run for mayor had convinced Gibson he was indeed built for the business, although he remained ambivalent for a considerable period of time about his role as a politician. He was not sure whether he was making a long-term commitment to the life of politics. He would often tell audiences that he was not a politician at all. Shortly after his election in 1970, for example, he announced, to the surprise of his supporters, that he would serve one term and then return to his profession as a civil engineer. On another occasion, at a luncheon with the publisher and editors of the *New York Times*, Gibson was asked, "Will it someday be Congressman Gibson, or perhaps Senator Gibson?" His reply, according to one of his aides, was, "I hate politics. Some people seem to enjoy all this wheeling and dealing. One of the councilmen called me last night at midnight and wanted to talk about trading jobs; all this in the middle of the night. I don't enjoy that kind of business."[5]

Gibson's avowed distaste for politics could not be taken too seriously. In several ways, he was a traditional urban reformer, shrewd and quite adept at communicating his message while building a base of support. However, his calls for improved services, efficiency in government, and an end to corruption stopped short of any bold or imaginative plans for reversing the patterns of decay in Newark. One might fairly consider his solutions as the most practical approach in light of the limited resources and entrenched opposition he faced, but his goals were often simplistic. For example, his answer for dysfunctional, resource-starved bureaucracies was simply to announce that the city needed to recruit better people. The problem with schools was that there were not enough good teachers. Leadership by example was his remedy for complicated institutional problems. The civil rights and Black Nationalist leaders as well as the liberal whites who supported him tended to have grand visions and expectations of political power. Gibson had a very limited view of the role of the mayor and the extent to which he could make significant change.

Initially at least, politics for Gibson seemed to be synonymous with corruption and personal enrichment at the public's expense. Although he indicated disrespect for what had become his own profession, there is another dimension, which one might call the political side: a willingness to bargain, compromise, and engage in the machinations of political life. He could not have entered the byzantine wilderness of Newark and New Jersey politics without some penchant for its excitement and glory, not to mention the late night phone calls. Even before the 1970 campaign, he often showed signs of cunning to further his political ambitions. For example, his decision to ally with Baraka's Committee for a Unified Newark, a militant group of Black Nationalists, showed a willingness to join a base of support far different in ideology than his own moderate approach to racial issues. During his campaign he accepted financial contributions from several individuals who presumed that they were purchasing easy access to the mayor's office. He said that a vice president of Prudential, the giant insurance firm headquartered in Newark, gave him a "wad of cash, more than $15,000" for his campaign. Another businessman paid for the rental of the Lincoln sedan that transported him around the city during the campaign.[6] Contrary to his frequent railings against corruption, in the latter part of his first term, it was discovered that he had stashed away $75,000 in a Swiss bank account, which had not been reported on his tax returns. He narrowly escaped the U.S. attorney's effort to have him indicted, apparently with a little help from his political allies in President Jimmy Carter's administration.[7] His performance on the Democratic Platform Committee during the 1972 National Convention, in which he conciliated such divergent groups as followers of the segregationist Governor George Wallace of Alabama and northeastern liberals, won him national acclaim. And by 1974, he was competing for high office in the U.S. Conference of Mayors. In 1976, he was elected president of that body, placing him center stage in the national conversation regarding the problems of urban America. In 1981 and 1985, he ran in the Democratic Party primaries for governor of New Jersey. He came in third both times.

In so many ways, Gibson was an odd fit for politics. He was a private man who related to a very small circle of friends. Gustav Heningburg, former president of the Greater Newark Urban Coalition who became a key advisor to Gibson, said, "By temperament and by training, he's an engineer accustomed to careful analysis . . . he's his own advisor. He listens and he absorbs and then he goes off somewhere to make decisions."[8] The point that Gibson was a trained engineer may help to explain his approach to decision making. An engineer is trained to appraise a task methodically and base his or her judgments on hard scientific analysis and precise measurements. The decisions and work of engineering are long-term: a road or bridge is built to last for a century or longer. On the other hand, a political leader must manage the very imprecise world of human dynamics and must often solve a problem for the moment. In some respects, politics is the polar opposite of engineering.[9]

At the end of his first term, and although he was well known across the nation, officials in the state's Democratic Party complained that Gibson followed his own political instincts. Political theorists have described the ideal politician as secure, reasonably familiar with, and trustful of, his environment.[10] But that was not Gibson. To many who campaigned for him and many who worked for him, he was an enigma, reluctant to take any person into his confidence or to allow anyone to assume that almost ordinary role of "advisor." In addition to Elton Hill, Gibson's childhood buddy, the person who became closest to Gibson during his 1970 campaign was Dennis Sullivan, a highly talented white undergraduate student from Princeton University. Sullivan, who had grown up in Oregon, joined the campaign as part of a civic internship program at Princeton's Woodrow

Wilson School of Public and International Affairs. Wise and savvy far beyond his years, Sullivan could deliver tough advice to Gibson that others could not or would not. Gibson treated him like a son. When the campaign got intense, the strain of Sullivan's long trips to Princeton, fifty-five miles from Newark, was abated by a sofa in the home of Gibson's parents. After graduating near the top of his class and earning a master's degree at Oxford, Sullivan returned to Newark and joined the Gibson staff.

While Sullivan won Gibson's trust, most people felt a strange aloofness around Gibson, which, nonetheless, did not damage his relationship with the larger black electorate. He won four consecutive elections and was strongly supported by black voters until his defeat in 1986. The perception of those who worked closely with him was that he distrusted many of the black activists he had recruited for his campaign and suspected that some of them would become political rivals, a threat that Dennis Sullivan and other white aides did not pose. Nevertheless, his white aides had limited ability to relate to the mayor's black constituency and thus did not help much in developing community support for the mayor's programs. For example, during the teachers' strike, which I discuss in this chapter, Sparky Jacobs, a black aide in the mayor's office, refused a request from two white Gibson aides that he attempt to calm a disruption at a school. Jacobs protested because he wasn't consulted sufficiently on handling the strike. Lower-echelon staff aides were black and handled citizen complaints; the aides closest to Gibson were white and helped to make policy.[11]

Although it is true that some of these traits hampered Gibson's efforts to realize even his modest goals of providing effective service to the residents of the city, he also brought considerable strengths to his office. Primary among them was a willingness to work very hard. He took pride in his jogging and marathon running, which seemed to symbolize his approach to politics and all of life. "I may be slow," he once said, "but I am awfully persistent." Some of his aides, noting his ability to remain calm amid chaos, joked that Gibson was a "type Z" personality. A telling example of this plodding, never-give-up attitude is the fact that he spent eleven years, interrupted by two years of military service, earning his degree in civil engineering from the Newark College of Engineering (now the New Jersey Institute of Technology).

Gibson's character was rooted in a strong family background in which hard work and self-improvement were fundamental tenets. He was born in Enterprise, Alabama, in 1932, and moved north with his family eight years later (a departure, according to Gibson, partly motivated by a search for a skilled surgeon who could extract a toy whistle from the young child's windpipe). His father, a butcher, appears to have been obliged to leave Alabama because his white neighbors resented his efforts to enjoy the benefits of middle-class life. According to Gibson, his father was a powerful but friendly "authority figure" in his home, who instilled in him the conviction that "we could do anything we wanted if we tried hard enough." At least on the surface, he brought those basic values to his politics. After a year in office, Gibson, in the eyes of many residents and officials, began to establish an improved reputation for City Hall as an honest and workable institution, an extraordinary accomplishment in Newark.[12] In time however, that reputation was to be sullied by poor judgment and a return to on old-style Newark politics by Gibson and the city council.

Indeed, it did not take long for Gibson to discover that mayoral power is severely limited, particularly regarding efforts to change long-standing bureaucratic behavior. No mayor, white or black, fully controls the various departments and bodies that provide services for the city. In addition, federal, state, and county governments are highly influential in local decision making. Civil service laws, for example, make it difficult to control, reorganize, or rid the bureaucracies of incompetents and dedicated opponents to a chief executive's policies. For a black mayor at that time, the problems were more difficult. Some whites working in government so resented the election of a black mayor that they openly attempted to subvert his efforts. Shortly after Gibson took office, a secretary at City Hall told one of Gibson's aides: "I want you to know that I worked for Addonizio's reelection. He lost but as far as I'm concerned, he is still my boss. Addonizio got me this job and he is still my boss."[13] A white senior employee at City Hall reportedly often referred to Gibson as "the nigger" when talking to other whites.[14] When Gibson's car broke down one day and his driver called for help, Gibson heard a policeman bark over the radio, "Let the bastard walk."[15] Hostility of this sort diminishes the capacity to control subordinates and often forces administrators to hire additional personnel just to bypass roadblocks and inert functionaries who sit and do as little as possible.

Paradoxically, the effort needed to stir a largely poor constituency to show up at the polls later complicated Gibson's ability to manage even the most modest reforms. Many black residents, no doubt, believed Gibson's campaign slogan "We will sweep City Hall clean" to mean he would clear out every old face within weeks. Previously, limited and token participation of blacks in the political process contributed to high and unrealistic expectations of what government could do, particularly in the short term. Unfortunately, in Gibson's first term there was often a rather shallow understanding of the limits of political power and how fragmented bureaucracies can resist control over them.

Blacks and Italians: The Struggle to Remake Newark

Going into the late twentieth century, Newark proved a powerful example of the racial and ethnic tensions that had been smoldering in urban America. Underlining those tensions, which were at the root of the widespread civil disturbances of the 1960s and much of the intra-community violent crime, was the shoddy and brutal treatment blacks had received for many decades in addition to the poverty and despair that remained. Economic hardship, made worse by continuing racially pointed disinvestments, was a painful reality for a substantial proportion of the entire population. Although blacks and Puerto Ricans were at the bottom of the ladder, unemployment among Newark residents was estimated to be more than 12 percent. More than 35 percent of white youth age sixteen to nineteen were out of work. As in many cities throughout America, Newark's racial and ethnic divisions were more than symbolic; they were rooted in an active and intense competition for scarce jobs and perquisites in a declining urban economy.

The city's population had become ethnically bimodal, with blacks and Italian Americans the two largest groups in the city. This dichotomy added to tensions in several ways. Matters that affected both groups, such as a tax issues, were frequently converted into racial skirmishes. In addition to the different neighborhoods of the two groups—most Italians lived in the North Ward and West Ward, with a few remaining in the Central Ward; blacks were concentrated in the Central and South Wards—a black mayor and Italian-dominated city council were apt reflections of the demographic and political divisions. Whites expected the worst from Gibson and quickly displayed stern resistance to his efforts. The resistance was most often voiced by the most powerful Italian American politicians, especially councilmen Ralph Villani, Frank Addonizio, and Anthony Imperiale. Steve Adubato said that the underlying reason for the conflict was fear: "Italian Americans thought blacks would treat them as they had treated blacks when they were in power." In Adubato's view, Italians feared that blacks would retaliate for the exclusion and hostility Italians had displayed. That, he said, made Italian Americans defensive and pushed them into the grips of the vigilante Anthony Imperiale.[16]

There were however deeper and more complicated reasons for the fears that beset North Ward Italians. They had in fact been left behind by their more successful neighbors, who had moved to the suburbs and southward to Jersey Shore communities. As a group, they held to old values emphasizing community and family. They bitterly protested the cost of government services for social problems, which they viewed as the result of personal failures instead of the consequences of discrimination or society's neglect. "Our taxes have been going up year after year," a resident complained, "but what do we get? I'll tell you what we get: More welfare and poorer schools."[17] Moreover, Italians were shoved out of the top office by blacks after a brief eight-year reign (not counting the years of Italian leadership during the years of commission government, which produced as much shame as the Addonizio scandals and revelations of mob influence). They found it hard "to relearn the role of minority," particularly in relation to blacks.[18] Imperiale, the stocky, rotund karate instructor who supported the Alabama segregationist George Wallace in the 1968 presidential election and won for himself a seat on the Newark city council, knew how to appeal to their fears and hatreds. "The good guys are prepared to shoot to kill to keep the peace if the Negroes come to burn our homes," he announced to North Ward residents.[19] In time, he learned that to be a political player, he had to abandon his blatant antiblack rhetoric and adopt a more sophisticated law-and-order appeal. For some time, to Newark blacks, he was an antiquated racist, Newark's own Bull Connor. For many Italian Americans, he represented the last defense of their neighborhoods.

So as Black Power arrived in the city of Newark, much of the remaining white community, including bureaucrats, the city council, the police department, and public employee organizations, lined up against Gibson. Authority to do anything was scattered all over the place and on all levels. The city was in financial crisis; the statehouse and the White House were both controlled by conservative Republicans, so little help could be expected from either source. Yet expectations were high that Newark's first black mayor would reverse the trend of the city's decay and deliver a payoff to the black community that had put him in office. However, Gibson was most eager to demonstrate that he was a fair and evenhanded leader. As such, he made concerted efforts to convince the white residents who remained that he was everyone's mayor—even to the extent of inadvertently signaling to blacks that he held no special obligation to use his power to advance their social and economic life. His professions of racial neutrality won him admiration among whites and large numbers of fans throughout the state and nation. For black Newarkers, however, he was increasingly an enigma and object of ridicule.

Council versus Mayor

The city council stood poised to combat Gibson on every front including personnel choices, programs, and policies. Ugly skirmishes continued throughout the major part of Gibson's first term and well into his sixteen-year tenure. Several white members of the council, and Earl Harris as well, were veterans of Newark politics and had grown accustomed to the graft and patronage operations of the past. Most of the white community expected their representatives to hold the line against the political ascendancy of the black community. Indeed, to many whites who remained in the city, the white council members were viewed as the last bastion of Italian American power. It was clear from the start that Gibson would face formidable challenges in dealing with them.

The council's opposition was not always based on race, although race was very often an important factor, at least during the first eight years. And it was not only the white block on the council that resisted Gibson. The three black councilmen, Earl Harris, Sharpe James, and Dennis Westbrooks, all of whom had run on the ticket of the Black and Puerto Rican Convention with Gibson, occasionally asserted their independence and at times publicly criticized the mayor. Much of the black community assumed that the black councilmen would give unwavering support to the new mayor. Such naïve hopes were quickly dispelled when Councilman Westbrooks joined the white councilmen in opposing Redden as police director on inauguration day. Other differences between Gibson and the black councilmen soon surfaced. As a result, several of the black councilmen often joined the six white councilmen in opposing his policies.

Councilman Harris had served as a Republican county freeholder. His political style, outlook, and experience resembled those of the white council members more than his black colleagues. He had changed his stripes and party as the movement for black leadership gained strength. Like most black politicians, he had campaigned for Addonizio in 1962 and later served as an administrative aide to Addonizio. According to Sam Convissor, a former Addonizio aide, Harris met with him after Addonizio was elected in 1962 and said, "Hughie told me that I could have the South Ward; it's mine."[20] In 1966, Harris ran for the South Ward council seat but lost in a runoff to Lee Bernstein. In 1968, he joined Baraka's organization, the United Brothers. After taking office, Harris stated, "The fact that I and two other black councilmen ran on the same ticket with the mayor does not bind us on every issue."[21] Sharpe James, the South Ward councilman and a physical education instructor at Essex County Community College who would later rise to the office of mayor, had no political experience before 1970. He was recruited by the convention committee after the Reverend Horace Sharper, the candidate expected to run for the South Ward seat, withdrew from the convention in sympathy with George Richardson. Differences between Gibson and James flared quickly and can be traced to the 1970 runoff election when Gibson was reluctant to endorse James, who was pitted against another black candidate. Although James won easily, he was left with the feeling that Gibson had not helped his (James's) candidacy.

Westbrooks, the Central Ward councilman, was closely allied with Baraka and had been active in civil rights protests and rent strikes. He was young and immature; he said his role was to "always expose the system and raise controversial issues." Shortly after taking office, he promised, "I'm never going to compromise. I'll always be in conflict."[22] It was no favor to the efforts of Gibson or the needs of his Central Ward constituency that he remained true to his promise. As the relationship between Gibson and Baraka fell apart, Westbrooks became more critical of Gibson. In August 1973, Westbrooks led a march to City Hall with three hundred residents from the Central Ward. Many of the protesters carried bags of garbage to highlight their complaints about poor sanitation services to their neighborhoods. The Newark police arrested several of the demonstrators, including James Nance, a black Newark police officer who had joined the protest. Nance, known as a critic of the department's racial policies, said he was beaten while in custody. Gibson charged that the demonstration was intended to boost the reputation of Westbrooks. "Newark is going to be a better place to live," the mayor said, "and the political activities of Dennis Westbrooks and Baraka cannot be allowed to stop this."[23]

The council had its own agenda, or, more accurately, agendas. It opposed Gibson on most major appointments as well as his efforts to reorganize government, and on matters that often had no apparent relationship to race. For example, Gibson was unsuccessful in his attempts to persuade the council to discontinue hiring an accounting firm that for over twenty years had audited Newark finances without discovering a single irregularity. City Hall rumors held that the firm annually granted each member of the council a payment of one thousand dollars to continue the deal.[24] The entire council opposed Gibson on this matter. Likewise, Irving Solondz, a white attorney who had provided numerous hours of volunteer service to CORE and civil rights causes, was nominated by Gibson to become a city magistrate. He was voted down by the council; the opposition was led by Earl Harris, who was miffed because Solondz had not contributed to his campaign.[25] Ultimately, one of Councilman Villani's nephews was appointed to the position. An effort to establish an ombudsman program in the city with federal funding was rejected by the entire council because the program would challenge past practices.[26]

In January 1972, mayor–council relations were at a low point. The federal government began a new program called Planned Variations and designated Newark one of ten cities in which the Model Cities concept would be expanded to cover an entire community. For Newark, it would mean $7 million in additional federal grants. However, the council knew the additional funds would strengthen the power of the mayor, and it was not pleased. It began its opposition by unanimously tabling action on accepting the first $1.2 million. Opposition to the proposal was led by James and Council President Louis Turco. James complained that the mayor would have sole authority in spending the money and the council would have no role at all. "The councilmen are totally ignored," he charged. They are "rendered powerless and policyless."[27] He also labeled Ira Jackson, an aide to the mayor imported from Boston who was slated to head the program, "a poverty pimp—someone who jumps from one poverty program to another trying to take care of himself."[28] Turco's view was that the mayor was going to use the program to build his political organization and enhance his political fortunes at the program's expense. "It would give the mayor," he charged, "in this program alone, a bigger press office than the governor of the state of New Jersey."[29]

Mayor Gibson countered by branding the councilmen with charges of "demagoguery" and of taking "cheap and irresponsible shots at me and members of my staff."[30] All of the councilmen, except Dennis Westbrooks, then introduced an ordinance granting the council control over all applications, contracts, extensions, personnel changes, audits, and reports of programs supported in whole or in part by outside funding. Gibson, who was increasingly a leader in calling for more federal assistance, would be made to look weak and ineffective if he could not even launch a federal program for which he had lobbied. In one of his rare uses of power politics, he issued dismissal notices to several city employees who had been granted jobs by councilmen. Included in the group were three relatives of Earl Harris, and Dr. Michael Petti, a close associate of Turco. The council and mayor were finally ready to compromise. The mayor agreed to scale down the $1.2 million for the initial phase of the project to $750,000. Councilmen were then granted one-third of the members of an advisory panel for Planned Variations. The council was also given a full-time staff member to "keep it abreast of policy decisions in the mayor's office."[31]

It was not only through their voting that the councilmen sought to defeat Gibson's efforts. Their behavior as opinion makers was also important. For example, Turco, the East Ward representative, helped to galvanize white opposition to the board of education and Mayor Gibson during the teachers' strike in 1971. The reality was that white councilmen often used their positions to intimidate Gibson with threats of inquiries. Council members frequently intervened in the affairs of departments, exploiting the continued presence of civil servants and personnel who had been placed in their jobs by the previous administration. When a student boycott occurred over the dismissal of an administrator at Vailsburg High School in the West Ward, the council called on the New Jersey Department of Education to investigate to embarrass Gibson.[32]

The demand for jobs and patronage often precipitated opposition among both white and black council members. In nonpartisan Newark, electoral success is largely dependent on the personal organizations of public officials and would-be candidates. To this day, Newark political leaders form clubs or associations for promotional and fund-raising purposes. The organizations are run and managed by associates of the political leader, and the lifeblood of such groups is the influence and jobs they control in government and city life. Following Gibson's election, the white councilmen were eager to demonstrate that they were still influential enough to get jobs for their constituents. Elton Hill, who headed the Kenneth Gibson Association and was hired to be assistant business administrator, said that two U.S. Department of Labor officials visited his office to inquire about charges that a federally funded employment project was being used for political patronage. In the midst of their discussion with Hill, Councilman Bontempo burst into Hill's office and shouted, "Where the hell are my jobs? I want my jobs. I want my jobs." The visiting federal officials were stunned to see such overt evidence unfold in their presence.[33]

In 1973, the Department of Labor had had enough when it verified that the Public Employment Program (PEP) had allocated a number of jobs to each member of the city council. The labor department accused the PEP in Newark of "disintegrating into a political

patronage system involving top city officials with some city councilmen filling at least 100 PEP jobs with persons of their choosing
in violation of government regulations." Federal officials demanded
that Harry Wheeler, who was director of the program, and Hill, the
assistant business administrator, be severed from all responsibilities
and activities related to the program. Mayor Gibson had no choice
but to agree. He explained that giving the council jobs to dole out
was a forced trade-off in order to get their approval of the program.
"I weighed allotting the city council ninety jobs against the city providing over 1,500 jobs for people who were in dire need. I decided to
allow ninety jobs in order to save the $7 million program we were in
danger of losing."[34]

Often the councilmen had heated exchanges and conflict among
themselves. On one occasion, Councilman Bontempo exchanged
insults with Westbrooks, ever the agitator, who said at a public meeting the council had only "eight and a half councilmen," and pointed
his finger at Bontempo, who jumped up from his seat and yelled
back, "You're a bum. This is not a jungle."[35] Westrooks frequently
burst into tirades against his fellow councilmen for being "partial
and biased" and joined a committee to recall councilmen at-large
Giuliano, Bontempo, and Villani.[36] Council president Frank Megaro
accused Westbrooks of "raucous, unruly, and irresponsible behavior" that caused "critical holdups" of urgent council business. Turco
charged that Westbrooks and other activists were "trying to achieve
anarchy in Newark."[37] Meetings were occasionally suspended as they
became unruly and close to violence.

Sometimes violence did occur, as in a meeting in March 1972.
Councilman Earl Harris struck Councilman Turco in the eye during a debate over a proposed raise for the city's corporation counsel. Harris later apologized for the attack, and Turco later requested
that the complaint he had filed against Harris be dismissed.[38] In 1976,
North Ward councilman Anthony Carrino, a former Newark police
officer who had been elected to the council in 1974, led a group of
seventy-five angry North Ward residents to Gibson's office to protest
the appointment of a police precinct captain for the North Ward who
did not live in the city. When they found the door closed, they kicked
it in, at which point they engaged in a shouting and shoving match
with Gibson and his staff. Carrino was accused of hitting one of the

mayor's security guards in the face and was later convicted of assault. He was fined and placed on probation.[39]

The conflicts manifested deep alienation and hostility between the races. The conflicts were also symptomatic of the pervasive and historic disregard for peaceful and orderly change in a community where government had little legitimacy. Members of the black community and their representatives had little confidence in the normal procedures of doing business. White councilmen, on the other hand, detested the reality that they now needed to share power with blacks. Blacks were bitter since their efforts were still thwarted by representatives of a minority of the population. In the years leading up to the election of 1970, lawful and sensible appeals to government for change had been ignored; disruptions at public meetings by black citizens during the Addonizio years became one of the more effective strategies for getting officials merely to listen. Public meetings during Gibson's first term resembled those held from 1965 to 1968, perhaps the period of highest tension in Newark's history.

Some of the mayor–council conflict, or the fact that it was often so prolonged, must be attributed to Gibson's failure or unwillingness to establish effective communications with the council. Unlike his predecessor, Addonizio, who met with the council weekly, Gibson initially delegated an aide to handle council relations. After the councilmen objected, Gibson decided to have pre-meeting conferences with the council. The councilmen then refused to allow Gibson to sit in on their weekly private discussions. It is also likely that mayor–council relations might have been more cordial if Gibson had been willing to continue the horse-trading practices at City Hall. Gibson's occasional public criticisms of the council angered them. In addition, Gibson's office was frequently delinquent in sending plans and federal grant requests to the council, which was interpreted as efforts to bypass them. Often, the delays and lack of communication were simply the result of sloppy management in the mayor's office.

The conflict impeded progress on many fronts. Business leaders complained that it prevented potential redevelopment. Federal authorities, wary of conflicts concerning applications for federal funds, notified City Hall that all requests must have prior council approval before submission to federal agencies, which marked a major victory for the council. A state task force criticized the conflicts and charged that they caused waste and inefficiency. Thus, establishing a working relationship with the council was a major challenge fueled by the council's tendency to be obstructionist and Gibson's mishandling of the relationship.

Gibson and Baraka

If managing the relationship of the nine-member city council was difficult, handling the charismatic poet Amiri Baraka would prove impossible. Gibson was concerned about sanitation and police services and efforts to dampen the conflicts that were spilling into neighborhoods and schools. Baraka, on the other hand, had big visions regarding Black Power and huge ideas about what could be done in Newark from his base of Black Nationalism. He had a cadre of several hundred men and women in Newark and ever-growing influence in the movement of cultural nationalists throughout the country. After Gibson's election, some members of CFUN expected Gibson to provide jobs and positions to committee adherents and advocate their brand of separatist politics. If they had been listening, they would have heard Gibson talking a very different line—pledging to unite all races and ethnic groups in Newark. The strains between the two began to show early. In October 1970, just four months after taking office, Gibson told *Jet* magazine, "Baraka is not a very good politician; he's more a theoretician and philosopher. When it comes to actual practice, he can't see why it doesn't work the way it's supposed to."[40]

Baraka saw Newark as a means to larger visions. He had developed a close association with Ron Karenga, the cultural nationalist in Southern California who created the organization called US. Karenga later defined a black lifestyle that included holiday celebrations like Kwanza and the Black Nationalist doctrine called Kawaida, meaning "tradition and reason."[41] It was through the doctrine of Kawaida that Baraka developed a plan to build a housing project—presumably for his followers—that would be an illustration of his values and commitment to the city. It would be called Kawaida Towers, a multifamily project designed to include services and facilities that would provide first-class domiciles. The site for the project was in the North Ward, in an area that had long been the stronghold of Italian

American political leadership, the ward where Italian American culture, business, and family life had flourished. Although Baraka had negotiated a deal with the city council that would have allowed white construction workers to build the project, Kawaida Towers became a focal point for Anthony Imperiale, who saw the project as an invasion of Italian American turf. Moreover, Imperiale had spread the false notion that blacks were at war with whites; thus having a project in their midst would be a danger.

From the day Baraka and city council members broke ground at the site, there were daily pickets and confrontations. The bitterness of this conflict spread to high schools and neighborhoods in other areas of the city. Police Director John Redden, whose police department members were caught in the middle, eventually resigned and publicly criticized Gibson and the political leadership of the city for creating the Kawaida situation. After months of bickering and conflict, the project lost the support of the majority of the council and Gibson became indifferent. Kawaida Towers was never built, and a foundation that had cost more than a million dollars was buried in the ground. It was a stunning defeat for Baraka and virtually ended the political relationship he had with Gibson. Gibson contends he was never in favor of building Kawaida Towers in the North Ward and said that he thought from the beginning the project would give Imperiale a launching pad.[42] However, the record shows that Gibson supported the project when it was before the council and apparently thought, like Baraka and others at the time, that the agreement to share construction jobs with whites would prevent the damaging struggle that occurred.

The Gibson-Baraka alliance was destined to end. It is true that Gibson used Baraka in many ways, such as his disciplined cadre of workers, his contacts with artists and celebrities, and his ability to excite the black community about political participation. Baraka, on the other hand, saw Gibson as his vehicle to real political power, access to resources, and ultimately legitimizing a national campaign for the control of other cities. It was largely a fantasy, devoid of any understanding that a Black Nationalist view of the world could not meld with the ways of a traditional accommodating urban political machine, not in Newark and not in places like Boston, Philadelphia, Washington, or Atlanta. Baraka, with all his literary brilliance and his unquestioned dedication to the improvement of the lot of black people, simply did not understand American urban politics. Neither did he comprehend that political sentiments in the black community were far closer to those of Kenneth Gibson than to his own. In the meantime, Gibson increasingly enjoyed his power and his stature in high places. The black community had embraced him. His challenge was to win the respect of the city's remaining whites, who were now in fear. He came to see Baraka as a liability. Out of his own political exigencies, he increasingly moved away from Baraka and his black activist supporters. His openness to the refugees from the Addonizio era seemed to bring him comfort and a new base of support.

In August 1973, Baraka held a press conference during which he called Mayor Gibson a "puppet." The mayor, he charged, "is one of a new clan of Negroes that control neither the means of production nor the productive forces in our city . . . they are the managers, the administrators of the political dumb-show that is supposed to trick black people and Puerto Ricans into thinking we are making real progress, while the orderly business-as-usual of the big insurance companies and big banks goes on."[43] Baraka still had plans to build in the city, and he carved out what seemed to be a more feasible plan to develop an already cleared urban renewal area of the Central Ward. He did not foresee that the leaders he had played a large role in ushering into public office, namely Mayor Gibson and council president Earl Harris, would conspire to deny his effort to build housing in the almost entirely black Central Ward.

By Baraka's account, he was encouraged to focus on a project in the Central Ward to get away from the North Ward disaster. John Notte, the executive director of the NHA, met Baraka in a restaurant in New York City to offer financing and support to undertake a development in an area already cleared in the Central Ward. After planning for his Central Ward project was well under way with a substantial financial commitment from the federal Department of Housing and Urban Development, Baraka recalled that Notte invited him into a private room at NHA headquarters and told Baraka the truth about the deal. To quote Baraka:

> At the Housing Authority, the son-in-law of a Mafioso was the director. He took me into a conference room one afternoon and told

me frankly. "You take this architect, this consultant, and this construction firm and you go forward tomorrow. Otherwise, nothing." I told him that was cool but how could I tell black people that I've been struggling for black development and then tell them that these are the people who're going to make a profit off this development. Gibson would do nothing but burp when he was told these things.[44]

The key to the project was getting sufficient subsidy through tax abatement, which was needed to stabilize and lower the rents so that the units would be affordable for ward residents. But tax abatement could only happen with the approval of the city council. Mayor Gibson's office sent a resolution for abatement to the council, but the measure met immediate resistance from council president Earl Harris and Central Ward councilman Jesse Allen, a former SDS organizer who had won the Central Ward seat from Westbrooks in the 1974 election. Allen, a man of considerable intelligence who had never learned to read, announced to the dismay of all that the city did not need any more housing. Harris said that he voted against the project because he had discovered that Baraka was a racial extremist and a dictator, and insisted "that Baraka's organization must never be allowed to build another development in Newark." Knowing that Baraka would bring an angry crowd to the next council meeting when the final abatement vote would be taken, Harris announced that "decorum would prevail at council meetings and slanderous remarks at council members would not be tolerated." Baraka's cadre had already showed up at earlier meetings with placards that alleged Harris was a "bagman" and "political pimp."[45]

On February 5, 1975, the council voted to deny the abatement; every member voted against it except South Ward councilman Sharp James, who said the issue was the need for housing and service, and not ideology. It was a sad spectacle when Councilman Harris ordered the arrest of Baraka and his wife, Amina, and five other people after Baraka angrily and profanely expressed his disappointment to the city council for their lack of support.[46] While Baraka was somewhat blind to the consequences of the friction that the Kawaida North Ward episode had created for the moderate politics of Gibson, the reasons both Harris and Gibson gave for their abandonment of the Central Ward development did not fit with the history. Baraka in fact had moved away from the rigid, I-can't-compromise politics of earlier years; Harris and Gibson had both joined him when he was more militant and less willing to compromise. In 1970, when some of Gibson's supporters asked that he sever ties with Baraka, I recall Gibson responding that Baraka was a tremendous asset to his campaign. He added, "I wouldn't ask him to step out because he gave me tremendous assistance. You have to have principles in politics or you won't be a good political leader." One has to ask, just what principle was at work in this case? Was there really good reason to so abruptly and brutally abandon Baraka's efforts? Baraka and his organization showed increasing signs of accommodation and willingness to work within the system. He had begun to make stronger efforts to allay fears of a black takeover while insisting on black advancement. He had showed a willingness to use white contractors and professionals on the Kawaida project as a manifestation of increased sophistication and an effort to accommodate to political realities.

Ultimately, none of that mattered. The Baraka plan was squashed by the combination of the old-line political forces who were now closer to Harris and Gibson than the reformers who fought for their election and the unrevealed actors who could tell Notte who should benefit from the largess of a development project in the Central Ward. Komozi Woodard, in his political biography on Baraka, rightfully concludes that the Kawaida episode marked the end of the Black Power experiment in Newark.[47]

The 1971 Newark Teachers' Strike

In February 1970, several months before the election of Kenneth Gibson, the Newark Teachers Union won the right to act as bargaining agent for Newark's 4,500 teachers.[48] The union had fought many years to replace the more moderate affiliate of the National Education Association, the Newark Teachers Association. At the time, no one was satisfied with the state of the schools and education in the city.[49] Facilities were old and decrepit; there were always shortages of textbooks and supplies; and the district was run in an old-fashioned, top-down manner by white men. Teachers were fed up with conditions, and it was not difficult to convince them to take action. At

their first mass meeting in response to their long-standing grievances about pay, school conditions, and their aim to participate in
school decision making, they decided to take to the streets, despite
state laws barring strikes by public employees. They struck for three
weeks, and more than one hundred teachers were jailed for violating
the state's antistrike law for public employees. The board of education and its negotiators finally gave in and gave the teachers adjust-
ments, binding arbitration, and relief from nonprofessional chores.
The teachers no longer wanted to monitor safety in the hallways and
school grounds, which they increasingly considered unrelated to
their classroom responsibilities.

The strike, like most public issues in Newark at the time, became
almost as much a racial issue as a labor issue. Baraka and several
community groups saw the union as another white institution,
although in 1970 it had elected a black president, Carole Graves. Fred
Means, the founder and president of the Organization of Negro Educators, saw the white-dominated union as an integral part of the city's
power structure. Nonetheless, the racial aspects did not predominate
because a good number of black teachers picketed with the union and
the union made several wise strategic moves to dampen racial antag-
onisms. For example, with the help of several black striking teachers,
union officials held a private meeting with Baraka to discuss issues.
Baraka did not support the strike, but he suggested the union should
join with the community in fighting the board, which was "running
some of the worst schools on the planet."[50] The union also invited
Bayard Rustin, the nationally known civil rights leader and organizer
of the March on Washington, to speak at a union strike rally

Still, there was deep sentiment among many black teachers and
black parents that the strike was an attempt by white teachers to
increase their power in the school system at the expense of its children. And across the river in New York City, the teachers' union was
embroiled in a widely publicized campaign against community control in the Ocean Hill–Brownsville section of Brooklyn. The notion
of teachers striking did not sit well with many parents who saw
schools as a safe place for their children while they are working, usually at nonprofessional jobs with no flexibility in work schedules.

The achievements were very important for the Newark Teachers
Union and many members, particularly those who had been arrested

and lost pay for several weeks, hoped that their sacrifices would pay off. However, the victory of the previous year led to war in 1971, a war that was to unleash ugly and violent hatred among union members, teachers who refused to support the strike, and black parents and community groups opposed to the strike. The "war," according to Steve Golin, the author of an excellent account of the Newark teachers' strikes, "pitted two grassroots movements against each other"; it also exposed Mayor Gibson's loose grip on the leadership of his city.[51]

The teachers' existing contract expired on January 31, 1971, and the board of education, with new members Jesse Jacob, the former president of the citywide Parents and Teachers Association, and Fernando Zambrano, a prominent leader in the Puerto Rican community, refused to negotiate with the union. The board ignored all communications from the union in the latter months of 1970. At a mass meeting of the union in late January, Carole Graves, the group's president, told members there was no choice but to strike. Graves and other union leadership realized that this time would be a much more bitter and difficult battle than 1970. With Gibson as mayor, the black community feeling a sense of empowerment, and Baraka and his followers asserting their nationalist views in every public conflict, surely there would be efforts to attack the union on racial grounds. The union was pressed for support. It received little from organized labor; union leaders in Newark supported the teachers, but the rank and file did not. The union accepted support from wherever it could get it, including from the Italian communities in the North, East, and West Wards, and from Anthony Imperiale.

Imperiale, the avowed and proud racist, had burst onto the political stage during the rebellion of 1967 as leader of a group of Italian vigilantes willing to use any means necessary to protect whites from black violence. While some of the union members were nervous about the association, Graves attempted to rationalize it by saying that it was not solicited. "As far as welcoming support," Graves said, "I think when someone is drowning and going down for the third time, you don't look at where that hand is coming from, or what color it is."[52] Whatever the reasoning, the open support from Imperiale for the union made it possible for the black community to justify claims that the union action was an effort to seize power from the black community. Furthermore, the black community argued that the union did not have the concerns of Newark's children as a central interest. Despite the fact that Graves was the president of the union, many blacks believed the community and its educational future were endangered.

Jesse Jacob believed that if the board maintained unity, it could take back the victory the teachers had won in 1970. However, he lost the support of white members of the board when he made clear he was out to bust the union. Nevertheless, with the backing of key political voices in the black community, a formidable bloc of opposition to the teachers emerged that was quite willing and able to match the bravado and recklessness of Imperiale as well as the violence of the union. A communal war was under way. The issues of binding arbitration, nonprofessional chores, and pay were virtually lost in the clouds of anger and mistrust that existed between the parties. Golin writes, "People looked through the lens of class and saw conspiracy: Gibson wanted to break the union and deprive teachers of their rights. Or they looked through the lens of race, and saw conspiracy: striking teachers were trying to undermine Gibson and prevent blacks from coming into their own."[53]

Violence occurred on the first day of the strike when a group of teachers heading to schools to picket were attacked by a band of about twenty black men. A white male teacher was severely beaten and hospitalized. Teachers who chose not to strike were pushed and shoved as they tried to enter school buildings. A campaign was launched to damage the automobiles of nonstriking teachers by breaking windshields and puncturing tires. Picket lines were often met by thugs who threatened and physically attacked strikers. Wheel lugs were loosened on cars with the intention of causing a breakdown, risking the lives of drivers and other people. In several instances, union members went to the homes of nonstrikers and damaged cars and fired weapons into their homes.

Behind the scenes, Gibson made several efforts to push Jacob and the board to settle with the union. He made entreaties to Baraka and Wyman Garrett, who had been appointed to the school board by Addonizio but became fiery and militant after Gibson's election. All the mayor's efforts to cajole the board to settle were to no avail. It would not have qualified as mutiny, but the board members appointed by Gibson were not interested in his view of the "war," and they ignored him. It was not the way school politics usually operated in Newark.

After almost three months of watching his city teeter on the brink of a disaster that could have surpassed the violence of 1967, Gibson decided to act. He enlisted the help of Clarence Coggins, perhaps the most astute organizer in the black community. Coggins, who had a long history of radical politics, had credibility with several key factions as a result of his Election Day field operations for Gibson in 1970. Gibson had also given him his first government job as director of neighborhood services. The crafty Coggins devised a peace strategy that first sought to isolate, as he said, "the nut element on each side" and bring together the forces that wanted to see a peaceful and fair settlement.[54] Gibson issued a statement, "The Call to Reason," which became the basis of an intensive public information campaign in the black community. The basic premise was that "only the moral pressure and action of the people can create an atmosphere which will lead both sides to a fair and just settlement."[55] In communications to the union, Gibson aides made clear that a fair settlement would keep binding arbitration, adding one arbitrator chosen by each side plus the neutral arbitrator for a total of three. It would remove the term "nonprofessional chores" from the contract that required elementary teachers to lead students from the building entrance to class and secondary teachers to stand outside the door of their rooms when students were changing classes. It would lift the suspensions of striking teachers.

Talks proceeded between Gibson and state union officials. Communications to the board reached behind and around Jacob to board member Charlie Bell, who had initially opposed any effort to settle. Coggins organized popular support in the black community for Gibson's appeal. Baraka, apparently sensing the Gibson/Coggins initiative, began to back off. As a settlement drew near, Imperiale seemed angry that the turmoil was about to end. He criticized Carole Graves, accusing her of "selling out to a bum," meaning Baraka. He preferred the chaos. Indeed, he announced that it was "time to declare war against Mayor Gibson."[56] At a large and emotional meeting at East Side High School, he called Gibson "an idiot" and urged people to take over his office. Board member Cervase, who had become a supporter of the union, unlike his position in 1970, urged the crowd to support Gibson. Steve Golin contends that Imperiale's performance "scared people into their senses," and he was pushed outside the circles of influence.[57]

During the negotiations at a hotel in downtown Newark, several hundred high school students organized by Larry Hamm, the senior class president at Arts High School, showed up. As Hamm told me, the students were worried that their time out of class would jeopardize their chances of graduation and entrance to college. Several hundred angry, raucous young men and women demanding that they be allowed to participate in the negotiations was a powerful message to the school board, the mayor's representatives, and the union negotiators. Gibson soon appeared and met with Hamm and a few of the student leaders. He promised them that the end was near.[58]

Meanwhile, Coggins continued to build community opposition to school board leaders. Jacob and Garrett were moved to the periphery, although they were unaware of the strategy that was being adroitly employed to isolate them. On April 18, a Sunday, Coggins brought hundreds of people he had organized to the board meeting, including many women who came in their church finery. Their purpose was to assure that the meeting was orderly; they reacted with disdain to any unruly behavior. It was the first board meeting in months that proceeded free of chaos and disruptions. The board voted six to three to approve the union contract, with Charlie Bell and Fernando Zambrana voting in favor of the settlement. Jacob would say at his defeat that he "received no support from anybody."[59] Gibson said the new contract "provides a firm basis for new and healthy relationships among board, union and community and a foundation on which we can rebuild education in Newark." While the agreement called for teachers to perform limited "nonprofessional" chores, in reality the contract made things like lunchroom duty voluntary.[60]

Although the strike was over, severe human and financial damage was felt on both sides and throughout much of the school system for a very long time. Jacob and Garrett attempted to prevent union teachers from entering their schools. They also continued to urge parents to fight against the union, prolonging the confrontations at school buildings. When teachers returned to their jobs, hostilities between strikers and nonstrikers erupted in the hallways and at staff meetings. The union paid $270,000 in fines. With loss of pay, many teachers expended their savings. There was deep racial polarization within the teacher corps. The quality of education in Newark continued to decline, and the union never became the force for improvement it promised as one of its goals. It had a key ally in Charlie Bell, who soon was elevated to president of the school board. In time, after the dust had settled, union leadership learned to work with the captains of the new regime in power, who also were primarily interested in enlarging and distributing the spoils of the system.

The Puerto Rican Riot

It was a bright, golden Sunday, a perfect ending to summer. A crowd of about 6,000 Puerto Ricans, including families with young children, assembled in beautiful Branch Brook Park on the north side of the city. It was September 1, 1974, the fifth time since Puerto Ricans had settled in Newark that they were permitted to use the park. Prior to that day, the park had often been declared off limits, ostensibly because the Italians of the North Ward often blocked their petitions. Violence and disorder were far from the minds of all. The plan was to enjoy a picnic, play games, eat some good food, and have a good time. Near the end of the day, things took an unexpected and unfortunate turn.[61]

A few Essex County mounted police officers came upon a dice game involving a group of Puerto Rican men who were apparently playing for money. The police officers knocked over the game table. Several nearby youth witnessed this unwise police action and were angered. Some began to hurl beer cans, rocks, and bottles at the officers. The police made things worse by riding their horses through the crowd, injuring several people, including a four-year-old child. As tensions escalated, emergency calls went out to the entire Newark police force and before long eighty patrol cars were at the scene. An emergency armored personnel carrier showed up, and within thirty minutes of the start of the trouble, Mayor Gibson, who left another Sunday outing, and Anthony Imperiale, who was now a state senator, arrived at the park. Two patrol cars and a motorcycle belonging to Senator Imperiale were set on fire. Shots rang out.[62] Imperiale, whose presence only further incited the crowd, suggested to Gibson that he "let the police do their job and rout everyone out of the park."[63] Rejecting that advice, which might have led to a massacre, Gibson, in his usual calm way, took over.

Gibson recalled:

> When I got there . . . it was like a stalemate. The cops standing on top of the hill and the kids out in the middle of the grassy area yelling and challenging the cops and the cops with their big sticks and Billy clubs and . . . shotguns. Well, the first thing I did was tell the cops not to make a move against the kids. There was an inspector in charge; I told him just hold the cops here, I'll deal with the kids. So I decided that the only way I could solve the problem, at least at that moment, was to get the kids out of harm's way because we had a bunch of cops there with shotguns but the kids had some rocks and sticks. So I told them, I think the best thing for us to do is have a meeting at city hall. I told the kids, I can't conduct business here in the middle of the park with guns at our back and you guys all excited. The best place for us to meet would be at City Hall. I said, well, the only way for us to get to City Hall is to walk. I said all bets off if there are any windows broken, if anybody gets hurt, or if you guys do the wrong thing on the way to City Hall. They said, well what about the cops? I said I'll take care of the cops. When I told the inspector, we're going to take these kids to City Hall, he said, man are you crazy? So when we got to City Hall, I sent somebody to see the kids who had been arrested. Then we brought the kids from the jail to show the crowd that they had not been beaten or injured; I told them the judge would set bail and they would be released. Then we agreed to meet the next day with designated leaders to discuss their grievances. Of course, the next day was another story.[64]

The leaders arrived the following afternoon, holding a list of issues to discuss, including the incident in the park, unemployment, health concerns, and substandard housing, which were the lot of poverty-stricken Puerto Rican neighborhoods. The negotiators were supported by a marching and singing crowd of nearly a thousand people, and Baraka was with them. The "young Turks," unmindful of the rifts that had occurred between Baraka and Gibson, welcomed Baraka and agreed to have him join their negotiating committee.

This deepened the existing divisions in the Puerto Rican leadership and led to the creation of two separate negotiating teams: one made up of the youthful protestors and Baraka, and the other of older, established Puerto Ricans who had been given jobs or appointments by Gibson. The younger group included Sigfredo Carrion, head of the Puerto Rican Socialist party, and Ramon Rivera, former head of the Young Lords in Newark who formed a new group called OYE (Listen). The older group included Deputy Mayor Ramon Aneses, Fernando Zambrano, who had been appointed to the board of education, and others who ran social service agencies. The two negotiating teams sat in different rooms. As expected, the older group was the "establishment" and was irrelevant to what was occurring with the thousand or so restless demonstrators outside.

The mayor was incensed: "I don't know, whoever told them kids to come back down to City Hall, in my opinion, did a disservice to the community and to the kids." He said some of the issues the group wished to discuss made good sense, but he described others as "stupid." The Puerto Rican leaders who met with Gibson inside City Hall were disappointed. Gibson said he would limit the discussion to what had happened in the park. At one point he told them, "I have no control over the economy. I can't do anything about unemployment."[65] It was largely true, but not what the group wanted to hear and it surely was not the most judicious way to treat the representatives. They left the meeting and went outside to the crowd and told them that the discussions with the mayor were not productive.

Sigfredo Carrion joined the group in the trek to City Hall on Monday, although he was not in the park the previous day. He recalled the unfolding events in an interview for the oral history project on the Puerto Rican Riot:

> The day had worn on, we weren't getting anywhere, more and more police were arriving, and they [the demonstrators] could see that they were being surrounded. Police were massing in this place, massing in that place, snipers on the roofs, and people were getting nervous and getting angry. He [Mayor Gibson] finally did agree that, "All right, I'm going to talk to you but [looking at the demands] this, we can't do any of this. All we can do is some of these things we can study them," lying about how he didn't think it was a good idea

to have a police community board and he didn't think that the city council would buy it and didn't think that it was viable and that kind of thing. . . . So, all of a sudden, just as he was saying, "I'm through with you guys, you're not getting us anywhere, you're not bringing anything to the table" all of a sudden his windows in his office just shattered. . . . He then said, "Well that's it. There is nothing else to talk about."[66]

Carrion continued,

I said, "Look. If you talk to us in earnest, we can make some progress on this, we'll try one more time to keep the crowd under wraps, we'll go and report to them." . . . We went down and talked to the crowd, we said we cannot guarantee we have total control, but we'll try. So we went down and [told] them, "Listen, we have to show him that we are your representatives, that you respond to us, so give us a little bit more time and we'll go back and talk with him." We went back inside . . . but he really wasn't prepared to do anything. He wanted us to calm them, he sort of took the defensive. Disperse everybody, send people home, we'll meet again at another date, but essentially he wanted us to surrender and break this up and he was pointing out to us, "Look at the police, I can't control them, they're already on the roofs, they have snipers, it's going to be a massacre." . . . So we went back down, we said, "All right, we're not getting anywhere. He refuses to negotiate in earnest and this is what we propose." We said "Let's have demonstrations, we're going to continue the pressure on the mayor until he listens to us, but he's not ready to listen now. . . . We have to get out of here because the police want an excuse to continue attacking us and then put the blame on us for being violent."[67]

It did not work. While most of the crowd assembled in a march to return to their neighborhoods, a sizable group stayed and began to bombard City Hall with rocks and bottles and anything they could get their hands on. Then the police attacked the people who were attacking City Hall as well as the others who were leaving peacefully. Mounted police and patrol cars broke into the march with police flailing their clubs at anyone within striking distance. One young man, later identified as Angel Perez, was struck in the head and died a few days later from multiple fractures of the skull. The mass of demonstrators returned to their neighborhood that evening and tore it apart. They firebombed and looted stores; for the most part, unlike 1967, the police ignored the looting and seemed unwilling to arrest anyone. The police were praised for their inaction by Puerto Rican leaders and condemned by local merchants. Sadly, another young man was shot and killed that evening; his body was found near the North Broad Street train station.[68]

The following evening and for two more days, bands of teenagers from the Latino neighborhood near the Columbus Homes housing project along Seventh Avenue looted stores and hurled stones at automobiles passing through the area. Ramon Rivera said, "The events of Labor Day weekend are the result of several years of isolation, abuse, and frustration of the Hispanic Community."[69] Percy Miranda, a spokesman for the Hispanic Emergency Council, called on political leaders at the city and county level to "share the responsibility of providing for the needs of the Hispanic community."[70] Mayor Gibson blamed the breakdown in communication and the uprising on Baraka and a group on his followers who joined the demonstration and "were determined to start trouble."[71] Gibson sounded like the Addonizio regime during the Newark rebellion of 1967. Carrion said Baraka played a supportive role to the Puerto Ricans. His presence "was so important and Baraka was very . . . helpful because he . . . has political perspective and he tried to say 'Look, we have to formulate demands. We have to be careful.'"[72] One week later, when the Puerto Rican leaders held a mass rally in Military Park, Baraka was the main speaker.

On September 4, three days after the incident in the park, the *Star-Ledger* described the North Ward area, which housed a large share of the Puerto Rican population, as a "neighborhood full of bitterness and confusion." Residents decried the loss of services and businesses. "Foodtown is gone," said Dorothy Workfield, a resident of Columbus Homes. She added, "The disturbances hurt nobody but ourselves."[73] Some people thought the violence should continue until the city met their demands. An owner of a local pharmacy had nothing but praise for two Newark police officers who tried to protect his store from looters and handed over to him several hundred dollars that had been left in the cash register.[74]

As was true in Newark in 1967 and in cities elsewhere, the roots of the violence were poverty and inaction by government and authorities. The social and economic problems of the community were as severe as or worse than those of the black population. Unemployment rates were 25 to 27 percent, and the school dropout rate was 42 percent. The leadership was divided by age and even by the philosophical issue regarding independence or statehood for Puerto Rico. And there was no Puerto Rican representation on the city council.[75] Tensions had been simmering for several years between Puerto Rican leaders and the Gibson administration. The riot represented a turning point for the Puerto Rican community of Newark and for Puerto Ricans throughout the state.

Puerto Rican Representation

The lack of representation in city government was a major challenge for the Puerto Rican community. More opportunities emerged in tandem with the growing political influence of the black community. Indeed, the black community was generally in favor of including more Puerto Ricans in efforts to capture City Hall. Specifically, in an effort to establish a strong coalition between communities, the Black and Puerto Rican Convention had endorsed Ramon Aneses to run for an at-large seat. Aneses did not draw enthusiastic support from Puerto Rican voters, however, and of the convention's candidates, he drew the least support of all the at-large candidates.[76] Puerto Ricans felt that the black community did not fully support Aneses. On the other hand, some members of the black community felt that the support expected from the Puerto Rican community simply did not show up. In any event, Gibson made Aneses a deputy mayor and Gibson also appointed Fernando Zambrano to the board of education. These moves were an effort to hold the alliance together and to show concern and sensitivity to the issues facing the growing Hispanic community.

Like the token concessions Addonizio made to blacks in the 1960s, the gestures by Gibson were not enough. In the second year of Gibson's tenure, a group of Puerto Rican leaders visited his office to plead for more jobs and more representation in city government.

The meeting became very tense as the Puerto Rican leaders began to shout at Gibson; a security officer ordered the group to quiet down as he tried to remove one of the most disruptive members of the group from the meeting. Several shoving matches ensued, and the meeting broke up with both sides concluding that it was a failure. The incident cost Gibson the support and trust he had from key leaders such as Hilda Hidalgo and Ramon Rivera. Following the incident, on March 9, 1972, Hildalgo, one of the most highly respected Puerto Rican leaders in the entire state, wrote a letter to Gibson expressing "frustration, and disappointment [at the] lack of sensitivity of the Gibson administration to respond with equity and compassion to the just demands of the Puerto Rican community." The letter further charged that "leaders were maltreated and physically attacked by your personal staff . . . and the incident could perpetuate an unreconcilable [sic] gap" between the mayor and a large segment of the Puerto Rican Community. Hildalgo called for "actions, not words, to restore a sense of confidence and to promote a sense of cooperation between your administration and the Puerto Rican community." Her final words in the letter were, "Please act."[77]

It did not help that Aneses was considered a token by his community. After Aneses resigned, Gibson always had a Puerto Rican on the mayor's staff, but there were never a significant number of high-level appointments in the departments of city government. More significantly, Gibson never attempted to organize a constituency among the growing population of Puerto Ricans in the North Ward, thus leaving the political future of the area in the hands of North Ward boss Steve Adubato. In 1988, when Gibson launched a campaign to become Essex County executive, several key Puerto Rican leaders endorsed his Republican opponent. They said, "Under Gibson, we got nothing."[78] Many of the city's Hispanic leaders concluded that the treatment of Puerto Ricans by blacks had been no more enlightened than the treatment blacks received from the Italian-led administration of Hugh Addonizio. It would be very hard to refute that charge. Puerto Rican leaders came to recognize that while there might be efforts at coalition, ultimately they would have to organize, struggle, strategize, and work in their own behalf to gain respect and power as other groups have done over the years.

As Italian Americans in the North Ward increasingly joined the exodus out of the city, the wise and astute Adubato began a vigorous effort to recruit disaffected Puerto Ricans into his organization. He began to hold meetings between Italian Americans and Puerto Ricans to raise scholarship funds for Puerto Rican students. Puerto Ricans ran for district leader and became part of the Adubato machine; he provided them entrée to political jobs and appointments in the city, the board of education, and the county. By the end of Gibson's tenure, the balance of power in the county had shifted and Adubato had fashioned a political network more influential than any other in the city. While Adubato's organization could not easily dominate most citywide elections, it could, with its tighter and superior organizational skills, win most seats on the elected school board and a few seats on the city council. In time, Adubato would emerge as the most powerful nonelected political operative in Newark. Puerto Ricans would provide a significant bloc of his political machine. It was indeed an ironic twist for a city with a majority black population and a black mayor in City Hall.

The Gibson Legacy

After about two years in office, Kenneth Gibson was no longer the reform mayor who had taken over the city in 1970. Initially, he fought to improve government, reform the bureaucracies, find good people to serve on the school board and other agencies, and ensure that young black professionals were given an opportunity to work in Newark's government. Junius Williams, fresh out of law school, was hired to run the Model Cities program, the cornerstone of the city's federally funded redevelopment effort. The young student leader Larry Hamm, at the age of seventeen, was appointed to the school board. At some point, however, Gibson seemed to decide that the battle he had to wage to get anything done was a fight he could not win. Gibson changed from an arguably good government, public service type to a calculating politician, wheeling both on the local and national levels. The Gibson administration began to look more and more like the one it had replaced, although it did not have the obvious ties to the rackets and underworld that turned out to be true of Addonizio. Williams, only twenty-six years old at the time, might have been over

his head with the mammoth Model Cities effort, but it was under-
standable that he would be angry when Gibson tried to place former
Addonizo aides on the Model Cities payroll.[79]

The Model Cities program became the target of congressional investigations. Although there was never any evidence of wrongdoing,
Williams was fired. Harold Hodes, a former staff aide to Addonizio,
became an aide to Gibson. Domenick Miceli, who handled the supplementary cash fund for Addonizio, found a place on the Gibson
team. Imperiale quipped when Miceli, called "The Hammer" by insiders, joined the Gibson team, "Why isn't that guy in jail with the
rest of those people?"[80] Donald Malafronte, the bright and loyal aide
to Addonizio, became a consultant to Gibson for Model Cities' program activities. Dennis Sullivan, the white Princeton student who
worked on Gibson's 1970 campaign, returned to Newark in 1972 to
enter city government. "When I got back," he said, "everything had
changed." The people who had talked about changing government
and making it work for the citizens were gone. The sharp operators
from the Addonizio administration were now on staff or close to the
mayor, and they were pretty much calling the shots, he said.[81]

Why the change? One might blame Baraka for pushing Gibson
to a more accommodating position with his own Black Nationalist
agenda. That, however, would not fully explain the transformation.
Also important was the reality that the departments were largely influenced by civil servants—most appointed by the previous administration—and that Gibson needed better relations with them. And
as the racial polarization of the 1967 rebellion period receded or
diminished, it became increasingly important for Gibson to look like
a political leader who was serving everyone. In his 1974 reelection
campaign, Imperiale was his opponent, so it did not take much to
motivate and turn out black voters. Gibson won handily. The major
issues for Gibson were now balancing the city budget, garnering as
much state and federal aid as possible, and trying to achieve more
effective policing in a city with major crime problems.

It is hard to know the extent to which underworld influence and
threats on Gibson's life by criminal elements affected his political outlook. Several things are worth considering. The notorious
and murderous Campisi gang was based in the West Ward and was
known to have connections to Newark police and other officials.[82] In

Left, top: Leo P. Carlin (*left*) was the first mayor elected under a new charter establishing mayor–council government in 1954. He is being sworn in by City Clerk Harry Reichenstein. (Courtesy of Newark Public Library)

Left, bottom: Hugh J. Addonizio left a seat in Congress to become mayor of Newark in 1962. He was defeated in 1970 by Kenneth A. Gibson in 1970, a year when Addonizio was convicted of extortion and sentenced to ten years in jail. (Courtesy of Newark Public Library)

Above: Joel R. Jacobson, president of the New Jersey State Industrial Union Council, AFL-CIO, hands over a check to Tim Still (*center*), Newark community leader, and businessman George Haney, who organized a trip to Washington, DC, to protest restrictions placed on community participation in the antipoverty program. (Courtesy of Newark Public Library)

Newark celebrated its three hundredth anniversary in 1966 with hope and confidence for a peaceful future. A Mutual Benefit float recalls the firm's prominence in New Jersey and its faith in Newark. (Courtesy of Newark Public Library)

Left: Poet and playwright Amiri Baraka (LeRoi Jones) returned to Newark, his hometown, to lead a black nationalist political movement to capture City Hall. (Courtesy of Newark Public Library)

Below: CORE leader Robert Curvin attempts to calm an angry crowd before a violent outburst at Fourth Precinct in Central Ward protesting the police beating of black taxicab driver on the night of July 12, 1967. (Associated Press Photo)

Left: Kenneth A. Gibson became the first black mayor of Newark, and the first to head a large northeastern city, in 1970. Anthony Imperiale entered politics as an avowed racist and vigilante, and often challenged and provoked Gibson. Eventually Imperiale learned to play politics. In 1986 he endorsed Gibson in his race against Sharpe James. (Courtesy of Newark Public Library)

Below: Charles Bell, president of the Newark Board of Education from 1972 to 1976 (and board member until 1982), made the schools a political machine according to several of his board colleagues. (Courtesy of Newark Public Library)

Mayor Sharpe James served five terms, from 1986 to 2006. He promoted major developments downtown and new housing in the neighborhoods. After he left office, he was convicted of fraud in a land deal with a friend and sentenced to twenty-seven months in federal prison. (File photo of the *Star Ledger*)

Newark residents crowd Symphony Hall to hear a report regarding the impending take-over of the Newark Public School District by the New Jersey Department of Education. (File photo of the *Star Ledger*)

Steve Adubato, executive director of the North Ward Center and political boss, at a press conference to support school board president Carl Sharif, who was indicted for assaulting an alleged intruder into his private office. Adubato is joined by Nellie Grier, director of the Emanuel Senior Citizens Day Care Center, and Ramon Rivera, executive director of La Casa de Don Pedro (August 31, 1982). (File photo of the *Star Ledger*)

Top: Beverly Ayres and Jesse Wright (*left to right*), two of Newark's homeless, sit in Penn Station and eat meals provided by the American Islamic Book Store. (File photo of the *Star Ledger*)

Bottom: Monsignor William Linder, founder of the New Community Corporation, which led much of the rebuilding of the Central Ward following the 1967 rebellion, with Irene Cooper Bosch, executive director of the Victoria Foundation, and Etta Rudolph Denk, executive director of the Bank of America Foundation. (Photo by R. Curvin)

Top: New housing has replaced the high-rise William P. Hayes Public Housing Project, across the street from the Fourth Precinct, where the rebellion began in 1967. (Photo by R. Curvin)

Bottom: The New Jersey Performing Arts Center, opened in 1995, has been a major boost to downtown rebuilding. (Photo by R. Curvin)

Art Ryan, former chief executive of Prudential, joined volunteers to mulch trees and clean up Branch Brook Park. Few Newark business executives are directly involved in the civic life of the city. (Photo by R. Curvin)

Top: Cory A. Booker and Cary Booker, his father, meet Lady Sheard, a Republican district leader in the South Ward of Newark, May 20, 1999, on a campaign stroll. (File photo of the *Star Ledger*)

Bottom: Gloria Buck, a public school social worker, founded the Newark Black Film Festival in 1974. The annual festival is a highly popular feature of the city's lively cultural scene. (Photo by R. Curvin)

Walter Chambers, a Newark native, was the first black executive hired by the New Jersey Bell Telephone Company, following CORE demonstrations over minority hiring at the company in 1964. (Courtesy of Walter Chambers)

1974, a car parked across the street from Gibson's home was blown up in the middle of the night.[83] And according to a former high-level official in the New Jersey Department of Criminal Justice, a meeting was held with Gibson and high-level criminal enforcement officials to discuss serious threats that Gibson had received. "He really thought they were going to kill him," the official recalled, "and he was in tears." From all indications, the gangland behavior of groups like the Campisi family was so pathological that any threats would have to be taken seriously.

Despite the turmoil and the divisions between supporters and allies, there were important achievements. Gibson appointed the city's first black police director, business administrator, finance director, and corporation counsel. Several blacks were appointed city magistrates as well as directors of other departments and large federal programs. And Gibson built sufficient ties with Democratic Party leaders so that several Newark magistrates were elevated to judgeships in the Essex County Superior Court. Many observers in Newark praise Gibson for deftly guiding the city through several crises. Steve Adubato, for example, said that "the city owes Gibson a lot for the way he handled things. We could have easily gone back to 1967."[84] Elton Hill, who served as business administrator, said, "All we did was fight each other," referring to the intra-community conflict between Gibson and Baraka. "Under the circumstances, he did all he could do, which was a lot."[85]

The racial divisions were increasingly uncomfortable for Gibson personally and politically, not to mention very damaging to the city's image. In 1976, Gibson was asked by a *New York Times* reporter, "How black can you be in this city?" His answer seemed almost 180 degrees from where he had positioned himself during his 1970 campaign: "In my opinion you cannot be black at all. You need coalitions and your own black people don't like black politics as black politics. We are probably one of the most conservative of all ethnic groups."[86]

When Gibson became active on the national scene, he was an effective ambassador for the city and won major grants from state and federal sources, which allowed Newark to bring many minority workers into government. By 1976, the Newark area had received $480 million in federal aid programs, which were largely the result of Gibson's lobbying and grantsmanship. Between 1973 and 1976, the

Gibson team reported that it had created 6,500 jobs with $54 million in federal and state subsidies.[87] Gibson is most proud of the system of neighborhood health centers built in the Central, East, and North Wards. The centers, according to Gibson, were funded by federal dollars and led to a 50 percent reduction in the rates of venereal disease and tuberculosis. The city also gained substantial federal support to rehabilitate housing in residential areas. When the program was announced in 1976, Mayor Gibson said, "We hope this program will breathe new life into these neighborhoods and lead to a new recognition of the vitality and variety of our residential areas."[88]

Gibson was also able to reduce the real tax rate. In 1970, Newark had one of the highest tax rates in New Jersey. Over the years, with state and federal aid, and thanks particularly to the state's adoption of an income tax and decision to assume a major share of the costs of schooling in poor districts, the mayor was able to reduce the real tax rate by 50 percent. In fact, Gibson was often more focused on the tax rate than anything else. He used revenue-sharing dollars to subsidize police and fire operations to cut overall budget expenditures, thus holding down tax rates. When Washington cut back on many of the federal programs that helped urban centers, Newark was hit very hard and was forced to cut staff to avoid raising taxes. Gibson cut budgets when he had to and reduced staff. From 1974 to 1980, total employment for the city experienced a 27.6 percent reduction. Five municipal services, including garbage collection in one ward, were contracted out to private vendors.[89]

In the area of redevelopment, the achievements were modest but important. Several actions undertaken in the Gibson years helped to lay the groundwork for the heightened development activity that occurred under the administration of Mayor Sharpe James. Although the most prominent physical downtown buildings were to come later, several important downtown developments did occur under Gibson's watch. The university campuses virtually exploded in growth: Rutgers began to expand its programs and infrastructure, and Seton Hall built a new law school in the city. The Gateway project, sponsored by Newark-based Prudential Insurance Company, was started before Gibson took office; in subsequent years, Prudential made significant investments in Gateway to expand the project, demonstrating its faith in the future of Newark. Public Service

Electric and Gas (PSE&G), the state's largest utility, rumbled about leaving Newark in the 1970s. It was, however, all about getting the best possible deal. Gibson quietly lobbied PSE&G's top executives, as well as members of the Board of Public Utilities, the state regulatory agency, to keep the utility in Newark. It remained in Newark and built a new, modern glass structure that towers over the downtown business district. The building cost $75 million, but because of the generous tax abatements afforded the project there were limited returns to the city. The initial phase of Society Hill, which featured thirty-one units of townhouses, got under way during the latter years of Gibson's tenure. It was the first market-rate housing built in the Central Ward in over forty years, and it provided housing for professionals and employees working at the burgeoning New Jersey College of Medicine and Dentistry.

Today, one of the leading jazz radio stations in the region is located in downtown Newark, call letters WBGO. When Gibson assumed office, one of his aides discovered that the Newark school system owned a radio frequency for the purpose of offering educational programs to classrooms. Like many other things, the station equipment had been ignored for years. In fact the station, if it could be called such, was located in a small closetlike room in the attic of Central High School. The moribund frequency was taken over by a government-organized nonprofit, which later became a part of the National Public Radio network. Mayor Gibson was supportive of the effort from the beginning, and the city provided resources for the startup. WBGO now provides a wonderful and varied program of American jazz, community news, and discussions. It is today one of Newark's precious assets, and with the development of Internet technology, its programs are heard throughout the world.

In 1974, Gibson hired Alfred Faiella, a young lawyer, to work on development issues. In time, Faiella became the sole dominant force in the economic development programs in Newark. His official job was director of the Newark Economic Development Corporation (NEDC), a quasi-governmental agency that was governed by members of the business community and city officials. In reality, he was a czar who was able to reshape development in Newark in the manner of a Lou Danzig. A corporate board oversaw the work of the NEDC, but the board members were either asleep at the switch or were not

bothered by Faiella's excesses. Curiously, Faiella served as chief economic development officer for the adjacent town of Elizabeth while
serving as the head of redevelopment in Newark, creating a trans-
city example of double-dipping, unique even for New Jersey. With
his board's obeisance, Faiella used his position to further his own
personal interest by structuring deals that gave him a financial stake
in development projects subsidized with public monies. He also used
his position to solicit campaign contributions from developers doing
business with the city. Faiella became even more powerful in Sharpe
James's administration, but the terms of his engagement and the lee-
way he was afforded occurred under Gibson and his board of downtown corporate executives.

While leadership is important and a mayor can help to improve
circumstances over time, the politics of Newark are shaped primarily
by deeply entrenched social, economic, and political forces. Strong
and strategic mayoral leadership can use the levers of government
and its power in Trenton to make small but significant changes and
gains for its constituencies. And if the stars are favorably aligned for
a mayoral leader, such as having good economic times nationally
and regionally along with having a reasonable amount of harmony
within the city's legislative body as well as the support and encouragement of the business community, a mayor can reach for larger
changes. Gibson ruled in difficult times. The stars were not favorably aligned for him. In addition to the local conflict, national economic problems were severe. A foreign oil crisis had deeply affected
energy and food prices. The average annual inflation rate increased
to 11 percent in 1974. Washington was now in the hands of a conservative Republican, Richard Nixon, whose administration cut deeply
into the flow of federal dollars to cities. It was not a good time for
urban development.

Nonetheless, it is fair to ask whether if conditions had been more
favorable, was Gibson the type of leader who might have done more
to move Newark's economic and social recovery forward. Not likely.
It is true Baraka made things difficult for him, but many of the values that Baraka promoted were sensible and important. Baraka believed in fighting for the children, avoiding the shady wheeling and
dealing that had been going on for decades, and making education
for all children a priority. Gibson could surely justify moving away

from Baraka's uncompromising politics and programmatic ideas that would deepen division of the city's people. But he could not justify moving away from the vision that had been espoused at the Black and Puerto Rican Convention and throughout his campaign, which had been honored with the support of Martin Luther King Jr.'s family and other major forces of reform. The notion that black and Puerto Rican citizens could use the levers of government through politics to advance their lives was at the heart of the 1970 campaign.

On the basis of the three important characteristics for effective mayoral leadership, Gibson might fairly receive an okay for management. However, on the matters of vision and integrity, he failed. After winning his fourth election in 1982, besting Councilman Earl Harris, it appeared that the drive of his administration (which was not highly energized to begin with) ground to a slow and tired pace. Mayor Gibson became less visible and less in charge. The quality of service declined, workers often failed to show up, and those who did often left shortly after lunch. Gibson had run out of steam, but he also was facing personal tragedy. Muriel Gibson, his wife of many years, was diagnosed with cancer and Gibson spent much of his time caring for her. Mrs. Gibson died in December 1983. As the 1986 election approached, Gibson seemed to be running on cruise control, set at a very slow speed. In an effort to fill the leadership void, executives at Prudential created a civic collaborative organization called the Newark Collaboration Group to stimulate a more comprehensive development program.

Kenneth A. Gibson earned a special place in Newark's history as the first black mayor of the city on the "Passaick." He assembled a campaign of the politically disaffected and the cadre of the social movements that had flourished during the 1960s. He campaigned in an atmosphere of raw tension as the city's remaining white ethnics often called him vile names and waged a racist campaign against him. He withstood it all while also deftly managing a chaotic campaign into which Imamu Baraka injected unrealistic visions of black power. By Gibson's own account, by the time of this glorious victory, his relationship with Baraka was already strained. The political complications at the outset were crippling.[90]

There was surely unease among his other supporters early on in the campaign. Gibson turned out to be an enigma and a surprise.

He could not develop lasting and trusting relationships with the black leaders who supported him and made his victory possible. Ted Pinckney, who ran for an at-large seat on the convention slate said, "When he got in office, he ignored us. He was afraid of black people."[91] Gus Heningburg, who spent many hours with Gibson, said he simply lacked certain skills a mayor needs, such as knowing how to work with business leaders.[92] Al Koeppe, who ran the large state utility based in Newark during Gibson's years in office, said, "Gibson never asked us for anything."[93]

The racial tension in the city made things difficult, but it was also an ironic blessing. In the name of black unity, Gibson maintained solid voter support against the prospect of returning the leadership of the city to Anthony Imperiale or other white politicians. Except for the Puerto Rican riot, he managed occasional eruptions of racial conflict extremely well. He proved to be most effective in soothing the disgruntled whites who remained in the city. On occasion, he gave Anthony Imperiale a big handshake in public. In 1980, he signed an appeal with other mayors asking the courts to release former mayor Addonizio before serving the remainder of his prison sentence.

There was peace, but there was no grand vision of repair of the city. There was no creative positioning of blacks in the larger political arena in Essex County and the state. At the end of Gibson's sixteen years as mayor, there was a view among the press and others that Gibson's major achievement was to usher Newark out of its backward movement from the civil disturbances of 1967 toward a better day for the city, not quickly, but in the slow, deliberate way of Kenneth A. Gibson.

Sharpe James, the councilman who frequently opposed Gibson, was now running faster and with more focus, vision, and energy than Mayor Gibson, offering voters a "Sharpe Change." During the 1986 mayoral campaign, Gibson appeared on a television program and in response to a question about his future plans to improve the city said, "I'm going to do exactly what I have been doing." Voters had tired of what he had been doing and not been doing. They gave Sharpe James the opportunity to show his stuff, by a large margin. James won all five wards with more than 55 percent of the vote, Gibson got merely 40 percent, and two other candidates divided the rest.[94]

After his defeat in 1986, Gibson established an engineering consulting firm, and he ran for Essex County executive in 1998.[95] Neither engineering nor political campaigning worked out well for him. He lost the race for county executive to Republican James Treffinger. In 1996, he was indicted for bribery and tax evasion involving a $50 million contract with the Irvington, New Jersey, school board. Court proceedings ended in a mistrial as a result of a hung jury.[96] As he approached a retrial on the charges in 2002, Gibson pleaded guilty to tax evasion and was sentenced to three years of unsupervised probation. The judge said that he spared Gibson the jail time because of his age and health problems. Gibson said that he accepted the plea agreement so that he and his codefendants (including his domestic and business partner, Camille Savocca) could return to normal lives. All charges against Savocca were dismissed. Gibson said that "the nightmare that we have suffered through for seven years, the long ordeal of a government investigation and a twelve-week trial in which the jury could not convict us of any offense, mounting this retrial, have made me weary."[97] It was sad to see the life of Black Power's pioneer, the first black mayor of Newark, take such an ignominious turn.

⟨7⟩

The Dancing Mayor

*Our mission is to serve and protect the citizens who
have placed their trust in us, and to prove worthy
of their vote and support.*

—Sharpe James as president of the National League of
Cities in Minneapolis on December 2, 1994

*I*T WAS INEVITABLE that one of the black members of the city
council would successfully seek the mayor's position. Earl Harris, the
old fox who had convinced the council to raise salaries and enlarge
the perks of council members, had tried and failed in 1978 and 1982.
Councilman Ralph Grant was planning for a run in 1982, before he
was ensnarled by a federal sting operation and caught taking bribes
(he was convicted and went to jail). Donald Tucker thirsted for the
role but never got to mount a campaign before his death in 2006.
Sharpe James, however, had deeper ambition and fire, and had long
resented Kenneth Gibson for his lack of support in James's initial
council run in 1970.[1] Victory over the incumbent mayor in 1986
would be especially sweet.

During the campaign, James attacked Gibson for his failure to create a spark for rebuilding. He told voters Gibson was unresponsive to
the city's plight and had done little to lead a recovery from the damage and decline of decades. He pointed out that Gibson did not work
well with the city council and, given his own long tenure on the body,

186

he was the perfect candidate to establish a cooperative relationship that could move Newark forward. With his leadership the city would see a "Sharpe Change," which became his battle cry. Gibson had no clue of the depth of dissatisfaction voters now felt toward his slow and methodical leadership, which was compounded by his failed attempts to seek the governorship in 1981 and in 1985. James won handily, capturing over 55 percent of the vote to Gibson's 40 percent.[2]

In important ways, the stars were neatly aligned for Sharpe James. The economic recession of the early 1980s had abated as boom times hit the Northeast Corridor. In New York City, Wall Street soared, neighborhoods were being refurbished and commercial strips were scaling up and expanding. The regional economy was so heated that cities in New Jersey such as Hoboken and Jersey City reaped a significant share of the spillover. Newark also felt the economic vibrancy as the early signs of renewal that had begun to show under Gibson gained momentum. Also playing to James's favor, the South Ward, his base, now had the larger number of black voters, replacing the Central Ward as the key power bloc for blacks.

As of 1982, the racial makeup of the city council had gone in complete reverse from its 1970 iteration. The council now had six black members and three white members. The debilitating racial conflict common during the early Gibson years had come to an end; no longer were Anthony Imperiale and Amiri Baraka key players. In 1984, a civic group spearheaded by Prudential executives brought together a broad swath of local and regional leadership to create what was called the Newark Collaboration Group (NCG). The NCG developed an extensive blueprint for change and reform, which, in a way, highlighted the lack of leadership and vision of the Gibson team. Following his inauguration in June 1986, James joined the executive committee of the NCG and promised to serve as a link between the group's work and city government.[3]

Early Years, Early Visions

Sharpe James was born on February 20, 1936, in Jacksonville, Florida. His mother, determined to escape an abusive husband, moved from Jacksonville to Elizabeth, New Jersey, when James was eight years old. The family later moved to the Newark, where James attended public schools and excelled in sports. When James was a young child, his mother had to be at work at an early hour, so she would take him to school and leave him on the doorstep. After a while, a gym teacher noticed this young person each morning and decided to invite him into the school, even before school had opened. The young James was given the chore of helping to set up the equipment and taking out the balls for play time. The gym teacher's caring and mentoring may have had something to do with James's later decision to become a physical education instructor.

James went on to earn a bachelor's degree in physical education from Montclair State College and a master's degree in human physiology from Springfield College in Massachusetts. When he decided to enter a life of politics and run for councilman of the South Ward, he was a physical education instructor at nearby Essex County College. James has often talked about his involvement in the civil rights movement, but his record shows he was more of a neighborhood activist, and a very effective one. In the early 1960s, after a bitter fight, he was elected president of the Weequahic Community Council, a network of block groups in the South Ward that advocated for improved services and upkeep of properties by residents. He was also active in the antipoverty program, and in 1964 he won a heated race in his neighborhood to control the local area board, which provided services to residents of the neighborhood.[4] Like many others who were active in civic affairs, he joined the United Brothers, the Black Nationalist political organization founded by Amiri Baraka around 1968. Unlike Gibson, who assumed the mayoralty with no previous political experience, James spent sixteen tumultuous years on the city council. During that time, he learned a great deal about the inner workings of Newark politics.

James was always an easygoing, fun-loving guy, at times exhibiting a tendency toward showmanship. He held a deep passion for sports, particularly tennis, at which he was superb. Former staff members and associates tell many stories of how his mayoral meetings were laced with reviews of recent sports events, many of which he attended. According to one of his former aides, despite the distractions and diversions in meetings, he was always on point, insightful, and knowledgeable when the group returned to business. Politics came naturally to him. His service as a council member afforded him a chance to meet key political players on the local and national stage; people warmed to his hopeful and energetic demeanor. He also never forgot a friend who had helped him or an opponent who did not. He was the life of any party, and if there was music, he was the first on the dance floor, out-dancing every man in the crowd. His yearly fundraising birthday parties—attendance was required to win his friendship—became so successful in part because his followers had a good time, and James, at the peak of the evening, always led everyone in the electric slide. Everyone knew that Sharpe James also had, as one writer put it, a "soaring ego."[5] He had charisma, a quick wit, and knew Newark and its people as well as anyone. When this joyful, upbeat politician took the oath of office on June 1, 1986, most voters had great hopes for Newark and high expectations for the new mayor.

Within the first weeks of his tenure, the public noticed a difference from the previous administration. James showed a burst of energy for which people had been looking. He seemed to be all over the city, speaking out on every issue, always expressing optimism about Newark and planting seeds of hope in residents and corporate leadership alike that long-awaited improvements would take place. Voters now expected that there would be more planning and direction, and with more alacrity. James was not at all reluctant to reach outside the boundaries of the city for his new team. For example, he recruited Richard Monteilh, who had worked in the business office of the city of Atlanta, to become his business administrator. Joanne Y. Watson from New York became an assistant corporation counsel. Glen Grant, who grew up in nearby Union Township, became corporation counsel. William Celester was recruited from Boston to head the police department, though he was eventually convicted and jailed for thirty months for stealing funds from the department. Mayor James then appointed Joseph Santiago as police director, the first Hispanic to serve in that position in Newark. Overall, James began his tenure with solid appointments on the basis of merit, shunning pressures to appoint cronies and campaign workers. An exception to his early stance on merit was the appointment of Jackie Mattison, his wife's cousin, as chief of staff; he later got in serious trouble with the law.

In a show of concern for integrity in government, and sadly, it turned out to be just a show, James announced that all top-level appointments in his administration would be subjected to "extensive police, credit, academic and financial background checks."[6] After James had been in office for one hundred days, the *New York Times* noted the "air of optimism" he had brought to the city of Newark. The article noted that James had spent his first three months as mayor talking to community leaders, business leaders, and visiting state officials in Trenton in efforts to gain assistance with Newark's fiscal problems. Although James had to give pink slips to 150 city employees two months after he took office, shortly thereafter he was able to draw a $4 million grant from the state to hire more police officers. Some observers were complimentary but cautious. Stanley Winters, a professor at the New Jersey Institute of Technology, said, "The first 100 days look good. There's a different tone, definitely. I don't think miracles have been accomplished but it's still early." A leader of the Newark Chamber of Commerce echoed the view of the majority of Newarkers when he said, "There is a general mood that the government is more accessible, that attention to detail is starting to happen and there seems to be a game plan taking shape. Everybody views that as a good sign."[7]

The first term saw a dazzling list of new development projects, often initiated by the state or by private local development and business interests. Several were promoted by the Newark Collaboration Group. Nonetheless, Mayor James took credit for them all. At the end of his first term, he issued a report card on his performance in fifteen areas. He gave himself an A-plus for reorganizing the city's administrative offices, which entailed establishing a program to go after $5 million in unpaid traffic tickets. He gave himself an even higher grade for his contributions to economic development, citing the building of the $75 million Legal and Communications Center by the Port Authority of New York and New Jersey, the disbursing of $500,000 for small business development, and the planning for a neighborhood movie house on Springfield Avenue. New housing was built in the Central Ward. He announced at the end of his first term that he had "definitely made the dean's list."[8]

Other new developments included the addition of seven hundred units of market-rate condominiums, with a number set aside at affordable rates, in the Society Hill project at the eastern edge of the Central Ward, adjacent to the downtown business district. Empty parcels on Springfield Avenue were filled with several national fast food and auto parts franchises, a Home Depot, and a new post office and Social Security Administration building. A major health research institution moved into the city. Several major corporations including MBNA and IDT sited facilities in Newark, and the high-speed communications capacity of the city was made as modern as anywhere. Several Rite-Aid and CVS drugstores moved into the city. Construction began on a long-awaited light rail downtown to connect Penn Station with the city's major cultural institutions and the Broad Street New Jersey Transit station to the north. Also, as a result of litigation against the Newark Housing Authority filed by Legal Services of New Jersey representing several housing authority tenants, some crime-ridden high-rise projects were demolished, making way for lower scale, more attractive, and more manageable housing units.[9] Rutgers University, the New Jersey Institute of Technology, and Essex County College undertook extensive building and growth plans as well. As in other urban areas, the city's crime rate began to decline and the police department hired more officers.

While some of the council members praised the mayor for the city's progress, Councilman Donald Tucker, whom James considered his nemesis, did not agree with the mayor's "lofty self-appraisals." Tucker said he had not seen any positive results from the mayor's reorganization of city agencies. He complained that not much had happened in the neighborhoods and more needed to be done in the areas of law enforcement and housing development. It was true that most of the major development efforts occurred in the downtown business district, but the neighborhoods were changing as well. The New Community Corporation built additional low-income housing and several commercial facilities in the Central Ward. Observers began to talk about a recovery, to some a renaissance, that was beginning to take shape. James said, "If nothing else, we've created a new sense of excitement about being in Newark."[10]

World-Class Arts Center "in the Middle of Nowhere"

The upward trend continued for several years with a steady stream of new projects, good news, and more bold promises. Fortunes for

Newark, and for Mayor James, received a major boost when the state announced that it would build a new performing arts center—in downtown Newark! The decision to build the center in Newark was by no means a simple matter. There were the expected objections from suburbanites that an arts center in Newark would have difficulty persuading audiences to visit for fear of crime and the absence of downtown restaurants. Some legislators predicted that the project would be obstructed by politicians at City Hall, who would see an arts center as simply another source of jobs and patronage. Others, inside and outside the city, wondered where the money would come from.

Fortunately, the idea of an arts center in Newark inspired Raymond Chambers, a New Jersey philanthropist who was already a key force behind efforts to rebuild Newark. Chambers grew up in the West Ward of Newark in a working-class Catholic household. He attended Rutgers University, where he earned a degree in accounting and a master's degree in business administration. For several years, he worked with the investor and former treasury secretary William E. Simon in a buyout firm called WESRAY. Chambers made a considerable fortune, which *Forbes* magazine estimated at $200 million in 1986.[11]

Beginning in the early 1970s, Chambers began shoring up the fiscal and organizational management of the Newark Boys and Girls Clubs, which he felt had given him and some of his childhood friends the caring and mentoring that contributed to their success. He then branched out to support numerous other community-building activities, including scholarships, mentoring programs, and worthy nonprofits. Chambers has been critically important to many of Newark's efforts at transformation, although people who know him say that he is shy and prefers to avoid the limelight. He has argued that Newark must have constant human traffic in the form of economic and entertainment activity downtown to become a healthy community. He had a key role in making the arts center happen. When state officials challenged private sources to come up with $35 million for the project, Chambers kicked in the first $5 million and guaranteed the remaining $30 million. The project was then a go. In the end, the performing arts center won broad support from local and national foundations and corporations. Construction was accomplished with an effective affirmative action program monitored by Gus Heningburg, a private consultant and former head of the Greater Newark Urban Coalition. While running the coalition, Heningburg had created a widely acclaimed program to create apprenticeships for minorities in the construction trades.

The New Jersey Performing Arts Center (NJPAC) is now the home of the New Jersey Symphony Orchestra and its seasons are filled with world-class music, dance, and theater. The 2,800-seat main hall is usually packed, as is the smaller venue, which holds 500. Architecturally, NJPAC is a break from most of the fortresslike, defensive buildings that had been constructed in downtown Newark since the rebellion of 1967. The center displays a brilliant openness, with generous portions covered with glass. The acoustics have been touted by experts as among the best in the nation. A famous maestro who brought his symphony orchestra to the center was heard to say, "Look at this beautiful place, in the middle of nowhere."

When Ray Chambers was tasked to look for a manager to oversee the development of the center, he found Lawrence Goldman, a Princeton University Ph.D. who was employed as the chief real estate development officer at Carnegie Hall in New York City. Goldman knew a lot about Newark; as a Princeton University administrator, he had recruited student interns to work in Kenneth Gibson's campaign in 1970.[12] Chambers and Goldman built a strong team and recruited smart and powerful corporate executives to join the board of directors. Art Ryan, the chairman and chief executive officer of Prudential, joined the board and became one of its key leaders. Roy Vagelos, the retired chairman and chief executive of Merck Pharmaceuticals, and Leonard Lieberman, the retired chairman of Supermarkets General, also joined the board. The corporate bigwigs were in a position to drum up support from their organizations, although they gave generously from their own coffers as well. They were also powerful political allies for the center and helped to make it one of New Jersey's top nonprofit recipients of state and philanthropic funds.

The New Jersey Performing Arts Center is technically a project of the state. Nonetheless, as Lawrence Goldman testifies, it is also a product of the city of Newark. In that sense, the support and cooperation of Mayor Sharpe James was key. According to Goldman, when critics cried that Newark had too many other problems to be concerned about building a performing arts center, James stepped up for the city. The project needed the support of local government for land assembly; permits and approvals; and for police, fire, and sanitation services. Whatever Goldman needed, the city delivered. James became a major booster. He countered the negative voices of some community leaders who complained that the center would drain Newark's limited financial resources and require a large police presence, taking desperately needed coverage from residential neighborhoods. James also endorsed the idea of building a police substation directly across the street from the entrance to the center, which has helped to create a crime-free zone. He also helped to gain approval from the city council to provide to the arts center a share of revenue of the parking garage at Military Park, directly across from the center. The city paid $6 million to upgrade the garage. And another highly important contribution made possible by Mayor James's support was the designation of the area around the arts center and extending through much of the downtown business district as a special development district, which in effect helps to shield the institution from local political interference. In 2002, as Mayor James began his fifth term in office, he received the Local Arts Leadership Award from the U.S. Conference of Mayors. Lawrence Goldman noted on the occasion, "Simply stated: No Sharpe James, no Performing Arts Center in Newark."[13]

Trouble in the Mayor's Office

Through all the excitement and cheering about what appeared to be a new beginning, troubling issues of finance and judgment emerged, continuing through James's several terms. Between 1986, the year he was elected mayor, and 1991, James purchased $850,000 in condominiums in Florida, South Carolina, New Jersey's Hunterdon County, and Newark, as well as a $300,000 vacation home in Brick Township, New Jersey. Two of the condominiums were bought from developers who received tax abatements from the city and contributed to the mayor's fund-raisers. In December 1994, the *Bergen Record* reported that the Sharpe James Civic Association, described by the mayor's office as a charitable organization, had received more than $10,000 in donations from development companies that had received tax breaks on Newark properties. The article also stated that James had been involved in personal real estate transactions with all three of the developers and that he had purchased a two-bedroom house in Port St. Lucie, Florida, at a discounted price from the K. Hovnanian Company, the firm that was building the previously mentioned condominiums in Society Hill.

The *Record* also reported that a failing bank, Metrobank, had made a $10,000 contribution to James's civic association just before being granted a $28 million tax break.[14] James's former police director, William Celester, whom he had personally recruited from Boston, pleaded guilty to misusing police funds and was sentenced to jail. Jackie Mattison, James's chief of staff and first cousin to his wife, was convicted of receiving $17,000 in bribes to steer board of education and city contracts; FBI agents had raided the home of Mattison's girlfriend and found $100,000 under floorboards.[15] The civic association put sizable checks, frequently made out to "cash" and often as much as $5,000, into the hands of close associates of James. Moreover, the association provided huge loans to James's campaign organization. In 1989, the civic association made four loans to his campaign fund totaling $400,000. Only $65,000 was paid back and the remainder was forgiven when the civic association was dissolved in 2000. An investigation by the New Jersey Election Law Enforcement Commission of James's political fund-raising revealed sloppiness, bad record keeping, and strong hints of deception in handling the books. In 1995, a fine of $41,000 was levied against the James campaign fund-raising organization by the New Jersey State Election Commission.[16] The fine set a new record; the previous record was $12,000. The complaint by the commission included twenty-seven counts and accused James of operating his organization as a political action committee "while skirting many rules intended to insure that such groups inform the public how they handles the money." William H. Eldridge, chairman of the commission, said, "I wish there were a way to reduce the influence of money in the election process. Given what we have seen in Essex County and other areas I think when people raise very large sums of money there are often a lot of temptations not to handle it properly." Mayor James insisted that he and his group never broke the law and that prosecutors were focusing on him because he was black.[17]

In 1998, following his victory over Councilman Ronald Rice, who was also a state senator, James hired the controversial Alfred Faiella, director of the Newark Economic Development Corporation (NEDC), to serve as deputy mayor while also overseeing the NEDC. James argued that Faiella could accelerate development throughout the city from a strengthened position in City Hall, but it was already known that Faiella had been taking political contributions from his friends and developers on behalf of the mayor. Faiella was unpopular among civic organizations for operating NEDC as a private fiefdom with virtually no transparency and making unsupported claims of job gains. His presence at Newark City Hall signaled that Mayor James was most eager to expand his fund-raising at the expense of his reputation, and the city's as well. During his years at City Hall, Faiella was both the city's chief development officer and the mayor's chief fund-raiser.

James brushed aside growing suspicions and scandals as he continued to solidify his standing in the city and his power throughout the state, taking credit at times for cooperating with authorities in the investigations of his former police director and chief of staff. In 1990, James had no opponent. In the 1994 mayoral election, James won by a large margin over William Payne, the brother of Congressman Donald Payne. James's three-to-one margin of victory over Payne, who was thought to have a large following in the South Ward, was more evidence of James's entrenched power. By 1995, James was into his third term, and although his fund-raising raised many questions, it had become highly successful. City employees were asked to contribute $250 to his campaign war chest at his annual birthday parties; tickets to the event cost upward of $500. The birthday celebration was a must for anyone working or doing business with the city. One prominent organization leader told me that one year he did not show up for James's birthday bash and James did not speak to him for a year. Hundreds of people did attend each year and his coffers grew. He also gained attention nationally as a spokesman for cities and in 1993 was elected to leadership positions in the U.S. Conference of Mayors and the National League of Municipalities.[18] In June 1999, he was granted a seat in the New Jersey State Senate, filling a vacancy created by the death of Senator Wynona Lipman. He won election to that seat the following November and in 2001 was elected to his first full term. A senate post in New Jersey carries a lot of weight; by virtue of a long-standing political practice, any state appointment by the governor within a senator's jurisdiction, such as a county prosecutor, must be endorsed by that senator. James could also introduce legislative proposals to support his aims at the city level. On several occasions when the city council tried to usurp his mayoral power, he introduced bills that were subsequently approved by his colleagues to clarify his powers over such matters as land distribution in Newark. He continued to hold dual offices until he ended his mayoral career in 2006. In 2007, he retired from the state senate.[19]

In 1996, the *Star-Ledger* reported that Newark's City Hall had been inundated with about two hundred subpoenas in the past two years from several law enforcement agencies, including the FBI, IRS, U.S. Postal Inspection Service, and federal prosecutors. James claimed the scrutiny had come as punishment for his unwillingness to alter the city budget calendar as requested by Governor James Florio and various state officials. But the mayor was drawing lots of attention for his purchase of a home in Barnegat Bay in 1991, a pretty large and expensive sailboat, which he named *Executive One*, and of course, his birthday parties, which were raking in lots of cash. Federal and state officials did a lot of poking around, but, seemingly, the conviction of Mattison, his chief of staff, kept James out of more serious trouble. Since Mattison did not throw his boss under the bus, his staff and friends thought he would no longer be pursued by state and federal investigators. Nonetheless, James continued to push the envelope. He acquired a used Rolls-Royce and, on occasion, joyfully cruised around his poverty-stricken city. The chatter about corruption did not slow him down. In 1998, he won reelection over State Senator Ron Rice and Mildred Crump.[20]

With his loyal Newark voter base and the added influence he acquired by holding a seat in the state senate, Mayor James became one of the most powerful politicians in New Jersey. An intriguing competition over the Democratic Party nomination for governor in 2001 gave him the opportunity to flex his political muscle. James McGreevy, mayor of Woodbridge, New Jersey, who had worked for years building support among labor and civic groups, had lost to the

Republican Christine Whitman four years earlier and was the presumed choice of the Democratic Party for 2001. U.S. Senator Robert Torricelli, also a Democrat, who had become a powerhouse in the Senate for his prowess at fund-raising and was well known for hobnobbing with celebrities, decided that he wanted to become governor of New Jersey and thus began to recruit party leaders to his cause. McGreevy called his friend in Newark for help and Mayor James delivered. James, as convener, along with others he had marshaled, held a press conference and announced that the assemblage of mayors, black and white, was solidly behind McGreevy's campaign. Senator Torricelli realized a campaign without the support of key black leadership and urban mayors would be futile. He ended his candidacy. McGreevy went on to win the governorship. James's intervention played a large role in sealing a victory for McGreevy. It was a major victory for James also, who was then recognized as a big-time kingmaker throughout the entire state, an unprecedented position of power for a black politician from Newark. And it was expected that when McGreevy became governor, he would pay James back, in a political sense.[21]

Go Devils!

In addition to his rescue of McGreevy, a victory in a long legal dispute gave James the opportunity to add another major development to the Newark business district. Ray Chambers owned a significant share of the New Jersey Nets and the New Jersey Devils, both major professional sports teams, and he was eager to get them out of their antiquated arena in the New Jersey Meadowlands. Building a new arena in downtown Newark for the teams would definitely be a double victory, boosting the fortunes of the teams and perhaps those of the the city as well. The initial proposals, which surfaced in 1998, called for the construction of a huge "arena district," a sports facility surrounded by extensive entertainment and commercial development. Throughout the nation, cities often plead for the presence of a national sports team, usually considered proof of a healthy and safe community that fosters both civic pride and promises of financial benefits to residents and the city. Nonetheless, the reigning experts on the economics of sports facilities, Roger Noll of Stanford University and Andrew Zimbalist of Smith College, contend the benefits of sports facilities are slight, if there are benefits at all. They have written:

A new sports facility has an extremely small (perhaps even negative) effect on overall economic activity and employment. No recent facility appears to have earned anything approaching a reasonable return on investment. No recent facility has been self-financing in terms of its impact on the net tax revenues. Regardless of whether the unit of analysis is a local neighborhood, a city or an entire metropolitan area, the economic benefits of sports facilities are *de minimus.*[22]

The Newark venture was particularly risky: the marketing analysis was quite clear that an arena would need at least one professional team and would be negatively affected if the Meadowlands Arena continued to operate.[23] Nonetheless, Sharpe James was not to be denied, so the press and corporate leadership joined the bandwagon. In an artful display of co-optation, the mayor convened a commission to review the arena proposal and evaluate the likelihood of the venture's success, the economic benefits to the city, and compare the Newark proposal to others. Patrick Hobbs, dean of the Seton Hall Law School, chaired the group and said upon receiving the assignment: "We are being asked to review this project and opine on whether or not the benefits are fair, achievable, and real."[24] As everyone expected, the commission endorsed the project, ignoring the reams of evidence that sports facilities have seldom provided the benefits promised. Under the leadership of Governor Christie Whitman and her interim successor, Donald DeFrancesca, the state would not contribute sufficient funds to make the project feasible. The governors could face major political risk for favoring a project in Newark that would undercut the viability of the Meadowlands arena, an arena considered economically important to the more suburban Bergen County.

Now with his pal James McGreevy in the statehouse and owing James big time, the prospects for making the arena happen became real. Before the project could be finalized, however, McGreevy resigned as governor and announced that he was a "gay American," living a dual life as a married man with a young child while also having sexual relationships with other men. Without McGreevy's presence in Trenton, there would be no major help from the state for the project. In addition, Chambers and his partners sold their interest in the Nets to Bruce Ratner, a developer in New York City, who announced that he would move the team to Brooklyn, where his firm would build a new arena. If the Newark arena was to be built, it could only rely on the Devils, an ice hockey team with staggering financial problems, and Seton Hall University's basketball team as regular users. With only two sports tenants, the economics of the arena made little sense, especially since the Meadowlands arena was still operating and holding a lock on most of the entertainment events that the Newark arena would need to sustain itself. Residents also wondered if the people of Newark would attend hockey, and there was widespread question of whether suburban and New York City hockey fans would come to Newark. But again, things fell in place for Sharpe James who wanted more than anything to have a sports facility in downtown Newark added to his legacy. The results of a protracted legal battle over rent and fees paid to Newark by the Port Authority of New York and New Jersey, the agency that operates the region's seaports and airports, led to a settlement that required remuneration of back lease payments to the city of Newark of over $400 million. Even without a major financial contribution from the state, James was prepared to put as much as was needed of the Port Authority windfall into the development of a new arena. The project would move forward.[25]

It is not easy to find residents willing to stand up to the government in Newark, but with the support of the Reverend William Linder of the New Community Corporation, a group of residents filed a lawsuit against the city asking that the project be put to a voter referendum. However, with Ray Chambers and other powerful business interests supporting the plan, the legal challenges that Linder's group brought forward were eventually dismissed. A lopsided agreement was struck between the city and the Devils, which required that the city pay most of the costs and receive very little direct benefit in return: the cost of the arena was approximately $375 million; the city was to contribute $225 million and the Devils $100 million. The city, in addition, had to expend its $225 million before the Devils were required to invest its money. Newark's subsidy, which also gave the Devils ownership of much of the surrounding land, was one of the largest ever granted to a privately owned professional sports team. The headline of this story should read: "Poor, Near Bankrupt City Builds Arena for Fiscally Troubled Professional Hockey Team." The arena, named the Prudential Center as required by a $104 million twenty-year naming agreement assigned to Devils' coffers, opened in 2007, after James had left office. As of the end of 2012, significant development was occurring around the arena, and Devils' fans (mostly from out of town) filled the arena on game nights.[26]

Sharpe James always considered the arena his major contribution to the city. The extent to which it can be considered a "major contribution" remains to be revealed. Thus far, the Devils get much better turnouts for their games than they had at the Meadowlands arena, and the team has been a strong contender in the NHL. Financially, the team is not in great shape. While the value of the franchise has appreciated in recent years thanks to the new arena, in 2011 the Devils had a debt/value ratio of 112 percent, gate receipts fell about 25 percent below player expenses, and operating income was only about $1.5 million for the preceding two years.[27] From the opening in 2007 to 2012, the Devils organization refused to pay rent for the arena, a sum of $2 million per year, claiming that the city of Newark had not met its obligations under the agreement for development of the surrounding area. The dispute over rent payments was eventually sent to a mediation panel, which ruled in the Devils' favor. Considering the financial straits of the Devils, it is not clear what Newark will get out of this investment other than more visitors and traffic downtown. In 2001, an official of the Federal Reserve Bank of St. Louis wrote: "When studying this issue, almost all economists and development specialists (at least those who work independently and not for a Chamber of Commerce or similar organization) conclude that the rate of return a city or metropolitan area receives for its investment in a sports facility is generally below that of alternative projects. Evidence suggests that cities and metro areas that have invested heavily in sports stadiums and arenas have, on average, experienced slower income growth than those that have not."[28]

The hockey arena raises a deeper question: What is the contribution of the city's redevelopment program, which has been touted as fueling a renaissance of Newark for over the last twenty-five years? Columbia University economist Brendan O'Flaherty took a look at the results of economic development efforts during this period of improvement and recovery in Newark; his analysis reveals the short-comings of development policies and practices in the city of New-ark, covering the years 1982 to 1997. He finds that Newark's economic development policies did not accomplish their claimed goal of bring-ing jobs and people to Newark.

It is worth digging a bit deeper into O'Flaherty's analysis for a fuller picture of Newark's economic decline. Specifically, using New Jersey State Labor Department data, O'Flaherty finds that between 1990 and 1997, the number of private-sector jobs in Newark covered by employment insurance fell by 8 percent. Between 1982 and 1997, covered private employment fell by 12.2 percent. Resident employ-ment (the number of Newarkers who have jobs, no matter where they work) fell between 1990 and 1998 by 6.8 percent; between 1980 and 1998, the decline was 9.0 percent.

O'Flaherty speculates that a boom in new construction (which is almost always tax abated) would show up as an increase in the money the city realizes from payments in lieu of taxes (PILOT). Between 1990 and 1998, PILOT rose only 1 percent, whereas between 1993 and 1998 it fell more than 20 percent; the rise was small enough to be attributable mainly to automatic escalators in some of the abate-ment contracts. Taken together, the data on PILOTs indicates that the value of real property in Newark almost certainly declined from 1990 to 1998, a period when downtown boosters and officials were proclaiming resurgence. Was the Newark record on jobs and PILOTs sufficient, O'Flaherty asks, to establish that something is wrong with Newark's economic development policies? Might forces of subur-banization and deindustrialization work so strongly against Newark that even the smartest policies could not stop the pace of decline? To check in a rough way whether this argument is plausible, O'Flaherty compares Newark with the next five largest cities in New Jersey plus Camden and Trenton. While all of these areas are not affected by the same national and international trends as Newark, most are affected by the same regional trends and state policies. Few of these places have Newark's transportation advantages and none has Newark's his-tory of financial leadership. But by measure after measure, Newark ranked near the bottom.

In resident employment, O'Flaherty demonstrates that Newark

is clearly at the bottom of the pack. In a broader comparison that includes New Jersey cities plus areas in New York, Newark is the only one of the ten places that lost in every category over both time periods. In fifty-four possible two-way comparisons (six measures with nine other places), Newark comes out better only seven times. The Bronx, Brooklyn, Jersey City, Woodbridge, and Edison do better than Newark on all measures; Paterson and Elizabeth on most. O'Flaherty concludes there was no renaissance in Newark during the period from 1982 to 1997.

O'Flaherty's analysis invites the question of whether, in a city like Newark, with such a large concentration of poverty, it takes longer for recovery to take hold and show results. So what happened in the period from 1997 to 2008? I looked at the data on private sector employment in Newark, resident employment, and changes in the business payroll tax payments for those years (see tables 7.1, 7.2, and 7.3). I found that the period presents a changing story that is not as dismal as the period from 1982 to 1996, but it still doesn't qualify as an outright renaissance. Private-sector insurance-covered employment increased by 1.3 percent from 1997 to 2008; resident employment declined by 4.8 percent. The huge surprise is that payroll taxes paid to the city increased from $25.4 million in 1996 to $38.7 million

───────────────〈 TABLE 7.1 〉───────────────

Private-Sector Employment Changes,
1982–1997

	1982–91	1990–97
Edison	+63.0%	+16.2%
Jersey City	+29.6	+13.9
Woodbridge	+10.7	+5.3
Bronx*	+10.6	+0.8
Brooklyn*	+5.9	0
Trenton	−10.1	−9.3
NEWARK	−12.2	−8.0
Paterson	−13.3	−11.9
Camden	−13.6	−18.6
Elizabeth	−15.4	−9.8

Source: Brendan O'Flaherty, "Newark's Non-Renaissance and Beyond," February 13, 2000.
*Includes government employment

⟨ TABLE 7.2 ⟩
Resident Employment Changes, 1980–1998

	1980–98	1990–98
Edison	+49.7%	+8.9%
Woodbridge	+20.1	+8.9
Jersey City	+15.1	−2.1
Paterson	+15.0	−1.2
Brooklyn	+8.9*	−3.9†
Bronx	+6.9*	−2.6†
Trenton	+4.8	−1.9
Elizabeth	+4.2	−2.6
Newark	−9.0	−6.8

Source: Brendan O'Flaherty, "Newark's Non-Renaissance and Beyond," February 13, 2000.
*April 1980 April–December 1999
†April 1990–December 1999 (from O'Flaherty 2000)

⟨ TABLE 7.3 ⟩
Employment in Four Cities

	Private-sector employment changes, 1997–2008	Resident employment changes, 1997–2008
Newark	+1.3%	−4.8%
Camden	+1.2	−18.4
Jersey City	+18.5	+2.9
Trenton	+20.8	−7.1

Source: New Jersey Department of Labor, lwd.dol.state.nj.us/labor.

in 2008, a gain of 52.3 percent. So how could there be such a major jump in payroll taxes, far more that what can be accounted for by inflation, and at the same time, virtually no expansion of jobs?[29]

The data reaffirm the evidence found over the years that jobs created in urban areas are most likely to go to people who live outside of the cities. Despite the slight employment increases in Newark and Trenton, for example, employment of residents declined by 4.8 percent and 7.1 percent respectively. The reality is that important changes and growth did take place in Newark through the 1990s and up to

2006, when Sharpe James led the city. But the expanded construction activity meant little for the mass of Newark's population. It is true that hard bargaining produced some jobs for minority workers in the construction of the medical school and expansion of the airport in the 1970s, but the world of commercial and banking affairs is beyond the ken of many unemployed Newarkers. The kinds of jobs created by these new or extended operations are not open to the unskilled or poorly educated. Additional jobs in the white-collar ranks do little to help the bulk of the unemployed or underemployed city dwellers. The importance of the expanded or new facilities in commerce, banking, or entertainment is not in the jobs they add but rather the taxes they pay and the added commerce they stimulate. But even with taxes, there are problems lurking.

As it turns out, the apparent tax advantage of commercial development projects is minimal. All of the major industrial-commercial development projects in the city over the past fifty years were built on the basis of agreements regarding taxation worked out under the state's Fox Lance Act.[30] Under that law, a developer can get an abatement of taxes by agreeing to pay a stipulated sum in lieu of taxes, a sum that must exceed the amount of taxes received prior to the development (or renovation). A fifteen-year tax abatement as an incentive to locate in Newark (or to remain in Newark) is unquestionably a boon to the business involved. The assurance of no rise in tax rates and the need to pay (in lieu) only from about 20 to 40 percent of what full taxation would yield are strong inducements. It is, of course, commonplace for states and cities to compete with each other for development through such arrangements, but it is noteworthy that New Jersey in past years let the whole weight of the tax concession fall on Newark's already dangerously low assessed property values.

One distinctive feature of the city's abatement policy is that everything is discretionary. The mayor and the council approve every tax abatement individually and no one has to give a reason for rejection or approval (although none that reach the formal council stage are ever rejected). The statutory limits on how generous development deals can be are fairly easy to evade through dummy corporations and separate subsidies, for instance; no one has to explain why one deal is more generous than another.

The right to develop a property at abated taxes is valuable, but Newark gives it away for promises that local benefits will follow.[31] The people who dole out Newark's abatements don't seem to have a clue as to what enterprises can produce the results to which they agree. As O'Flaherty points out: "Fast food restaurants on major thoroughfares get abatements, as do hotels next to the airport and major New Jersey corporations like PSE&G and Blue Cross."[32] City officials have never published or made clear their methodology for awarding abatements. Political money and lobbying seem to count for a lot more in the tax abatement process than calculations of investment sensitivity. During Sharpe James's tenure, the man who negotiated all tax abatements was Deputy Mayor for Development Alfred Faiella— the same person who was the mayor's chief political fund-raiser. Notably, the largest and most innovative abatements seem to cluster around extremely savvy corporations such as Blue Cross, PSE&G, and IDT, which declared bankruptcy in 2011 despite winning some of the most generous abatements and subsidies a decade earlier. It is also true that some developers simply avoided the city when word circulated that the process was dangerously discretionary.

O'Flaherty contends that not only does the development activity fail to produce benefits for local residents but it actually slows down the process of development and eventually impedes the likelihood of development for those who do not get an abatement. If you own land that you want to develop and ask for abatement but you are turned down, it is highly unlikely you would proceed without the abatement. You will either change your plans to make them appear more attractive in the press, make a few carefully placed campaign contributions, sell your land to someone better connected politically, or simply wait and hope your side wins the next election so you can get an abatement. Newark's abatement process is so haphazard and byzantine, it would be impossible to get enough information to explain fully how it works. O'Flaherty calls it a discretionary, random system, which not only slows development but forces a continual upward spiral of abatements. It is rationalized to the public with highly exaggerated claims of job generation and benefits to the city. For example, when the Devils arena was first announced, there were claims that the facility would produce "8,000 permanent jobs." When the arena opened in 2006, the managers announced that

1,000 jobs would be available. They then failed to mention that the majority were part-time sales jobs for refreshments and beverages in the arena on game nights or when other events took place. Political leaders want to be able to claim that they have contributed to "development impact" during their terms of office, and developers want to reduce their costs, or, as they do at times, enrich themselves. In O'Flaherty's words, "Newark's policies don't combat blight, they create it."[33] The scholarly evidence from other cities shows little or no support for the notion that huge subsidies to developers in poor cities make a difference.

Creating more jobs in Newark does not necessarily help Newark residents very much. The overwhelming majority of jobs and work opportunities in the regional labor market are not located in Newark. Moreover, putting a job in downtown Newark doesn't guarantee it will be more accessible to Newarkers. Getting to Livingston or Irvington can be easier for most residents of Vailsburg than commuting downtown; Hillside, Irvington, and Union may be more accessible for people who live in the South Ward or Weequahic. Even a more successful economic development program is not likely to alter the job prospects for a good number of unemployed Newarkers. What would help? Certainly improved education and training to make job seekers more capable of operating in a twenty-first-century workforce would make a difference. However, the kind of human development strategies needed are costly and take time; they also require the strong support of political leaders. Unfortunately, Newark's political leaders have cared more about the abatements flowing to large corporations than the kind of education the city's children receive. Improved local bus service and more frequent service to employment centers would also do as much or more in providing jobs to Newarkers as a $15 million tax break to a corporation. A policy that acknowledged that the employment benefits of development policy were modest at best and offered less generous subsidies as a result would probably produce more jobs for Newarkers.

This is not an argument to close down the development office. Despite the lack of success Newark's development program has had in providing jobs and increasing income for Newark residents, there are other benefits that flow from rebuilding that should not be overlooked. For example, downtown developments have brought visitors to the city. The construction of new housing has improved the appearance of the city, and, over time, new development makes the city more attractive for future development. Development activity can also create a ripple effect and encourage other agencies and institutions to upgrade.

The Last Dance

The new sports arena did not open before James had to fight for his seat as mayor in the 2002 election. For most of his years in office, Mayor James faced very little competition, and in 1990 he ran unopposed. In 2002, however, he was challenged by a young newcomer named Cory Booker who in 1998 wrested the Central Ward council seat from longtime council member George Branch. Booker, only thirty-three years old at the time, was a graduate of Stanford University and Yale Law School as well as a Rhodes scholar. He had arrived in Newark seeking a place where he could "give back." James's race against the well-financed Booker ultimately was not close, but it was rough and dirty, reminiscent of the street clashes between the Addonizio and Gibson forces in 1970. Following the 2002 victory, James's leadership began to fade and his behavior became odd. He dismissed his unpopular deputy mayor, Al Faiella, but hired in his place State Senator Ronald Rice, who had challenged him for the mayoralty in 1998. Rice brought further opprobrium to the James administration when it was discovered that he simultaneously held a paid position as a public relations consultant to a Newark developer, thus making him a triple-dipper, with salaries from his state senate position and his job at City Hall.[34]

It may be that the hard-fought victory over Booker embittered James, for following the campaign, he put on a display of old machine-type vindictiveness that raised eyebrows in hardened corridors of City Hall.[35] He was brutal and inhumane in punishing those who did not support him. He cut off funding for a transitional residence for homeless families and a youth recreation program run by the New Community Corporation, the organization headed by the Reverend William Linder. Linder had supported Booker in 2002. The city's director of neighborhood services was demoted and forced to take a pay cut because he had not shown sufficient loyalty. Police officers who backed Booker were given onerous transfers; developers who sided with Booker learned that their projects were stalled by red tape or "lost" paperwork.[36] These tactics were not new to the James administration's style of politics, but they became more frequent and more targeted after 2002. Mayor James denied responsibility for the reprisals, but the evidence supporting the claims of the victims was undeniable.

As the 2006 election approached, James seemed unsure whether he would run again. Then one day, wearing a straw hat, bicycle shorts, and a tight tank top, he rode a bicycle into City Hall. Carrying his reelection petitions, he looked more like a circus clown than the chief executive of a major city. A picture of James's antics in the local paper led some residents to wonder if he had lost his grip. Ultimately, filing the petitions had no meaning. On March 27, 2006, eleven days after he had filed his petitions, he announced that he would not run for mayor again. He said, "Under my leadership, Newark has climbed the rough side of the mountain and has become a renaissance city with pride, prosperity, and progress. Newark is now a destination city with planned programs and economic projects that will surface over the next decade."[37]

Sharpe James probably knew it was time for him to remove himself from the limelight. Federal investigators had been prying into city affairs for several years. On July 12, 2007, Christopher Christie, the United States attorney who had already put more than a dozen crooked New Jersey politicians behind federal bars, announced that Mayor James was being indicted for criminal misconduct. The indictment contained thirty-three separate counts of alleged violations of federal laws, but the sum of the charges boiled down to two damning issues. First, there were charges that the mayor had misused city funds by traveling to places like Florida, Brazil, and the Dominican Republic simply to have fun and had falsely reported that such trips were for city business. On several of the excursions, according to the charges, he was accompanied by girlfriends who traveled at the city's expense. The second and most serious issue was the charge that Mayor James had arranged for the sale of several parcels of land at steeply discounted prices to a particular girlfriend, Tamika Riley, who had not rehabilitated the properties as required in the sale agreement but instead had quickly resold them, reaping extraordinary profits that she had not reported in her tax filings. Riley was also indicted on an unrelated fraud charge and income tax evasion.[38]

In March 2008, Mayor Sharpe James and Tamika Riley were put on trial in federal court before a jury with Judge William J. Martini, a former congressman and county freeholder, presiding. Several former city council members testified on James's behalf and stated that the mayor did not have sole authority to sell city property. It was pointed out that other developers also received generous prices on city land deals and had, like Riley, made hefty profits on the transactions. Prosecution witnesses stated that the mayor and Riley had more than a business relationship, and one city official testified that the mayor had personally requested that he make special concessions to her on land sales. A security aide to the mayor testified that Mayor James had directed him to install an air conditioner in Riley's apartment, and James's former secretary testified that Riley got special attention when she called the mayor's office.

Still, it was a very curious trial. The judge frequently challenged the prosecutor's theories and at one point asserted that he discerned no aggravated behavior on James's part. Although the evidence against James on the land deals seemed murky and weak, it appeared that he would have an impossible mountain to climb defending himself on the charges of misuse of city credit cards and the hotel receipts documenting his travels.[39] On April 18, 2008, the jury returned a guilty verdict of fraud for conspiring to rig the sale of nine city lots to his friend, Tamika Riley. It was, as described by the *Star-Ledger*, "a potentially staggering blow to the legacy of James."[40]

During the sentencing hearing, federal prosecutors seemed to irk the judge when they asked that James be sentenced to thirty years in prison. When Assistant U.S. Attorney Judith Germano attempted to justify the request for such a severe sentence, she began, "There has been a history . . . ," but before she could complete her sentence, Judge Martini interrupted and said, "Don't talk in terms of the history of corruption unless you've proven that. You didn't prove that in this courtroom as far as I was concerned."[41] When all the testimony and arguments were finished, the jury found both James and Riley guilty, and both were sent to prison. James received a sentence of twenty-seven months.

A Few Words from Sharpe James

In August 2009, I wrote to Sharpe James, who was incarcerated in a federal prison in Petersburg, Virginia, and asked him to respond to seventeen questions regarding his experience as a councilman and mayor of Newark.[42] He responded promptly with sixty pages of handwritten comments. Some of the remarks were helpful in understanding the complications of running the city; others were frankly unsubstantiated charges against his political enemies, seemingly efforts to settle old scores. For example, he expressed his anger at former governor Jon Corzine, perhaps because Anne Milgram, New Jersey's attorney general, participated in his prosecution. He criticized Corzine for spending most of his time in New York City, "paying off his campaign staff," and giving $6 million to a former girlfriend, Carla Katz, who courted the governor while also serving as the leader of a state employee union. James correctly predicted that Governor Corzine would lose to Chris Christie, the former U.S. attorney who had put James behind bars. He also alleged that Mayor Cory Booker, while campaigning for Governor Corzine, "secretly worked for Christie." While none of these accusations were substantiated, they illustrated the thinking of a man who was deeply embarrassed by his imprisonment but yet did not comprehend how much he had contributed to his own downfall.

James considered himself a political prisoner. He attached a cover page to his response listing his name among world figures such as Gandhi, Martin Luther King Jr., and Nelson Mandela, all of whom had been persecuted for fighting for justice for their people. He was adamant that he was convicted for executing land transactions that were approved by the city council and were not substantially different from land deals involving others. Imprisonment did not diminish his view that he had made a singular and major contribution to Newark's development. That was indeed true, which highlighted the tragedy of the circumstances that led to his political demise.[43]

According to James, it was Earl Harris, as president of the council from 1974 to 1978, who engineered the move to have council membership declared a full-time job, thus raising salaries to executive levels. Harris, he said, persuaded the city to purchase automobiles for each council member and had the city increase support staff for each member to five. Council members now earn $89,000 per year, have individual offices, and each one receives $8,500 to distribute for summer recreation programs. In 2005, the *Star-Ledger*'s Jeffrey Mays analyzed the pay and perks of the Newark City Council for the preceding year. He found that Jersey City, with a population of 239,000 to Newark's 277,000, spent 32 cents per resident compared with Newark's $1.23 per resident. The seven council members in St. Paul, Minnesota, population 287,000, are allowed about $7,000 per year; in Raleigh, North Carolina, population 276,000, the eight council members each get $1,200 per year added to their paychecks for expenses, and the entire council shares an $18,000 travel budget. In Newark, council members received an average of $19,615 in personal reimbursements for expenses, not counting the in-lieu-of-expenses payments that are added to their $64,766 salaries. Jersey City council members, by contrast, made between $30,000 and $32,000 per year. Each has one aide.[44]

Sharpe James's envious opponent and competitor on the city council was Donald Tucker, an at-large member who lived in the East Ward. It was Tucker who had upset tradition and denied James the presidency of the council when James was the leading vote getter in the at-large council race in 1982. And it was Tucker who had emerged as the fiscal authority and often contested the mayor's proposals. In 1997, the bitterness between James and Tucker broke into the open. James had criticized the council for their spending and lack of cooperation on several development projects in his state-of-the-city speech, deeply upsetting council members. Tucker then denounced the mayor for trying to act like "King James." He reminded the mayor that the city was not a kingdom run by an executive or a kingdom run by a city council. "It is a democracy," he said.[45]

The Sharpe James Legacy

The era of Sharpe James is fraught with complications and tragedy, but the bottom line is that a lot of things got done in the downtown business district as well as in the neighborhoods. The city worked its way out of the malaise and turmoil it experienced during the Gibson years. Of course James would like to take credit for all the good things that happened, such as NJPAC and the Prudential sports arena as well as the thousands of units of new brick-front housing dotting the streets in every ward. And he insists that the improvements that have been made truly represent a renaissance. However, while the changes have been significant, it would be an exaggeration to suggest that Newark's turnaround was anywhere near complete.

Sharpe James deserves credit for marketing the city, for being a spirited booster who probably gave considerable push to the development drive. He was also an effective facilitator, as in the case of NJPAC, and he was a driving force and organizer of the support he needed on the council to get the arena built. He often used his power in the legislature to benefit Newark. The fact that his housing strategy—virtually giving away idle and abandoned properties to jumpstart a building surge—led to his downfall is tragic and ironic, for the new housing construction is one of the most important positive changes since 1967, and even since 1997. Whether he can legitimately take credit for the increased interest in commercial real estate is less clear. Market forces in the region helped make Newark's vacant commercial spaces available at bargain prices, but Mayor James may have done as much to dampen those market forces by mixing political fund-raising with development business. The construction of the waterfront building that has become the headquarters for the FBI represents one of the oddest and most unwise planning decisions in the history of Newark, a symbol of a city's total disregard for planning. The building will constrain future development of the precious waterfront in many costly ways.

In 1994, at the opening of the National League of Cities' annual convention in Minneapolis, Minnesota, James, who was serving as president of the organization, told the delegates: "Our mission . . . is to renew our oath of office to serve and protect the citizens who have placed their trust and confidence in us; to prove worthy of their vote and support; to make our cities and towns better, and I believe we can meet that challenge."[46] Did Sharpe James meet the challenge? How can one explain his actions and behavior, a person who had to know well what a fallacy it is that one can forever escape the arm of the law if it is violated? He had witnessed the fate of Mayor Addonizio and he had seen at least four of his council colleagues convicted of wrongdoing. What happened to the racial pride James expressed back in the early 1970s when he joined the city council after being nominated and supported by the Black and Puerto Rican Convention? And what happened to the rules and standards James announced at the time of his ascendancy to the mayoralty when he said all of his major appointments would be subjected to strict background checks and would be expected to avoid any moral issues as long as they worked in his administration? Apparently the preachment was for others.

Up to the time of his departure from City Hall in 2006, almost all of the projects and developments that had taken place in Newark during the previous twenty years, which included a minor league baseball stadium, the New Jersey Performing Arts Center, and the Prudential Center arena, can be considered achievements of James's leadership. But his record is terribly marred in several ways. First there is the stain of his conviction and the transgressions for which he was not tried that continue to leave impressions of abuse of a public trust. Then there is the flaunting of conspicuous symbols of wealth like a Rolls-Royce, which is not a crime but certainly not something to convince the people of Newark he is worthy of their support. His record is also marred by his meanness and ruthless retaliation against organizations that did not support him. It is especially spoiled by his failure to focus on the needs of Newark's poor citizens, particularly children. His administration never developed any consistent, comprehensive strategies or policies that might have addressed the needs of residents. For example, there was never a serious effort to gain the most out of the developments downtown or along Springfield Avenue. Never was there an effort to adopt models of linkage like Boston's programs to extract payments from large-scale developers for the support of affordable housing. Newark's federally funded employment and training programs were mediocre at best, and James never showed any concern for their effectiveness. Like others before him, he used them for patronage.

James fought hard against the decision of the state to take control of Newark's school district but his principal concern was again the occasional jobs he could squeeze out of the school bureaucracy, not a concern for better education. Sharpe James, who was always willing to play the race card when it seemed to his advantage, in the end betrayed his race as well as those of all races who supported him. He talked often in his speeches about the history of suffering of black

Americans and frequently made reference to his participation in the civil rights campaigns of the 1960s. His joining with Baraka's Black Nationalist organization was a manifestation of smart politics, but it was also a statement of racial pride. Could it have been that the respect and devotion he often professed for the advocates of black advancement were smothered by his love for material trophies of wealth like the Rolls-Royce, the sailboat, and the numerous properties he acquired? Or did he simply believe that his considerable political power and influence would protect him from the retribution to come? Sharpe James had a chance to have one of the most successful mayoral tenures in Newark's history. Sadly, he will be most remembered not for the development that occurred under his twenty-year leadership from 1986 to 2006, not for his vigorous championing of his city, and not for his lively dancing. Rather, he will be best remembered for adding another bad example of leadership to Newark's history.

The much-debated question of whether Sharpe James would have bested Booker in 2006 cannot be answered. As history would have it, Booker ran and won against Senator Ron Rice. The city was ready for the young, untried, charismatic visionary with the golden connections and silver tongue who declared that he would lead the old place to a new future and create a shining city on the hill.

───<8>───

Black Mayor on a White Horse

All of us are bursting for a messiah. Me too.

—Steve Adubato Sr., quoted in the *Newark Star-Ledger*,
October 3, 2000

NEWARK NEVER HAD a mayor like Cory Anthony Booker. For more than fifty years, Newark's mayors have emerged from the city's ethnic neighborhoods. Booker is a New Jersey native but not from the city. When he arrived in Newark sometime around 1995, shining with the brilliance of an Ivy League education, he said he was seeking a place to "give back." While his words referred to giving service to the community for the fortunes that have come one's way in life, his critics said he was really looking for more fortunes, a place to launch a political career destined to end far from Newark.

In early 2013, Booker made it known that he would not run again for mayor of Newark. Instead, he planned in 2014 to seek the U.S. Senate seat held by the eighty-nine-year-old Frank Lautenberg, who announced that he would retire at the end of his current term.[1] But Senator Lautenberg died on June 3, 2013, thus forcing the question of who would complete his term and who would succeed him after the 2014 election.

To answer the first question, Governor Christie scheduled a primary vote for August 8, 2013, and a special election on October 16, with the winner of the contest to hold the seat on an interim basis until 2014. Booker vied against three other candidates in the Democratic primary race: Congressman Frank Pallone Jr. of Long Branch, Congressman Rush Holt Jr. of Princeton, and Speaker of the New Jersey Assembly Sheila Y. Oliver, who lives in East Orange. Booker won handily.

In the October 16 special election, Booker ran against Republican Steve Lonegan, businessman and former Bogota mayor, who was closely allied with the conservative Tea Party wing of his party. Booker did not win the landslide that had seemed likely at the beginning of the contest, but he won by a comfortable margin, garnering 54 percent of the vote to Lonegan's 44 percent. He went to Washington to complete Senator Lautenberg's term, and will run for the full term in 2014. Cory Booker is the first African American to serve as a U.S. senator from New Jersey, and the first Newark mayor elevated to higher office in more than one hundred years. He achieved exactly what many residents expected when he arrived in Newark: a higher office far from the poor, resource-starved city he led for almost eight years.[2]

So how did Booker fare in Newark, where he promised to set a new standard for urban transformation in the nation? Booker's is a story of significant material gains for the city, but also one of an absent mayor who failed to connect to the people of his city while he was being highly praised and celebrated elsewhere.

The Super Kid

Cory Booker was by no means an average child growing up in Harrington Park, a northern New Jersey upper-class suburb. Harrington Park, at the time Booker was growing up there, had a population of about 5,000 with a handful of minorities and virtually no one living in poverty. Booker's parents, Cary and Carolyn, spent long careers at IBM. They instilled in him and his older brother, Cary II, a sense of caring and concern for the historical plight and journey of black Americans. As Booker explained, his parents taught him and his brother that everything they achieved was not of their own making. "Somebody at the Urban League helped to open doors in business so that they could be hired at IBM. People at a fair housing council—blacks and white working together—made it possible for my parents to buy a home in Harrington Park."[3] They were dutiful parents who stressed the importance of education and set a very high bar for their children. Cory and Cary always reached the bar, and better. Cary is an educator who runs a charter school in Memphis, Tennessee. Cory's excellent grades and football talent in high school got him to Stanford University on a football scholarship, where he was more of a student campus leader than a standout on the football field. He was red-shirted the first year (which meant in Booker's case that he was on the practice squad) and he was never a varsity starter. He had a few heroic moments in a game in 1989 when Stanford upset number-one-ranked Notre Dame, and he scored a critical touchdown in a game in which Stanford put up a gallant but losing fight against highly ranked University of Southern California. However, in his fourth eligible year, he reluctantly took the advice of Stanford football coach Dennis Green and devoted his time and energy to campus politics, an area which he already seemed to have more natural ability and success. He had been elected president of his senior class that year. Booker's release from the squad caused anger and disappointment among some of his student supporters. Booker said later that Green did him a favor by forcing him to think more seriously about life and the problems of society.[4]

Following graduation from Stanford, Booker was named a Rhodes scholar and went to Oxford to spend two years studying history. It was there that he met his close friend and sometimes spiritual advisor, Hasidic Rabbi Schmuley Boteach, who had founded an organization of Orthodox Jewish students at Oxford called the L'Chaim Society. As the story goes, Booker stopped by a meeting of the society one evening to meet a friend, but when the friend did not show up, he was invited to stay, join the meeting, and have dinner with the group. Booker stayed, intrigued by the conversations he heard; he then decided to learn more about Judaism. He kept going back to the L'Chaim Society, which occasionally sponsored lectures by world figures such as former U.S. secretary of state Henry Kissinger, former Russian president Mikhail Gorbachev, and Britain's prime minister, Tony Blair. Booker eventually became a regular member of the group, and he and Rabbi Boteach became close friends. Boteach invited Booker to become chair of the society. Booker agreed to serve as a cochair. Booker helped to build the L'Chaim Society, which was not a part of the university, into one of the largest student groups at Oxford.

Upon his return to the United States, Booker continued his close relationship with the Lubavitchers as well as his friendship with Rabbi Boteach. In September 2007, Booker was honored at a dinner held by the Rabbinical College of America, the institution that trains Hasidic rabbis, and granted an honorary degree. In 2008, he was a guest speaker at the American Israel Political Action Committee (AIPAC) summit; Rabbi Boteach introduced Booker to the audience and said, only two years after Booker's elevation to mayor, Booker was the "most preferred speaker in the Jewish community." In 2010, Booker was the keynote speaker at the AIPAC annual convention, where he delivered a stirring, emotional speech detailing the common interests of Israel and the United States.

Booker has said that he has prayed at the gravesite of Menachem Schneerson, the Lubavitcher leader who died in 1994 and is considered by his followers to be an iconic figure but somewhat of an oddity to many non-Hasidic Jews. There are many different views among Hasidim concerning the meaning of Schneerson's demise. Some, for example, believe he will return as the Messiah; others believe he is merely hidden. Some followers continue to visit his resting place, apparently in belief that "the righteous, in their passing, can bless those in this world more so than during their lifetimes."[5]

Booker's experience with the L'Chaim Society and his close friendship with Rabbi Boteach and the Hasidim, perhaps the most conservative wing of Judaism, would have little significance if Booker had not chosen to lead a largely black and Latino American city. I and others in Newark wonder, what did this relationship mean? Was it about curiosity? Faith? Spirituality? Opportunism? Or could it have been, as some of Booker's opponents charge, that Booker was an agent of people who wanted to exploit the pickings of a hard-pressed city? Or, might it have been about nurturing a black voice that would agree with conservative economic and foreign policy interests? The Reverend David Jefferson, the pastor of Newark's Metropolitan Baptist Church, where Booker became a member after his arrival in

Newark, saw a positive in the relationship, however. "Booker is an attentive churchgoer," Reverend Jefferson said, "whose interest in Judaism helps him better understand Christianity's roots, and, in a different way, helps the city." A former Oxford colleague, Harvard law professor Noah Feldman, sees no hidden agendas. In his view, it's mainly about Booker's intellectual curiosity, charisma, and leadership abilities. "If Booker had similarly walked into a Buddhist meeting," he said, "he would have become a participant and leader of that Buddhist organization." Feldman's comment points to the fact that Booker does have an extraordinary range and depth of curiosity, an intellectual breadth rarely found in local politicians.[6]

I asked Mayor Booker why one would visit the gravesite of Menachem Schneerson, a person considered by many non-Hasidic Jews to be an oddball and, more important, from a sect whose social values are narrow and regressive. "Look," Booker said, "No religion is perfect. I have complaints about my own religion, which is Baptist. They preach intolerance against homosexuality." As the conversation went on, I later realized that Mayor Booker had adroitly steered me off topic to a very different discussion, a tactic he frequently employs when asked a question he does not wish to answer. I still do not know why he prayed three times at the gravesite of Menachem Schneerson.[7]

Booker is much admired by followers among all faiths, but it is clear that he has had a special relationship with Hasidic Jews. The booking agency that represents Booker, as well as hundreds of other celebrities, for speaking engagements offered joint appearances of the rabbi and the mayor.[8] Rabbi Boteach is hardly as significant to Booker's political future, however, as are the mayor's relationships with the big-time powers and celebrities who have lined up behind him. Booker's greatest talent may be the ability to reach people and make them believe in his vision as well as his ability to realize that vision. He can, like former president Bill Clinton, look you in the eye, engage you for a few minutes, and make you think you really know him. He is a superb speaker, often citing the lessons of great writers and leaders like Hillel, George Bernard Shaw, James Baldwin, Adam Smith, and Martin Luther King Jr. I have listened to many of his speeches and have been impressed with his talks to college students, which are sermons on brotherhood and community and the importance of giving to others.[9]

Booker Comes to Newark

When Booker arrived in New Jersey's tired but raucous city, he made the rounds, doing due diligence on Newark while also displaying his charm, good looks, and smarts. One of his most significant conversations was with the ubiquitous Raymond Chambers, the wealthy investor who became a major supporter of efforts to rebuild the city. Although other local foundations may have more capital, Chambers is a far more significant player because he has roots in Newark and much of his private business interest is also focused on Newark. He once was a principal owner of the former New Jersey Nets, an NBA franchise, as well as the New Jersey Devils hockey team.[10] Chambers has said he immediately realized Booker had unusual leadership talent and urged him to run for mayor of Newark. Booker readily credits Chambers with changing his focus from trying to build the best nonprofit in the city. Booker also jokingly adds that in pushing him into politics, "Chambers ruined my life and my parents are going to sue for damages."[11] Chambers envisioned that Booker would become the kind of leader Newark needed—an honest man with the vision and skills to move the city forward. I suspect that one way or another, Booker would have entered Newark politics. The nudge from Chambers, I think, merely affirmed his already designed path.

Booker's initial instinct was to run for mayor but he decided instead to try for a council seat to establish a base and reputation first. In 1998, at the age of twenty-eight, Booker won his first campaign for public office as city council representative of the Central Ward, for many years the heart of Newark's black community. He beat the civic-minded former amateur boxer George Branch, who had held the position for sixteen years. Branch staunchly defended the interests of his ward but also occasionally engaged in some of the unseemly behavior all too common for members of the council.[12] It was not an easy victory for Booker. In the initial election, Branch led by more than 300 votes, but since no candidate had a majority, there had to be a runoff election. Political boss Steve Adubato then poured all of his troops behind Booker. "We were all looking for a Messiah. Me too," he told the *Star-Ledger*.[13] The newcomer won the run-off by 659 votes. Arguably, the Booker/Adubato relationship has been the most critical factor in building a path for Booker's future victories in Newark. Adubato may in fact be Booker's most important horse. The wealthy and celebrity supporters could cheer and send money, but they could not deliver votes the way Adubato has done.

As a member of the city council, Booker was best known for his dramatic public displays of disgust at the flourishing illegal drug markets operating in his ward, which Mayor Sharpe James called grandstanding. On one occasion, he and a group of young followers pitched a tent in an area adjacent to Academy Spires, a large, worn-down housing development that had become a major site for drug dealing. Booker announced that he was going to stay in the area, in fact sleep overnight in the tent, and fast until the city cleaned up the place. Two of his former supporters who participated with Booker in the demonstration said that Booker seldom stayed in the tent overnight but would often leave after dark and return early the next morning. The press was led to believe that he camped at the site overnight. Darrin Sharif, the son of Carl Sharif, Booker's campaign manager in 2006, was an early Booker supporter and participated in the action at Academy Spires. He eventually left the demonstration worried that they would all be embarrassed by Booker's deceptive tactics.[14]

Booker was often absent from council meetings. He spent a great deal of time propping up his reputation around the nation, attending meetings of the Stanford University Board of Trustees, of which he was a member, and giving speeches on college campuses. His reputation blossomed outside Newark. What became apparent in his travels was a tendency to spin heroic tales that occasionally could not be verified or, in the case of the now infamous "T Bone" story, seemed to be bold fiction. Booker claimed that he had a dramatic and frightening confrontation with a drug dealer named T Bone, who threatened to harm Booker physically if Booker dared to look at him. Booker said that he and T Bone got to know each other despite his earlier threats, and that eventually, T Bone, with tears in his eyes, asked Booker to help him change his life. When a few reporters swarmed the area in search of T Bone, including chatting with undercover narcotics police officers, they could not find anyone who knew a T Bone. When a reporter circled back to Booker, he then said T Bone was not really a person, but a composite of a number of characters he had met. But Booker had told the T Bone story to audiences all over the country. In an attempt at deflection, Booker responded that those looking for a real T Bone were missing the point of his story.[15]

It seems Booker has a penchant for finding dramatic and heroic moments, or, to say it another way, turning the tragedies of poverty, violence, and urban life into tales that make him look brave and entitled to the Superman outfit TV host Ellen DeGeneres tried to give him. He held a dying teenager in his arms and tried to stop his bleeding from gunshot wounds before he was taken to a hospital, where he died. Booker did indeed charge into a burning house to carry a woman to safety, although the woman said she does not know who carried her out.[16] Rahaman Muhammad, the head of the Service Employees Union in Newark who was also part of the young group that supported Booker early on, said that he believes that there is a part of Booker that truly wants to help people. However, stories of Booker's heroism, the concocted ones and the real ones, also supported the impression that the city of Newark is nothing but a crime-ridden hellhole. The stories brought admiration on college campuses and plush fund-raising parties, but many people in Newark thought their leader should try to give the larger public a more balanced picture of city life.

In 2002, after one term on the city council, Booker challenged Mayor Sharpe James, who had already won four terms. Booker lost in a nasty race, full of extreme rhetoric and name calling. James's workers tore down Booker's posters. Booker's workers retaliated. The campaign looked like a contest between a choirboy (Booker) and a clubhouse brute (James). James won by a comfortable margin. But James, beleaguered by federal investigations into his dealings and travels, quit prior to the 2006 mayoral contest, leaving the task of defending City Hall from the upstart Booker to Ronald Rice Sr., his former deputy mayor and a state senator.[17] Rice was not a strong opponent for Booker, although he had long served the Newark community as a police officer and civic leader prior to being elected to the city council and later to the state senate. The Booker team had a campaign fund of over $6 million while Rice raised about $250,000. Booker did not have much to run on except his well-publicized demonstration against drug dealers. Rice had been a fairly low-key, I-will-fix-your-potholes kind of politician. He was well liked by those who had directly benefitted from his service, but his message was nothing unusual. It certainly did not provide a spark. He was no match for the high-octane, well-financed Booker campaign. Moreover, many voters saw Rice as a continuation of the worst of Sharpe James, which was not hard to understand, given that while he served as deputy mayor to James, he also held another post as a public relations aide to a private housing developer in the city.[18]

Booker was by this time approaching celebrity status as a result of the documentary *Street Fight*, which covered his unsuccessful race against James in 2002. The film was produced by Marshall Curry, one of Booker's friends and a scion of the Curry family, owners of the investment firm Eagle Capital. The Currys were among the most generous contributors to Booker's campaigns and to the city following his election as mayor. Booker won in a landslide, capturing 72 percent of the vote, and all the city council candidates who joined the Booker team also won, thus sweeping out several members who served during the tenure of James. One of the victorious council candidates was Ronald Rice Jr., who supported Booker against the candidacy of his father, Ronald Rice Sr., showing that in Newark, politics can be thicker than blood.

Cory A. Booker, Mayor of Newark

"The future is now. . . . The future is Newark," Booker proclaimed on July 1, 2006, when he was sworn in as the city's first new mayor in twenty years. The central theme of his inaugural address was the city's crime problem. He implored residents to join him in reclaiming the streets from the bloodshed and violence that stained the city. "Will you stand with me?" he loudly exhorted his carefully handpicked audience, who needed tickets to attend the event at the New Jersey Performing Arts Center. Again, he shouted, "Will you stand with me?" And the audience rose to their feet, and yelled, "Yes, yes!"[19]

Booker promised to introduce a package of reforms that would change the city's organizational chart. His administration would not be run on "politics or patronage, but on professionalism." He vowed to introduce new legislation on ethics. In the short run, with the council members and mayor bound together by the hefty donations Booker received from his friends throughout the country,

STREET FIGHTS ARE NOT UNUSUAL

Street Fight is a slick film that portrays Cory Booker as a visionary young man who wants to clean up one of the worst cities in the nation. He is thwarted by this thuggish, undemocratic, unfair, name-calling mayor, Sharpe James. To heighten the drama and capture the concern of supporters outside Newark, the film suggests that James's kind of tough, below-the-belt campaign is a rarity, perhaps a new threat, in American politics. The film, hyped to the heavens, was nominated for an Academy Award and won Booker lots of campaign cash and sympathetic followers. When I saw the film at the Tribeca Film Festival in New York City, it was introduced by a young woman who said the film showed "major violations of human rights that had occurred right here at home, right across the river." While James did play hard with Booker and foolishly displayed anger often enough to make the film credible, the election was typical of thousands of local, hotly contested ethnic and racial elections that have taken place through the ages across America. The film was treated as though it was based on objective reporting. *Street Fight* became an important tool for Booker and showed the young politician's particular ability to tell his story, at times with grand embellishment and convenient distortion. In the 2010 reelection campaign, the Booker team used some of the same tactics Sharpe James was condemned for in the film.

the team approach lessened the potential mayor–council conflict that characterized the administrations of his predecessors.[20] (For a time, it also removed the constructive tension between the executive and legislators.)

Booker's key appointments to department heads brought new talent to the city. Booker quickly revealed that he thought differently about the racial distribution of jobs and positions that had prevailed under James, who clearly favored hiring African Americans. He named Bo Kemp from New York, an African American and a graduate of Yale University and Harvard Business School, as business administrator; Aneh Chandy, an Asian American, was named to corporation counsel; and Toni Griffin, an African American from Washington, DC, was appointed as director of the planning department.

Booker then took a very bold step in choosing Garry McCarthy, a high-ranking white officer from the New York Police Department, to become police director. McCarthy stayed for one term and then landed the job heading the police force in Chicago. His replacement was another risky pick, Samuel DeMaio, who had been in the department for twenty-three years. Until Booker became mayor, Newark had not had a white police director since the early days of the Gibson administration in the 1970s. Whites were also chosen as finance director, deputy mayor for redevelopment (Stefan Pryor, one of Booker's classmates from Yale), and directors of the fire department and engineering department. Pryor left after three years and was replaced by an insider, Adam Zipkin. Maria Viscarrondo, a Latino and native Newarker and former United Way chief executive officer, was appointed to head the health and welfare department; and Pablo Fonseca, who headed the code enforcement department under Sharpe James, was Booker's initial chief of staff. Ronald Salahudeen, who had been active in Newark and Essex County politics for many years, was appointed deputy mayor for public safety. Salahudeen distinguished himself by being the first member of the Booker administration to get caught taking bribes to fix demolition contracts for the new arena site. Salahudeen was convicted and sentenced to one year in jail.[21]

While the top echelons of appointments seemed balanced, it was not long before blacks in Newark began to complain about the cadre of outsiders Booker had recruited.[22] To fill lower-echelon jobs, more nonresidents were brought to the city. As in Gibson's administration, the appointments went to a mix of whites, blacks, and Latinos. Newark does not have an abundance of highly trained professionals among its residents. There is talent within the black and Latino neighborhoods, but those who are well educated and have skills are likely to be already employed in the region or in New York. It is a difficult balancing act for any chief executive of a poor city to mix and blend locals with outsiders, who are an absolute necessity. How messages are conveyed and whether or not insiders and outsiders are treated in the same manner, with the same opportunities for advancement and with the same pay scales, is one of the trickiest challenges. The perception among many Newarkers, and supported by people who work at City Hall, is that Booker clearly favored outsiders over local people, and when he hired local people for city jobs, there was a clear tilt toward Latinos.

The fact is that Booker hired Latinos, blacks, and whites, but Latinos received a greater number of key jobs than they had in the past. For example, the heads of the municipal court, the workforce development agency, and corporation counsel were Latino, and there were key Latino operatives on the mayor's staff. The stronger and broader presence of Latinos has served to deliver more benefits to the Latino community. For example, more workforce and training contracts went to Latino organizations. This approach can be understood in political terms, for Booker's major support for mayor came out of the North and East Wards, both heavily populated by Puerto Ricans and other Hispanic groups. Latinos are the emerging force in Newark politics and make up the major bloc of the Newark base of Steve Adubato's political machine. On the other hand, blacks are declining in numbers (as a percentage of the population) in Newark and have lower levels of voter registration and turnout, although they remain the largest group in the city. Booker had what might be called a tenuous relationship with the black community. While his appointments seem balanced, and perhaps represent the changing demography of the city, they represented a new political alignment and a sensitive issue for black voters.

Following Booker's inauguration in 2006, in addition to his continued focus on crime, he unveiled a sweeping array of reforms and proposals, including ethics reforms (all of which were quickly approved by the city council). There were plans for new housing as well as new and refurbished parks. The ethics reforms required disclosure of contributions by contractors, an end to developers making political contributions within a year of doing business with the city, and an end to candidates for office taking campaign contributions from city employees. Mayor Booker seemed serious about a transformation.

Newark, USA

In 2008, two historic events profoundly affected American life and opportunity and the political fortunes of Newark and Mayor Booker:

Barack Obama, an African American, was elected president of the United States and the American economy went into a recession that was deeper than at any period since the Great Depression of 1929. President Obama's elevation to the White House was an extremely inspiring occurrence for many citizens of all races. It was also a major sign of encouragement for Newark, since Mayor Booker had campaigned nationwide for Obama and the new president had spoken passionately about the urgency of addressing poverty and the problems of urban areas. President Obama also had highlighted "green jobs" as a key feature of his economic policy agenda, which Mayor Booker also considered an important goal in Newark. The city surely would have friends in Washington. Obama's election also invited increased speculation that someday Booker too might lead the nation.[23]

The economic story was a different matter. Newark, like the entire state, was hemorrhaging jobs from 2008 to 2010. During that period, Newark's unemployment rate went from 7.4 percent to 14.5 percent. In numerous cities across the nation, many struggling families could not meet their mortgage payments and thus lost their homes to foreclosures. The crisis hit Newark very hard, beginning in 2006. Defaults often occurred in the newly built homes that a few years earlier political leaders had pointed to as signs of the city's recovery. There were fourteen hundred foreclosures in Newark by 2009, and several hundred families were behind in mortgage payments. Default rates soared to 20 and 30 percent, and credit systems were frozen, leaving many of Booker's new development ideas with no financing.[24] IDT, a communications company located in downtown Newark, which had been touted as a symbol of an emerging high tech sector in Newark, went bankrupt in 2010. The major residential renovation at 1180 Raymond Boulevard, which brought middle-class professionals to downtown, as well as the adjacent commercial building at 744 Broad Street, went into bankruptcy. Symbolically, the July 2008 departure of the Starbucks coffee shop on Broad Street in the center of the downtown was a devastating blow. The loss of the Starbucks was reported in the New York Times in a story that hinted at a reversal in the city's struggle to recover.[25] The plans for a large new hotel next to the Prudential Center fell off the table, as did other plans. A large pharmacy that was part of the Springfield Avenue revitalization closed operations.

Not Easy to Please the Voters

Booker was not deterred from voicing his ambitious ideas and persuading wealthy donors to support activities in the city. One might have thought that by espousing an ambitious agenda that addressed Newark's challenges in creative ways, Booker would have won over every community in the city. However, after two years in office, Booker's political support, particularly in black neighborhoods, was fragmented and uncertain.[26] Adubato said that Booker's first year was the worst he had ever seen. Al Keuppe, president of the Newark Alliance, a business-supported nonprofit that focuses on education, public safety, and development, said that "when you are on the outside looking in, the problems look a lot simpler. When you are on the inside, the problems have another character." Amiri Baraka said, "Some people around the city are beginning to call this place 'occupied Newark.'" After one year, Booker admitted, "I'm worn. Everything is hard. I've been losing my temper more."[27]

The most vocal complaints came from the South Ward, the bastion of Sharpe James. It may be fair to say that no effort, no matter how significant for the improvement of Newark, could completely stamp out the intense loyalty James's constituency holds for him. It was also likely that James's backers as well as other residents of the city shared an intense sense of xenophobia, and for some people, Booker, the outsider (although he had been in the city more than fifteen years), could do nothing right. I am often reminded that Newark may be New Jersey's largest city, but it remains a village.

Booker did not live up to his promises not to run a government based on favors. Shortly after he took office, contracts were issued to law firms that had been among his major supporters. He has not balanced his need to recruit loyal outsiders to his team with the need to show a degree of confidence in local people (with one exception — Pablo Fonseca, who had been a city employee and political operative for many years, has been a close confidant of Mayor Booker). For

the most part, he has appointed people who have impressive educational credentials but lack the toughness and wisdom needed to
run a city. His weekly activities—when he was in town—were built
around announcements, press conferences, and media events boast-
ing of improvements, many yet to materialize. "He can't sit still for a
day without having a press conference or giving a speech," said Carl
Sharif, his former campaign manager.[28] Some of his press and media
ventures do not help him at all, like the photos of him escorting
young males to the movies. "Can't our mayor find a better use of his
time?" a neighbor asked me, not recognizing that this kind of photo
op was intended to give the impression that the mayor is really connected to the people of Newark.[29]

A five-part Sundance Channel series called *Brick City* caused
outright anger among many Newarkers. Produced by Marc Levin,
who over the years has been strangely fascinated with the under-
belly of black life, *Brick City* glorifies gang life, makes the police and
Booker look good, and makes Newark look very bad. In one particular scene, a high school vice principal spoke of a young girl with
an obnoxious body odor explained by the fact that "they found used
condoms in her vagina." That was in episode two, the point at which
many Newarkers I know said they had enough and refused to watch
another minute of it. There is not a single hard-working family in
the series. The young people who want to do better are mentored by
a gang girl who clearly needs some heavy-duty mentoring herself.
As one review of the series noted, "The middle class of Newark are
simply left out."[30] In Levin's *Brick City*, there is no presence of business organizations. Mark Levin told me that Booker and his advisors participated in the editing of the series, but ultimately, "we were
interested in making a good movie for Sundance. We are not the
Chamber of Commerce."[31]

Shortly after the airing of *Brick City*, there was condemnation of
the series from Newark's schoolteachers, community activists, ministers, and business leaders. Then, conveniently for Booker, Newark
was ridiculed on a late night talk show hosted by Conan O'Brien.
In response, Booker proclaimed that O'Brien would be barred from
ever visiting Newark, as though he had the authority to carry out
such a silly threat. After the back and forth went on for a few days,
O'Brien announced that Booker would appear on his late night

show, thus giving Booker a chance to promote his city to millions of people and override the flap about the *Brick City* series. When he did appear, O'Brien, after some additional vacuous joking, handed Booker a check for $50,000 to be used for Newark programs. It is not clear why and how all this happened, but one interesting related fact is that Cory Booker and Conan O'Brien are represented for speaking engagements and appearances by the same company, Greater Talent, owned by one of Booker's donor friends. At one point during their on-air exchange, O'Brien said to Booker, "You handled this very well."[32]

The Cultural and Political Gap

Booker, with more than 1.3 million followers on Twitter, is clearly a man of the media, and used every modern technology to promote himself and his vision of transforming Newark. His frequently voiced large and clever tales have made him much like a tabloid newspaper whose bold headlines are often several times removed from reality. The following story is another example of Booker's clever but deceptive use of the media.

In December 2010, a major snowstorm hit the city. The snowplows had not arrived on my block in the West Ward, although the storm had ended several hours earlier. So I called Mayor Booker on his cell phone, and within a few minutes he called me back. I told him of our neighborhood's problem, and he said, "We are going to get the plows there. Give us an hour or so." The plows never arrived that evening. Later I turned on the television and was shocked to hear a report that the mayor of Newark was out shoveling driveways for elderly people. He had used Twitter to respond to calls from residents to help them dig out. The next day, I drove through the entire ward and much of the Central Ward. The areas I observed were in very bad shape. Very little, if any, plowing had been done. The management of the cleanup effort was a near disaster. However, on the airwaves and in the newspapers, Booker was being praised as a leader who knew how to handle a snowstorm. One news report suggested that Mayor Michael Bloomberg of New York, who also faced difficulties with his snow removal effort, could learn a few things about handling snowstorms from Cory Booker. As a result of Booker's timely snow shoveling, the city of Newark was given an award as the Best Government Twitter feed![33]

Booker's thirst for a photo op, a media appearance, a chance to make a speech has become well known among his City Hall colleagues as well as other political leaders, and several were eager to share their observations on this point with me. A former aide to former governor Jon Corzine learned of this during his tenure when Booker virtually took over one of the governor's press conferences. When Booker attended the Democratic National Convention in 2008, he spent most of the week in press meetings aimed at boosting his national profile. According to one of his staff members, he arrived at the convention with twenty-one scheduled newspaper, radio, and television interviews. Booker has, however, learned that sometimes things can backfire. For example, in speaking before a white audience in Summit, New Jersey, a town more like Harrington Park than Newark, he spoke about a Newark woman who was a school advocate and had recently died. He said the woman had taken a hundred-dollar bribe from Sharpe James, that her front teeth were missing, and she cussed a lot. The next morning, Newarkers saw the speech on YouTube. The woman's family was enraged. Booker's critics cited this as evidence of his lack of understanding of the community and disrespect for black residents. Booker apologized, but the damage had been done.[34]

One afternoon, I talked to Rahaman Muhammad, a Newarker raised in one of the city's housing projects, who offered an interesting interpretation of Booker's political life and why he has not tried to court the black residents of Newark. Muhammad is from a troubled family. He quit school at the age of sixteen but later went back to earn a general education diploma. He joined the union (Local 617, Service Employees International Union) as part of the maintenance staff of the Newark Housing Authority, and in 2009 became the local's president. It has three thousand members in the Newark unit, all of whom live and vote in Newark. Muhammad, who also holds a seat on the statewide American Federation of Labor–Congress of Industrial Organizations governing board, represents a major force.

Muhammad was also a member of the Newark Youth Coalition, a group that embraced Booker when he first moved to Newark in the 1990s. The coalition, according to Muhammad, helped to plan and stage most of the public protests Booker engaged in during his years on the council. "I understood early on," said Muhammad, "that Booker was not the person he was made out to be by his supporters. I felt, however, that if he got elected, he would build a team that could deliver on his promises. Booker hired a lot of people from outside of Newark who not only did not understand the city, but sought to take revenge against the older leaders of Newark. I was not always in agreement with those leaders, but you cannot deny the service they rendered." Muhammad said that Booker had a narrative that was given to him by an elite group of people who foresaw him as a governor or president someday. Booker, he said, "was so locked into the long-range narrative that he did not even bother to establish relationships with the people who supported him." Muhammad added, "Sharpe James understood the community. Booker does not."

Muhammad's final story helps to explain why Booker has made so little effort to befriend black voters. He said that after Booker was elected, he began to hear so much criticism of the mayor among members of the black community that he decided to make Booker aware of the situation. Much to his surprise, Booker simply said: "Don't worry about it. I only need 30 percent of the black vote." Muhammad said that he realized that the mayor was not incorrect. But as a black mayor of Newark, New Jersey, "Why would you say it, and why would you want that?"[35] It may be that Booker's main interest was simply numbers and demographics. Since he was out of the city so often, he would not have a lot of time to cater to constituents who did not turn out in force for him. I asked a person at City Hall who was given a top job by Booker, "What could Booker do to improve his connection to the city and its people?" He said, "He just needs to be here more."

Getting Local

The most difficult challenge for Mayor Booker was to build a political constituency at the neighborhood and ward levels. Political leadership, as opposed to office holding, rests in the ability to control local districts and thus have a say in choosing ward chairs of the Essex

County Democratic Party. For example, the family of late Congressman Donald Payne had a loyal following of district leaders who controlled the South Ward for many years. Ron Rice Sr. has long held sway over the district leader selection in the West Ward. The Central Ward has in recent years been hotly contested by several factions, but for many years the district leadership was controlled by a cast of older black politicians. Adubato dominates over the North Ward and in recent years, he has also played a role in electing a ward chairman in the Central Ward. The East Ward is dominated by Joe Parlavecchia, a long-time political operative and former county freeholder who is closely tied to Adubato.

Booker made several efforts to build a base of support after the 2006 election. In March 2007, he began by backing a slate of candidates to run for the Democratic nomination for assembly and senate seats in the state legislature. Standing hand in hand with six legislative hopefuls seeking to capture seats in the state senate and four in the assembly in a June primary, Booker said, "It's time to bring new ideas and energy, but more importantly, it's time to bring in people who are willing to work together."[36] One of the senate aspirants was Teresa Ruiz, who was pushed into the race by Adubato. The strength behind her candidacy included all the political functionaries of the Adubato machine, plus the forces aligned with County Executive Joe DiVincenzo, who is also a product of the Adubato machine. Ruiz won by a landslide, beating Assemblyman William Payne to run for the senate seat vacated by Sharpe James. State Senator Rice beat back a candidate supported by Booker. The race made it ever clearer that Adubato, not Booker, was the decisive power; Booker produced little support for his own candidates. Adubato said the performance of Booker's forces in the race was "pathetic."[37]

In June 2007, Mayor Booker fielded a slate of candidates for district leader in the South Ward and in the Central Ward. In the South Ward he was defeated by a slate backed by the Payne family; Booker's candidates won only ten slots out of eighty. In the Central Ward, where Booker hoped to have his deputy chief of staff become chair of the ward Democratic Party, the Booker slate did better but not nearly well enough. A slate of candidates backed by Adubato won about thirty-two slots and a slate backed by Booker won seventeen. Adubato was jubilant in recounting the story to me. "We kicked Booker's ass," he said.[38] A slate fielded by Blonnie Watson, a county freeholder who held the position of Democratic Party ward chair, produced fifteen winners. Adubato, who was critical in helping Booker become mayor, said he got involved in the Central Ward races because he did not want Booker to gain power over the ward. Adubato was eager to promote Booker as the leader of the city, but he did not want to help him build a base in the city, thus assuring that Booker would remain dependent on his machine. Watson and Adubato joined forces to pick the chair, a staff member at Adubato's North Ward Center.[39]

In November 2008, Booker had another opportunity to test his strength in the Central Ward. Dana Rone, the council representative who had taken office in the Booker team sweep in 2006, was removed from her position because she had attempted to dissuade a police officer from carrying out his responsibility. Charles Bell, who had previously served on the council, and had, during the Gibson years, served as president of the school board, gained the support of Adubato in a race for the seat. Again, Booker had his own candidate, Eddie Osborne, an official in a local union. Bell, clearly of the old guard, draped his candidacy in the garb and slogans of President Obama, and with Adubato's machine behind him, defeated Osborne by a large margin.[40]

Chambers and Adubato to the Rescue

As the 2010 election approached, Booker began to worry, and so did one of his important supporters. While his national popularity was reaching new heights, his local power was in question. Everyone who attempted to win anything with the mayor's support met defeat. Adubato made signs that he thought Booker might be finished in Newark and considered not backing him for reelection. Ray Chambers, sensing the difficulty Booker would face without the political boss's support, brought Booker and Adubato together, got them to mend their fences, and brokered a renewed alliance between them.[41]

Shortly after the Adubato–Booker fence mending was complete, the Oprah Winfrey Foundation sent $2 million to Cory Booker to be distributed by Newark Now to nonprofits doing good work. By any measure, Steve Adubato's organization would qualify, for his programs are excellent. His charter school received $500,000 from the gift.[42] The timing was exquisite. For Adubato, the alliance made a lot of sense and was perhaps inevitable. Since 1970, when he emerged as the responsible voice among the frightened and angry Italians in the North Ward, Adubato has made peace and forged a working alliance first with Gibson and then with James. Holding a grip on Newark politics is a central feature of his power, although his range of influence extends throughout Essex County and through much of the state. His power is built on three things: a network of highly successful social programs (including one of the nation's best-performing charter schools, which serves the predominantly Latino North Ward); a disciplined cadre of election workers who are superbly trained and are expert at getting their constituents registered and out to vote on Election Day; and a network of loyal politicians and carefully placed government workers, including the key staff at the county election commission, who owe their paychecks to Steve Adubato.[43]

The social programs give the North Ward Center an honorable cause; Adubato's political network gives the center raw power. His power delivers foundation grants and government funds, which in turn rationalize and enhance his power. All of this is managed by Adubato himself with a daily routine of wheeling and dealing, exchanging favors, and building his political strength. Adubato has extraordinary political intuition and stays on top of his domain, even at the age of eighty in declining health. He is admired and feared by many; he is particularly loathed by some politicians and activists in the black community who bristle at his bad manners and occasional crude outbursts. The bottom line is that they envy his empire. He will remind all who will listen—and any conversation with him is frequently interrupted by his command to "listen to me"—that blacks have had political dominance of the city since 1970 and the worst schools in the city are in the black neighborhoods. One of his mantras is "Many children are dying a bloodless death in the public schools." It is hard to argue with him on that point, although through the years, he has been a major player in patronage distribution and the seedy politics of the school board.[44]

The Reelection Campaign

With Steve Adubato behind him and the polls indicating that his opponent, Clifford Minor, a sixty-eight-year-old former Essex County prosecutor, had virtually no support beyond the black voters of the South and Central Wards, Booker cruised to victory. Minor was uninspiring, and voters wondered why he had waited until such an advanced age to run for public office.[45] His workers included a cadre of old Gibson supporters and some community activists who had been behind Sharpe James. Their battle cry seemed mainly a plea to take the city back from Mayor Booker and strong criticism of the police director for the high rate of crime in the city.

Booker raised a staggering sum of $7.6 million for his team, which included all nine members of the city council, among them Charlie Bell. Booker's war chest would pay for their campaigns and free them of the rigors of fund-raising. The Booker team drew maximum contributions of $26,000 from the likes of Oprah Winfrey, Gayle King, singer/entertainer Stephanie Mills, Ravenel Boykin Curry III, Ravenel Boykin Curry IV, and Mayor Michael Bloomberg of New York City. Booker was so confident of victory that he appeared at only one candidates' forum. When the returns came in on election night, by the numbers, Booker won a decisive victory, winning every ward except the South Ward, which Minor won by 1,000 votes (see figure 8.1). However, the vote revealed the sharp polarization that had developed in the city between the areas most populated by blacks and the areas most populated by Latinos and whites. The distribution of the vote also highlighted the critical role Adubato played in Booker's victory.

Two of the council races produced huge surprises. In the South Ward, Ras Baraka handily beat Councilman Oscar James, the incumbent and member of the Booker team. James (no relation to Sharpe James), with the Booker campaign cash, outspent Baraka by at least 20 to 1. But Baraka, a principal of one of Newark's high schools and the son of the writer and poet, Amiri Baraka, is an astute organizer; his volunteer team of campaign workers out-hustled and outsmarted the well-heeled James and Booker forces.

In the Central Ward race, Charlie Bell faced Darrin Sharif. With two other candidates in the race, Bell led the pack by better than

──────────⟨ FIGURE 8.1 ⟩──────────

Newark Mayoral Election, 2010

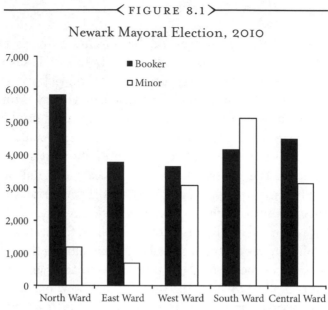

Source: Office of the Newark City Clerk, 2010 citywide election results

1,400 votes but did not receive the majority needed for victory. Thus there had to be a runoff election. Few thought that Sharif had a chance, except for Sharif himself, who proceeded to undertake an old fashioned, door-to-door canvassing of every home in the Central Ward. Ras Baraka's volunteer force moved into the Central Ward to help Sharif, which was both a significant message for the future and a key factor in strengthening Sharif's campaign. The Booker team pledged to invest $1 million in the effort to save Charlie Bell; Sharif had about $250,000 for both races. Adubato's forces worked for the Booker team and were expected to aid Bell in the run-off contest. Bell was hurt by the revelation that his claim that he had graduated from Rutgers University was fraudulent. When the final runoff votes were counted, Darrin Sharif upset Charles Bell by eleven votes.[46]

Overall, Booker's victory was seriously tarnished. With the massive sum of cash, four years of incumbency, and invitations to the hottest talk shows on television, the mayor had to rely on Steve Adubato once again; he could not protect his team members in the two wards of the city most heavily populated by blacks. How can a mayor promise that he will set a new standard for urban transformation in America if he is not capable of establishing a political base in the city and cannot have political dominance in the neighborhoods and communities that are most in need of transformation? The election left Booker to face that very question.

Booker was utterly upstaged by his city council at the inauguration that marked the beginning of his second term. Ras Baraka gave a fiery speech castigating "political leaders who are more adept at pleasing Hollywood than the people of Newark, and who would sell our precious assets away to people who only want to exploit the city." Gayle King, Oprah Winfrey's sidekick and Booker's friend, sat on stage as one of Booker's guests. Baraka's stiff lecture emboldened other members to declare their independence and remind the mayor he could not run the city alone. The Booker team approach was showing deep strains.[47] Through the following few months, the mayor tried to get the council to approve the establishment of a municipal utilities authority (MUA) to manage the city's water system and assets (more on this later in this chapter). The council turned him down. The defeat on the MUA led the *Star Ledger*, in a jolting editorial, to ask the question: "If Cory Booker cannot manage a city well and has led to such divisive politics in Newark, is it possible for him to succeed to higher office?"[48]

Renewing Development

The new decade brought much better economic times, and despite Booker's lack of support at the neighborhood level in parts of the city, he had impressive successes in moving the city's development program forward. Booker and the council created the Brick City Development Corporation to replace the discredited Newark Economic Development Corporation, which was left in shambles by Al Faiella. The Newark Housing Authority completed several projects during Booker's first term, but the thousand units the mayor claimed to have added during his tenure were difficult to find, if they could be found at all. Thus Booker could not push the development of any major projects during his first term. His staffing patterns in development were weak, but the broken economy made it unlikely that any new ventures would be implemented.

In 2010, Booker persuaded several prominent businesses to locate operations in the city; these included Audio.com, an audiobook company; Pitney Bowes, a packaging and shipping company; and Manischewitz, a kosher products company. Booker also resurrected a hotel project adjacent to the arena that had been planned during the James years, although the final rendition was a scaled-down version. The development of a Teachers Village in downtown spurred a larger plan to build market-rate housing in several locations to attempt to repopulate the city with a mix of middle-class working professionals. In 2011, the Panasonic Company announced that its U.S. headquarters would move from Secaucus to Newark, and the company would build a new office tower downtown. In 2012, Prudential announced plans to build a new $444-million office tower a few blocks north of its present headquarters.

It is difficult to apportion credit for major developments such as the Panasonic or Prudential office towers. State economic development policy has made a timely difference. An economic development grant can provide 20 percent of a project's financing, and the Urban Transit Hub Tax Credit can provide a 65 percent saving on rent for companies that move to a built-to-suit location in nine New Jersey cities. It was this credit that paved the way for the Panasonic development as well as the Prudential tower. Clearly, some of the developments, such as the restaurants and new housing adjacent to the arena, are the result of the revitalization potential of the entire area around the facility. Both new business towers are subsidized by hefty state tax concessions—$125 million for the Panasonic building and $250.8 million over ten years for the new Prudential tower—made available through two state initiatives to spur development. Moreover, the city granted the Panasonic project a thirty-year tax abatement.

Some of the development that took place should be seen as continuing the pace of downtown growth that goes back to the construction of the first Gateway project as well as the PSE&G headquarters in 1977. Still, Booker can rightfully claim credit for making a strong case for Newark: he did not tarnish the process with underhand deals and had his staff facilitate the development process. More to the point, a business leader told me that the Panasonic project was initially started by the president of a local university, but, ultimately, the chief executive of Panasonic said he admired Cory Booker and thought it would be a good idea for his firm to be in his town. Clearly, the Booker factor helped to close the deal.

Development manifested in other forms, too. In providing services to neighborhoods and poor families, cities primarily rely on the traditional departments—police, fire, sanitation, and health—and the jobs and health programs funded by the state and federal governments. While all of these efforts are essential to the well-being of communities, they often do not provide easily accessible services in poorer neighborhoods. The Booker administration initiated an impressive program to bring counseling and other services to poor neighborhoods through the Family Success Centers.[49] The centers, run jointly by the city and Newark Now, were new efforts in some cases; in other cases they were piggybacked on to existing service centers run by nonprofit organizations like the North Ward Center and the New Community Corporation. They are funded in various combinations by the city of Newark, the county, the state, and the Nicholson Foundation, a private charity that has taken a strong interest in Booker's administration. Other local foundations have also contributed to the centers. While the centers are not uniform in structure, size of budget, or capacity, all of them are reaching needy families and children, and in some cases, helping them to find a better path. The centers have helped a range of people, including a mother of a seven-year-old daughter who needed a pair of glasses after she lost sight in one eye as a result of domestic violence. The centers provide blood pressure screening; community forums on child abuse; and collaborations with other agencies to provide classes on nutrition, family health issues, and HIV/AIDS testing.[50]

Mayor Booker also intended the centers to have a political role, in terms of helping him reach out to the communities and win electoral support. That is perhaps the reason Newark Now was given the role of being the intermediary and given oversight of the centers. Center staff attempted to mobilize residents to support administration political battles. The centers are clearly an important innovation, but the oversight of the centers by Newark Now and the reliance on grant money raises the obvious question: What will happen to the centers after Booker? Perhaps they will survive, perhaps not. If the resources are available, services can be more accessible and closer to where they are needed. The issues of crime and safety are, however, far more complicated.

Fighting Crime and Managing the Police

In December 2006, about six months after he assumed office, Mayor Booker spoke to a group of regional business leaders at the New Jersey Performing Arts Center. He spoke of the often-forgotten message of Adam Smith that capitalism had the obligation to spread wealth and well-being for everyone, and said his goal was not simply to reform City Hall but also to make the city economically robust again. He spoke of the absence of leadership that had rendered the city unaccountable and promised that his major focus would be on safety and security because "nothing is more important." The drug problem was tearing Newark apart, he said, and "every single murder in the last year has been related to drugs." He would direct his new police director, Garry McCarthy, to start a vigorous enforcement of the law, going after quality-of-life crimes that often lead to more serious offenses. The city would strengthen community policing and put more officers on the streets.[51]

High crime in cities is the costly payback of social isolation, poverty, and hopelessness, the outcome of limited opportunity and inferior education. Crime was prevalent in America's ghettos in the nineteenth and early twentieth centuries when the inhabitants were European immigrants. And so it is today when the ghettos are populated mainly by Latinos and descendants of slaves. Oppression, poverty, and crime go hand in hand, whether in Detroit, Baltimore, Atlanta, New Orleans, Philadelphia, or Newark. All the cities I just named have poverty rates that hover around 25 percent or above. We are often led to think about crime in personal terms, a criminal and an unlucky victim. But crime has devastating effects on the life and health of a community. The costs weigh heavily on city budgets. It is a major impediment to economic development; it can make the pathways to schools unsafe. Crime creates fear and isolation for elderly people, who are often vulnerable to violent street crime. The late George Hicks, a reformed addict and criminal, once explained to me that "any thug seeking to rob will likely target someone in-capable of fighting back—an aged person is the best target." There are numerous and powerful reasons for any mayor to worry about the rate and impact of crime and to try to do something about it. But to be successful at it, the police department has to be managed effectively. And that is no small order in Newark, where the police department has a long history of mismanagement, abusive behavior, corruption, and staunch resistance to change.

McCarthy was a seasoned, high-ranking police official, with a record of leading innovative strategies to fight crime. He had years of experience working in some of the toughest areas of New York City's South Bronx and Upper Manhattan. Nonetheless, his entry into Newark was met with traditional patterns of dislike of outsid-ers, and a bit of backdoor politics at City Hall. When Mayor Booker announced that his police director was a white official from New York City, there were many voices of dissent in the black community, including some members of the city council. While McCarthy had a good record of fighting crime in New York, he had just prior to his appointment been involved in an altercation with a Palisades Park-way police officer who had ticketed McCarthy's daughter for illegal parking. McCarthy apparently went into a "protective dad" mode and spun out of control. Some Newarkers justifiably thought that Booker was taking one of the NYPD's bad cops who did not seem ready to fit into Newark's challenging scene.

Booker initially had his way with the council, and McCarthy was approved. The confirmation vote was just the beginning of the battle, for there was considerable resentment toward McCarthy in the upper echelons of the department. Indeed, in the department and among several political insiders, the expectation had been that Anthony Campos, a career officer, would win the director's job. Campos had to be satisfied with the post of police chief. Soon the question of who really runs the department, the police director or the police chief, came into play. McCarthy, after reviewing the strength and deploy-ment of the department's personnel as well as crime patterns in the city, ordered the reassignment of several dozen police officers. Before the new assignments could take place, Campos issued an order to rescind them, apparently persuaded to do so by Booker's chief of staff, Pablo Fonseca. The conflict quickly hit the news columns of the *Star-Ledger*; Booker faced his first internal crisis. A showdown occurred in the mayor's office with Fonseca and a few of the mayor's assistants present. Booker ordered Fonseca not to interfere in the police department, and told him that McCarthy was responsible for all administrative decisions, including personnel assignments. Fonseca had a tantrum and told the mayor that he had a majority of the votes upstairs, referring to the offices of the city council. Fonseca left the meeting licking his wounds and disappeared from City Hall for a few days, during which time he refused to take calls from City Hall.[52] Fonseca apparently got over his pique, and so did Booker. When Booker began preparing for his 2010 reelection campaign, Fonseca left City Hall to become Booker's campaign manager.

McCarthy was now positioned to launch the crime war that Booker had promised. Despite the perceptions and Booker's high-decibel focus on lawlessness, crime had declined significantly over the previous fifteen years, although the city's murder rate has always seemed to have a trajectory of its own. From 1997 to 2006, the violent crime rate in Newark declined by almost half, from 83.30 to 43.17, measured in incidents per 1,000 (see figure 8.2). During those years, homicides showed their customary jagged trend line (see figure 8.3).[53]

In 2006, while the overall crime rate was declining and just before Booker took office, the homicide rate spiked by almost 60 percent. Police Director McCarthy explained that rising homicide rates are partly the effect of more efficient weapons. The Magnum 9, for instance, holds nine rounds that can be fired rapidly, thus increasing the odds that a round will hit a critical part of the target's body. These more lethal weapons are readily available on the streets. In addition, Newark has numerous illicit drug markets, street turfs claimed by various gang-related drug dealers. According to police sources, Newark's gangs are not tightly knit organizations like those in Los Angeles or Chicago. Very often, according to McCarthy, a gang member could be associated with the Bloods, and a week later might belong to the Crips. Contests and violent struggles over turf occasionally occur between members of the same gang. It is the power of the money earned in the drug trade that drives the competition and violence, not the sense of brotherhood and family found elsewhere. A large percentage of the homicides in Newark occur between a shooter and a victim who know each other.[54]

Violent Crime per 1,000 Residents—Major New Jersey Cities

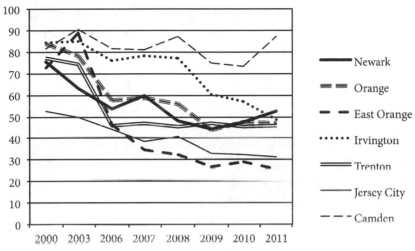

Source: New Jersey State Police Crime Statistics, 2000–2011, www.njsp/info/stats.html

Homicides per Year, Newark, 1997–2011

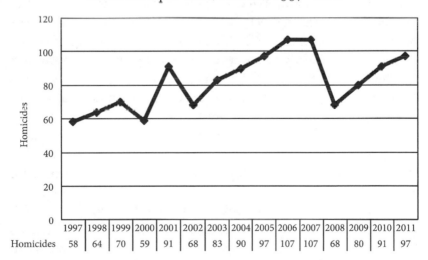

	1997	1998	1999	2000	2001	2002	2003	2004	2005	2006	2007	2008	2009	2010	2011
Homicides	58	64	70	59	91	68	83	90	97	107	107	68	80	91	97

Source: New Jersey State Police Crime Statistics, www.njsp.org/info/stats/html

A NEWARK TRAGEDY SHOCKS THE NATION

The night of July 13, 2007, was one of the worst nights in Newark history. Four young men and women, three already enrolled in college and one on his way, entered a schoolyard in the Ivy Hill section of the city simply to hang out and listen to music. Shortly after they arrived in the yard, a group of six males, ages fifteen to twenty-eight, also entered the yard. The group of men began to threaten the students with a machete and a pistol. The two women in the group were sexually assaulted. Under the threat of death, the young people begged and prayed to be spared, but they were lined up and shot in the back of the head. One of the victims miraculously survived because the bullet lodged in her skull. That the victims were African Americans and all of the people who assaulted them Latino except for one (who was black) led to speculation and threats of retaliation. For weeks, Mayor Booker worked tirelessly to console the families and calm the community. The officers of the law did their job well, and within weeks, apprehended all of the people responsible for the heinous crime. The homicides added strength to the negative perceptions of Newark and concern about public safety in the city. This particular crime, however, was unusual even for Newark, an aberration in almost every respect. First, it occurred in an area of the city with a very low crime rate. There were no drugs involved in the incident and it was clearly not over turf. Law enforcement investigators concluded that the killers belonged to a Latin gang, M-13, active in New York City, and may have been carrying out an initiation order. The only positives of this story are that one of the victims miraculously survived a bullet wound to her skull, and that the assailants have either pleaded guilty or have been tried and convicted. All of them have been sentenced to extremely long sentences, which for almost all of them will be their entire life.[55]

The anticrime campaign took on new meaning for the city following this horrific event. Surveillance cameras and shot-detection technology were installed in high-crime areas. McCarthy increased patrols to high-crime spots and shifted personnel from daytime duty to night patrols, the time when most crime occurs. McCarthy took charge of the Compstat meetings and brought increased depth and analysis to the sessions.[56] He also initiated an approach that he had employed in New York in which strong efforts were made to destroy and disintegrate drug markets that were the source of the competition and crime. Major drug sweeps were conducted. Coordination with other law enforcement agencies increased. The campaign required new equipment and additional personnel, and Mayor Booker diverted funds from other departments to support the drive. Private donors paid for the purchase of surveillance cameras. In the face of impending budget deficits, additional officers were added to the force. "For too long," the mayor said, "Newark has been seen by people as a city of violence and crime, and I will not tolerate it anymore."[57]

Mayor Booker has said his anticrime strategy reduced crime in the city by 40 percent, although McCarthy is more precise and says the city reduced *shootings* by about 40 percent. The only statistic that has shown a significant decline that might be attributed to the anticrime push is the murder rate for 2008. In 2007, there were ninety-seven murders in the city; in 2008, the number dropped to sixty-seven, a number approaching the all-time low of fifty-nine in 2000. That was clearly a major victory. However, since 2009, the rate has moved upward. Booker deserves credit for recruiting a tough, smart cop, which McCarthy surely is, and putting his passion and energy behind the director to make changes. He does not deserve credit for organizing automobile caravans to ride through poor neighborhoods, which had no impact on crime and were nothing more than an insensitive gimmick. The data indicate that in six years of the Booker administration (2006–2011), the reductions in crime generally tracked the trend occurring around the country and in other New Jersey cities. In some New Jersey cities, the rates of crime reduction clearly surpassed Newark's performance, and without the high-profile attention to strategies carried out in Newark. Booker undoubtedly raised awareness about crime in the eyes of the public, both for residents and suburbanites. One might argue that the efforts of Booker and McCarthy, and Samuel DeMaio after McCarthy's departure, put into the anticrime drive prevented things from getting worse. But the data show that only in a few cities did crime increase during the years of Booker's first term.[58] Andra Gillespie, political scientist and author of *The New Black Politician: Cory Booker, Newark, and Post Racial Politics*, offers a detailed analysis of violent and property crime rates for Newark compared to national trends and the trends in other peer cities:

> Overall, the data seem to suggest that the Booker administration's record on crime is mixed. In the case of property crime, the rate began to fall years before Booker became mayor of Newark. Therefore, the Booker Administration can take credit for continuing the progress that began in the previous administration. The changes in the violent crime rate have been inconsistent. . . . No one should begrudge the Newark police director's decision to change the department's personnel policies . . . but by the summer of 2010, those policies had not consistently yielded the desired effect.[59]

The frequent claims by Booker, repeated by Oprah Winfrey, that something extraordinary has occurred in crime reduction in Newark under Booker's leadership cannot be supported by the data. It would be great for Newark, and for the potential in other cities, if those claims were true. But the reality does not reflect negatively on Booker; his upbeat analysis of the crime fight was typical of what many politicians do. Nonetheless, the exaggerated claims ignore the hard truth that crime, and particularly homicide, are not easy to diminish because they are related to long-standing and deeply entrenched problems of poverty and isolation compounded by the easy availability of firearms. That is to say, crime can be abated by well-organized and sustained police strategies, for effective policing does matter. There is much stronger evidence of that in nearby East Orange, where an outstanding anticrime campaign has reduced crime and boosted the public's perceptions of the city in significant and measurable ways.[60]

POLICE–COMMUNITY RELATIONS

In September 2010, the New Jersey Chapter of the American Civil Liberties Union filed a petition with the U.S. Department of Justice (DOJ) requesting that the federal government begin an investigation of the Newark Police Department's practices in handling citizen complaints regarding mistreatment of citizens and misconduct of officers. The petition further asked that the DOJ impose changes in

the manner in which complaints are handled by the Internal Affairs
Division, and also, to appoint an independent monitor to ensure that
any recommended changes would be followed.[61]

The ACLU petition made serious allegations of mistreatment
of citizens and provided evidence of abusive treatment, including
harassment of minority and female officers by superiors. The cases
cited in the petition overlapped both the James administration and
the Booker administration. It was surprising, however, to see the
considerable number of examples of alleged mistreatment—mainly
against African Americans—that had occurred after Mayor Booker
took office and McCarthy took leadership of the police department.[62]

The ACLU focused its investigation on a two-and-a half-year
period during Booker's leadership, from January 1, 2008, to July 1,
2010. The study found that for the 261 complaints filed in the time
frame with Internal Affairs, only one had been sustained. Moreover,
the Internal Affairs Division did a poor job of maintaining records of
its activities and failed to follow procedures for reporting as directed
by the office of the state's attorney general. The petition cited 407
allegations of police misconduct, most of which involved false arrests
and use of excessive force. And from January 2008 to mid-2009, the
city paid more than $4 million in at least thirty-eight litigation settle-
ments and other agreements resulting from lawsuits for police misconduct. The city had been sued more than fifty times over deaths,
false arrests, excessive force, the failure of the Internal Affairs Division to do its job, improprieties, employment discrimination, and
similar matters. The citizens of Newark, the petition said, turned to
the U.S. Department of Justice in a last resort to obtain the relief that
they had been unable to obtain locally.

The ACLU petition, which was almost entirely based on cases that
had already been adjudicated or settled, revealed that there was little
control of abuse from within the department. The lesson of 1967 had
long been forgotten. In May 2011, the DOJ announced that it would
investigate the charges issued in the ACLU petition and appoint a
monitor to oversee a transformation and improvement of the regulations as well as the training and behavior of the Newark police
department. Director McCarthy was vehemently opposed to a monitor, and Mayor Booker has strongly criticized the ACLU's effort.
They both argued that McCarthy was already reshaping the behavior

of the force and a monitor would be an obstacle to improvement. Booker said the ACLU action would end the cooperative relationship his administration had established with the ACLU.[63]

In Newark, the absence of police discipline and respect for the rights of citizens, particularly minorities and the poor, had been an issue for more than half a century. Such matters date back to the 1950s when the Newark Commission on Intergroup Relations noted that the negative views about the police among black citizens could have costly consequences.[64] It is clear that a department with such extensive problems of serious and violent misconduct is very costly to the taxpayers of Newark. Also, a department with such frequent incidents of conflict and confrontation with citizens is not likely to get the maximum out of its crime-fighting efforts, which may help to explain why McCarthy's leadership and introduction of new strategies in the war on crime produced such modest results.

Since McCarthy's departure in 2011, the appointment of Samuel DeMaio, and the presence of the DOJ investigators, the complaints of mistreatment of citizens have declined. Although the department size was reduced by 167 police officers in 2010, it has made improvements in policing and management. The lush pool of overtime pay that had bloated the department's budget was cut back by more than 50 percent. DeMaio added deeper knowledge of the department and the community to the technical advances McCarthy introduced. He reached out to community groups and was more responsive to community concerns. While crime continued to present a major problem to Newark, DeMaio's leadership was much closer to the standards of police management—tough and aggressive, but respectful of citizen's rights—that civic groups have fought for over many years. The DOJ intervention had made a difference, although it has not at the time of this writing in August 2013 issued a report on its finding.

Budget Woes and the MUA Proposal

Immediately following the election of 2010, Mayor Booker announced that the city was in dire financial straits and that the budget for the year 2010 had a deficit of about $83 million. In order to balance the budget, which is required by state law, the mayor proposed that the city establish a Municipal Utilities Authority (MUA) to manage the city's water and sewer assets. An MUA would have the power to borrow against the assets of the city's extensive water system. The plan was to convert a troubled nonprofit, the Newark Watershed Conservation and Development Corporation, into the MUA, thus giving an organization with highly suspect financial discipline increased power and less accountability. It would pay the city about $70 million up front, and make annual payments of $5 million to the city. It would have sufficient funds remaining to pay for much-needed repairs and an upgrade of the antiquated system.

If the city election had not turned out as it had, Booker might have been able to get immediate approval of the creation of the utility authority. But the victories of Darrin Sharif and Ras Baraka profoundly altered the political dynamics of the council. Other members became cautious regarding the notion of an authority; when the new council members proposed public hearings throughout the city on the issue, a majority of the council consented. During the course of one week in August 2010, a hearing was held each evening in successive wards. In every ward, including the North and East Wards where Booker had overwhelmingly prevailed in the election, the opposition to the water authority was strong, indeed intense. A few city employees and a group of young people rounded up by Newark Now showed up with signs supporting the authority. But they were decidedly outnumbered and outshouted by a very large margin.

Balancing the budget with the establishment of an independent authority to operate the water system was a dubious policy step. The major benefit was the one-time payment of $70 million, which would have helped for one year, but even the potential annual donation to the city was contingent on the money's being available. There was no guarantee. Moreover, the authority would have the power to set water rates without any accountability to the voters of the city, the reason many homeowners opposed the idea.[65]

The Newark water system is a unique treasure, and over the years Newark residents have become increasingly aware of its value. Its major reservoirs are located in suburban and semirural jurisdictions far from the city, surrounded by hundreds of acres of priceless, underdeveloped land owned by Newark. Newark's water supply is so abundant that it provides water to several nearby municipalities.

It was the city's plentiful and advanced water system that attracted many of the major beer companies to Newark in the nineteenth century. In the 1960s, Mayor Hugh Addonizio attempted to sell off the water system and watershed lands to private companies but was stopped by legal action initiated by an aspiring young politician named Kenneth A. Gibson. The Sharpe James administration tried to turn over management of the system while the city kept ownership, and that idea met furious opposition.

The budget crisis was not the sole making of Mayor Booker. Sharpe James had run a profligate administration and significantly enlarged the city payroll. James also decided to invest $225 million from the Port Authority in an arena for the New Jersey Devils, and the city spent another $110 million on infrastructure improvements—money that surely could have been spent more wisely to benefit the city. The impending crisis, also fueled by the economic downturn, was not a surprise. Although the financial situation was news to the larger public, the mayor and council members had known for years that the city would face a major financial problem in 2010, since annual payments from the Port Authority would be substantially diminished and state aid was also declining. Nonetheless, Mayor Booker did not plan for it. He kept the facts about the budget from the public and had no plan to address a structural deficit that reached more than $100 million in 2011. An informal budget advisory group set up by the city council, on which I participated as a member, developed an analysis that showed how the city could, with a combination of higher taxes and reductions in the city workforce, balance the budget for five years. The mayor and the council would not countenance a tax increase of around 20 percent, so they preferred to muddle through.

In 2011, the city's budget problems increased. At Governor Christie's urging, the state imposed a 2.5 percent cap on property tax increases, thus limiting the amount of money that could be raised by a tax increase. Curiously, Mayor Booker stood by Governor Christie's side and supported the imposition of the cap on real estate taxes, a policy his own city would not be able to live by.[66] Booker meanwhile continued to press for a municipal utilities authority. In 2012, when the MUA idea surfaced yet again, the Newark Water Group, a civic organization, fought the proposal by petitioning the city council to pass an ordinance that would require a public voter referendum in order to create a MUA. More than five thousand voters signed the petitions asking for such an ordinance, and the council passed the measure by unanimous vote. The Booker administration filed a suit challenging the validity of the ordinance, arguing that it was drawn too broadly and was too restrictive. The court ruled in the administration's favor and said the ordinance could not restrict forever the mayor and council's authority to create such a body. The Newark Water Group, in turn, appealed the ruling, and the case will eventually work its way through the legal system. The MUA drive was checked. As Booker neared the end of his second term and the end of his mayoral leadership, he showed no interest in continuing the battle for an MUA. In early 2013, after Booker had declared his intention to run for a U.S. Senate seat, he filed a lawsuit against the Newark Watershed Conservation Development Corporation (NWCDC), charging the agency with financial improprieties and asking the court to order the return of the functions and assets of the NWCDC to city government. This was a startling development since Booker was the chairman of the governing body of the NWCDC, and the Water Group and the *Star-Ledger* had reported improprieties years before. Booker might have won the battle for an MUA if he had majority support on the city council, which is why he tried so awkwardly and so hard to have a supporter fill a council vacancy.

An Ignominious Battle

In March 2012, Congresswoman Donald Payne Sr. died after serving twenty years in the U.S. Congress. As expected, his son, Donald Payne Jr., an at-large member of the Newark City Council, easily won his father's seat, thus creating a vacancy on the council. The younger Payne had served as council president for two years.

The stakes in the replacement were high for Mayor Booker. The Booker team splintered after the 2010 election, and Donald Payne Jr. voted with a five-member faction that had stopped the implementation of an MUA and opposed the mayor on other actions. If the mayor could get a supporter on the council in place of Payne, the split would shift 5–4 in favor of Booker. All four black members (Baraka, Crump, Sharif, and Rice) favored appointing John Sharpe James, son of former mayor Sharpe James. John James had placed fifth in the 2010 election, just short of winning a seat. In the backroom dealing over the bargaining for position, Councilman Quintana, a Latino who has enjoyed strong support in the black community and usually voted with black council members, decided he would not support James. Instead, Quintana joined Ramos, Gonzalez, and Amador in supporting a black woman, Shanique Speight, the wife of the Central Ward Democratic chair, who worked for Steve Adubato. With the groups split, Mayor Booker thought he could appear and invoke a seldom-used statute that allows for a mayor to cast the deciding vote on appointments if the council is evenly divided.

The James supporters, knowing the mayor's authority in the event of a tie, decided that one of the black members would not attend the meeting and several others would abstain on the vote, thus negating a tie result. When the meeting was held, Mayor Booker made a highly unusual personal appearance to cast the deciding vote with his council allies, none of whom, ironically, were black but were united in support of a black woman for the position. The mostly black audience became angry; after the vote, many stood and chanted, "Cory's gotta go!" When Speight was escorted by police to the dais to be sworn in, a group of residents, led by Rahaman Muhammad, president of Local 617 of the Service Employees International Union, stormed the dais and appeared to lunge toward Speight and her eight-year-old son. Police attempted to restrain the group, but when the demonstrators did not retreat, a police officer doused Muhammad and others with pepper spray. Muhammad was charged with assault and inciting a riot. Councilman Sharif blamed Booker for the fracas. He said, "The mayor, who goes all around the country to talk about democracy . . . literally was in the back of the room, hiding in the shadows." A Star-Ledger editorial called the effort to abort the swearing in "an act of thuggery."[67]

The black councilmen challenged the appointment of Speight in court, arguing that under the prevailing statute, the mayor did not have the authority to cast a vote since there was no tie vote. The court agreed with the black council members and the selection of Speight was ruled invalid.[68] (The seat remained vacant until a citywide election in November 2013.) Aside from the legal questions, it was difficult to determine what side offered a candidate who would add substance and sound judgment to the deliberations of the council. James's claim to recognition was that he was an army reserve major and had served a tour in Afghanistan. He had no convincing portfolio of civic activity or leadership. On the other hand, Speight's claim to recognition was that she had twice won a seat on the advisory school board as part of tickets backed by Adubato. In discussions at the school board, she contributed little. What she would have to offer to the city council, other than to vote as told by Adubato and perhaps to back Booker, was a mystery to me.

The council episode was not a pretty moment for Mayor Booker. There he was, pitted against the preference of the black members of the council, who may have backed a weak candidate but nonetheless represented the majority of residents of Newark. Once again, he demonstrated that the horse he had to ride was Steve Adubato. A mayor with political strength of his own might have been able to fashion a deal without organizing and participating in what turned out to be just another shameful Newark circus.

The Power of Celebrity

To many powerful outsiders, from bankers on Wall Street to stars of television and movies, Booker became a noble cause. If you care about people, and particularly if you care about the decay of American cities and the plight of poor people in urban areas, Cory Booker makes you believe that finally, there is hope. William Ackman, the head of Pershing Square, a multibillion-dollar Manhattan hedge fund, has written large checks to help buy new equipment for the Newark Police Department. Ackman said his first meeting with Booker was one of the most inspirational moments of his life.[69]

"I don't know what else to say. He inspires me," said Drew Katz, who owns a billboard company in Cherry Hill, New Jersey, and donated $100,000 when Booker called after the murder of three young college students in a schoolyard. "He's got tentacles that reach throughout the country in ways that very few mayors of cities of this size have."[70] Oprah Winfrey called Booker a rock star. Bon Jovi, the pop singer, helped to finance a housing project in Newark. Shaquille O'Neal, the former NBA star, and Tiki Barber, the former NFL running back, are also in the Booker loop. Booker has carefully cultivated this following of moneyed and well-known people who have visions of him in the White House someday. Mayor Booker's elevation to the United State Senate is likely to deepen their hopes. They presume they are financing a race to greater heights, and the old city on the Passaic River was merely a stopover. They are his happy horses; he is their gifted jockey. It could be said that in Newark, Steve Adubato's political machine was the lifeline for Booker's Newark political career. Nationally, however, his network of the wealthy and the famous constituted a different kind of political machine, one that has helped him build his own celebrity as he waits in the wings for bigger things to come.

The celebrity game has been an important feature of Booker's tenure as leader of New Jersey's largest city, but it has been a mixed blessing for the city. The city has gained much more media attention during Booker's leadership, and the coverage is more balanced. Celebrity power has brought Newark huge financial gains in the form of new housing, refurbished parks, new businesses, and a record-setting pledge of $100 million for school reform. One would have to conclude that much of this development success was tied in some way to Booker's glittering friendships and his access to big-money players in the financial centers of America. On the other hand, managing a celebrity network, as Booker has done, is another big job, and his absences and celebrity distractions weaken him as a leader of the city. That is why a *New York Times* reporter wrote, "Back in the battered beauty that is Newark, his golden shine has accumulated tarnish at an alarming rate. The budget is busted, he has laid off cops, and crime is climbing. And the political bosses sit snug as ever in their lairs." The writer added, "The mayor's troubles look a lot more self-inflicted. He appears not so adept at the daily bread and butter of running a city."[71]

Grading Mayor Booker

Cory Booker was born in 1969 and grew up at a time when the overt racism of American society that previous generations had witnessed was gone. In understanding politicians like Booker, it is important to note that they did not experience the direct pain of racism. They did not, for example, face insult and exclusion, did not see firsthand the sacrifices blacks and their allies made in the struggles to eliminate the most egregious forms of hate and discrimination. In Booker's youth, there were profound differences in the attitudes of white Americans as contrasted with the period in which Ken Gibson and Sharpe James were reared. Indeed, both Gibson and James grew up as struggling kids in Newark. Booker's generation was bequeathed a society with different formal and informal rules about race, and far greater opportunity. Booker could view the political arena through a different lens, one that presented a picture of a more open society in which it seemed not only possible but imperative to forge political coalitions with other groups. In this new age, some have argued, blacks were essentially like other ethnic groups. Without significant obstacles to hurdle, they could move into the political mainstream. It was, according to some observers, a postracial world, and Booker was a postracial politician. The postracial advocates might ask, "Where's the old racism, if a black man can be elected president of the United States?"

There is however an old adage in politics that says a leader should never abandon his base. Defining, or identifying, Booker's base is not a simple matter. Prior to this age of postracial politics, it was presumed, with few exceptions, that the major base of any black elected official was the black community. When he won his first race for the city council, Booker's base was indeed the black community of the Central Ward, where there were only a handful of Hispanics, and fewer whites. But Booker, as mayor, did not see himself as a candidate carried into office by black voters. Indeed, even for the council runoff in 1998, it was the Steve Adubato machine that came to Booker's rescue. And it was the Adubato machine that later helped to secure Booker's victories for mayor.

William Julius Wilson at Harvard (*The Bridge Over the Racial Divide*) and Edward Glaude at Princeton (*In a Shade of Blue*) both contend that class is becoming far more important in understanding inequality in American society than race.[72] There is surely much evidence that the substantial black middle class in America opens new possibilities and profoundly alters the political landscape. It is also true, as both Wilson and Glaude argue, that cross-racial and

cross-ethnic coalitions are likely to achieve more than blacks working alone or in isolation. However, it is not yet the time to ignore race
and to act as though it is no longer a significant factor in social and
political life. Tim Wise argues that "race neutral policies cannot possibly solve persistent racial inequities, because so many of those disparities are caused by racial discrimination—not merely the residue
of past racism but ongoing racial discrimination in the present day.
Universal efforts, though valuable, will prove insufficient."[73]

In some ways, Booker is a puzzle. Despite all of his visionary
rhetoric and frequent reference to the historic injustices blacks have
experienced, it is not evident that he identifies with black life and
black culture. He has close ties to conservatives and principals at
the Manhattan Institute, a conservative think tank, and some of his
donors are staunch Republicans. He has been a persistent advocate
of school vouchers, clearly a conservative cause. In 2012, during the
presidential campaign, much to everyone's surprise, he defended an
investment firm known for slashing jobs on a Sunday morning *Meet
the Press* show. In the process, he criticized President Barack Obama's
campaign for attacking the firm, formerly run by Obama's opponent,
Mitt Romney. He said the Obama camp's attacks on Bain Capital
were "nauseating."[74]

In 2002, when Cory Booker was running for mayor against Sharpe
James, Martin Kilson, emeritus professor of political science at Harvard University, was surprised to read that George Will, the conservative columnist, had written an essay alerting his conservative
right-wing network about the promising leadership of Cory Booker
in Newark. "Any celebration of Cory Booker's campaign by George
Will and his ilk," wrote Kilson, "must be viewed automatically as bad
news for black people of Newark."[75] In an interview with Bill Moyers
in 2008, Booker was asked about his strategy to deal with the problems that burden America's large cities. His response was, "Don't look
at government to do it, don't look at somebody else, look in the mir-
ror and ask yourself, I benefit from this nation. What am I willing to
do to make a difference in this nation?" Moyers then asked, "You're
saying that to these black kids who are being arrested and being sent
to prison?" Booker stated, "Absolutely. And I've sat with those kids.
. . . We as Americans have to understand that change will never roll
in on the wheels of inevitability. It necessitates sacrifice and struggle."

Moyers responded, "Is that money? Do you need more money?" Booker said, "That's a knee-jerk reaction to spend more money."[76]

Booker then continued with a commentary on the impressive voluntary efforts that he saw as more of an answer to the problems of the city than the infusion of government aid would be. Needless to say, this exchange and Booker's responses could have come right out of a conservative handbook. Was this right-wing politics, or was he simply playing to the national demographics and his long-term interests? He could have said that we both need more resources to address some of the entrenched problems that private efforts will not reach and more civic engagement and action to address some of these issues. Booker has not been bad news for Newark, but it has not been easy to figure out where he stands politically.

Booker brought to Newark a grand vision of urban transformation. He has not, by his personal behavior, raised suspicions of his integrity, although there have been several cases of wrongdoing in his administration. But in governing and managing the city, he has been weak. He displayed little of the political skill necessary to get things done in the city's complicated and byzantine environment. When Booker took office, he preached about a state audit that pointed to a plethora of management failures during the James administration. Since Booker assumed office, a similar audit has found a long list of problems and violations of regulations and city ordinances, many indicating that there is little or no competent supervision in many areas of the city.[77] The much publicized new ethics rules that Booker strongly advocated were ignored by his own office. Shortly after he became mayor, his administration granted contracts to several law firms that had supported his campaign. He gave the son of his campaign manager a sole source contract to develop a website for the city, although the firm was new to the business. The city invested more than $2 million in the project and then had to hire another firm to clean up the job.[78] Booker's nonprofit organization, Newark Now, apparently became the place for donations by contractors who sought business from the city. A report in the *Star-Ledger* found that the donor roll of Newark Now for a golfing charity event listed nine contractors who together gave the nonprofit $19,500. Within a year of making the donations, the companies received $21.5 million in city contracts, according to city records.[79] Booker said that "neither I nor anyone in my administration, to my knowledge, knows that these donations were made and who made them."[80]

While Booker has been mediocre in managing the city, he ironically has more potential than any Newark mayor elected in its modern history. In some respects, that conclusion comes as a result of the shortcomings of Addonizio, Gibson, and James. It is also a conclusion earned by Booker's talents, ambitions, and the results of his daring to lead one of the most complicated and poverty-stricken cities in America. The people in Newark, who initially bought into the vision and the inspiring promises of Booker, ultimately saw a leader who overpromised, did not remain true to his pledges to avoid the traditional shady deals, was not around that much, and could not win the support of the African American community, partly because he did not need it.

Without the Italian American political boss of the North Ward and the friendship of the wealthy Ray Chambers, Booker would have been lost. His constant harping on the negatives of the city was obviously intended to make him appear heroic, but they offended Newark residents and business leaders. Worst of all, he ignored the impending fiscal crisis and made it worse by continuing to add personnel, including some high-level positions, to the city payroll. His unwillingness to give up the effort to establish a Municipal Utilities Authority kept council meetings in turmoil for several years. By the time he decided he was ready to aim for higher office, there was widespread disaffection throughout the city for the celebrity mayor.

In fairness, Mayor Cory Booker faced hard times. The collapse of the economy not only stalled the development momentum the city had under James, it reversed many of the successes. I once described Booker as "idealistic and naïve." The idealism remained strong and it has been appealing to many. However, it also suggests a shallow understanding of the depth and complexity of problems that exist in Newark and urban centers in general. His speeches are more platitudes and dreamy hopes than solid, practical formulas for change. Former New York governor Mario Cuomo once said, "Politicians campaign in poetry, but govern in prose."[81] The problem with Booker was that he both campaigned with poetry and tried to govern with poetry. Dealing with poverty and poor schools requires focus, sustained attention, and leadership; traveling all over the country will not help to negotiate better and fairer contracts with the employee unions. A journalist writing about development almost thirty years ago said, "Most cities learned the hard way that you don't need a charming . . . talker for mayor. You need the toughest, canniest, obsessive son-of-a-bitch in town. You need someone who's going to make it his life."[82] Newark was not Cory Anthony Booker's life.

Booker could have been the kind of mayor many of his supporters outside of Newark believed he was. But he was just too busy looking to that next step.

‹ 9 ›

Pity the Children

Until such time as these reading and arithmetic levels come up, there isn't anyone who can say in the city of Newark . . . we are doing a good job, because these children just can't read or do arithmetic.

—Harold Ashby, president of the Newark
Board of Education, to the Governor's Select
Commission on Civil Disorder, 1968

SCHOOLS ARE THE LENS through which one can understand how a city's leadership carries out its special obligation to children, and to its future. In fact, a city that has suffered extreme loss of its economic base and much of its middle class cannot accurately claim that it has been transformed if a large share of its schools are dysfunctional. That is why I have devoted an entire chapter to education in Newark, a story of school politics and governance that spans more than a half century.

Since the violent summer of 1967, much has changed regarding the organization, management, governance, and financing of Newark's schools. In 1982, Newark voters approved a referendum to install an elected school board, wresting from the mayor the authority to appoint school board members. In 1995, in response to continuing problems of mismanagement and educational failure, the state's board of education took control of the Newark public school district. In 1985, the New Jersey Supreme Court ruled in the case *Abbott v. Burke* that the state had a constitutional responsibility to provide a "thorough and efficient" education for each child, an important victory for the children of Newark and other poor urban districts. Newark was one of thirty-one school districts affected by the *Abbott* decision, which ultimately eliminated the wide disparities in funding between poor and wealthier districts.[1] In 2009, after years of stark differences, per pupil expenditures in urban systems matched those of most wealthy suburban districts; the allocation per student in Newark was $18,378 compared to an average of $15,168 for the state.[2] Still, despite state supervision and the elimination of funding inequities, the Newark school district remains a failing institution.

Newark has the largest school district in New Jersey, with a total of seventy-five elementary and secondary schools and a steadily declining school population of around 35,000. In 2010, the school budget was $940 million; the state pays 72 percent, the city pays about 20 percent, and about 10 percent comes through federal aid.[3] One can find examples of excellence in the district and among the teaching and administrative corps; there are many gifted, dedicated individuals who each day produce outstanding results. However, in more than fifty years, there has been no system-wide improvement; schools with heavily black populations are consistently in the lowest tier of performance. Overall, the system shortchanges the overwhelming majority of children who enter its classrooms. In 2010, merely 36 percent of fourth-graders were proficient in language arts, and 54.5 percent were proficient in mathematics. In several highly segregated elementary schools, proficiency rates in language arts and mathematics were around 25 percent (see table 9.1). Only slightly more than 50 percent of students who enter the ninth grade receive a diploma at the end of four years. The district has one of the highest absentee rates, and in some areas, personal safety within and around the schools is a serious concern.[4]

Only about 17 percent of teachers in the system live in Newark, but the major problems have not been residence but the long-term practices of hiring unprepared personnel, not getting rid of teachers who cannot teach, and having a weak and ineffective administrative system. One parent advocate said, "We see a lot of misfits who come

────────────────────────⟨ TABLE 9.1 ⟩────────────────────────

Newark Charter and Public Schools in Comparison with State Public Schools

	Newark charter schools	Newark public schools	State public schools
Enrollment	5,354	34,086	1,362,596
Percentage receiving subsidized meals	84	82	32
4th grade—percentage proficient in language arts	41	40	63
4th grade—percentage proficient in math	54	54	73
8th grade—percentage proficient in language arts	78	56	83
8th grade—percentage proficient in math	69	42	72
Average cost per student	$13.5	$18.4	$16.2

Source: Advocates for Children of New Jersey, Newark Kids Count, 2010, www.ACNJ.org

to teach in Newark. They know nothing about the social environment."[5] In 2012, almost three hundred teachers were deemed unfit or unable to teach but still drew their paychecks. Issues of performance and failure are widespread, particularly in schools located in the South, Central, and West Wards, where the vast majority of poor black and Latino children attend school.

Since the early 1960s, politicians viewed the schools, which had larger budgets and more jobs than city government, mainly as a source of patronage and deal making. Shortly after his election in 1962, for example, Mayor Hugh Addonizio began to exploit the patronage opportunities at the board of education. As a reward to black voters, he appointed Verner Henry, an African American who worked for the state parole board, to the board of education. Addonizio then quickly engineered Henry's election to the presidency of the board. Addonizio also appointed Harold Ashby, an African American lawyer, to the school board, and a year later, Ashby replaced Henry as president. At the same time, Addonizio arranged for a good number of his supporters and campaign workers to be placed in key education-related positions. He kept tight control over the actions of board members and met with the entire body each month.[6]

A great deal of money flowed from federal programs that were meant to improve the education of poor children. Federal funds simply meant more patronage, however. In 1965, for example, federal and state auditors found that eligibility requirements for receipt of federal funds were occasionally ignored as the money was spread to white middle-class areas at the periphery of the city, areas that were not eligible for the programs. "They were spreading the money around to their friends," a federal official charged.[7] Quay Whitlock, a retired school social worker who joined Newark's board of education in 1968, recalled that rumors concerning payoffs for jobs were rife at the time. Fred Means, a teacher who founded the Organization of Negro Educators (ONE), recalled, "The word around town was that promotions were for sale." Former Newark teacher and administrator Theodore Pinckney said, "The system was corrupt and everyone knew it."[8]

When school board president Harold J. Ashby spoke before the Governor's Select Commission on Civil Disorder during the investigation of the 1967 rebellion, he told the group, "These children just can't read or do arithmetic. Until they are able to accomplish that on a broad base and we have more than six out of every 100 above the national norm, I don't think we can say that we are doing a good job." He added, "I think we are going to have to halt all the camouflage that has gone on for the past ten, fifteen, and twenty years."[9] The commission, headed by Robert Lilly, the chief executive officer of New Jersey Bell Telephone, recommended that the state inject major levels of new resources—money and personnel—into the Newark system. The recommendation fell on deaf ears at every level of government.[10]

Gibson and Education

As Kenneth A. Gibson campaigned for mayor in 1970, his constant refrain was that "children are our most important asset; they are our future." He promised to use the power of the mayor's office to improve education. Through appointment of board members and budget-making authority, the mayor clearly was the most powerful figure in running the schools, although, like any mayor, he had to contend with pressures from other sources such as parents, teachers and their union, and civic groups. It did not take long to realize how strong the pressure could be.

Between 1970 and 1978, when the city council was dominated by white members, Gibson learned that he could not function without the support of the entire body. Consequently he was often a party in discussions with white council members who sought promotions for their constituents. Disputes often arose over personnel decisions, fueled by the allies of the old regime and/or residents of the fringe areas of the city that contested the mayor's power over the schools. If a black person was assigned by the administration to a school in the North or East Wards, the council representative would call Gibson to protest. Gibson would then stop the appointment by calling other members of the school board. This political bargaining often led to sharp criticism from black residents, who were usually surprised to learn that Gibson did not have the power to resist the demands that came from the white councilmen.

Nonetheless, Gibson did not ignore blacks. They continued to gain more teaching, administrative, and supervisory positions. Gibson increased the number of black members on the board of education from three to four. In 1979, three years before the mayor-appointed board was abolished, the nine-member board consisted of two whites, five blacks, one Latino, and one Portuguese American. The president of the board was Charlie Bell, an African American, who became a dominant force in Newark school matters for several decades.[11]

THE NEWARK BOARD OF EDUCATION

Unlike other boards and commissions in city government, the mayor's choices did not require approval by the city council. Therefore, school officials often considered the board an independent agency. But that was not the case: the board's budget was set by a five-member Board of School Estimate, which was chaired by the mayor with two council members and two school board members. Moreover, some board members received their appointments as a result of the support of council members. If a board member had a council member's blessing, he or she was expected to have a good memory when the council member sought a favor.

Life on the board was about politics, trading votes, and favors. School governance in Newark has never been like Robert Dahl's New Haven or Essex County's Montclair, where school board members are classic volunteers. As Dahl wrote of the New Haven school board, they were "unpaid, with career goals, and standards of their own." Likewise, in Montclair, board members have careers or professions unattached to the schools. Their influence and reputation in the community are enhanced by school board membership, but their standing is not solely dependent on board activity. In places like New Haven and Montclair, board members do not feel beholden to the mayor.[12]

In Newark, under mayoral control, most board members were not civic volunteers, but professionals and politicians themselves who served to promote their own political and financial interests. By virtue of the politicking, board members had considerable influence on school decisions. They not only participated in making school policies but also had some say about how financial resources were allocated. In addition, under state law, board members had to approve all personnel actions, from principals to janitors, which rationalized for some board members direct involvement in hiring and firing. The model for board operations was very similar to the old city commission. Through a board committee system, the money, contracts, and jobs were assigned to board members who then controlled decisions in their respective areas.

In examining the roles of members of the board and their voting records between 1974 and 1975, two factions emerged.[13] The two sides, which I label resource distributors and change agents, clearly had different approaches to the board's role and function. Resource distributors were cast in the mold of the classic patronage-dealing political operator; they bargained and dealt for certain advantages and viewed their status as an opportunity to further their own interests or those of their allies. They might have at times supported positive educational initiatives and voted along with the positions of the change agents. However, for them, the game remained the same. The goals of the change agents were more substantively oriented and primarily concerned about the operation of a school system that was in trouble by every conceivable measure. The change agents wanted the board to focus on issues of education; their concern with personnel policy was less about particular individuals and more aimed at the development of policies that would increase minority hiring in the schools and deliver more contracts to firms owned by minorities. They resented the mayor's effort to influence their decisions, and often simply ignored his instructions.

Attachment to one group or the other could change over time. For example, Carl Dawson (later known as Carl Sharif) once sided with the change agents but eventually voted with the resource distributors. In most instances, board members needed no instruction on how to vote since most business was routine. In 1976, of 165 resolutions before the board, 100 were not discussed and 110 were approved by unanimous votes. Nonetheless, the board was far from a unified body. By examining the decisions in which there were split votes, a pattern becomes clear. In twenty-two divided votes taken by the board at public meetings that year, all members I identified as resource distributors agreed with each other at least eighteen times, and three of the five members of that bloc voted together twenty times. On the other hand, the change agents voted together in sixteen out of the twenty-two divided votes. The resource distributors were solidly together in reelecting Charlie Bell as president of the board, while the change agents voted against him. The resource distributors opposed the superintendent's effort to reduce the payroll during a financial crisis; the change agents supported him. The factions were not drawn in an ironclad fashion. However, every change agent position almost always lost. In one particular case, as described to me by a former board member, the resource distributors supported the change agents on a matter with the understanding that the change agents would support the appointment of a particular person as principal of an East Ward school.

One might ask why the mayor appointed Fred Means, a dedicated activist who had been in the forefront of the civil rights struggle, to the board of education; or Vickie Donaldson, leader of a black student takeover of a classroom building at Rutgers University to force school authorities to admit more blacks; or Helen Fullilove, a grand and principled lady, fiercely independent, and dedicated to the city's children. Such appointments were important to the mayor, strange as it may seem. They gave the appearance that he was trying to create a high-quality board, and such stellar appointments gave the board a degree of legitimacy. But the important point is that change agents were *always* in the minority. And despite their commitment to good education and responsible leadership, the mayor would often attempt to enlist them to support his political deals with other board members. According to Means, "Mayor Gibson appointed some good people and asked them to do bad things."[14]

From the time that Verner Henry assumed the role of board president in 1962 and until the shift to an elected school board, all board presidents were black. There was no other president like Charlie Bell, an ardent resource distributor who served four terms as president and essentially converted the Newark school bureaucracy into a political machine. It was somewhat ironic that Bell became a staunch supporter of the Newark Teachers Union, since he had lost his job in the labor movement when he failed to vote for a proposed union contract during the 1971 teachers' strike. The board of education became Bell's life until the appointed school board was abolished. Bell enlarged and expanded the board president's powers and virtually made the board of education his personal fiefdom. Some teachers referred to him as "King Charles." Gene Campbell, who served as executive superintendent from 1985 to 1995, said, "Yes, Charlie was about making deals."[15]

Bell took over the presidency of the board during a period of rather chaotic transition. The superintendent during the Addonizio regime, Franklyn Titus, left his job as a result of a scandal. The interim superintendent, Dr. Edward Pheffer, a thoughtful and dedicated gentleman who had spent many years in the system, could control neither the turmoil from the teachers' strike nor the unrest created by a movement of high school students who eventually ransacked his office. In the face of continuing chaos, Pheffer seemed powerless. Bell stepped in and obliterated the line between governance and administration. Bell wrote directives to department heads, visited and inspected schools, assigned and reassigned personnel, and, on occasion, negotiated contracts. When Bell left the presidency in 1976 (though he remained on the board), the Office of Board Affairs, which up until Bell's leadership had a very small staff and simply saw that board members received materials and their mail, took on a much larger role and became a force in school management.[16] When Bell became a key player in the Newark school system, it was already in disarray. His leadership made it worse, however, for his major concern, despite occasional pleas for better education, was to politicize the system for the benefit of adults. The children of Newark did not fare

well by Bell's life on the school board. Neither did the school superintendents, whose ability to lead was frustrated by Bell's domination
of the system.

A PARADE OF SUPERINTENDENTS

In a school system that produces massive failure, and where management principles are distorted or ignored by political interests, a
superintendent is likely to become the scapegoat. This was a fairly
well established pattern in Newark. Stanley Taylor, a brilliant educator, was the first black superintendent and was chosen shortly after
Gibson's election in 1970. Before coming to Newark, Taylor was a district superintendent in Brooklyn, New York. Outsiders begin with a
significant weakness because they are not likely to have a constituency of parents or civic leaders to support a policy direction. Outsiders also need to know how to relate to and manage the political
system. Taylor simply did not understand Newark politics. He cut
himself off from the resource distributors and he surrounded himself
with a bevy of black junior aides, all from his previous position in
New York. Newark may be a majority-black city, but political relationships and alliances have almost always been mixed, even when it
is not so obvious.

Charlie Bell was president when Taylor was hired, and he negotiated the terms of Taylor's contract. After Taylor signed on to take the
position, Bell opposed the board's efforts to provide Taylor the staff
and resources he had been promised, as well as opposing all of Taylor's efforts to discipline teachers. Former board members recall Bell
occasionally proclaiming when disciplinary issues came before the
board, "I'm a union man." As Taylor tried to change outmoded and
unworkable patterns, pressure mounted for his removal.[17] When the
state commissioner of education appointed a task force to investigate
the condition of Newark schools, Taylor was doomed. Predictably,
the task force highlighted the horrible conditions of the district, the
same problems that had existed for decades. The public was told the
problems were the result of Taylor's incompetence. In 1977, the city
council called for Taylor's resignation. Despite his earnest and strong
efforts to improve the quality of education in the system, he was out.

Then there was Alonzo Kittrels, who had been hired by the district in 1976 to head the human resources department, but was elevated to the superintendent's job on the departure of Taylor. As a result of a new state law that was recommended by a state auditor who thought Newark schools needed business leadership, school superintendents no longer had to be certified as educators. Kittrels conceded that he knew nothing about education but promised to help the board improve teaching and schooling by applying business principles to the management of the district. The business principles never arrived, as the district overspent its budget year after year under his leadership. Board members continued to devote most of their meeting time on job distribution and vendor contracts. Kittrels resigned in 1982 but appeared shortly after as a full-time consultant.

And then came Columbus Salley. Salley had been an assistant superintendent in Chicago. He began his tenure with a burst of activity. He installed learning centers to assist students with homework and launched a campaign to improve attendance for students and teachers. For most of his tenure, he was in a pitched battle with the Newark Teachers Union, which objected to his program to determine why the attendance record of teachers was so low.[18] But Salley had a falling out with Carl Sharif, which put his position at risk. And then he committed an ethical blunder that led to his suspension by the board in 1982. He formed a corporation to purchase fast food restaurants, and his partners in the endeavor were his chief of staff, a lawyer doing work for the school board, and a member of the school board. Most members of the board were irate. After he was suspended he filed legal action and won his job back but instead of returning to it received a hefty settlement of $600,000 and left the system. There was a public outcry regarding the cost of the agreement, and the state promised to investigate. It never happened. Charlie Bell lauded the payout and said it had been necessary to allow the board to refocus on the children.[19]

Next the board hired Eugene Campbell, who had started in the Newark schools as a grade school teacher and moved up through the ranks in the post-riot era when the schools were under great pressure to place more minorities in administrative positions. Campbell was well intentioned, but the reality was that Charlie Bell (followed by Carl Sharif) ran the system and did whatever he wanted. Campbell, for the most part, was a bystander. As the school system faced increasing political pressure on the state house and legislature from suburbanites unhappy over the growing costs of urban education, it became increasing clear that the Newark system would face closer supervision and oversight.

TEACHERS AND ADMINISTRATORS UNITED

The only forces that can rival the politicians and the bureaucrats who run the Newark schools are the teachers and administrators, represented by the Newark Teachers Union (NTU) and the City Association of Supervisors and Administrators (CASA), both affiliated with the American Federation of Labor. The rise of both unions as major forces in school politics was the result of broader economic and demographic developments that altered the distribution of political power in city politics—not just in Newark. Many decades ago, decision making in public school systems was so highly centralized that school boards would yield little, if anything, to teachers or any other group. Teachers had legitimate complaints and often had to contend with arbitrary administrators and ineffective management. However, as the black population of Newark and large cities elsewhere grew to significant proportions, blacks and other minorities demanded a share of the system's jobs and resources. They were often joined by civil rights activists as they recruited parents and neighborhood organizations to protest the poor conditions in the schools or the absence of minorities in key jobs. School officials frequently responded with concessions mainly aimed at stemming further disruptions. In turn, white teachers and professionals often viewed any capitulation, no matter how minor or just, as a threat to their security. As community demands increased, sometimes over a principal or administrator who was considered to be insensitive, the board would often pacify protestors by simply moving a teacher or official to another school.

In 1968, in the aftermath of the civil disorders, every public bureaucracy in the city was under strong pressure to open more opportunities to blacks and Latinos. The school board promoted ten blacks to principal and vice principal over white candidates who were higher on the civil service promotional list. At the same time, the board agreed to end the written and oral exams for promotion, thus eliminating the tools used for years to deny blacks promotional opportunities. The Newark Teachers Association, an affiliate of the National Education Association (NEA), which then represented teachers in the Newark school district, did not challenge the promotions in court. In fact, NEA representatives, cognizant of the historic patterns of exclusion, conferred with board leadership as the promotions were planned and rendered a quiet endorsement of the action. The fledgling NTU saw in this an opportunity. The union brought legal action on behalf of the twelve white teachers who had been passed over for the promotions. Although the NTU did not win the case, the union's aggressive action in support of the white teachers won broad support among the teacher corps and helped it to become the bargaining agent for Newark teachers.[20]

A union has a lot of muscle and political money to dole out; a union can profoundly affect educational practices through its influence in school policy and its strong connections to elected officials, particularly in the state legislature. In exchange for agreeing to provide labor, a union can extract costly concessions that citizens may be unaware of but pay for by provisions found to be common in most union contracts. Unions can severely limit the ability of school leaders to innovate and change some of the most onerous practices that impede reform efforts. This has led much of the public to believe that unions have reoriented the schools to the interests of adults, not schoolchildren. Much of the authority regarding discipline, in-service training, and the assignment and transfer of employees resides in Newark union contracts for both teachers and administrators. The contracts also require that personnel receive financial compensation for what were once considered routine obligations. Since the NTU won binding arbitration in 1971, virtually any matter can be submitted as a grievance. A school official once said, "We have more grievances than a steel factory."[21]

The Newark Teachers Union has not done much to oppose the mismanagement that was so evident at the board prior to the state takeover. On at least one occasion, it joined the party. In the agreements following the prolonged teachers' strike, a supplementary fringe benefit trust was established to provide employee benefits through an insurance provider. The trust was governed by a four-person board, with equal representation from the union and the school board. For the first few years of its operation, the trust kept administrative expenses under control, and by 1976 it had built a reserve fund of $3 million. But in 1984, the New Jersey State Commission on Investigation (SCI) held a series of hearings to examine allegations that the trust was misusing public funds by supporting activities that were fiscally irresponsible and, in some cases, outside of the law.[22] Joseph Visotski, who served as executive vice president of the NTU local, also became the fund's executive director, holding both jobs at the same time. The SCI said that expenses increased as the director led an effort to enrich himself. He sent the trust's board members on frequent junkets to places like Florida, Bermuda, Las Vegas, and San Diego. A major beneficiary of the junket spree was former superintendent Alonzo Kittrels, serving as consultant to the board after he left the superintendent's job. In one year, Kittrels made eleven trips to conferences out of state. Visotski was paid $75,000 to manage the trust, an additional sum to oversee fund investments (which were placed safely in certificates of deposit at a local bank), and a fee to manage the building the fund had purchased to house operations. The SCI concluded that the fund was unnecessary and that the staff of the board of education could handle its functions. The commission expressed its hopes that "this public hearing will discourage any attempt to establish again anywhere in this State a trust entity capable of the flagrant abuses the SCI found at the Newark fund." It called for its abolition and urged the sale of the downtown building, which it characterized as "the single most expensive boondoggle undertaken by the fund." The fund had purchased the building for $80,000 and spent $470,000 on renovations.[23]

Energetic, creative, dedicated teachers who know their subject matter can make wonderful things happen in a classroom, even under the most difficult circumstances. But adequate pay is a necessity in order to have competent teachers. Ideally, there should be no conflict between community and teachers over salaries. Teachers are entitled to reasonable levels of job security; the nation does not honor or pay teachers enough. At the same time, the public, particularly parents and taxpayers, do not want ineffective or incompetent teachers to be shielded by union rules that ignore the interests of children. Good education is a service to the nation, but more fundamentally, it is a service to children, who require it to be able to live productive lives.

Teaching children from backgrounds of poverty and hardship is far more demanding than teaching children who are not hampered by such disadvantages. So while teachers have won release from certain duties, the objective conditions demand more, not less from teachers. Unions have convinced their members that they should resent having to perform "nonprofessional chores," such as walking children to a school bus or supervising a lunchroom.

Provisions in union contracts that allow only one faculty meeting per month and one departmental meeting per month, not longer than fifty minutes, provide an example of how union and school administrators have enabled the schools to be run for the benefit of adults. It is difficult to imagine how any organization could manage under such constraints. The provision in the CASA contract that limits a principal's workday to six hours simply does not make sense. The results of such policies are predictable. When state-ordered education improvement programs are offered, school leaders must always ask, "Would the new program violate the contract?" In-service training workshops have abruptly ended when teachers simply get up and walk out because the time allotted in the contract for such meetings expired.[24] It is regrettable that children in poor communities do not have an organization as powerful as the union on their side.

The Puzzle of School Financing

In 1973, attorney Harold Ruvoldt started a revolution by filing a lawsuit in behalf of a child in Jersey City. The complaint (*Robinson v. Cahill*) argued that the taxpayers and the students of Jersey City were placed at an unfair disadvantage because the city's property valuation per capita was much lower than in more affluent communities. Therefore it was necessary for Jersey City and similar cities with large numbers of poor residents to finance education with a much higher property tax rate than was required in well-to-do jurisdictions. To raise $1,000 for education in a town with average property values of $100,000 versus a town with an average property value of $50,000 meant that the tax rate in the more affluent town would be half the rate in the poorer town. The result was much higher tax rates in poorer cities. There was no way out of this problem as long as the property tax provided the major source of funding.[25]

When the case wound its way through the judicial system, the court held that the state had an obligation to guarantee an "educational opportunity . . . to equip every youngster for his role as a citizen and a competitor in the labor market." Later, the New Jersey Supreme Court found that relying on the property tax to finance education violated a provision of the state constitution mandating that the state "provide a thorough and efficient system of free public schools for the instruction of all children in this state."[26] It was then up to the legislature to make laws to comply with the court's ruling. The legislators did not act until the court took the most drastic action possible: it ordered the closing of all public schools in New Jersey until the legislature developed a school financing plan. Within ten days of the court's drastic action, the legislators adopted a school financing plan in accord with the *Robinson* decision. Thus began a significant shift of the burden for financing schools away from the property tax and placing it more squarely on the general taxation of the state. And that meant, for the first time in its history, New Jersey would have an income tax.[27]

The income tax had several important consequences in addition to providing more resources to urban communities. It led to a new relationship between the department of education and the Newark school board. The department of education increased oversight and supervision of urban districts. The major impact, however, was that the income tax lowered the tax burden for urban homeowners. And finally, it led to increased pay for teachers. As for the quality of education in the district, as measured by student performance, there were ultimately marginal changes. Overall performance in the larger urban districts hardly budged.[28]

As the income tax increased the state allocations for education and poor districts received $300 per pupil more in state aid, the share of state aid allocated to Newark decreased. Between 1972 and 1976, urban districts had received 24 percent of the total, a loss to the poor districts of 9 percent under the new law. While state aid for education in Newark increased from $53 million in 1974 to $84 million in 1975, the schools did not end up with more resources because the city administration lowered its contribution to education from $51 million in 1974 to $37 million in 1975, thus passing the benefit from refinancing to homeowners. Over time, it became clear that *Robinson v. Cahill* did not address the more fundamental issues regarding the significant gap in education quality between poor urban districts and wealthy suburban districts.[29]

A series of reports from academic researchers had concluded that the law enacted in response to the *Robinson* case had led to the lion's share of benefits going to the middle class. Although the school funding pie had expanded (from 1977 to 1978, the state was spending $449 million more than it had two years earlier), poor districts had received only 12 percent of the new money, while middle-income districts had received 68 percent. Little of the new money for poor communities had reached poor children. Rather, the cities used much of their windfall not to increase school spending but to reduce property taxes, effectively replacing local money with state money. Although tax rates had been lowered in places like Newark, Camden, and Paterson, school spending and disparities had hardly moved and in some cases had widened. According to one analyst, "The broad outcome of the new law in operation has been almost negligible; district wealth is still the major factor in determining the level of educational expenditures in New Jersey."[30]

Abbott v. Burke

Robinson v. Cahill had taken school financing as far as it could go. It was not enough. As Ruvoldt moved on to other projects, it was left to the Education Law Center (ELC) to carry the school financing battle. The ELC, with offices in Newark and Philadelphia, was established by Rutgers law professor Paul Tractenberg in 1973 through a $475,000 grant from the Ford Foundation. It was one of those exceptional grant actions that was to have deep and sustaining impact on social policy. In 1979, the ELC hired Marilyn Moreheuser, a civil rights activist and former nun, who was to make New Jersey's school financing case the passion of her life. More importantly, she provided the wisdom and dedication necessary to wage a historic legal battle that would force a very reluctant citizenry to pay attention to an issue crucial to the state's future.

In 1981, based on the dismal outcomes achieved through *Robinson v. Cahill*, Moreheuser and her colleagues at the ELC filed a complaint in New Jersey Superior Court on behalf of twenty students from Camden, East Orange, Irvington, and Jersey City, as well as students in other poor and underfunded districts in the state. The complaint, *Abbott v. Burke*, charged that the state's school financing formula, which was still based on property taxes, denied poor children the same educational opportunity granted wealthy public school students in suburbs like Glen Ridge, Princeton, and Cherry Hill. The underlying argument was that funding disparities between wealthy and poor districts have a direct correlation to the quality of education provided to students.[31]

The debates concerning the quality of education had three camps. Some observers, particularly suburban residents and their elected representatives in the legislature, said the failure of education stemmed from the mismanagement and corruption of urban education systems in cities throughout the state. Others blamed the deep and entrenched poverty and disarray often found in poor communities. The ELC lawyers steadfastly viewed the financing of public education in cities as the major problem. There was ample evidence to support each of the three positions. But strategically, if you were going to fix the financing problem and change what was happening in poor districts, it was absolutely necessary to do something about the shortage of resources. Arguments about bad management, corruption, or poverty did not help the case against financial disparities. Steve Block, who worked at the Education Law Center, was told by his colleagues at the ELC to "shut up" about the corruption that he thought was so prevalent in the Jersey City school system.[32]

Courts can create revolutionary change, but they do so in a process that is agonizingly slow. It was not until 1985, four years after *Abbott v. Burke* was filed, that the justices spoke to the complaint. To establish the facts surrounding the case, the court sent the case to an administrative law judge who, after a series of exhaustive hearings, gave ELC, in the words of one analyst, "everything it had hoped for, and rejected virtually all of the State's case."[33] The opinion, issued in August 1988, filled 607 pages. "The expenditure differences," it said, "are in some cases greater now than before the present funding law was enacted. I have concluded that the funding law contains systemic defects which contribute to the continued inequity." And then the ruling struck the hammer against inequality: "New Jersey's poor urban school districts are shortchanging their students, and fundamental flaws in the school funding law were to blame. The system is not 'thorough and efficient' because opportunity is determined by socioeconomic status and geographic location."[34] The decision for *Abbott v. Burke* also noted that the mismanagement and corruption that existed in the urban districts were secondary issues. "Plaintiffs have proved that the system is broken."

Abbott I, as this case later came to be called, marked the beginning of what may be the longest ongoing legal contest the Supreme Court has ever considered. In *Abbott II* and in subsequent rulings, the court ordered the state to ensure that urban schoolchildren receive an adequate and constitutional education through comprehensive programs and reforms, including standards-based education supported by parity funding, supplemental programs, preschool education, and school facilities improvements. In 2011, thirty years after the filing in 1981, matters relating to the implementation of the *Abbott* rulings remained before the court. The *Abbott* ruling had profound effects on the politics of the state. It intensified the discontent of suburban homeowners over escalating property taxes, and as a consequence heightened criticism of urban governments. Legislators, particularly those from conservative districts, resisted because their constituents were angered by the rising cost of education. Governor Brendan Byrne was supportive of the efforts to equalize funding as a result of the *Robinson v. Cahill* decision. Democratic governor James Florio (1990–1994) embraced the goals of *Abbott*, and proposed the Quality Education Act, which led to increased funding for poor districts and middle income districts, despite strong opposition from higher income areas. But governors Christine Todd Whitman (1994–2001), a Republican, and Jon Corzine (2006–2010), a Democrat, did all they could to limit the state's financial obligation to the *Abbott* districts. Governor Corzine successfully pushed for an alteration in the court ruling that converted the *Abbott* obligation from a commitment to poor districts to a commitment to poor children, thus effectively bringing an end to the *Abbott* case.

The ELC victory revolutionized school financing in New Jersey and set a new standard for education reform across the nation. The impact of *Abbott* has been very significant, although the results in academic performance are modest and uneven. Smaller districts such

as Hoboken, Long Branch, and Union City have done best at closing
the racial and class gap in test scores, but Jersey City, Paterson, and
Newark still lag significantly behind state averages. Debates continue
over what is at the root of poor performance in urban areas since
the funding disparities have virtually disappeared. Surely one of the
issues seldom addressed is the exodus of more upwardly mobile families to suburban communities as well as the siphoning of the more
highly motivated students into charter schools, which did not exist
when the saga of *Abbott v. Burke* began. Most important, there is still
the huge puzzle for policy makers, educators, and political leaders
of how to marshal the human resources and design the programs to
effectively educate poor children.

The End of Mayoral Control

After Gibson had served two terms, Council President Earl Harris
began to eye the mayor's office. According to one of Harris's former
aides, Harris considered the mayor's control over the school bureaucracy as the fulcrum of his power. Gibson, contrary to his pledges to
change the schools, had resorted to the same old power politics that
had been practiced since Addonizio. He had Carl Sharif at the helm
of the school board, he appointed each of the school board members as the old guard cycled off the board, and he had tight connections to the resource distributors. The jobs pool and budget were rich
with opportunities for favors and trade-offs. Harris thought that the
mayor's control over the schools gave him an unbeatable advantage,
and he sought to change that. He persuaded his fellow council members to place before the voters a referendum to determine whether
they would prefer to change to an elected school board.

Gibson warned that although an elected board appeared to be
more democratic, it had several key weaknesses that would render
it undemocratic. For example, he explained, elections would be held
citywide and thus small ethnic groups would not be able to compete. He warned that those who could raise large sums of money
and already had political connections could control the election of
board candidates. Gibson said he would support an elected board if
the law were changed to allow for a combination of ward elections

and at-large elections. In addition, he called for the passage of a law that would provide campaign financing for school board elections. Gibson, however, would not say a word about the school board referendum during the course of his reelection campaign for the simple reason that he did not want to lose the support of voters on either side of the question. The referendum passed by a margin of four to one.

What seemed shocking was that few citizens understood the implications of having an elected school board. The city council was also in the dark regarding the rules and regulations of the new arrangement. They were not aware that with an elected board, they would have no direct role in constructing the school budget. No one knew just how a new elected board should be installed. (The New Jersey Department of Education determined that there would be an election for three seats, and holdovers from the appointed board would remain until replaced by elected members.) Faced with the reality that an elected board diminished its powers, the council passed a resolution to reinstate an appointed board. The action was forestalled by a restraining order sought by Anthony Carrino, the North Ward councilman.

In 1983, Charlie Bell and Carl Sharif, along with several members of the NTU, formed a coalition promoted as an effort to reform the schools. Many civic activists and parent groups joined, and the coalition became known as People United for Better Schools (PUBS), an unusual amalgam of resource distributors and change agents. In the 1984 school board election, PUBS fielded a slate of candidates for the school board—the Reverend Oliver Brown, a minister at Roseville Avenue Church; Edgar Brown, a high school PTA leader from the South Ward; and Joseph Stecher, an allied union organizer. All three PUBS-supported candidates won. However, the school board refused to seat the Reverend Oliver Brown and Edgar Brown, invoking a rule that apparently prohibited a school board member from filing a legal action against the board. The Reverend Brown and Edgar Brown had jointly filed a complaint against the board in 1983 contending the board had violated the law requiring adequate public notice of meetings. Eventually, the state commissioner of education ruled that the Reverend Brown and Edgar Brown would have to be seated, and that the school board had to pay their legal fees.[35] PUBS

was further strengthened by the ruling and the board was now controlled by PUBS adherents. NTU leadership heavily invested in the
coalition because it realized that the elected board would control
decision making as well as contract negotiations—without domination by the mayor. With the support of its friend Charlie Bell, PUBS
was classic Newark theater: Charlie Bell, who had surely helped
to deepen the politicization and mismanagement of the school
board, was now heading a movement claiming that it would reform
the schools.

Marcia Brown, a lawyer and administrator at Rutgers University–
Newark, was a young PUBS activist in the 1984 campaign. In a presentation she gave to the Abbott Institute at Rutgers Newark in
January 2009 she said that PUBS morphed into a strong campaign
organization, well oiled and full of energy, determination, and
hope. She said that the PUBS members canvassed door-to-door in
every neighborhood and told anyone who would listen that the city
had an opportunity to reaffirm the right of the residents to elect
their representatives.[36]

There are conflicting accounts as to when and why Steve Adubato
joined the group, but it is clear that he and Sharpe James were key
decision makers in determining how the spoils of victory would be
distributed. However, the first order of business for PUBS was to
drive out the change agents. At one of the PUBS meetings near the
end of the campaign, Charlie Bell and the resource distributors took
over, strongly supported by union members. Marcia Brown recalled
that the people who really wanted to improve the schools faced red-
baiting and other name calling. "We were eventually ushered out of
the critical meeting when it was time to discuss follow-up and strategies."[37] She said that when Amiri Baraka, who also believed that real
reform was possible, protested, he was accosted by a big, crude union
guy who grabbed Baraka and threw him to the ground, repeatedly
calling him the most vulgar epithet possible. The coalition fell apart.
The resource distributors had their way.[38]

If the behavior of the appointed board was at times self-interested
and ethically challenged, the elected board pushed bad behavior up
a notch or two. One board member billed the board for $6,000 for
food to cover daily lunches. It was an odd request since this person
had missed most of the board meetings during the year. Another

board member spent $8,700 on meals; at least she attended most of the board sessions.[39] For the Newark Teachers Union, the payoff was immense. In 1985, the board of education approved a contract that gave the union the house: a 23 percent pay increase over three years, far outstripping the inflation rate and the average 5 percent increases granted other city employees. The agreement also called for the city to assume total costs of the supplemental fringe benefit program, and, for the first time, teachers would be able to get paid for sick days they did not use. In addition, the contract gave the union authority to offer its own in-service course for teachers, which would qualify them for pay increments and promotions.[40]

Mayor Gibson was angry. He said the agreement would cost the city over $30 million in two years. "The board has surrendered its management prerogatives to the Union. I think it is clear that the political support offered by the NTU to those who won [the school board election] is being demonstrated in this contract," he charged. Carole Graves, the union president, showered the board with praise, and "hailed the board negotiators for bargaining in good faith." She said that the contract would have a positive effect on education in the Newark schools.[41]

In 1988, federal investigators swarmed board headquarters with dozens of subpoenas asking for personnel records. Several people who have worked in the system or have served on the board told me that there was strong reason to believe that the promotion system had been corrupt for a long time. A former district superintendent told me, "I have seen bad teachers become bad vice principals, and ineffective principals become ineffective administrators. Sure, I think people were paying for jobs." Former board member Vickie Donaldson said everyone assumed that "money changed hands on personnel decisions." One former board member said that he had been offered $10,000 to help a person (not the caller) get a principal's appointment. Newspapers reported that federal investigators were following up on rumors of corruption in Newark, and in other districts in the suburbs as well. Federal authorities indicted Malcolm George, a member of the elected school board, for soliciting payments from board employees who sought promotion. George pleaded guilty to four counts of bribery and was sentenced to twenty-seven months in federal prison.[42]

The State Takeover

Throughout the 1980s and 1990s, the Newark Public School District was subjected to several state department of education comprehensive audits that delved into everything from quality of education to efficiency in management and governance. Each audit found the district deficient in almost every category, prompting the state to initiate a Comprehensive Compliance Investigation, a final step prior to the state's taking control of a local school district. To give the state investigators a degree of credibility in Newark, Rebecca Doggett, one of Newark's most admired civic leaders, was hired to serve as auditor general for the Newark school district. It was a state position but located on-site at the Newark school board central offices. In the early 1960s, Doggett was the architect of the Newark Preschool Council, which established a network of Head Start centers under the antipoverty program. Her leadership and skill at organizing helped to make the preschool network of Newark one of the most effective in the nation.

As the investigation proceeded, Newark school leaders scrambled for ways to avert a takeover. First came outright resistance and efforts to defy the state investigators. Hilda Hidalgo, also a well-known Newark activist and Rutgers professor who served as a deputy commissioner in the state department of education, was literally barred from entering a school and was arrested by Newark police for trespassing. Files and records at the school board disappeared. As a last-ditch effort to prove that the city could handle its own problems, Superintendent Eugene Campbell hired a team of consultants who were assigned to give the Newark schools a complete overhaul. It was much too late.[43]

The findings of the investigation could not have been more damning. The investigators found that members of the school board were unengaged in the education problems of the district, and several could not even identify the critical challenges facing the schools. The team called the board "misguided" and mainly concerned with staff assignments and job security issues. The board's committee structure served to limit discussion of important issues and merely "promoted faster movement of the agenda at meetings of the full board." There were no efforts by the board to encourage parental involvement.[44]

In 1993, only one-quarter of high school juniors in Newark passed the first phase of the state-mandated graduation test. The percentage of children meeting state minimum achievement levels on standardized tests of basic skills was lower at grade six than at grade three. While this pattern occurred in a number of other districts in the state, the gap between grades three and six was greater in Newark than in any other district in New Jersey. "The majority of youngsters who remain in Newark schools," the report concluded, "are in danger of leaving high school without diplomas." Average daily school attendance was about 90 percent, one of the lowest rates in the state, and the team discovered numerous examples of faulty records, and in some cases, no attendance data at all.[45]

School buildings and classrooms were "filthy and in disrepair," despite the presence of a bloated maintenance workforce. The investigators found that on the opening day of school in 1993, most school buildings had not been cleaned and tidied up since the close of school the previous June. A team report said, "The toilets had not been cleaned during the summer and the halls in some schools reeked with the odor of urine."[46] Students lacked books, and science laboratories lacked adequate equipment. The investigators noted that some teachers did not have an understanding of the subjects they were teaching and were passing out misinformation for children to copy into their notebooks. The district had established a "Superintendent's Scholarship Fund," to which vendors doing business with the board were asked to contribute one thousand dollars. The fund was not registered with the state attorney general, as required by law. The Comprehensive Compliance Investigation found that the school board had failed to hold the district's chief administrator accountable. "The Newark Board of Education," it concluded, "has failed or has been unable to take corrective action necessary to establish a thorough and efficient system of education . . . the State must withdraw its delegation of that important responsibility to the Newark Board of Education."[47]

When the report was filed and made public, the Newark Board of Education hired a prominent defense attorney, Raymond Brown, who asked the court to prevent the state from taking over the district. When the matter was heard in court, the judge, after reading the investigators' report, issued a summary judgment that the state take

A REAL ESTATE STORY

In 1994, the New Jersey Department of Education had received complaints that two Newark school board employees owned a building that was leased to the board. In 1977, in fact, Joseph C. Parlavecchio, a principal at Dayton Street School and an Essex County freeholder, and Alphonse Rossi, a principal of an alternative school in the district, the owners of the building in question, had presented affidavits to the board stating that they had sold the property to Mutual Investment Associates Inc.

Department of Education investigators searched the property records and found that a mortgage filed in 1977 purported the sale of the building, known as the Roberto Clemente Annex, to Mutual Investment Associates, of which Frank Marsella was president and Francis Acquaro was listed as secretary. When investigators interviewed the eighty-six-year-old Acquaro, he stated that he had no knowledge of Mutual Investment Associates, had never heard of the Roberto Clemente Annex, and when asked if he knew Alphonse Rossi, he responded, "Alphonse is my son-in-law." When shown a copy of the mortgage, he said, "That is not my signature." It was clear that a conduit relationship was established whereby Mutual Investment Associates received lease payments from the board, which in turn were paid to Parlavecchio and Rossi. The yearly rental fee for the building escalated from $98,577.14 in 1987 to $212,920.00 in 1988. It was lowered to $177,987.00 in 1994.

In January 1996, Parlavecchio and Rossi were tried in federal court on charges of conspiracy, mail fraud, and money laundering, related to the Annex transaction. They were acquitted of all charges. The jury was apparently persuaded by defense arguments that the unconventional transaction was motivated by a need to sell the property quickly.

Source: New Jersey Department of Education Comprehensive Compliance Investigation Report of the Newark Public School District, July 1994, 1038–1043.

over the district immediately. The state board of education affirmed Commissioner Dr. Mary Lee Fitzgerald's recommendation shortly thereafter. The elected school board was dismissed, as were Executive Superintendent Campbell and several of his aides. The state officially took control of the Newark school district in July 1995.

Rebecca Doggett, as the state's auditor general, had observed the system from up close for several years. She said, "Given the cronyism and the deep level of corruption, reform would not take place from within." In her view, the whole system was a jobs mill, and educators who wanted to do a good job were saddled with teachers not even interested in teaching. Few parents were active in the schools because the leadership of the district bought off the parents who protested by giving them jobs. Sadly, she said, "Community groups had simply given up; foundations were totally frustrated; they wanted to help but they were kept at arm's length."[48]

State Management

Local political leaders were horrified by the notion of the state running their school district, although the problems the state investigators identified were extremely serious and impossible to ignore. Several of the school board members accused the state of having no respect for local autonomy, and some shouted racism. The opponents of the takeover made claims that they were improving the schools despite overwhelming evidence that the schools had a prolonged period of dysfunction.

Shortly after the state took control, Beverly Hall, a deputy schools chancellor from New York City, was selected to become the first state-appointed superintendent to head the district. She was a smart and highly competent educator, but the hurdles before her were very high. There certainly was no welcome mat in Newark for Dr. Hall. The resentment among political leaders, union officials, and community activists was intense. Hall quickly realized that leadership at the school level was sorely lacking. Within a year, she removed a third of the system's principals and installed more able, and energetic school leaders. Most of the new hires were younger and brought new ideas to the classrooms. She established a comprehensive in-service training program to upgrade the skills of elementary school teachers, and she campaigned to improve attendance. She eliminated service jobs and put the savings into preschool programs. She ordered an old-fashioned housecleaning of the schools. She never had a chance to carry out a sustained effort to upgrade the district, however. She was resisted at every turn by the bureaucracy and particularly by the teachers and administrators unions, which blunted efforts to have teachers participate in in-service training programs.

The city's political leaders, including Mayor Sharpe James, paid lip service to cooperation. However, James helped fuel the discontent of community leaders who railed against outsiders. At a public school board meeting, someone called Dr. Hall profane names. She received anonymous treats and warnings to leave town. State officials focused on reducing spending and forcing cutbacks. Ultimately, her downfall was that the state's skills at accounting proved to be sloppy and inept. When the administration faced a $73 million deficit, officials of the state education department blamed Hall.[49]

After four years of Newark, Hall had enough and took the superintendent's job in Atlanta, Georgia. Mayor James seized the occasion of her departure to denounce the state takeover as a failure. Joe Del Grosso, president of the Newark Teachers Union, said, "We don't believe that there's been any improvement in the Newark Public Schools." However, the state commissioner of education, Leo F. Klagholz, noted that there were indeed modest improvements under Hall's short term of leadership. He said, "Resistance is built into takeover, and when you use that opportunity for change, then that is compounded."[50]

The next state-appointed superintendent, Marion Bolden, had served as assistant superintendent for instruction for Hall. She landed the job more as a result of happenstance than intention. She said that the state was looking for someone from outside the district, and she was encouraged to apply because state officials wanted to be able to say local candidates were being considered.[51] When two favored outside candidates declined to take the job, Bolden became the only candidate standing. Marion Bolden's strength was that she knew the system better than anyone. She had graduated from Newark's South Side High School (now Malcolm X Shabazz High School) in 1962 at the very top of her class. After attending Montclair State College, she joined the Newark teaching staff in 1968 as a math teacher. For several years, she administered all math instruction in the district. And she was Hall's assistant. When she was appointed superintendent in 1999, she had already clocked thirty-one professional years in the Newark school system. She was also a member of the executive board of CASA, the school administrators' union. Marion Bolden was the quintessential insider.

Bolden concedes that it took at least two years for her to fully understand the superintendent's job. Nonetheless, she immediately tightened administrative and fiscal management of the district. Her relationship with state officials was rocky, and at times she instinctively opposed suggestions from state officials. Gordon MacInnes, who headed the state's Division of Abbott Implementation, recalled, "Newark was often difficult to deal with." As an example, he said the state offered a literacy program to districts for which the state would train the personnel. He said that Newark's response was, "We are already doing that." A year after the program was in place in other districts and showing positive results, Newark came back and said, "We would now like to do the literacy program."[52] On the other hand, the state, through constant efforts to cut costs and shift resources to charter schools, tried to impose changes on the district that Bolden and her staff found unacceptable. One year, for example, the state attempted to eliminate the position of department chair in all high schools. On several occasions, at Bolden's direction, the Newark district filed legal actions to challenge proposals considered contrary to the mandate of the New Jersey Supreme Court's *Abbott* decision.[53] It is also likely, given her close ties to CASA, that some of her resistance to the state was encouraged by the unions.

Bolden ran a system without scandal or controversy. She gained respect because she was clearly supportive of the children and was not at all reluctant to push back against the bureaucrats in Trenton. She took great pride in supporting the district's athletic programs, and she allowed student athletes to participate in varsity sports even if they had a scholastic average below C. Her defense of such a dubious policy was that "at least they would stay in school if they could play sports." Her focus on sports worked for West Side High School football, which had lost fifty-six games in a row when Bolden took the helm of the schools. In a few years, West Side had a strong, competitive football team, a cheering squad, and large attendance at its games, often including the superintendent. Regarding academic change throughout the district, gains were small and occurred in the lower grades. Serious problems of learning and discipline continued in the general high schools.[54]

Mayor James tried to force Bolden to leave the job in 2004 but was met by an avalanche of opposition from students and parents, community activists, and political leaders, including North Ward political boss Steve Adubato. James backed off after learning that Bolden was very skillful as a political organizer. In 2008, however, her position was weakened by Mayor Booker's public criticism of the schools and private criticism of her leadership. According to Bolden, she was also opposed by Art Ryan, the president of Prudential, who, she said, told officials in Trenton that Bolden was too stubborn. Bolden said that her relationship with Prudential was always icy, for when she took the job, she was approached by a representative of the Prudential Foundation and asked to turn over five schools to the Edison Corporation, a private firm that manages public schools for a fee. She said she rejected the idea because such a move would have severed her ties with the community and with the unions. With winds blowing in different directions, and at higher velocity, state officials offered Bolden a retirement deal. She accepted.[55]

Back to an Outsider

With the departure of Marion Bolden, Govenor Jon Corzine established an advisory search committee chaired by the highly popular Rutgers professor Clement A. Price. The committee recommended Dr. Clifford Janey, who had served as superintendent in Rochester and Washington, DC. Mayor Booker was not happy with the recommendation and tried to persuade Govenor Corzine not to appoint Janey. Nonetheless, Mayor Booker joined Govenor Corzine at a meeting to introduce Janey to the community. Covering his dissatisfaction well, Booker shouted to the audience, "This is my superintendent. We are brothers in the fight to improve education in Newark."[56]

Janey arrived with mixed reviews of his previous record. He was recognized as a big thinker, strong on innovative ideas, but weak on implementation. In his short (two-year) tenure in Newark, he seemed to be off to a good start. He invited scholars to study student performance, began a comprehensive learning and development zone in the Central Ward, and allowed several young teachers to manage a failing elementary school in the South Ward. His most important contribution was the creation of a strategic plan, a document that forthrightly outlined the deficits in learning and achievement in the district and provided rather ambitious targets for improvements. The plan, "Great Expectations, 2009–2013," was perhaps the first honest and thorough appraisal of the academic condition of the schools in more than four decades. "Great Expectations" called for improving proficiency levels by as much as one-third over a period of five years and aligning the district's curriculum with state standards. Janey also put Newark elementary students in uniforms, something that had been on the drawing boards for more than a decade. Finally, the plan called for sweeping changes in the high schools by replacing the comprehensive schools with theme schools.[57]

In the final analysis, "Great Expectations" was just a plan; a good one, but simply a document that defined what needed to be known as well as what needed to be done. To get the plan implemented would require strong leadership, building alliances within and outside the school system, getting maximum support from city and state officials, and having sufficient time to make change happen. The prospects were not good for getting the district to follow Janey's formula for change. Janey never reached out to staff and teachers in a personal way, to engage people, to discover potential allies. At times, he had little to say at public strategic planning sessions, leaving the interactions between school leaders and community representatives to others.

Much like Stanley Taylor, Mayor Gibson's school superintendent, Janey did not get to know the city's political leadership. He and Mayor Booker had little communication. Janey never got the time to prove that he could put his plan in play. At Booker's instigation, Governor Chris Christie, who was elected in 2009, notified Janey that the state would not renew his contract. Janey left the job, after two years. At his departure, the state had been in control of Newark's schools for fifteen years.

Grading the State

Rebecca Doggett concluded that the state did not do its job. Doggett, the state general auditor who had helped with the investigation, said that the state did not have a strategy to reengage parents and the community in school matters. And, Doggett pointed out, no fore-thought was given to how and when the district might be returned to local control. She said the most critical failure of the state was that it did not follow up and attempt to determine whether unlawful acts had been committed by school administrators or members of the school board. "When the bad actors realized that they would not be punished or removed from the system, they resumed their resistance to any efforts at change," she said. "There would have been more progress if the right message had been sent."[58]

Rutgers law professor Paul Tractenberg echoed many of the same criticisms. He said that the underlying purpose of the takeover should have been to build the capacity of the local system in order to return the system to local control. Tractenberg and his Institute on Education Law and Policy at Rutgers were retained by the state to review state intervention in Paterson, Jersey City, and Newark. The institute's final report had this to say: "[State authorities'] initial focus typically has been on correcting management and fiscal prob-lems, and often, the effort has dominated the first several years of takeover . . . the myriad programs and strategies initiated in the three districts lack any consistency or approach . . . the vision or theory of the programs in the state-operated districts is unclear . . . develop-ing capacity for local control does not appear to be among the pri-mary objects."[59]

On the surface, the takeover of the Newark school district was aimed at ridding the school bureaucracy of mismanagement and corruption so that efforts to improve learning would have a bet-ter chance to succeed. However, the state placed strong emphasis on management and budget controls and little emphasis on either building local capacity or strengthening the teaching and develop-ment of children. In recent years, there has been increased emphasis on education matters by the state, but the state has little to show after seventeen years.

The Gift and Prospects for Reform

To reform the Newark school district, to make it a system for learning for children and not an organization that operates first and foremost for bureaucrats, politicians, and ward leaders, would be a monumental task. The overwhelming majority of children in Newark's public schools live beneath the poverty threshold, and their readiness for learning is seldom what it ought to be. Their needs are extraordinary. Yet for over fifty years the school system and its leaders bastardized the educational process by stacking the personnel roster at all levels with people with weak or nonexistent qualifications. And for many years, the board of education ceded to the various unions excessive powers and prerogatives that hampered education. Deeply entrenched in the system was a political culture that resisted and undermined reform. School leaders who chose to merely dust the edges received full support from the leaders of this bankrupt system. Any top official who earnestly tried to change the manner in which the system operated would be denigrated and opposed. So creating real reform in Newark is certainly worth trying, but it would be, as Oprah Winfrey said, a challenge much like climbing Mount Everest.[60] (Nonetheless, it should be obvious by now that reforming Newark schools is a much harder venture than climbing Mount Everest. Some people have reached the top of Everest.)

So what might the Newark school system, with a budget approaching $1 billion and granted a gift of $100 million from Facebook founder Mark Zuckerberg, accomplish in reforming the schools over the next five to ten years?

The Zuckerberg pledge was announced in September 2010 on the *Oprah Winfrey Show* with Governor Chris Christie, Mayor Booker, and Mr. Zuckerberg in attendance. Governor Christie proclaimed that he was committed to school reform and would do all he could to make changes in Newark. Mayor Booker created two organizations in response to the pledge. The first was called PENewark, something of an ad hoc survey effort that convened scores of meetings throughout the city to hear what citizens expected in school reform. The PENewark strategy was the first clue that Mayor Booker was unclear about what the elements of a reform process should be. Many residents of the Central, South, and West Wards held a cynical view of the PENewark meetings. They speculated that the survey was really intended to provide a database for Mayor Booker for his future political campaigns. The surveys reaffirmed what everyone knew: the schools were troubled, there were wide variations in the quality of education by wards, and there was a dire need for strong and inspired teachers. When the public learned that the price tag for the survey was $2 million, and a good share of the money went to political consultants, the project was considered wasteful and a boondoggle for Booker's friends.[61]

Under the terms of the Zuckerberg pledge, Booker agreed to raise a dollar-for-dollar match, which would mean $200 million would be available for improving the Newark schools. The pledge was placed in the California-based Startup Foundation, Mark Zuckerberg's charity dedicated to education reform. The Startup Foundation was headed by Jen Holloran, a close associate of Facebook executives. For the match, Booker created the Foundation for Newark's Future (FNF), a new entity located in Newark. Booker hired Greg Taylor, a vice president at the Kellogg Foundation, to run FNF, for a salary of $382,000 a year. Taylor never moved to Newark and devoted three to four days a week (at best) to the job. Despite the very high pay, Taylor was not happy to discover that he was simply a figurehead, the head of an organization with strong instincts toward secrecy, and, worse, contrary to the public perception, it really had few discretionary resources. It had no clear purpose.[62]

The lack of transparency was challenged when the ACLU asked Mayor Booker to make public all the communications leading up to the pledge. Booker refused. The ACLU went to court and won. E-mails revealed a network of dozens of people from California to New York and New Jersey, fumbling over how to shape the initiative and how to raise the match to the Zuckerberg gift. Booker and his advisors decided that the board of FNF would have only donors who contributed $10 million, thus closing out the possibility of any local philanthropic or civic participation. Ray Chambers, arguably the most generous and significant donor Newark has known for more than forty years, offered to contribute $1 million toward the match. He was turned down. Barri Mattes, Booker's thorny fund-raising aide, said that the $1 million Chambers offered was too small. The e-mails revealed that Mark Zuckerberg thought that having a mass appeal for small and large contributions for the match would bring excitement and opportunity, not to mention allow many people to participate in the reform effort. Again, Mattes argued against it.[63]

Greg Taylor was put in the position of simply acting as a black front for a group of wealthy donors who really had their own agendas for Newark schools. While Zuckerberg was mainly interested in doing something to improve teaching, most of the donors of the match were only interested in supporting more charter schools. William Ackman dedicated his $25 million toward the match to Newark for charter school expansion, and he placed the funds in his own foundation at Pershing Capital. The Gates Foundation match contribution went to the New Ventures Fund in New York City and was also dedicated to charter schools. Jen Holloran of the Startup Foundation was the key decision maker for all of the money. Thus if most of the match money was dedicated to charters, Greg Taylor really had nothing to do for his lush salary. In response to community demands for transparency, FNF eventually organized an advisory board. It was not hard to understand the irrelevance of an advisory board for an organization that itself had no power or purpose. After less than two years on the job, Taylor left FNF for a job as director of external relations for the National Basketball Association.[64]

The Zuckerberg money did manage to support a number of innovations and improvements that are likely to make a marginal difference in the schools. For example, a teacher innovation fund was established, as was as a university-allied precollege high school. The money also paid for much of the data analysis that was necessary to get a fix on the rates of graduation and other information about the student population. The major impact of the grant money was the financing of the district's new contract with the Newark Teachers Union. There was much fanfare about the fact that the teachers' union agreed to a merit pay program, which would provide as much as $12,500 to outstanding teachers and bonuses to teachers who agreed to teach in the poorest-performing schools. However, the biggest chunk of the much touted $100 million pledge, celebrated on the *Oprah Winfrey Show* and described as a major effort to upgrade the schools for the children of Newark, was diverted for a different purpose. Since the teachers had been working on a contract that had expired three years before, they were entitled to back pay under the new agreement. Thus, $33 million of the $100 million pledge from Zuckerberg went to pay the state's debt to teachers. In other words, the major share of the money simply subsidized a state budget obligation. Covering the back pay of teachers is not education reform for the children of Newark.[65]

Can the Mayor Rule Education?

Mayor Booker was well positioned to have a major impact on the administration of the school system. He had the Zuckerberg gift, the prestige of being a celebrity mayor, and he had more access to the media than most other politicians at the local level. Unfortunately, his first effort to change the Newark schools showed little wisdom or know-how in approaching changes that would affect children and families. On a Friday afternoon in March 2011, Deborah Terrell, serving as interim superintendent after Janey's departure, assembled school principals and handed them a document created by the consulting firm Global Education Advisors. The document was a wide-ranging facilities plan that spelled out a number of proposals that would close several schools, consolidate populations in some cases, and co-locate five new schools, with separate staffing, in Newark public school buildings already housing school programs. It also called for co-locating eleven charter schools in public school buildings, an explosive idea given the emerging tensions over the allocation of resources to charter schools.[66]

Several elements of the plan, such as closing schools and consolidating declining populations, had certainly been done before. Other aspects of the plan were new, particularly expanding the number of alternative schools and the recommendation to place charter schools in Newark public school buildings. Moreover, some of the placements suggested for alternative schools were bound to generate opposition. When Terrell explained to the principals that the plan was to be fully implemented in less than nine months, the principals and administrators were stunned. Moreover, Acting Commissioner of Education Chris Cerf, who had been appointed by Governor Christie in 2010, had been a founding partner of Global Education Advisors. The firm's address registered with the state was Cerf's home in Montclair, New Jersey.[67]

The perception among many in the community was that a band

of unknown outsiders aligned with corporate elites was imposing a highly disruptive decision on Newark schools, primarily to support charter school expansion. There was no consultation with the community and families that would be affected, and the detailed planning needed for such a major reorganization had not been done. Mayor Booker denied knowing anything about the Global Education Advisors plan, although several people involved in education confirmed that aspects of the plan had been discussed with his advisors and had been reviewed in his office. The fee for the development of the plan was provided by the California-based Broad Foundation, whose principals said they had conversed many times with Mayor Booker over the grant and its purposes.

Considerable damage was done to the cause of reform and to the legitimacy of the state overseers. Democrats in the legislature viewed Cerf's appointment as a blunder by Governor Christie. Some residents of Newark saw a corporate conspiracy backed by Governor Christie, Acting Commissioner Cerf, and Mayor Booker. State Senator Ronald Rice, who had lost in the mayor's race to Booker in 2006, exercised his right to hold up action on any nominee from a senator's home county and pledged, "Mr. Cerf will remain acting forever."[68] After a year as acting commissioner, Cerf moved to another county, at which time he was promptly confirmed and granted the title of commissioner of education.

With the plan launched, meetings of the School Advisory Board of the Newark Public Schools became louder than ever, and shouting matches erupted between charter school parents and public school parents. A majority of the advisory board voted against the opening of several new schools, for no reason other than their pique at the state and the mayor. The uproar led to several alterations in the plan.

The White Lady from Harlem

In May 2011, Governor Christie named Cami Anderson the fourth state-appointed superintendent of the Newark Public School District. Anderson had run District 79 in New York City, an amalgam of dozens of alternative programs for special needs students, a population not all that different from the school population in Newark.

Anderson had also worked for Teach for America, and she had attended the Broad Foundation training program, which tries to enlist new talent for leadership roles in public school systems. She was relatively young and energetic and lived in Harlem with her infant child and partner. She also had a new commissioner and, supposedly, the Zuckerberg resources available to her. Governor Christie came to Newark to announce the appointment and promised her his full support. The liabilities were that she was white and had no roots in the black community of Newark. She had worked on the Booker mayoral campaign in 2002, but that was not necessarily a plus.

I had served on an advisory committee to review candidates and agreed that after a rather disorganized search, she was the most qualified person. I thus wrote an op-ed essay published in the *Star-Ledger* entitled "The White Lady from Harlem," in which I attempted to explain that since Newark had had seven consecutive black superintendents, the black community had won the representation battle. What it had not won was the fight against mediocrity and failure.[69] In my view, it was not a setback to black advancement to give a bright white woman who had deeply relevant cultural and organizational experience a chance to run the district. Still, to many in the community, more significant than anything was that she was just another representative of the state. By the end of 2012, Anderson had served for three semesters and the going was very rough.

Several of the advisory school board members opposed anything she suggested. In her first year, she forced another round of school closings, setting the community in turmoil again. She pushed new efforts to reorganize failing schools and gave principals the power to pick their own staff. She proved to be very strong in identifying the problems of learning and in conceptualizing new approaches to achieve better outcomes. Perhaps her biggest victory was the new contract with the Newark Teachers Union.

In all her endeavors, implementation was chaotic and unsuccessful, however, and because some of her outside advisors were paid by FNF, there were also issues of transparency. Anderson hired an army of consultants to take on various reorganization chores. The consultants became a major item of discussion among district employees, for almost all of them were white women from New York City. Like many of the perceptions regarding Mayor Booker's hiring, critics seldom noticed that Anderson also hired several blacks and Latinos to fill key positions. There was considerable antipathy toward the consultants. Staff members told me stories about consultants who had to ask employees how to do the work they were being paid to do. A consulting firm from California cost several million dollars, plus almost one hundred thousand dollars in expenses, to track graduation rates and to set up a system to track students' movements through the grades, work that was already under way at a local university. State officials continued to apply pressure for budget reductions, which led to proposals to eliminate key staff positions and other reductions in personnel. After it had made its deal on the new contract, the Newark Teachers Union began an all-out attack on Anderson's leadership and the state's supervision. Facing steep budget reductions in 2013, there were clear efforts to turn back the clock on the *Abbott* decision.

The Demand for Local Control

In 2011, the demand for local control of the district began to grow louder and more persistent. Paul Tractenberg had proposed a return to local control with the state and local universities having nonvoting seats on a local board.[70] To grant local control to an elected school board in its current form, however, would risk the return of the politics and behavior that led to the takeover in the first place. Newark needs to learn from its history. The people concerned with the schools and the future of their children might do well to remember how calls for more participation and democracy only perpetuated the dominance of the resource distributors.

In fact, many of the people demanding local control are the very same people who kept the schools devoted to jobs and patronage. Based on the overwhelming and long-term evidence of politics swamping the educational concerns of children in Newark, the state would be ill advised to return Newark to a completely locally controlled school board. However, some form of increased local participation is not only justified, but necessary; the other side of the coin is that the state is so concerned with the budget issues that it cannot be trusted to do what is best for the children of Newark. The best solution is a shared form of governance to provide for a mayoral role and a continued state role. A shared governance system could be achieved by creating a nine-member governing board made up of five ward representatives, two representatives appointed by the mayor, and two representatives appointed by the commissioner of education. A new system of governance would reflect the reality that financing for Newark schools is now provided mainly by general revenues from the state, approximately 70 percent of a budget of around $950 million. Given the realities and politics of school financing, it would seem prudent for the state to have a continued direct role in districts where state financing exceeds a defined threshold, perhaps 60 percent of a local school budget. The state would still have many other ways to exercise oversight of school spending and policies.

The reform of the Newark school district has many parts, and layers upon layers of complexity. Along with the horrible inner-city joblessness situation, the condition of the school district ranks as one of the most important issues facing the city. Continued failure will forever prohibit a meaningful recovery of Newark. The ultimate goal is to have competent teachers in every classroom, particularly at the early grades. That is much easier said than done. State supervision brought many of the bad fiscal and management behaviors to a halt, but state officials have not yet proved that the state has the tools or the competence to rid the district of the failures and mediocrity that existed before the takeover and undertake a sustained effort to upgrade the schools.

The major and possibly the most important contribution of the state thus far has been the introduction of early childhood education for all children, a result of the *Abbott* court decisions. Preparing young children to learn to read, which almost all middle-class families do by having books at home and reading to children, particularly at bedtime, is absolutely essential in efforts to overcome the burdens of poverty and disadvantage. The research is clear. Children who learn to read by the third grade have a better chance of finishing high school, staying out of prison, and acquiring a job or profession that enables them to live a decent life.[71] Unfortunately, the concentrated poverty found in the neighborhoods of the South and Central Wards does not produce many children who have been nurtured with reading lessons and bedtime stories.

If children do not get the basic skills to prepare them for school, the schools must still do their job. Urban schools are desperately in need of an organizational makeover. Some features of the traditional model of education should be jettisoned in favor of approaches that recognize that the task of educating children from poverty-stricken families requires more-intensive and higher-capacity learning systems than are provided in most schools today. The few exceptions to the general pattern of failure in Newark have in every case, among private schools and public schools as well as charter schools, enriched and expanded their learning systems to meet the challenges of educating poor children.

For Newark, a fundamental challenge is poverty, as it is for poor communities in Detroit, Chicago, Philadelphia, and Cleveland. As Ted Pinckney has written, "Urban schools that are asked to educate the children of families that are at the bottom rung of the economic ladder require more of everything, not just more money. They need better teachers, better supplies, better facilities, more time, and more attention paid to personal development and teacher competency."[72]

Epictetus, a Roman slave and philosopher (c. 55–135 A.D.), uttered a wisdom that will surely live forever: "Only the educated are free." In a global, technological world, the ability to be self-sufficient and have the knowledge to participate in the economic and civic life of a community and nation is the essence of a free life. That ideal is only possible with a sound education, which includes reading, reasoning, and computing skills, as well as appropriate character formation. The adults who have achieved position and power have a moral obligation to serve the children of their community and do whatever is possible to support the provision of a decent education so that they too can be free. The children of Newark cry out for leaders, at every level, who are dedicated to the cause of education and will not exploit and corrupt the school system to serve their own selfish interests. Only then can Newark proclaim transformation.

Conclusion

The Search for Transformation

*Our city has embarked on a program of renewing itself with
the initial objectives of eliminating existing slums and blight
and preventing the recurrence of such conditions.*

—Mayor Leo P. Carlin, 1961

*We will set a new standard for urban transformation
right here in the City of Newark.*

—Mayor Cory A. Booker, 2006

Since the end of the 1950s, city leaders have offered plan after
plan for a new and restored Newark. In 1958, Mayor Leo P. Carlin created a business-led economic development committee, and with the
impetus of the charter change in 1953, Newark witnessed a building
boom, with new public housing, new schools, a new YMCA building, and the major building projects of the insurance giants, Prudential and Mutual Benefit Life. Carlin declared at a public forum on
the city's future, "If in this day and age the residents are indifferent
to the physical conditions existing in their community, are content
to let the corrosion of time and changing economy take its toll, then
our older American cities like Newark are doomed to residential and

slum status."[1] Carlin promised that new structures would bring New-ark back to the vibrancy it had enjoyed decades earlier. The revival he hoped for never happened.

Mayor Hugh Addonizio made pretensions of building a revitalized city as well. His 1962 campaign theme was "Peace and Progress," by which he meant the absence of the disruptions that were occurring in other places and an increasing flow of dollars from Washington. As it turned out, the destruction of neighborhoods beginning with clearance in the South Ward for Interstate 78, in the Central Ward for the medical school, and the bisection of part of the North Ward for Interstate 280, as well as clearance for a midtown connector that was never built, all caused considerable damage to Newark. At least on the surface, Addonizio saw the development of a new medical school in the heart of the city as that single economic blockbuster to kick-start a resurgence. Below the surface he saw vendor and construction contracts that might fuel a campaign for the statehouse. His undem-ocratic pursuit of the medical school added tinder to an already combustible situation, a major factor in sparking a violent rebellion.

Mayor Kenneth A. Gibson was so often occupied with managing racial tensions that swelled in the city after 1967 that development did not rank high on his agenda until after his second term, which began in 1978. Still, by the time he left office, significant developments had taken place, including the first phase of the Gateway project, a new PSE&G building, and the first Society Hill units meant for middle-class professionals. Gibson handed to Sharpe James a city that was beginning to look different. Mayor James then oversaw a very active period of development with the expansion of Society Hill, develop-ment of Science Park in the Central Ward, construction of the New Jersey Performing Arts Center, expansion of the Gateway complex, scattered projects on Springfield Avenue, a push on housing in the neighborhoods, and, at the end of his tenure, the development of the Prudential Center arena.

In recent years, Mayor Booker has quickened and broadened the pace of the city's development program. While much attention has been focused on the North American headquarters of the Panasonic Corporation and a new Prudential building on Broad Street, there has also been an expansive housing and residential strategy in down-town that will bring a "Teachers Village" in one area, market-rate housing close to the university complex, and residential housing to Broad and Market Streets, the historic four corners of the city. There are a few other scattered housing developments on South Broad Street and in the Lincoln Park area. The expansion of various colleges and universities in the city and the expansion of Newark Liberty International Airport have continued to contribute significantly to growth and rebuilding in Newark,.

Throughout the last five decades, business leaders and elected officials have often pronounced an imminent turnaround of Newark, indeed a renaissance. The Newark Chamber of Commerce has occasionally gone beyond the exuberant boosterism common to representatives of business interests in painting a glowing picture of the city. For example, on the tenth anniversary of the 1967 rebellion, the Chamber published a pamphlet reviewing the achievements of the decade. It complained about the city's critics, claiming they presented an unwarranted image of consistent negativism. "Newark," the pamphlet asserted, "has consistently been cited as the classic example of urban decline. It has made everyone's list. On the best it is last, on the worst it is first."[2] Rather, the Chamber said, the city has experienced much economic development in commerce and transportation facilities, and it went on to describe how the city's financial situation had improved as a result of generous subsidies from Washington and Trenton. The Chamber cited improvements in housing and health, for which there was indeed some evidence. It also lauded progress in the school system, though in 1977 there really was not much to praise.

Other voices also proclaimed that Newark's turnaround was under way. The prestigious Regional Plan Association (RPA) issued a report in 1978 suggesting that the state's older cities were undergoing a renaissance of sorts. Unlike the Newark Chamber of Commerce, the RPA was cautious and more tentative about developments and noted, "Reversing the long trend of city decline will be hard to do."[3] It observed that nearly all New Jersey cities were losing population and that the rate of income in those cities lagged behind that of the state as a whole. The RPA pointed to the high unemployment rates and loss of industry by older cities and expressed concern about continuing failure of city schools. On the brighter side, the RPA cited the return to the cities of middle-class residents who "are restoring valuable residential housing."[4] There was a hope that gentrification, the process of nudging out the poor, would bring back to the city some of those middle-class people who had fled to the suburbs. However, gentrification always seemed unlikely to go very far in a city like Newark, with serious school issues and limited middle-class housing. Perhaps more significant was the RPA's contention that racial tensions, especially in Newark, were easing. Confrontation tactics, it said, were giving way to efforts to establish communications among the various ethnic and racial groups. Commercial construction in the central parts of the city impressed the RPA, and its report highlighted Newark's enhanced cultural life (noting that the New Jersey Symphony was performing at the "restored" Symphony Hall, which Newark residents knew was still in need of repair).

If the RPA report had a note of tentativeness about where Newark was heading, the editors of *New Jersey Monthly* threw all caution to the winds when they published in 1979 an issue devoted to Newark.[5] Contributors to the issue thought the city was uncommonly well administered and safe. They thought that Newark was a city of "ethnic harmony, where racial and ideological confrontations are almost unknown." It noted the worldwide reputation of Mayor Ken Gibson. An editor of the magazine drove around the city and reported on his observations in an essay titled, "The Wanderer Gets Off at Exit 14." The "Wanderer" admits to passing through some grim neighborhoods and finds along one access route into the city burned-out hulks of buildings "not even blessed with the dignity of boards and protective iron." Impressed with the parks and the better neighborhoods he visits, the "Wanderer" then goes to the central business district and is awed by imposing skyscrapers, newly built or under construction. He notices some "truly urban amenities. Not the least of these is crazy people." He finds "winos and mumblers galore." More noteworthy is the essay's complete lack of discussion of Newark's failing schools, high unemployment, and the unambiguous evidence in every central city neighborhood of a community ravaged by deindustrialization and a failed urban renewal program.[6]

Throughout the country, some cities were indeed improving and undertaking significant development projects. However, Newark was not on that list. In the mid-1970s, urban expert Richard Nathan attempted to ascertain trends in the economic health of cities, especially since the public was increasingly hearing of places that were doing better. Nathan found that the disparity between cities in relatively good condition and those in distress was widening. He and his colleague, Charles Adams, developed a set of measures of conditions that included unemployment, education, and income levels, poverty, and the percentage of citizens under eighteen and those over sixty-five without sufficient income (that is, citizens dependent on others for care). From these indicators they developed a composite indicator—the higher the number, the worse the condition. Newark stood at the top of the list with a composite indicator of 422, where the mean for the fifty-five cities in the study was 148. No other city reached the 400 level and only two exceeded 300.[7]

Such dismal realities helped to spark a more collaborative push for development. In 1984, as Mayor Gibson's fourth and last term was drawing to a sluggish end, Alex Plinio, a senior executive at the Prudential Foundation, with the backing Robert Winters, the firm's chief executive, created the Newark Collaboration Group (NCG) in an attempt to jump-start a broad development effort in the city. Plinio grew up in Newark, attended Newark schools, and graduated from Rutgers–Newark. It was not all that common for a Newark guy, reared in the city, to move high up on the corporate ladder in one of the city's large and increasingly global firms. Plinio knew and cared about the city, and he was highly regarded among Prudential's top leadership. "The city was a horror at the time," he said. "Nothing was happening; there was constant conflict between and among groups, and corruption was rampant."[8]

With broad representation from stakeholders throughout the city and region, the NCG set an agenda for change and acted as facilitator to get things started. For example, the group persuaded Prudential to provide a $2 million loan to an African American developer named Don Harris. In the Central Ward, Harris built forty units that later became Society Hill, a critical venture and the first market-rate housing construction in the Central Ward since the disturbances of 1967. Harris did not have the financial backing to move the project to the next phase, so the Hovnanian Company stepped in and built the condominium development up to 730 units. The NCG also pushed the idea of a performing arts center and helped to raise funding for a feasibility study on the project. It promoted the idea of a light-rail link to connect Penn Station with the major arts facilities as well as the train station at North Broad Street. The NCG was also involved in the development of new housing near the universities.[9]

The Newark Collaboration Group was a rare instance of corporate leadership—totally out in the open in efforts to change and improve the city.[10] Its focus on the downtown area led some critics to conclude that the NCG was born simply for the purpose of enabling the downtown business interests to get what they wanted, but for a city that seemed to be chronically depressed almost twenty years after a riot, it was a critical step forward. The momentum it created for increased development was important to the subsequent efforts of Mayor Sharpe James, who embraced the NCG after his election and joined its executive board.[11]

Nonetheless, the NCG's agenda could never move beyond downtown to address social concerns that stifled the city's progress. Conversations about schools, neighborhoods, and unemployment took place among the members, but they never went beyond the talking stage. In Plinio's view, it was strategic for the NCG to avoid taking on education; it had to establish itself and show results in a rather short time. After a few years, in 1986, Plinio gave up leadership of the NCG, and Saul K. Fenster, president of the New Jersey Institute of Technology, took his place. Fenster served for two years. He was succeeded by Mayor James. The NCG, without strong business and corporate leadership, sputtered to a slow end. In one respect, the NCG was a metaphor of the story of development in Newark: Good things can happen downtown, but they do not necessarily translate into improvements for the people who live in the neighborhoods.

Newark's downtown has been substantially renewed in the last forty-plus years. During the period of Mayor Cory Booker's leadership, many new projects have been brought to the city. The Panasonic and Prudential office towers will certainly enlarge the commerce and pedestrian traffic of downtown Newark. The question remains, though: Will these new developments provide jobs, housing, better health, and schooling for the people of the city?

This question cannot be addressed without discussing the role of the state and federal government. Cities like Newark, which house a disproportionate share of the nation's poor, cannot meet the extensive needs for services without help from Trenton and Washington.

Unfortunately, it is unlikely that American cities will ever again receive the kind of major subsidies they enjoyed in the 1960s and 1970s. Urban places do not matter as much as they once did, since people with higher and middle incomes have left the cities, leaving behind the poor. When the president of the United States and state and local politicians repeatedly voice their concern for the middle class, they are appealing to the areas of the nation where the votes are.

Moreover, at the end of 2012, the nation was still in the throes of the worst economic collapse since the Great Depression, rallying conservative forces eager to take aim at urban programs and, consequently, the poor who depend on those programs. President Obama was handed a nation in dire economic straits. Jobs disappeared in huge numbers and many citizens lost their homes because they could not pay their mortgage. Fortunately, the President was able to get the Affordable Care Act, his major domestic achievement, through Congress before Democrats lost their advantage in the House of Representatives. In 2010, his Democratic Party lost control of the House by a large margin and a divided Congress worked diligently to undercut his proposals. With limited options, Obama governed from a weak position, one from which he could barely fight. He offered compromises that were not as severe as Republican proposals, but they nevertheless continued Washington's several decades of cutting back support for cities and for poor people. Obama, caught in the midst of political gridlock, simply could not deliver on his campaign promise to make urban issues a concern of his administration. Throughout President Obama's tenure thus far, the Urban Policy Office and the Department of Housing and Urban Development have had limited funds and have been virtually invisible, quietly advocating local city–suburban partnerships that would be cost-free for Washington.

In the 2012 election campaign, urban issues and poverty were not discussed at either of the party conventions. Cities and poverty were not mentioned by either presidential candidate in the course of the campaign. The general antipathy to paying taxes has grown to a point where most candidates for public office fear voter wrath if they suggest the public should pay more to support services. The antitax sentiment at the state and federal level is staunchly against welfare and social programs and against providing adequate support for poor schools.[12] The ongoing shift of people from urban areas will continue to weaken the urban voice in Congress and state legislatures. In 2010, as a result of the drift of population toward the South and the West Coast, northeastern states lost several seats in the House. Their replacements are unlikely to be favorable to struggling cities. New Jersey lost one seat in the redistricting; Texas gained four.[13] Members of Congress who represent the northeastern states are more likely than in the past to represent either the suburbs alone or come from districts that are both urban and suburban. Policy choices such as allocations for low-income housing and social welfare programs will surely be affected, and not to the advantage of cities.

Given the declining support from the federal government and the state, the fact that the economy has yet to find a way to produce sufficient numbers of jobs, and the impact of strong competitive pressures on domestic enterprises as a result of globalization, the future for Newark and cities like it is not bright. Change and improvement, however, are still possible. There are mounds of academic studies that conclude that the major ills of urban life and the plight of urban poor are the result of national forces and policies that may be out of the reach of local citizens and their leaders. The view from those mounds is that local actors are powerless in the face of these external forces and that little or nothing can be done to improve the lives of citizens. That is a false argument. It does not recognize that even in the face of major disadvantages, local leadership really matters, that civic and political efforts on the local level can make substantial improvements in the functioning of a city. Leadership, working together, can ensure that government is focused on the needs of citizens. Local leaders can give order and reason to the processes of governance. Local leadership can help to improve the reputation of a troubled city in the larger regional community.

Throughout its history, ethnic and racial politics along with petty deal making and corruption have hampered Newark's social as well as economic progress. The city's reputation has often been damaged by its politics and destructive behavior by its officials. Some of Newark's leaders, certainly not all, have misused resources or have failed to plan and manage wisely. At times, Newark's elected leaders have made conditions worse. For example, it was Newark's own officials and leaders who so badly administered the public schools, making the school system a patronage pit that led to intervention and a takeover by the state. The people who mismanaged the Newark Watershed Conservation and Development Corporation were Newark's appointed and elected officials. Newark's own officials corrupted a federal jobs program during the Gibson years and made it a national example of government waste.

Newark's major challenges are clear, if difficult to confront. Concentrated poverty is the overarching problem; its complications are most prominently manifested in the dysfunction of the schools, the pervasive violent crime, and the reality of joblessness for thousands of people, many of whom are young and who have no legitimate options for a safe and crime-free livelihood. As Michelle Alexander, author of *The New Jim Crow*, notes, "Throughout the black community, there is widespread awareness that black ghetto youth have few, if any, realistic options, and therefore dealing drugs can be an irresistible temptation."[14]

The city's job training and workforce efforts hardly touch the depth of the problem. Newark's Workforce Investment Board is under the aegis of City Hall, and, according to federal regulations, the chair of the board is supposed to be an employer. But in Newark, the chair is an assistant director of the Newark Alliance, a corporate-sponsored nonprofit that serves as a facilitator in the areas of development and education. In 2010, the program had approximately $8 million to distribute to job training programs.[15] Of that amount, $2.5 million went to support local vendors to carry out training for the unemployed and $3.5 million went to support administration of the program, which includes a director, support staff, and a number of counselor and job development positions. According to a former senior employee at the agency, these jobs are often assigned to the politically connected, such as district leaders and campaign workers. As a former employee of the agency told me, City Hall would not only insist the agency hire this or that person but also dictate what the salary had to be, even if it was out of line for the job.

The director of the program said that the program served from twenty to twenty-five thousand people each year, meaning that they receive one of the several services offered.[16] By her calculation, the program reaches about one-third of the residents who need help in finding a job, which judging from the virtually static unemployment figures is a very generous estimate of what the program accomplishes.

There are a few exemplary job training programs run by community development corporations and other nonprofits. However, several program managers told of the difficulty of working with the Workforce Investment Board and said that its personnel attempt to push program operators to fudge their numbers by counting job referrals as job placements. The reality is that Newark and other urban communities need a massive public service and public works program that can provide work opportunities for any adult who can show up. While the Comprehensive Employment Training Act (CETA) program of years ago had its problems and was poorly managed, it showed that idleness can be addressed by such approaches, and, in the process, the civic groups that provided many of the placements can be strengthened.

A Modest Agenda

Newark can move forward if there is a new politics in which leaders clearly believe in democratic practices and encourage the participation of citizens. The city needs leaders who would say first and foremost that their mission is to improve the operation of the city on behalf of all of its people. Newark leadership cannot alone solve the problem of unemployment or the shortage of affordable housing. But local leadership can take actions to make the city a better place. Granted, there are some who will say that politics is politics and it will never change, particularly in a city that had been behaving the same way for almost a century. However, I have seen the good and strong people who continually try to make Newark a better place. There are many, but they need the help of others and they need better leadership. I offer the following suggestions to move Newark ahead:

1. The number one priority for the city should be to improve the operation and results of the Newark's public schools. This would be the most important feature of a real renaissance, but it may be the most challenging thing to do because close to 40 percent of the city's children live in relatively deep poverty, and neither local leadership nor state leadership has served the children well. The governance of Newark schools should be the responsibility of a hybrid

board that might be made up of five elected ward representatives, two members each appointed by the mayor and the commissioner of education. Ultimately, the traditional model of the American school system must be altered to meet the needs of Newark students. The problem of education in Newark is not the children, but careless politics, and the antiquated, ineffective approaches that are simply inadequate to meet the special needs of poor children.

2. The city needs broader and more organized civic participation and civic action. The schools, colleges, and civic organizations should undertake a concerted effort to encourage and teach citizens how their government works and how they can engage in civic improvement efforts. The citizens of the city should have a stronger and more informed voice regarding all activities of municipal government. Newark would profit by looking back in history to examples like the Business and Industrial Coordinating Council and the efforts of the Newark Collaboration Group, as well as to current efforts in other cities. In Cincinnati, Ohio, for example, a civic organization has begun to attack the problems of failing schools by mobilizing a broad consortium of more than three hundred leaders and organizations, including heads of private and corporate foundations, city government officials, school district representatives, presidents of universities and colleges, and related nonprofit and advocacy groups. STRIVE, the convening group, facilitates a process through which all agree on an agenda and the manner in which their efforts will be evaluated.

The STRIVE approach is based on the understanding that fixing one point on a continuum of problems in a troubled system is not going to create much difference unless there is an effort to work on all aspects of the problem simultaneously. It is also understood that no single organization, however innovative or powerful, can accomplish the reform of a system alone. Ultimately, the approach seeks *collective impact*, which has become the descriptive name of the process. The STRIVE approach is being attempted in Houston, Texas; Heyward, California; Indianapolis, Indiana; and Richmond, Virginia.[17]

Any endeavor of this kind would require exceptional leadership, a very inclusive strategy of participation, and the resources to fund and sustain an effort that is not looking for quick fixes.

Foundations are not accustomed to supporting efforts that attempt to mobilize large groups of people to seek systemic change. But if Newark is ever going to address its critical social issues, especially failing schools, job readiness, and crime, it will take the dedicated efforts of everyone in business, higher education, and the civic and nonprofit community to do so.

3. Newark needs a new civic organization to watch over the city's budget. Such a committee could be supported through local foundations and enlist financial expertise from local academics at Rutgers University, the New Jersey Institute of Technology, and Seton Hall University, as well as members of the financial staffs of corporations and local nonprofits. An organization like the Citizens Budget Committee in New York City or the citizens budget watchdog group in Chicago should be created in Newark, perhaps housed at one of the universities but based on a collaboration involving all higher education institutions and civic organizations.

4. Newark leadership should make more organized and directed efforts to establish collaborative arrangements with nearby jurisdictions. City leaders should explore the trade-offs of creating a regional fire department as well as integrating additional police services and explore possibilities for collaboration in purchasing and other services.

5. Right-size the Newark City Council. Newark's council is one of the highest-paid and heavily staffed local legislative bodies in the nation. Its duties and functions are important, but members do not deserve the exorbitant compensation they receive. The role of a council member has become in some cases more of a political plum to serve the financial interests of family and friends than a post of civic responsibility. Several of its members have other public jobs or private businesses. The following changes would help:

   ◇ Reduce the pay of council members to a reasonable sum that is consistent with a part-time job.
   ◇ Reduce the size of the staff of each council member to three, and return all research functions to the office of the city clerk.
   ◇ Establish a two-term limit for members of the council, which would encourage more participation. A council position should not be seen as a lifelong endeavor.

6. Establish a three-term limit for the office of the mayor. Term limits help to expand the participation of citizens in electoral politics. An elected office is intended to provide an opportunity for service to the community and society. There are term limits for the state governor and the nation's president. Why not for the mayor of Newark? Some argue that longer tenure provides for better and wiser leadership, giving those in office a long view of the city's problems. But along with the long-term view comes rigidity, excessive power, and loss of accountability. It's a trade-off, but the benefits of term limits would outweigh the negatives.

7. Establish a forum for civic conversation about the current conditions and the future of Newark. It should be a conversation that would include every segment of the community, including business, civic, political, and labor groups. The aim of such an effort would be to broaden and deepen the dialogue about the future of the city, particularly its children, with forthright discussion and vetting of ideas unfettered by personal and political agendas. In order to be effective, any new effort would require a broad and varied group of people, the likes of which has not been assembled before. Elected officials should be involved and have an opportunity on occasion to lead and voice their opinions. Public access television has the capacity to bring real-time conversations into the homes of residents. A major challenge would be to find the right parties to lead such an effort. They would have to be respected members of the community, such as a university president or chancellor, a highly placed business executive, or the leader of a civic or cultural institution. All stakeholders—residents, nonresidents, civic and business people—need to have a discussion regarding how Newark can have a more complete recovery.

Getting to a Better Place?

More than forty years ago, Bayard Rustin, perhaps the most strategic thinker of the civil rights movement, wrote that "the quest for equality of black citizens could not be satisfied within the framework of existing political and economic relations." The struggle for equality in America, he added, "is essentially revolutionary," which did not connote violence, he was careful to add. He meant however that there had to be "qualitative and transformative shifts which would significantly alter the structure of social and economic institutions." "The [civil rights] movement could not be victorious," he said, "in the absence of radical programs for full employment, abolition of slums, the reconstruction of our educational system, and new definitions of work and leisure."[18]

Rustin saw his vision of radical change arriving through a vigorous and highly mobilized political movement in which change-minded people captured political offices and then supported progressive ideas aimed at alleviating poverty and enhancing society's well-being. His thesis was that the vision and idealism of the civil rights movement would transform traditional political organizations to create a more democratic and reform-minded political system. Richard Hatcher, the first black mayor of Gary, Indiana, was the kind of visionary Rustin imagined. And there were others: Maynard Jackson, who served as mayor of Atlanta; John Lewis, a civil rights veteran who suffered the brutal violence of southern racists and won a congressional seat in Georgia; CORE activist Major Owens, from Brooklyn, who served in Congress and fought for a better society; and our own late congressman, Donald Payne, who served on the city council and, before being elected to Congress, always stayed close to his community while at the same time providing extraordinary service in the developing world. Like Payne, the late council member Donald Tucker never lost his devotion to the people of Newark and was not afraid to speak up against some who would abuse their power.

Somehow, however, the core values of the civil rights movement, which were at the heart of the initial Gibson campaign, got away from most of Newark's political leadership. Both Kenneth A. Gibson and Sharpe James talked about using their power to advocate and advance the economic and political position of blacks. However, Gibson was eventually angered by the expectations blacks had of him. Neither Gibson nor James did anything significant or effective to strengthen the political knowledge and position of the black community. Both eventually joined Newark's long tradition of petty deal making by operating close to or outside of the boundaries of legality. For both, the school district was about jobs and patronage, not the future of Newark's children. Several members of the city council also joined the old political games; some broke the law and went to jail. They vigorously defended their hefty salaries and large staffs but were virtually mute regarding the reality that they represented the worst areas of the city. The schools in their bailiwicks had the highest rates of failure and the neighborhoods they represented had the highest rates of crime and received the worst police protection.[19]

The old machine-oriented ethnic politics allowed Germans, Irish, Jews, and Italians to use the levers of the political system to move their families and neighborhoods into better jobs and circumstances. Black political ascendancy has not produced the same results because the economic foundations of the urban community have been drastically altered by suburbanization, economic decentralization, and, more recently, globalization. Furthermore, there are still pockets of racism that have targeted African Americans more consistently and intensely than any other "minority" or ethnic population.

Black political leaders have not been as effective as the leaders of previous groups in delivering to their community, partly because they have erroneously assumed that they could behave just as leaders of other groups had. Even worse, some of them emulated the venality of the ethnic leaders of earlier times. If Newark is to be a better place, it will have to have more civic engagement and elect leaders who are willing to serve the interest of the community. Newark needs leaders willing to fight for programs that aid poor families, who will ensure that the spoils of government are fairly distributed, who are willing to clearly state and to act upon the premise that the purpose of government is to serve its citizens. Perhaps when that kind of leadership emerges out of the neighborhoods of the city, Newark will have a chance to experience a genuine transformation.

Notes

1. ABOUT NEWARK

1. Timothy Crist, "Godly Government: Puritans and the Founding of Newark" (paper presented to the Newark History Society, meeting held at the New Jersey Historical Society, 52 Park Place, Newark, November 9, 2009), 1–15.

2. Ibid.

3. Ibid., 16nn.

4. Laurie Cohen, "'Tracking High School Graduation Rates in the Newark Public Schools" (unpublished manuscript, submitted for Graduate Seminar on Post Industrial Cities, Edward J. Bloustein School, Rutgers University, spring 2012).

5. American Community Survey, 2010, www.census.gov/acs/www.

6. Jean Anyon, *Ghetto Schooling* (New York: Columbia University Press, 1997), 53.

7. Stanley Winters, "Newark's Plight in Perspective," *Urban Consensus*, April 1972.

8. Mary Bruno, *An American River* (Vashon, WA: Dewitt Press, 2012), 23–43.

9. Michael E. Porter, *Opportunity Newark*, Initiative for a Competitive Inner City/ Newark Alliance, 2006, www.Newark-alliance.org/docs/media/1324-newarksummary.

10. Mike Kinney and Mark Mueller, "Two Suburban Schools Refuse Trips to Newark for Football," *Star-Ledger*, October 27, 2008.

11. Michael Danielson, *The Politics of Exclusion* (New York: Columbia University Press, 1976), 202–205; Kenneth Jackson, *Crabgrass Frontier* (New York: Oxford University Press, 1985), 210–212.

12. Kevin Michael Kruse, *Atlanta and the Making of Modern Conservatism* (Princeton, NJ: Princeton University Press, 2005), 61.

13. Beryl Satter, *Family Properties* (New York: Metropolitan Books, 2009); also Danielson, *Politics of Exclusion*.

14. George Sternlieb, *The Tenement Landlord* (New Brunswick, NJ: Rutgers University Press, 1966).

15. Satter, *Family Properties*.

16. William Frey and Dowell Myers, "Segregation in U.S. Metropolitan Areas and Cities, 1990–2000: Trends and Explanations" (University of Michigan, Institute for Social Research, 2005).

The causes of segregation are complex, and while there is little dispute regarding the role of discriminatory federal housing policies in contributing to segregation, the extent to which those policies remain causal in segregation and poverty concentration today is a matter of debate. The most significant determinant of segregation today is the matter of choice; most whites will not move into a neighborhood with a black population of more than 40 percent. The entrenched racism in American society (manifested in a wide range of housing polices and individual and institutional actions) created the foundations of urban residential segregation. Additional factors of institutional and personal behavior have served to sustain segregation and develop a housing and real estate industry in which racial considerations are deeply embedded, despite the fact that acts of discrimination are against the law. Nonetheless the role of the federal government is clear: "The Civil Rights Commission has reported that of all the sources of residential segregation, the federal government has been the most influential in creating and maintaining residential segregation." See Florence Wagman Roisman, "Intentional Racial Discrimination and Segregation by the Federal Government as a Principal Cause of Concentrated Poverty," a response to Schill and Wachter, *University of Pennsylvania Law Review*, May 1, 1995.

17. New Jersey Advisory Committee to the United States Commission of Civil Rights, "Public Housing in Newark's Central Ward," April 1968. This bound brochure is a report of public hearings.

18. Ada Louise Huxtable, "A Prescription for Disaster," *New York Times*, November 5, 1972. See also Tim O'Neil, "A Look Back: Pruitt and Igoe Started Strong, but in the End Failed," *St. Louis Post Dispatch*, July 25, 2010, www.umsl.edu—keelr/010/Pruitt—igoe.htm.

19. Michael B. Katz, *Why Don't American Cities Burn* (Philadelphia: University of Pennsylvania Press, 2012), 49.

20. Thomas Sugrue, *The Origins of the Urban Crisis* (New York: Columbia University Press, 1996), xx.

21. Frank Rich, "Fourth of July, 1776, 1964, 2010," *New York Times*, July 4, 2010, 8.

22. The fact that the poor have higher crime rates than people who are not poor does not mean that the poor have some innate propensity to commit crime. Social science research over the years has supported the notion that crime is related to opportunity and conditions in which the poor live. The poor often live in areas where crime has been common for a long period of time, where there are few or no family or institutional sanctions for youth who engage in crime, and where there are few if any positive role models. In addition, in the inner city the relationship of law enforcement agencies often deepens alienation rather than abating it. See Samuel L. Myers and Margaret C. Simms, *The Economics of Race and Crime* (New Brunswick, NJ: Transaction Books, 1988).

23. Alfonso Narvaez, "121-Story Office Tower Proposed for Newark," *New York Times*, August 17, 1986; Wayne King, "Developer's New Gift Unwanted in Newark," *New York Times*, September 29, 1989; also Marc Holzer, Elizabeth Strom, Lois Redman Simons, and Tony Gonzales, *Reinventing Newark: Visions of the City from the Twentieth Century* (Rutgers University, National Center for Public Productivity, 2005).

24. Prior to the changes required by redistricting, each county had one senator in the state legislature, and that senator was usually from the suburbs. With redistricting, a county like Essex can have as many as three senators in the legislature, and at least one of them is likely to represent a large swath of Newark. Thus, redistricting gave urban Newark voters a senator who would have the power to review any state appointment involving a resident of the county, or any appointment, such as a county prosecutor, for a job in Essex. As a result of redistricting in 1996 the New Jersey Assembly

went from sixty to eighty members and the state senate expanded from twenty-one to forty members.

25. Paul Hoffman and Ira Pecznick, *To Drop a Dime* (New York: G. P. Putnam's Sons, 1976).

26. New Jersey State Commission of Investigation, "Afro-lineal Organized Crime," 1991, section titled "The Family North," 3–7, www.state.nj.us/sci/index.shtm.

27. "Genovese Organized Crime Family Soldier and Associates Indicted on Racketeering Charges, Including Extortion of International Longshoremen's Association Members," United States Attorneys, District of New Jersey and Eastern District of New York, January 20, 2011.

28. "Views and Outlook," *Wall Street Journal,* July, 25, 2009.

29. Diana Henriques, "Practices of HFA Attacked," *Trenton Times,* August 14, 1980, 1; State Commission of Investigation, "Report to the Governor and Members of the Legislature of the State of NJ," March 23, 1981, www.state.nj.us/sci/pdf/njhfa.pdf.

30. Joe Ryan and Ted Sherman, "Massive N.J. Corruption Sting Targets Mayors, Legislators, Rabbis," *Star-Ledger,* July 23, 2009.

31. Joseph F. Sullivan, "Senator in Jersey Is Indicted on $360,000 Bribe Charge," *New York Times,* October 23, 1979; Alfonso Narvaez, "Jersey Legislator and Father Guilty of Taking Kickbacks; to Be Sentenced May 27," *New York Times,* April 12, 1980; Robert Hanley, "Fugitive Politician Ordered to Serve Prison Term," *New York Times,* December 30, 1987.

32. As Mayor Booker prepared for his Senate race, his administration filed a lawsuit against the Newark Watershed Conservation and Development Corporation, charging many of the same improprieties that the Water Group had voiced over several years. The mayor asked that the NWCDC be dissolved and that the responsibilities of the NWCDC be returned to the city. The court subsequently appointed an interim board of directors for the NWCDC with a mandate to carry out the mayor's request. See David Giambusso, "Booker Administration Files Complaint to Dissolve Watershed, Alleging Financial Improprieties," *Star-Ledger,* May 24, 2013.

2. WINDS OF CHANGE

An earlier version of this chapter was published as "Black Ghetto Politics in Newark after World War II," in *Cities of the Garden State,* edited by Joel Schwartz and Daniel Prosser (Dubuque, IA: Kendall/Hunt Publishing, 1977).

1. Fred Means, "A Time of Hope: Black Newark in the 1950s" (paper presented at a panel discussion by the Newark History Society, held at the New Jersey Historical Society, September 13, 2010).

2. Phillip Hauser, "Demographic Factors in the Integration of the Negro," *Daedalus* 94 (Fall 1965): 850.

3. The term "urban crisis" came into vogue in the early 1960s and generally meant the declining social and economic conditions resulting from deindustrialization. Thomas Sugrue's prominent study, *The Origins of the Urban Crisis,* explains in illuminating detail how Detroit, once one of the most vibrant manufacturing cities in America, became the embodiment of the "urban crisis" as a result of the flight of industry and capital and the combined forces of racism and anti-urban government policies. See Sugrue, *The Origins of the Urban Crisis* (New York: Columbia University Press, 1996).

4. Clement A. Price, "The Afro-American Community of Newark, 1917–1947: A Social History" (Ph.D. diss., Rutgers University, 1975), 40–62.

5. New Jersey Advisory Committee to the U.S. Commission on Civil Rights, "Public Housing in Newark's Central Ward" (U.S. Civil Rights Commission, April 1968), 1 (hereafter cited as New Jersey Advisory Committee on Civil Rights Statement); Housing Authority of the City of Newark, "Progress Report on Integration," June 1952, 1; "T.B. Deaths Increase in 18 Large Cities," *New Jersey Afro-American*, January 2, 1943, 11 (hereafter cited as *Afro-American*). A study by the American Tuberculosis Association found that in 1940 the overall death rate from TB was 42 per 100,000 and the rate for blacks was 203 ("Tuberculosis Deaths Cut; 3.3 Per Cent Lower in Nation and 0.3 Off in 42 Big Cities," *New York Times*, December 22, 1942).

6. Curtis Lucas, *Third Ward Newark* (Chicago: Ziff-Davis, 1946), 1.

7. Harold Kaplan, *Urban Renewal in Newark* (New York: Columbia University Press, 1963).

8. U.S. Bureau of the Census, *Census of Population: 1950, 1, Number of Inhabitants* (Washington, DC: Government Printing Office, 1952).

9. "Metropolitan Leads in Church Membership," *Afro-American*, March 22, 1947, 20.

10. "First Negro Named to Newark Bench," *New York Times*, October 19, 1958.

11. "Pettigrew to NHA," *Newark News*, April 24, 1955. Also "Carlin Praised on Pettigrew," *Newark News*, April 7, 1955; and "Ask Naming of Pettigrew," *Newark News*, January 27, 1963.

12. "Carlton Norris, 60, of Newark NAACP," *New York Times*, September 8, 1963. Also, interview with Walter Chambers, who as an NAACP member and volunteer handled Norris's correspondence. Chambers, interview by author, Newark, New Jersey, April 21, 2010.

13. James Pawley, former executive of Essex County Urban League, interview by author, Montclair, New Jersey, September 1975.

14. Richard Hofstader, *The Age of Reform* (New York Alfred A. Knopf, 1955), 9.

15. Stanley Winters, "Newark Blight in Perspective," *Urban Consensus* (April 1972).

16. Fred Cook, "The People vs. the Mob; or Who Runs New Jersey," *New York Times Magazine*, February 1, 1970, 11; Lester Velie, "The Man to See in New Jersey: From Rackets to Riches," *Colliers*, September 1, 1951, 48; U.S. Congress, Senate, *Investigation of Organized Crime in Interstate Commerce, New York and New Jersey*, Hearings before a Special Committee to Investigate Organized Crime in Interstate Commerce, Senate, pursuant to S.R. 202, 81st Cong., 2nd sess., 1950 and S.R. 129, 82nd Congress, 1st sess., 1951 (hereafter cited as *Senate Crime Hearings*); U.S. Congress, Senate, *Organized Crime in Interstate Commerce*, Final Report of Special Committee to Investigate Organized Crime in Interstate Commerce, Senate, pursuant to S.R. 202, 81st Congress, 2nd sess., 1950, as amended by S.R. 60 and S.R. 129, 82nd Congress,1st sess., 1951, 65–73 (hereafter cited as Senate Crime Committee, *Final Report*).

17. Testimony of Meyer Ellenstein and Jules Endler in *Senate Crime Hearings*, 219–260, 306–336, 773–778.

18. Charles Matthews, interview by author, Newark, New Jersey, October 1975.

19. Quoted in Cook, "The People vs. the Mob," 35.

20. Matthews interview.

21. FBI files, Zwillman, "Personal History and Background," June 7, 1950, 3–4, http://vault.fbi.gov.

22. Matthews interview.

23. Toussaint Ware, "Third Ward Political Evils in 1920's Left Ugly Scars," *Afro-American*, November 10, 1951, 20. Ware authored two additional commentaries on Third Ward politics in the *Afro-American*, November 17, 1951, and November 24, 1951.

24. Calvin West, interview by author, October 23, 2009.

25. Matthews interview.

26. Ibid.

27. Ibid.

28. State of New Jersey, *Manual of the Legislature of New Jersey* (Trenton: MacCrellish and Quigley, 1949), 520.

29. "Bowser Wins Assembly Seat," *Afro-American*, May 9, 1953.

30. Samuel Haskins, "Far Eastern Café Cited: Restaurant Flouts Civil Rights Laws," *Afro-American*, November 18, 1950, 1.

31. Based on tabulation of net change in the number of manufacturers listed for the years 1950, 1960, and 1969 in *New Jersey Industrial Directory* (Union City, NJ: Hudson Dispatch, 1950, 1960, and 1969).

32. Chester Rapkin, "Group Relations in Newark—1957, Problems, Prospects, and a Program for Research" (Mayor's Commission on Group Relations, 1957), 16–28. Newark is part of the tristate New York, New Jersey, Connecticut Standard Metropolitan Statistical Area (SMSA). The New York SMSA includes Essex, Morris, and Somerset Counties.

33. "Dr. McCarroll Breaks Bar, Joins City Hospital Staff," *Afro-American*, January 12, 1946; "50-Year Old Hospital Tradition Is Broken," *Afro-American*, September 1, 1951.

34. "Pastors Call Upon Mayor to Name Judge, Law Aide," *Afro-American*, April 26, 1952, 1; Samuel A. Haynes, "Mayor Makes 2 Offers Instead of Judgeship," *Afro-American*, May 17, 1952, 1.

35. "Mayor Insults Race on Judgeship," *Afro-American*, May 24, 1952, 1.

36. "Newark to Abolish JC (Jim Crow) Housing Policy," *Afro-American*, August 19, 1950, 1.

37. Hearings before the U.S. Commission on Civil Rights, September 11–12, 1962, held in Newark, New Jersey (U.S. Commission on Civil Rights, 1963).

38. "School Board Not Disturbed: 300 Parents Stage Protest," *Afro-American*, June 14, 1950, 1; "Board Surrenders, Pigeonholes Transfer Bill," *Afro-American*, July 1, 1950, 1.

39. "Voters to End Rule by Commission: Charter Group Cites Major Advantages Mayor-Council Rule Would Bring to City," *Afro-American*, August 15, 1953.

40. For a comprehensive discussion of charter change see Stanley Winters, "Charter Change and Civic Reform in Newark, 1953–1954," *New Jersey History* 118, nos. 1–2 (Spring/Summer 2000), 34–65; also Michael Decter, "Charter Reform in Newark" (senior thesis, Princeton University, 1969); and Phillip Douglass, "Reform in Newark, 1953–1972" (senior thesis, Princeton University, 1972).

41. Winters, "Charter Change," 47–48.

42. "74,000 Newark Citizens Forgotten by Planners: NAACP Censures Charter Study Unit," *Afro-American*, May 9, 1953.

43. Samuel A. Haynes, "5 New Wards Set in Newark: 'Central' Is Key Election District," *Afro-American*, December 5, 1953.

44. "Commission Eyes Mixup in Central Ward Population," *Afro-American*, January 9, 1954; Larry Coggins, interview by author, Newark, New Jersey, 1972.

45. Douglass, "Reform in Newark, 1953–1972."

46. Turner worked for the *New Jersey Record*, a black weekly that ended publication in 1947. According to one Central Ward/Third Ward old-timer, Turner mainly "hustled" for advertisements for the publisher.

47. "Councilman from Ward Drive Gains," *Afro-American*, December 26, 1953, 1.

48. William Payne, interview by author, Newark, New Jersey, October 3, 2008.

49. "Yancey, Hazelwood Endorsed as Councilmanic Candidates," *Afro-American*, February 27, 1954; also editorial: "No Unity, No Funds," *Afro-American*, February 27, 1954, 1.

50. Alan V. Lowenstein, *Alan V. Lowenstein: New Jersey Lawyer and Community Leader* (New Brunswick, NJ: Rutgers University Press, 2001), 227.

51. Coggins, interview by author, Newark, New Jersey, 1974.

52. Gerald Pomper, "A Report on Newark Politics" (Rutgers University Urban Studies Center, September 17, 1963, author's files).

53. "Councilman Turner Raps Landlords," *Newark News*, January 4, 1956.

54. Sam Convissor, interview by Linda Jones, Newark, New Jersey, April 1972; Convissor, interview by author, South Orange, New Jersey, March 1, 2010; Kaplan, *Urban Renewal Politics*, 153–154.

55. "Negro Leaders Criticize Turner," *Newark News*, February 12, 1956.

56. Louis Danzig, interview, Newark, New Jersey, October 1976.

57. According to Danzig, both Irvine Turner and Timothy Still objected to the Newark Housing Authority's announced policy on integration in 1950. For Turner, integration was a threat to his solid black base in the Central Ward. Timothy Still, the widely respected leader in the Hayes Homes, also objected to the effort to integrate public housing. Danzig interview.

58. Kenneth B. Clark, *Dark Ghetto* (New York, Harper & Row, 1965), 163.

59. Edgar Litt, *Ethnic Politics in America* (Glenview, IL: Scott, Foresman, 1970), 60–65.

60. "Sugrue Denies Police Raids Discriminatory," *Newark News*, April 20, 1957; "Turner Offers an Apology," *Newark News*, April 25, 1957.

61. "Councilman Turner Gives Carlin Plan for Changes," *Afro-American*, August 14, 1954, 1; Coggins interview.

62. On Oscar DePreist see Harold F. Gosnell, *Negro Politicians* (Chicago: University of Chicago Press, 1967), 190–195. On Adam Clayton Powell, see James Q. Wilson, "Two Negro Politicians: An Interpretation," *Midwest Journal of Politics* 4 (November 1960).

63. Rutgers University, Business Executive Research Committee, "Economic Development of the Greater Newark Area: Recent Trends and Prospects," 1958.

64. Ibid., 5–7.

65. Rapkin et al., "Group Relations in Newark—1957."

66. Jean Anyon, *Ghetto Schooling: A Political Economy of Urban Educational Reform* (New York: Teachers College Press, 1997), 93–95.

67. Ibid., 95.

68. Ibid.

69. Fred Means, interview by author, Monroe, New Jersey, August 19, 2008, and Walt Chambers, interview by author, Newark, New Jersey, April 21, 2010. Sharpe James interview by Glen Marie Brickus, Krueger-Scott Cultural Center, African American Oral History Project, December 3, 1996, and December 17, 1996.

70. Rapkin, "Group Relations in Newark—1957."

3. THE COLLAPSE OF THE MACHINE

1. Recent scholarship on Dwight Eisenhower's presidency has suggested that Eisenhower was far more active and was more of a world leader than earlier scholars had given him credit for. The revised view is that he was successful in leading the nation through a very difficult period. Jim Newton in *Eisenhower: The White House Years* (New York: Doubleday, 2011) points out that under Eisenhower, the interstate highway system was built and Russia was stared down, and that Eisenhower had courage and foresight to warn the nation about the inherent problems of the military-industrial complex. There is no evidence to support an argument that Eisenhower was supportive of racial advancement, however. On this point, see August Meier and Elliott Rudwick, *From Plantation to Ghetto* (New York: Hill and Wang, 1970).

2. Taylor Branch, *Parting the Waters* (New York: Simon and Schuster, 1988), 679. See also David Levering Lewis, *King: A Biography* (Urbana: University of Illinois Press, 1978), 235.

3. Branch, *Parting the Waters*, 679.

4. John Cunningham, *Newark*, rev. ed. (Newark: New Jersey Historical Society, 1988), 306.

5. Sam Convissor, interview by author, South Orange, New Jersey, March 1, 2010.

6. Alan V. Lowenstein, *Alan V. Lowenstein: New Jersey Lawyer and Community Leader* (New Brunswick, NJ: Rutgers University Press, 2001). Lowenstein reveals in his autobiography that Carlin assigned him to search for a new police director and he identified Weldon.

7. Tom Giblin, interview by author, West Orange, New Jersey, February 27, 2012.

8. Robert Bender, former director of the Essex County chapter of Americans for Democratic Action and former CORE activist, interview by author, Plainfield, New Jersey, August 5, 2008.

9. Gerald Pomper, "A Report on Newark Politics" (Urban Studies Center, Rutgers University, n.d.), 2, copy in author's files.

10. Ibid.

11. Harold Kaplan, *Urban Renewal Politics* (New York: Columbia University Press, 1963), 61.

12. Ibid., 65.

13. Duane Lockard, *The Politics of State and Local Government* (New York: Macmillan, 1963), 118.

14. Stanley Winters, "Charter Change and Civic Reform in Newark, 1953–1954," *New Jersey History* 118, nos. 1–2 (Spring/Summer 2000): 35.

15. Hugh Joseph Addonizio, en.wiki.org/wiki/HughJosephAddonizio.

16. Mark Pizzaro, "Irish Make Last Stand with Carlin against Addonizio," *PolitikerNJ*, March 17, 2010; also Donald Malafronte, interview by author, Roseland, New Jersey, October 2010.

17. "Addonizio Pledges Support for Negro Aims," *Afro-American*, March 17, 1962.

18. Steve Adubato, political boss of Newark and Essex County, founder of Robert Treat Charter School and a network of other services, interviews by author, Newark, New Jersey, October 22, 2009, and May 26, 2011.

19. Malafronte interview.

20. Ibid.

21. Convissor interview.

22. Adubato interview, October 22, 2009. It is well known that Steve Adubato Sr. is the father of Dr. Steve Adubato Jr., a radio and television personality in the New Jersey–New York region. From here forward, I will use the name Steve Adubato, referring to the father.

23. CORE, which grew out of an organization named the Fellowship of Reconciliation, practiced the philosophy of nonviolence and applied Gandhian tactics of nonviolent direct action for nearly two decades before the civil rights movement burst onto the national scene in 1960.

24. Bender interview.

25. George Richardson, interview by author, New York City, September 22, 2008.

26. Julia Rabig, "The Laboratory of Democracy," in *Black Power at Work*, ed. David Goldberg and Trevor Griffey (Ithaca, NY: Cornell University Press, 2010), 51–59.

27. Ibid.

28. Ibid., 55.

29. Ibid.; also Harry Burke, "Building Trades Reject Demands: Arbitrary, Says Essex Unit," *Newark News*, July 24, 1963.

30. Richardson interview.

31. Bender interview.

32. New Jersey Bell Telephone Company, "CORE Launches Press Attack Against Company Charging Discrimination against Negroes," Information Bulletin No. 6, March 23, 1964. Letter from J. W. Helmstaedter, Personnel Director, New Jersey Bell, to Richard Proctor Jr., Chairman, CORE subcommittee on employment, March 24, 1964. Both documents are from author's files.

33. Data sheets provided by New Jersey Bell, author's files.

34. New Jersey Bell Telephone Company, "CORE Launches Press Attack Against Company Charging Discrimination against Negroes."

35. "CORE Sets Moves Against N.J. Bell," *Newark News*, March 25, 1964.

36. This account was conveyed to me by Gene Felker, former vice president of New Jersey Bell. Felker and I served on the board of the Victoria Foundation, a local Chubb family foundation.

37. Chambers interview.

38. Comment made to me by Donald Stevens, an executive of New Jersey Bell, in 1964, during period of negotiations between CORE and New Jersey Bell.

39. Douglas Eldridge, "Interracial Action: A Series of Articles," *Newark News*, March 22–26, 1964. Also Convissor interview.

40. Affirmative Action reports, author's files.

41. Convissor interview.

42. Affirmative Action reports.

43. Richardson interview.

44. Ibid.

45. Ibid.

46. "Richardson Cites Vote," *Newark News*, November 8, 1963,

47. "Carey Rebuffs Richardson," *Newark News*, March 10, 1964.

48. "Richardson Slate Dies," *Newark News*, July 9, 1964.

49. "Richardson Slate Garners 10,000 Votes; Impact Unclear," *Newark News*, November 14, 1965.

50. The invitation to the meeting leading up to the ERAP project was sent by Stan-

ley Winters; the meeting at Winters's home was attended by Stanley Aronowitz, a scholar/labor activist who was an enthusiastic advocate for SDS.

51. Warren Grover, professor of history and Newark expert who served as director of Newark SDS project in 1964, interview by author, Newark, New Jersey, October 21, 2011.

52. Jennifer Frost, *"An Interracial Movement of the Poor": Community Organizing and the New Left in the 1960s* (New York: NYU Press, 2001).

53. Ibid.

54. David Milton Gerwin, "The End of Coalition: The Failure of Community Organizing in Newark in the 1960's" (Ph.D. diss., Columbia University, 1998).

55. NCUP leaflet, author's files.

56. Malafronte interview.

57. Steve Block, former NCUP member and education advocate, interview by author, Rhinebeck, New York, August 18, 2008.

58. "All About Essex," *Newark News*, August 31, 1964. (Turner's comments were made in a local television interview.)

59. "Turner Says NAACP Should Lead All Civil Rights Groups," *Newark News*, June 10, 1963.

60. Harold Baron, "Black Powerlessness in Chicago," *Trans-Action,* November, 1968.

61. Calvin West, first black elected citywide, and political advisor to mayors and governors, interview by author, Newark, New Jersey, September 2009.

62. Kenneth B. Clark, *Dark Ghetto* (New York, Harper & Row, 1965), 196.

63. Comment made to me in personal conversation by Newark Branch executive board member, 1963.

64. Members of Newark Branch of the NAACP: 1962—1,454; 1963—1,687; 1964—3,422. During the three-year period, membership increased by more than 100 percent. Former *Newark News* reporter Douglas Eldridge showed me a file that included a communication from "Current" (presumably Closter Current who was then the executive in charge of local branch activities) to *Newark News* managing editor William R. Clark indicating the membership for this period. A copy of Douglas Eldridge's note in file of author.

65. Editorial, "Blame Yourself," *Afro-American*, June 29, 1963, 1.

66. "Norris Critics Ask Him to Resign NAACP Presidency," *Newark News*, June 10, 1963.

67. "Cantrell Named County Sheriff's Chaplain," *Star Ledger*, December 29, 1963.

68. Douglas Eldridge, "Vote Rules Hailed by NAACP Camps," *Newark News*, January 28, 1965.

69. Douglas Eldridge, "Mayor Denies Role in NAACP Voting," *Newark News*, February 24, 1965.

70. Lewis M. Killian, "The Significance of Extremism in the Black Revolution," *Social Forces* 20, no. 1 (Summer 1972), 42.

71. Douglas Eldridge, civil rights reporter for *Newark News* in 1960s, interview by author, Newark, New Jersey, April 12, 2008.

72. Lee Johnson, "Inside Newark," *Afro-American*, October 5, 1963. (It has been known for some time that Lee Johnson was Stanley Winters, the white professor and activist who led the Clinton Hill Neighborhood Council.) At the beginning of the Community Action Program, "maximum feasible participation," was interpreted to mean a majority (50 percent plus 1) on the governing boards of the local programs.

73. The Newark antipoverty program was strongly influenced by the HARYOU experience in Harlem. HARYOU was one of the nation's first antipoverty programs; its leaders organized a system that allowed for extensive participation of community activists and residents. The noted black psychologist Dr. Kenneth Clark was an advisor to the program.

74. The Vailsburg section, still almost entirely white at the time, was the only area that resisted the establishment of a neighborhood center or area board.

75. I served on the governing board of the UCC and chaired the personnel committee for a few years. I left my position at the county welfare board to take a top position at the Rutgers University Community Action Training Program, funded by the Office of Economic Opportunity. The Rutgers program was housed at the Rutgers Labor Education Center in New Brunswick and recruited neighborhood organizers and union shop stewards, initially for a year-long course in community organization. Each of the trainees received a monthly stipend and met at the Labor Center for classes each Friday. One entire weekend each month was spent in classes, where students studied labor history, politics, and economics, and often heard lectures from major leaders of the labor and civil rights movement. Donald Tucker and Charlie Bell, who became major players in Newark politics, were trainees in the program.

76. Richardson contends that Newark police director Dominick Spina told him that Hassan had five thousand followers. Richardson interview.

77. See Komozi Woodward, *A Nation Within a Nation: Amiri Baraka and Black Power Politics* (Chapel Hill: University of North Carolina Press, 1999).

78. The Gibson campaign is discussed in chapter 5.

4. REBELLION AND CITY POLITICS

1. Several works have documented the story of the Newark 1967 disorders. The most comprehensive and useful are *Report for Action* (Governor's Select Commission on Civil Disorders: State of New Jersey, February 1968) and the *Report of the National Advisory Commission on Civil Disorders* (New York: Bantam Books, 1968), also known as the Kerner Report (for its chair, Governor Otto Kerner). *Report for Action* looks in depth at Newark, Plainfield, Englewood, and other New Jersey cities. The Kerner Report focuses on Newark, Detroit, Milwaukee, and other U.S. cities. See also Kevin Mumford, *Newark: A History of Race, Rights, and Riots in America* (New York: NYU Press, 2007). Readers should be aware that Mumford's book is riddled with small and major errors of identification and reporting of events, however. Also see Tom Hayden's *Rebellion in Newark* (New York: Vintage Books, 1967); Nathan Wright's *Ready to Riot* (New York: Holt, Rinehart, Winston, 1968); and Ron Porambo's *No Cause for Indictment* (New York: Holt, Rinehart and Winston, 1971; Hoboken, NJ: Melville House, 2007). For an excellent general and theoretical discussion of urban disorders and violence, see Ted Gurr, *Why Men Rebel* (Princeton, NJ: Princeton University Press, 1970).

2. Wright, *Ready to Riot*, 11.

3. Gurr, *Why Men Rebel*, 22–58.

4. The point should not be lost that in the Newark rebellion, Elizabeth Artis, Rebecca Brown, and Eloise Spellman were shot and killed while in their homes, where they certainly had reason to believe they were out of harm's way. See listing of homicides in *Report for Action*, 138.

5. Stanley Lieberson and Arnold R. Silverman, "The Precipitants and Underlying

Conditions of Race Riots," *American Sociological Review* 30, no. 6 (December 1965): 887–898.

6. Ibid.

7. Henry Bienen, *Violence and Social Change: A Review of Current Literature* (Chicago: University of Chicago Press, 1968). In a conversation with the Columbia University historian Kenneth Jackson, he asked whether calling a civil disorder a rebellion, which means an attack against the state, might justify in the minds of some the harsh and brutal response measures. Since the labeling occurs after the event is over, it is clear that those who were unsympathetic to the rioters (for example, law enforcement forces and jury members who heard details of the killings) supported harsh and brutal responses without concern or attention to what the disturbances were called. However, for the larger society, Jackson raises an important point.

8. Wright, *Ready to Riot*, 11.

9. Albert Bergesen, "Race Riots of 1967: An Analysis of Police Violence in Detroit and Newark," *Journal of Black Studies* 12, no. 3 (March 1982): 273.

10. John T. Cunningham, *Newark* (Newark: New Jersey Historical Society, 1966), 314. In a later edition of the volume, Cunningham expressed his regret for the overly optimistic analysis of the potential for disorders in Newark in his 1966 edition.

11. *Report for Action*, 104–125, presents a chronicle of events from the beginning of the disorder on July 12, 1967, to the end, when law enforcement and control forces were removed.

12. Ibid.

13. *Report for Action*; Hayden, *Rebellion in Newark*; Porambo, *No Cause for Indictment*.

14. Anthony J. Carbo, *Memoirs of a Newark, New Jersey Police Officer* (Bloomington, IN: Trafford Publishing, 2006).

15. John Wefing, *The Life and Times of Richard J. Hughes* (New Brunswick, NJ: Rutgers University Press, 2009), 171.

16. Carbo, *Memoirs*, 125.

17. *Report for Action*, 125–129. Newark police officials advised Colonel Kelly, the head of the state police, in a June 1967 meeting that "everything was under control and they could contain and handle any situation" (127).

18. Carbo, *Memoirs*, 117.

19. Malafronte interview.

20. *Report for Action*, 135.

21. Ibid., 22.

22. *Kidd v. Addonizio* (DC#899–67) July 12–16, 1967: Pls.—"Negroes charge Newark police, in concert with state police and Nat'l guard, deprived Negroes of enumerated rights, with brutality, killings and other indignities. Seek injunction." Brief filed by Attorney Morton Stavis of the Constitutional Law Center, and the NJ American Civil Liberties Union. The case was dismissed in 1972.

23. *Report for Action*, introduction and 199; see also Michael Lipsky and David Olson, *Commission Politics: The Processing of Racial Crisis in America* (New Brunswick, NJ: Transaction Books, 1977), 244.

24. Lipsky and Olson, *Commission Politics*.

25. Sanford Jaffe, interview by author, December 10, 2008.

26. Ibid.

27. Ibid.

28. *Report for Action.*

29. Lipsky and Olson, *Commission Politics*, 381.

30. Ibid.

31. Malafronte interview.

32. Jaffe interview.

33. Although Essex County prosecutor Joseph Lordi said that the investigation was turned over to federal authorities because they had more resources to protect witnesses, there was also a view that the county investigation was dragging its feet.

34. Charles Grutzner, "Addonizio Balks at All Questions in Newark Inquiry," *New York Times*, December 10, 1969.

35. Charles Grutzner, "U.S. Indicts Mayor of Newark, 9 Present or Former Officials, on $253,000 Extortion Charges," *New York Times*, December 18, 1969; Grutzner, "Addonizio Balks at All Questions in Newark Inquiry," *New York Times*, December 10, 1969; Grutzner, "2 Jersey Judges Relieved of Duty in Crime Inquiry," *New York Times*, December 30, 1968; Thomas Brady, "Addonizio and 4 Convicted of Extortion by U.S. Jury," *New York Times*, July 22, 1970; Walter Waggoner, "Lacey to Expand Investigations in Jersey," *New York Times*, July 24, 1970.

36. Lipsky and Olson, *Commission Politics.*

37. PBS.org/WGBH/mjk/sf_video_pop_04B_tr_html.

38. Harold Kaplan, *Urban Renewal Politics: Slum Clearance in Newark* (New York: Columbia University Press, 1963).

39. David Levitus, "Planning Slum Clearance and the Road to Crisis in Newark," *Metro*; www.newarkmetro.rutgers.edu/reports/display.php?id=173.

40. In the matter of the Public Hearing in re: Negotiations on Relocation of New Jersey Medical School in Newark, New Jersey. Hearings held at State Office Building, 1100 Raymond Boulevard, Newark, on February 13, 17, 19, 21, 26, and March 1, 1968. In author's files; slso available at the Rutgers University Medical School Library in Newark, NJ (formerly University of Medicine and Dentistry of New Jersey.)

41. Ibid., February 19 hearing.

5. POLITICAL MOBILIZATION IN BLACK NEWARK

1. Jeffrey K. Hadden, Louis H. Masotti, and Victor Theissen, "The Making of Negro Mayors 1967," *Transaction* (January/February 1968); see also William Nelson, "Black Political Mobilization" (Ph.D. diss., University of Southern Illinois, 1972), for a case study of Richard Hatcher's campaign. Also see Elliott Moorman, "Toward a Black Model of Organization: The 1970 Mayoral and Councilmanic Election in Newark, New Jersey" (senior thesis, Princeton University, 1970).

2. Fred Waring, interview by author, July 18, 2012.

3. George Richardson, interview by author, September 22, 2008.

4. Kenneth Gibson, interview by author, March 5, 2009.

5. Richardson interview; Joe Scrimmager, interview by author, October 10, 2010.

6. Sanford Gallanter, friend of Kenneth Gibson, interview by author, Newark, New Jersey, November 15, 2010.

7. Komozi Woodward, *A Nation Within a Nation: Amiri Baraka and Black Power Politics* (Chapel Hill: University of North Carolina Press, 1999).

8. The Sunday morning meetings occurred monthly but sometimes with longer

intervals. In addition to Gibson, those who usually attended included Stanley Winters, leader of the Clinton Hill Neighborhood Council and a history professor at Newark College of Engineering; lawyer and businessman Sanford Gallanter; William Mercer, a manager at the local utility; and Elton Hill, a close buddy and friend of Gibson who was employed at the Newark Housing Authority.

9. Memorandum to community leaders on the organization of a black convention, author's files.

10. Richardson interview. Richardson's strong commitment to integration—after all, he had organized the first true rainbow political coalition in the area—probably would have made it difficult for him to participate in a black separatist event like the Black and Puerto Rican Convention.

11. Convention registration tally, author's files.

12. The election for candidates at the convention was supervised by the Community Dispute Resolution section of the American Arbitration Association, which volunteered personnel for the event.

13. William Nelson, "Black Political Mobilization" (Ph.D. diss., University of Southern Illinois, 1972), 37.

14. Robert Curvin, "The Persistent Minority" (Ph.D. diss., Princeton University, 1975).

15. See chapter 1 for discussion of Coggins's role in the election of Irvine Turner; see also Robert Curvin, "Black Ghetto Politics after World War II," in *Cities of the Garden State*, ed. Joel Schwartz and Daniel Prosser (Dubuque, IA: Kendall/Hunt Publishing, 1977).

16. "Gibson: Issues Revolve Around Municipal Services," *Newark News*, May 8, 1970, 13.

17. Tex Novellino, "Gibson's Plan to Improve City Hall Performance," *Star-Ledger*, April 14, 1970.

18. Ron Porambo, *No Cause for Indictment* (New York: Holt, Rinehart and Winston, 1971; Hoboken, NJ: Melville House, 2007). Dominick Spina, a police inspector in 1962, was appointed police director when Addonizio took office that year. For the city's blacks, he came to symbolize both the harsh brutality of the police and the corruption prevalent in the Addonizio administration. When FBI tapes were made public during the Addonizio trial, mobsters Angelo "Gyp" DeCarlo and Tony Boy Boiardo were heard in conversation agreeing that their choice to head the Newark police department was Dominick Spina. At one point, DeCarlo's advises Boiardo, "It's your call." See "Excerpts from F.B.I. Transcripts of Tapes Released at the DeCarlo Trial," *New York Times*, January 7, 1970.

19. Douglas Eldridge, "Indictments Strengthen Addonizio Opposition," *Newark News*, December 19, 1969.

20. Ibid.; see also Homer Bigart, "Cynicism and Sorrow Prevail in Newark in Scandal's Wake," *New York Times*, December 19, 1969; Charles Grutzner, "Newark Officials Under Inquiry," *New York Times*, December 19, 1969; and Thomas P. Ronan, "Blacks Drive for Mayoralty in Newark," *New York Times*, December 19, 1969.

21. L. H. Whitmore, *Together* (New York: Morrow, 1971).

22. Ron Rosenbaum, "Newark, First Real Test of the New Black Politics," *Village Voice*, April 16, 1970.

23. Woodard, *A Nation Within a Nation*, 148.

24. Ronald Sullivan, "Racism Issue Grows in Newark," *New York Times*, June 6, 1970.

25. Tex Novellino and Roger Harris, "Gibson, Addonizio in Run-off," *Star-Ledger*, May 13, 1970, 1.

26. Peter Bridge, "Gibson, Mayor Seek Votes Rivals Won," *Newark News*, May 14, 1970.

27. Addonizio Says Divisive Forces at Work in Newark," *Newark News*, May 8, 1970. *Newark News*, June 11, 1970.

28. John C. Waugh, "Tom Bradley's Non Partisan Bi-Partisan Campaign," *Black Politician* (October 1969): 9–11.

29. Douglas Eldridge, "Addonizio Charges Gibson is Front for Baraka," *Newark News*, June 4, 1970, 1.

30. Ibid.

31. Ronald Sullivan, "Newark Mayoral Contest Reaches a Bitter Climax," *New York Times*, June 14, 1970, 77.

32. Peter Bridge, "Gibson Wins by 12,000," *Newark News*, June 17, 1970, 1

33. Ibid.

34. Kenneth Gibson interview.

35. "Six New Members in City Council," *Newark News*, June 17, 1970, 8.

36. Kenneth Gibson interview.

37. Douglas Eldridge, "Voters Evenly Matched," *Newark News*, December 19, 1969. Estimate of black voters in Newark.

38. Bridge, "Gibson Wins by 12,000." In the North and West Wards, Councilman Giuliano outpolled Addonizio by 19,382 to 18,737 and 12,262 to 11,616 respectively. However, in the Central and South Wards, both overwhelmingly black, there was a sizable drop in the vote for black councilmen, compared to the Gibson vote. Thus, some white voters either cast ballots for Gibson and white council candidates or voted for white council candidates only. On the other hand, many black voters failed to vote for black council candidates. This is why black council candidates did not do as well as Gibson.

39. Bridge, "Gibson, Mayor Seek Votes."

40. Walter Waggoner, "Unity Behind a Vote-Getter Urged in Mayoral Race," *New York Times*, March 15, 1970.

41. Bridge, "Gibson wins by 12,000." Of the 101,230 (out of 133,000) registered voters who went to the polls; only 98,183 voted for mayor.

42. Edward Higgins, "Newsmen Attacked by Addonizio Backers," *Newark News*, June 17, 1970, 8.

43. Mamie Bridgeforth, interview by author, January 29, 2010.

6. THE ARRIVAL OF BLACK POWER

1. Robert Curvin, "The Persistent Minority" (Ph.D. diss., Princeton University, 1975). See also Phillip Thompson's excellent study of New York mayor David Dinkins's administration, *Double Trouble: Black Mayors, Black Communities, and the Call for a Deep Democracy* (New York: Oxford University Press, 2005).

2. U.S. Census 1970 and supplementary survey of distressed neighborhoods. The survey found that of 85,000 poor residents in Newark, 78 percent lived in low-income areas. About 30 percent of the residents of low-income areas were below the poverty level, compared to 11 percent of those living elsewhere. About 88 percent of the city's

blacks and 77 percent of poor Hispanics lived in low-income areas as compared to 48 percent for non-Spanish whites who were poor.

3. Carl B. Stokes, *Promises of Power: A Political Autobiography* (New York: Simon and Schuster, 1973), 272.

4. Quoted in Kenneth G. Weinberg, *Carl Stokes and the Winning of Cleveland* (Chicago: Quadrangle Books, 1968).

5. Ira Jackson, former aide to Kenneth Gibson, interview by author, Newark, New Jersey, May 8, 1971.

6. Kenneth Gibson interview.

7. Joseph Sullivan, "U.S. Jury Studying Gibson's Finances," *New York Times*, October 1, 1979; Leslie Maitland, "Trial Reveals Refusal to Indict Gibson for Tax Fraud," *New York Times*, January 25, 1981; Maitland, "U.S. Prosecutor Finds No Crime in Gibson Taxes," *New York Times*, April 11, 1981; Maitland, "Con Man in White Hat," review of *The Sting Man Inside Abscam*, by Robert W. Greene (New York: E. P. Dutton, 1981), *New York Times* Sunday Book Review, June 7, 1981.

8. David K. Shipler, "Gibson Finds Corruption Exceeds His Fears," *New York Times*, September 20, 1970, 168.

9. Craig Montouri, "Study It, Live It, and Love It: Why Do Very Few Engineers Enter Politics?," www.quora.com, September 26, 2012.

10. Robert Lane, *Political Life* (New York: Free Press, 1959), 163.

11. Eric Richard, "The Mayor's Office: Its Intra Politics in Newark, NJ" (paper submitted for Politics 310, Princeton University, December 1971).

12. Fox Butterfield, "Gibson Is Widely Considered Successful in Restoring Integrity to City Hall," *New York Times*, October 3, 1971.

13. Ira Jackson interview.

14. Eric Richard, interview by author, Newark, New Jersey, June 1972.

15. Ira Jackson interview.

16. Adubato interview, October 22, 2009.

17. Peter D. Dixon, "The Sources of Italian Politics, the North Ward of Newark" (senior thesis, Princeton University, 1973). Quote from the *Philadelphia Inquirer*, February 2, 1972.

18. Dixon, "The Sources of Italian Politics," 80.

19. Ibid., 102–103.

20. Convissor interview.

21. Marge McCullen, "The Newark City Council: Finding Itself," *Newark*, May/June 1971, 45.

22. Nathaniel Sheppard, "Gibson Says Political Rivals Plotted Clash," *New York Times*, August 17, 1973.

23. Ronald Smothers, "Gibson Denounces Protesting Group," *New York Times*, August 21, 1973.

24. A *New York Times* editorial commenting on the conviction and sentencing of Mayor Addonizio noted that the "legacy that official looters have left to Gibson is sad and grim. . . . The books in Newark for years have been audited by an accounting firm employed by the reputed head of organized crime in the city, a man who was indicted with the former mayor. . . . Gibson's sensible effort to subject the city's books to an independent review has been blocked by a backward council which pleads inadequate funds for the project while simultaneously providing a new $6,100 automobile for one

of its own members." "Public Office, Public Trust," *New York Times*, September 26, 1970.

25. Irving Solondz, conversation with author, Newark, New Jersey, October 2008.

26. William B. Gwyn, "The Failure of the Newark Ombudsman" (Ombudsman Activities Project, Santa Barbara, California, University of California, 1973).

27. Joseph Sullivan, "Gibson Assails City Council in Newark," *New York Times*, January 7, 1972, 10.

28. Black councilmen often expressed the black community's resentment of Gibson's white aides and the high number of officials from outside of the city. See "Gibson Attacked for Having Out-of-State Aides," *Star-Ledger*, October 12, 1972.

29. *Information*, August 21, 1972. Published by the City of Newark. Publication ended in 1979. The complete set of twenty issues is in the personal files of Douglas Eldridge, who served as the organ's editor. Douglas Eldridge, interview by author, October 14, 2013.

30. "Gibson Fights Back at Council," *Star-Ledger*, December 30, 1972.

31. Joseph Sullivan, "Gibson and Council Compromise on Newark Model Cities Funds," *New York Times*, February 16, 1972.

32. The Vailsburg conflict was characteristic of Newark's racial polarization at the time. Black students had demanded the removal of a black administrator who they alleged was harsh and punitive toward black students. White students demonstrated and boycotted in support of the black administrator. "Council Asks State to Investigate Vailsburg Conflict," *Star-Ledger*, February 8, 1973.

33. Elton Hill, interview and conversation, Newark, New Jersey, 1972

34. "Gibson Yields to U.S. on PEP Cash, Firings," *Star-Ledger*, June 13, 1973.

35. "Newark Council, in a Raucous Session, Votes to Keep Turco Despite Guilty Plea," *New York Times*, October 20, 1973.

36. "Council Committee Seeks Gibson and Harris Recall," *Star-Ledger*, December 30, 1972.

37. "Newark Council, in a Raucous Session, Votes to Keep Turco Despite Guilty Plea." Councilman Turco had pleaded guilty to income tax evasion charges; five white council members voted against a motion to remove him.

38. "Council Debate Ends in Violence," *Star-Ledger*, March 3, 1972.

39. Walter Waggoner, "75 Invade Office of Mayor Gibson," *New York Times*, March 24, 1976; "Carrino Fined in Invasion of Mayor Gibson's Office," *New York Times*, June 17, 1976.

40. *Jet* magazine, October 15, 1970.

41. Komozi Woodard, *A Nation Within a Nation* (Chapel Hill: University of North Carolina Press, 1999), 72. Ron Karenga was a mentor to Baraka and his organization. Karenga's philosophy and teaching shaped much of Baraka's approach to politics. Woodard provides an illuminating narrative on the relationship of the two leading cultural nationalists. Baraka eventually abandoned black nationalism for Marxism, and said that "nationalism, no matter how justified, was not justifiable." See *The Autobiography of LeRoi Jones* (New York: Freundich Books, 1984).

42. Kenneth Gibson interview.

43. Joseph Sullivan, "Gibson Called a 'Puppet' by Baraka in Open Split," *New York Times*, August 18, 1973.

44. Jones, *Autobiography of LeRoi Jones*, 302. See also Woodard, *A Nation Within a Nation*, 244–255.

45. Woodard, *A Nation Within a Nation*, 249.

46. Tex Novellino and Stanley Terrell, "Baraka and Six Are Arrested at Council Meeting," *Star-Ledger*, February 6, 1975, 16. Also see Woodard, *A Nation Within a Nation*, 250–255.

47. Woodard, *A Nation Within a Nation*. While the episode divided the already damaged coalition of forces that had merged for the Black and Puerto Rican Convention, it did not diminish the significance of race in the political arena. Race continues to matter in daily political organizing and decision making. There is no postracial politics in Newark. The weight of various factions has surely changed. The most critical levers of power are in business, the university, and the major civic institutions. With few exceptions, they are dominated by whites, with blacks in secondary or tertiary positions.

48. Steve Golin, *The Newark Teacher Strikes: Hope on the Line* (New Brunswick, NJ: Rutgers University Press, 2006); Robert Braun, *Teachers and Power* (New York: Simon and Schuster, 1972).

49. For an excellent review of the state of education in the Newark school district, see Paul L. Tractenberg, "Pupil Performance in Basic Skills in the Newark School System since 1967," in *Newark, 1967–1977, an Assessment*, ed. Stanley B. Winters (Newark: New Jersey Institute of Technology, 1978). Also see Jean Anyon, *Ghetto Schooling* (New York: Teachers College Press, 1996).

50. Golin, *Newark Teacher Strikes*, 110.

51. Ibid., 102. M. A. Farber, "Teachers Ratify Pact in Newark," *New York Times*, February 26, 1970.

52. Golin, *Newark Teacher Strikes*, 144.

53. Ibid., 142.

54. Ibid., 170. See chapter 2 for discussion of Coggins's role in the election of Irvine Turner.

55. Golin, *Newark Teacher Strikes*, 177.

56. Ibid.

57. Ibid.

58. Larry Hamm, former student leader and organizer, leader of People's Organization for Progress, interview by author, April 12, 2012.

59. Fox Butterfield, "Newark School Strike Ends as Gibson Plan Is Backed," *New York Times*, April 19, 1971.

60. Ibid.

61. Olga Weigenheim, Keynote Address, on the 25th Anniversary of the 1974 Puerto Rican Riots in Newark, New Jersey, October 14, 1999. Archive and oral history of the Puerto Rican riots is available at the Puerto Rican Archives Project, Newark Public Library.

62. Ibid., 3.

63. Kenneth A. Gibson, interview by Cassandra M. Katner, March 22, 2000.

64. Ibid.

65. Sigredo Carrion, interview by Hildegarde Rivera for Oral History Project, March 21, 2000.

66. Ibid.

67. Ibid.

68. Weigenheim address.

69. Alfonso Narvaez, "Some Link Rioting to Chronic Neglect," *New York Times*, September 4, 1974.

70. Ibid.

71. Kenneth Gibson interview by Katner, 8.

72. Carrion interview.

73. Richard Coniff, "Incidents Strike Fear into Hearts of Newark Residents," *Star-Ledger*, September 4, 1974, 7.

74. Ibid.

75. Alfonso A. Narvaez, "Some Link Rioting to Chronic Neglect," *New York Times*, September 4, 1970.

76. Douglas Eldridge, "Black Convention Shows Its Worth," *Newark News*, May 14, 1970, 1.

77. Hilda Hidalgo's letter to Kenneth Gibson, copied to Gus Heningburg and Robert Curvin, author's files.

78. "Hispanic Leaders Won't Back Gibson in County Exec Race," *Star-Ledger*, April 10, 1988.

79. Junius Williams, interview by author, Newark, New Jersey, November 13, 2010. Williams was the key organizer for the medical school fight and had been an SDS organizer when he came to Newark in 1965.

80. Curvin, "The Persistent Minority," 230.

81. Dennis Sullivan, former aide to Gibson, interview by author, New York City, April 14, 2011.

82. Paul Hoffman with Ira Pecznick, *To Drop a Dime* (New York: G. P. Putnam's Sons, 1976).

83. Joan Cook, "Bomb Explodes Near the Home of Gibson, But No Tie Is Seen," *New York Times*, July 27, 1974.

84. Adubato interview, May 26, 2011.

85. Elton Hill interview.

86. Thomas A. Johnson, "Gibson Ministers to Newark's Needs with Large Amounts of Federal Aid," *New York Times*, February 23, 1976.

87. Ibid.

88. Walter Waggoner, "Newark Program to Aid House Repairs," *New York Times*, June 26, 1976.

89. Memorandum from Thomas A. Banker, Assistant Business Administrator, to Elton Hill, Business Administrator: "Economy Measures 1975–1980," March 24, 1980, copy in author's files.

90. Kenneth Gibson interview, March 5, 2009.

91. Theodore Pinckney, interview by author, Newark, New Jersey, July 13, 2010.

92. Gus Heningburg, interview by author, March 12, 2008.

93. Al Koeppe, interview by author, Newark, New Jersey, March 10, 2012.

94. Joseph Sullivan, "Gibson Loses Bid for a Fifth Turn," *New York Times*, May 14, 1986.

95. Ronald Smothers, "Ex-Newark Mayor Seeks to Pioneer as County Executive," *New York Times*, April 14, 1998.

96. Ronald Smothers, "Mistrial for Ex-Mayor of Newark," *New York Times*, November 29, 2001.

97. "Kenneth Gibson, Former Mayor of Newark, Pleads Guilty to One Count of a 17-Count Indictment, Ending Seven-Year Federal Case; Gibson and Co-Defendant Receive Non-Custodial Sentence of Probation from U.S. District Judge," thefreelibrary

.com, October 31, 2002; Ronald Smothers, "Newark's Ex-Mayor Admits Tax Evasion and Avoids Prison," *New York Times*, November 1, 2002.

7. THE DANCING MAYOR

1. In 1970, Sharpe James, who had run with the Black and Puerto Rican slate, made it into the runoff against Leon Ewing, who held the position after the white councilman, Lee Bernstein, was ousted by a recall vote. Gibson did not want to take sides in the runoff because he wanted the votes of Ewing's backers as well as those who supported James.

2. Paul Horvitz, "In Newark, a New Style Takes Over," Philly.Com, May 15, 1986; Daniel Walker, "Newark Mayor Loses Bid for Fifth Term," Associated Press, apnews archive.com, May 14, 1986.

3. "James Stresses Revitalization, Boosts Goals of Collaboration Group," *Star-Ledger*, June 11, 1986.

4. Sharpe James oral history for the Krueger-Scott Cultural Center, African-American Oral History Project, interviews by Glen Marie Brickus, December 3, 1996, and December 17, 1996, available through Newark Archives at Rutgers Newark (three discs). See chapter 3 for discussion of organizations of Newark antipoverty program and role of area boards.

5. John McLaughlin, "In the Face of Blistering Bluster from James, Byrne Retreats," *Star-Ledger*, August 17, 2000, 17.

6. Angela Stewart, "Newark Mayor-Elect Orders Checks to Avoid Scandal in Top Level Posts," *Star-Ledger*, June 20, 1986.

7. Alfonso Narvaez, "Mayor James Brings Air of Optimism," *New York Times*, October 3, 1986.

8. Adrienne Fox, "James 'Report Card' Shows High Marks," *Star Ledger*, April 20, 1990.

9. A federal lawsuit was filed against the Newark Housing Authority by tenants of public housing (represented by Legal Services) to prevent the authority from demolishing public housing without replacing it. The matter was heard by District Judge Dickinson Debevoise and was settled in an agreement that required the NHA to replace each demolished unit with new housing. The court appointed Gustav Heningburg to oversee the implementation of the court's agreement.

10. Alfonso Narvaez, "100 Days in Newark, Mayor James Brings Optimism," *New York Times*, October 6, 1986.

11. Judith Miller, "A Self-Made Man Takes On Newark: Shy Philanthropist Gives His Time and Money to New Arts Center," *New York Times*, October 14, 1997.

12. I met Larry Goldman during the 1970 Gibson campaign, and it was he who introduced me to Professor Duane Lockard at Princeton University. Lockard was instrumental in persuading me to attend Princeton for graduate studies; he became my mentor and thesis advisor while I worked toward a Ph.D. in the Politics Department.

13. Jeffrey C. Mays, "James Applauded for His Role in the Arts," *Star-Ledger*, June 16, 2002, 34.

14. Bruce Locklin, "Newark Mayor Urged Tax Break for Contributors," *Bergen Record*, December 4, 1994.

15. Neil McFarquhar, "Raids Yield $100,000 In Newark," *New York Times*, Novem-

ber 11, 1995; John Sullivan, "Mayor's Aide in Newark Is Indicted," *New York Times*, January 26, 1996; Ronald Smothers, "Ex-Official in Newark Is Convicted," *New York Times*, March 22, 1997.

16. Clifford Levy, "Vote Panel Cites Mayor of Newark," *New York Times*, February 22, 1995.

17. Ibid.

18. Marian Courtney, "Coping with 'Crisis Times' for Cities," *New York Times*, December 26, 1993.

19. Nearly one-third of New Jersey's legislators hold another elected office that is funded by the public, an arrangement that most states prohibit. Local officials commonly hold county jobs, and in some cases legislators also serve as teachers and school officials. For example, a member of the city council in Newark is a high school principal and serves as chair of the city council's education committee. Governor Jon Corzine signed legislation to ban double office holding effective in 2008. However, those who already held two elected positions were grandfathered in. See Politickernj.com on dual officeholding.

20. Ronald Smothers, "Newark Mayor Wins Vote, Defeating 2 for 4th Term," *New York Times*, May 13, 1998.

21. McLaughlin, "In the Face of Blistering Bluster from James, Byrne Retreats."

22. Andrew Zimbalist and Roger Noll, eds., *Sports, Jobs, and Taxes: Are New Stadiums Worth the Cost?* (Washington, DC: Brookings Institution, 1997).

23. Jeffrey C. Mays, "Project Price Tag Nears $500m," *Star-Ledger*, October 15, 2007.

24. Jeffrey C. Mays, "Mayor Appoints Commission to Study Arena Proposal," *Star-Ledger*, October 15, 2007.

25. Clifford Goldman, a consultant and former New Jersey state treasurer, fashioned the Port Authority contribution. The Port Authority wanted to avoid making a direct payment to the City of Newark so the payment was made to the State of New Jersey and then passed to the Newark Housing Authority, which nominally became the developer of the arena. Cliff Goldman, interview by author, Princeton, New Jersey, November 11, 2010.

26. Sarah Portlock, "New Newark Businesses to Sprout Up in the Rock's Shadow," *Star-Ledger*, March 28, 2011.

27. "The Business of Hockey," Forbes.com, November 11, 2009.

28. Adam M. Zaretsky, "Should Cities Pay for Sports Facilities?" Regional Economist, Federal Reserve Bank of St. Louis, stlouisfed.org, April 2001.

29. Brendan O'Flaherty, "Newark's Non-Renaissance and Beyond," February 13, 2000, New Jersey Room of the Newark Public Library, files.

30. See chapter 3, in which Sam Convissor, former employee of Newark Chamber of Commerce, recalled how Chamber executives drafted the Fox-Lance legislation.

31. O'Flaherty, "Newark's Non-Renaissance and Beyond," 13.

32. Ibid., 14. Todd Swanstrom, in his study of development in Cleveland, wrote: "Central cities have a strong market position with regard to certain forms of economic activity; they need not approach the bargaining table with hat in hand. The reason for this is that not all economic activity is hypermobile. While there are deep centrifugal forces in the economy dispersing manufacturing and routine back office service sectors, at the same time there are deep centripetal forces pushing certain forms of service activity into central business districts." *Crisis of Growth Politics: Cleveland, Kucinich, and the Challenge of Urban Populism* (Philadelphia: Temple University Press, 1988), 237.

33. O'Flaherty, "Newark's Non-Renaissance and Beyond," 13

34. Jeffrey Mays, "No One's Home: Newark and Builder at Odds over Housing Project," *Star-Ledger*, July 6, 2006.

35. Andrew Jacobs, "Victory with a Vengeance," *New York Times*, November 27, 2002.

36. Ibid.

37. Damien Cave, "After 5 Terms as Newark Mayor, James Opts Not to Run Again," *New York Times*, March 28, 2006. It was soon announced that Mayor James would return to Essex County Community College to head a new institute on urban affairs. His salary of $150,000 per year would be paid through a donation from the philanthropist Raymond Chambers, perhaps an act of gratitude for James's role for financing the new home for the New Jersey Devils in Newark, or an inducement to get James out of the way for Cory Booker, who looked to Chambers as a counselor and strong supporter.

38. "Sharpe James Indicted on 33 Counts of Corruption," Politicker NJ.com, July 12, 2007.

39. Bob Braun, "Competing Arguments in Sharpe James Trial," *Star-Ledger*, April 9, 2008.

40. "Sharpe James Convicted," *Star-Ledger*, December 8, 2009.

41. Bob Braun, "A Judge Who Chafed at the Advice He Got," *Star-Ledger*, July 30, 2008.

42. Robert Curvin to Sharpe James, August 18, 2009.

43. Sharpe James, reply to Robert Curvin, August 31, 2009.

44. Jeffrey Mays, "Newark Council Tab Dwarfs Other Cities," *Star-Ledger*, April 10, 2005.

45. "Councilman Tucker Blasts James in Election Preview," *Star-Ledger*, February 6, 1997, 37.

46. Sharpe James, "Let's Provide Leadership for New Ideas, New Opportunities" (address to National League of Cities), *National Cities Weekly*, December 12, 1994, www.nic.org.

8. BLACK MAYOR ON A WHITE HORSE

1. Ryan Hutchins, "It's Official: Cory Booker Announces Candidacy for U.S. Senate," *Star-Ledger*, June 8, 2013.

2. David Giambusso, "Cory Booker Makes History As He Defeats Steve Lonegan in U.S. Senate Election," *Star-Ledger*, October 17, 2013; also Politico, "New Jersey Special Election Results 2013—Map, County Results Live Updates," www.politico.com/2013-election/results/senate/new-jersey.

3. Interview of Cory Booker by Oprah Winfrey, *Oprah's Next Chapter* @OwnTV #Next Chapter, May 27, 2012.

4. Corey Booker, interview by author, Newark, New Jersey, March 2011.

5. Peter Shafer and Mark R. Cohen, eds., *Toward the Millennium: Messianic Expectations from the Bible to Waco* (Leiden: Brill, 1998).

6. Nakita Stewart, "A Man on a Mission: Cory Booker," *Star-Ledger*, October 3, 2000.

7. Booker interview by author.

8. Greater Talent website, www.greatertalent.com.

9. A good number of Mayor Booker's speeches are available on YouTube. See also Nan Hu, "Newark Mayor Calls for American Unity," *Princetonian*, October 2, 2008.

10. Judith Miller, "A Self-Made Man Takes On Newark," *New York Times*, October 14, 1997.

11. Booker made this comment at a dinner hosted by Ray Chambers at Le Bernardin, a restaurant in New York City, to discuss plans for a visit by the Dalai Lama to Newark. At other times, Booker made claims that it was the late Virginia Jones, an elderly lady who headed the tenant's association in Brick Towers, Booker's former place of residence, who pushed him into politics.

12. "A Newark Councilman Is Charged with Graft," *New York Times*, May 18, 1988.

13. Stewart, "A Man on a Mission: Cory Booker."

14. Rahaman Muhammad, president of the Newark local 617 of the Service Employees International Union, interview by author, Newark, New Jersey, February 10, 2011. Mr. Muhammad is also a member of the New Jersey State executive board of the AFL-CIO. Interview by author, Newark, New Jersey, April 2010, and Darrin Sharif, interview by author, Newark, New Jersey, May 2010.

15. Jeffery Mays and Katie Wang, "For Booker, Often Told Tales Turn into Trouble," *Star-Ledger*, August 6, 2007. See also Scott Raab, "The Battle of Newark, Starring Cory Booker," *Esquire*, July 1, 2008. Booker said: "T-Bone is an archetype of an aspect of Newark's woe . . . he's a real person, 1000 percent." Professor Clement Price responds, "Of all the creations you're gonna come up with to depict Newark, why this guy? Why contribute to that mythology?" It was not lost on the residents of Newark that in the movie *Colors*, a gang character played by Damon Wayans was named T-Bone. In 2013, in a statement to the *Star-Ledger*, Professor Price said that Mayor Booker confessed to him that he had made up the T-Bone story. See David Giambusso, "The Tale of T-Bone: Cory Booker's Past Statements Haunt Him on Campaign Trail," *Star-Ledger*, August 29, 2013.

16. David Giambusso, "Cory Booker Recounts Risking His Life in a Dramatic Fire Rescue of Newark Neighbor," *Star-Ledger*, April 4, 2012.

17. Ron Smothers, "With Usual Flourish, Sharpe James Pulls Curtain on a Career and an Era in Newark," *New York Times*, April 11, 2007. James announced that he had quit the race and would set up an urban studies center at Essex County College. The new center was to be partly financed by Raymond Chambers.

18. Jeffrey Mays, "Newark Mayor Asks Advice on Deputy's Job," *Star-Ledger*, January 5, 2005.

19. Bruno Tedeschi, "Newark Mayor Cory Booker, Taking Oath of Office, Urges City Forward," *Star-Ledger*, July 2, 2006.

20. Ron Smothers, "Booker Has 100 Day Plan for Newark Reorganization," *New York Times*, July 11, 2006; "Mayor Booker Launches Massive Ethics Reform for Newark Municipal Government Employees," *U.S. Federal News Service*, November 1, 2006.

21. Joe Ryan, "Former Aide to Newark Mayor Cory Booker Is Indicted on Extortion, Corruption Charges," *Star-Ledger*, March 4, 2010.

22. Ted Pinckney interview, July 13, 2010; Rahaman Muhammad interview, and Amiri Baraka interview, May 11, 2009; all interviews by author, Newark, New Jersey.

23. Gaby Wood, "The Next President of America?" *London Observer*, February 9, 2009.

24. Kathe Newman, "Geographics of Mortgage Market Segmentation: The Case of Essex County," *New Jersey, Housing Studies* 19, no. 1 (2004).

25. Kareem Fahim, "To Starbucks, a Closing; To Newark, a Trauma," *New York Times*, July 23, 2008.

26. Andrew Jacobs, "Newark's Mayor Battles Old Guard and Rumors," *New York Times*, July 3, 2007.

27. Katie Wang and Jeffrey C. Mays, "Newark Mayor Cory Booker's First Year a Wearying Journey," *Star-Ledger*, January 18, 2008.

28. Carl Sharif, interview by author, Newark, New Jersey, February 2012.

29. Daniel Gibson, interview by author, Newark, New Jersey, February 27, 2012.

30. David Giambusso, "Newark Middle Class Is Overshadowed by Brick City Documentary," *Star-Ledger*, October 16, 2009.

31. Marc Levin, film producer, interview by author, New York, October 26, 2009.

32. See www.greatertalent.com. I have no evidence to suggest there was deception in this matter or that it was staged; it did however illustrate another example of Booker's use of celebrity and his knack for courting the media.

33. "City of Newark Receives Second 'Shorty' Award for Mayor's Twitter Feed," *Local Talk Weekly*, March 31–April 6, 2011.

34. Bruno Tedeschi, "Newark Mayor Apologizes for Remarks at Summit Fundraiser," *Star-Ledger*, August 2, 2007.

35. Rahaman Muhammad interview.

36. Andrew Jacobs, "Booker Tries to Unseat Legislators, Dividing Party," *New York Times*, March 20, 2007.

37. Adubato interview, May 26, 2011.

38. Ibid.

39. Jeffrey Mays, "Booker Sees Slate of District Leaders Fall Short," *Star-Ledger*, June 5, 2008.

40. Jeffrey Mays, "Charles Bell Wins Newark Central Ward Seat," *Star-Ledger*, November 4, 2008.

41. Conversation with Ray Chambers at Robert Treat Hotel. See Josh Margolin, "Stephen Adubato and Cory Booker Bury the Hatchet," *Star-Ledger*, June 22, 2009. As Margolin makes clear, Adubato may have been bluffing about withdrawing support from Booker. Adubato always pushed for a better deal, more patronage, or more money for his programs. He admitted to Margolin that money was a factor in the renewed alliance.

42. Ted Sherman, "Oprah Winfrey Donates More Than $15 Million to Five Newark Nonprofits," *Star-Ledger*, February 1, 2009. Saint Benedict's Prep and Integrity House also received $500,000, and Newark Now and Apostle House, a women's shelter, received donations.

43. Richard Cammarieri, Newark activist, interview by author, Newark, New Jersey, April 2009; see also Brian Hohmann, "Adubato Agonistes: Stephen Adubato, White Ethnicity, and the (Re)Construction of Public Selfhood" (master's thesis, Rutgers University, 2010). See also, Rebecca Casciano, "'By Any Means Necessary': The American Welfare State and Machine Politics in Newark's North Ward" (Ph.D. diss., Princeton University, 2009).

44. Adubato interview, May 26, 2011.

45. Ted Sherman, "Essex County Prosecutor Clifford Minor Sentenced to Federal Prison for Jailhouse Plot," *Star-Ledger*, October 24, 2011. Minor was indicted in September 2010, less than six months after the election. He was charged with perjury, obstruction of justice, and falsification of records.

46. Rohan Mascarenhas, "Sharif Pulls Out Central Ward Council Victory by 11 Votes," *Star-Ledger*, June 17, 2010.

47. David Giambusso, "Newark Inauguration Speeches Signal Tense Relationship between Mayor Booker and Council," *Star-Ledger*, July 1, 2010.

48. Tom Moran, "Newark Mayor Booker Faces Worst Crisis of His Career after Council Dismisses MUA Proposal," *Star-Ledger*, August 8, 2010. This was an entirely unusual statement from Tom Moran, who, as head of the *Ledger* editorial board, provided strong support for all of Booker's policies.

49. Family Success Center website, newarkfamilysuccess.org; interview with John Welch, coordinator of Success Centers for Newark Now, March 29, 2010; also interview with center operator at New Community Family Success Center.

50. Family Success Center website, newarkfamilysuccess.org.

51. I attended this breakfast meeting of the Regional Business Alliance at NJPAC in September 2006.

52. Fonseca worked in the administration of Sharpe James as director of code enforcement; since Booker won a council seat in 1998, Fonseca has been at his side, either as an aide or as a key political advisor. The conversation was recounted to me by Carl Sharif, who had served as campaign manager of Booker's 2006 race, and remained for a while as an advisor to Booker.

53. New Jersey State Police Uniform Crime Report, www.njsp.org/info/stats/html.

54. Newark Police Director Garry McCarthy, interview by author, Newark, New Jersey, August 31, 2010.

55. Nate Schweber and Fernanda Santos, "Shooting of 4 College Friends Baffles Newark," *New York Times*, August 6, 2007; Alexi Friedman, "Chilling Details Emerge in Newark Schoolyard Murders, As Suspect Pleads Guilty," *Star-Ledger*, December 24, 2011.

56. Compstat is a policing tool that brings together top commanders to examine patterns of crime in specific geographic areas of the city. The officers use extensive data analysis and are pressed to explain and develop strategies to abate criminal activity. The approach was introduced in New York City by former commissioner William Bratton. McCarthy told me that prior to his arrival, the Newark police department was not using the approach effectively. He said, "There's Compstat, and there's Compstat!"

57. Sharon Adario, "Newark Police Department Graduates 115th Recruit Class," *Star-Ledger*, March, 2010.

58. New Jersey State Police Uniform Crime Statistics, www.njsp.org/info/stats.html.

59. Andra Gillespie, *The New Black Politician: Cory Booker, Newark, and Post-Racial America* (New York: NYU Press, 2011), 128.

60. New Jersey State Police Uniform Crime Statistics, www.njsp.org/info/stats.html; also East Orange Police Director Jose Cordero, interview by author, East Orange, New Jersey, November 3, 2010.

61. "American Civil Liberties Union Accuses Newark Police of False Arrests, Excessive Force," *Star-Ledger*, September 8, 2010. I am very thankful for several opportunities I had to meet with Deborah Jacobs, former executive director of New Jersey ACLU, regarding issues of justice in Newark and the petition filed seeking Department of Justice intervention in Newark.

62. "American Civil Liberties Union Accuses Newark Police of False Arrests, Excessive Force."

63. Ibid.; see also Politifact, New Jersey, *Star-Ledger*, June 22, 2011, which examined

the facts regarding Booker's claim that he opposed the ACLU request to the Justice Department because it asked for supervision of the NPD, without an investigation. Politifact concluded that Booker was wrong; the ACLU had indeed asked for an investigation first. See also Joshua M. Chanin, "Pattern or Practice Reform: Evidence from Four Police Departments" (paper delivered to the Public Management Research Conference, Columbus, Ohio, October 1–3, 2009). Since 1994, when the provision allowing the DOJ to monitor local police departments (a result of the Rodney King beating and subsequent riot in Watts, Los Angeles, in 1992) that had a record of continuous violation of the rights of citizens was written into law, New Orleans has been the only jurisdiction that invited DOJ intervention. All others resisted DOJ intervention, including Pittsburgh, Cincinnati, Washington, DC, and Prince Georges County, Maryland.

64. City of Newark, *Newark: A City In Transition*, vol. 2, book 1, "Residents' Views on Inter-Group Relations," March 1959, 97.

65. Dan O'Flaherty, "Newark Mayor Cory Booker's Water Plan Would Lead to Worse System," *Star-Ledger*, March 13, 2012; David Giambusso, "Municipal Authority Could Bring Millions to Newark," *Star-Ledger*, June 20, 2010; Giambusso, "Newark Mayor Cory Booker, Council Clash over Timeline of Municipal Utility Authority," *Star-Ledger*, July 14, 2010. Interview and conversations with Dr. Dan O'Flaherty, an authority on Newark's economic history and an advisor to the Newark Water Group, February 5, 2010.

66. Claire Henninger, "Newark Mayor Cory Booker Backs N.J. Governor Chris Christie's 2.5 Percent Tax Cap," *Star-Ledger*, June 21, 2010.

67. David Giambusso and James Queally, "Chaos Erupts at Newark City Hall Meeting," *Star-Ledger*, November 20, 2012; "Newark City Council Video Appears to Show Thuggery," *Star-Ledger*, editorial, November 21, 2012.

68. David Giambusso, "Judge Rules Cory Booker Did Not Have Authority to Vote for Open Newark Council Seat," *Star-Ledger*, December 11, 2012.

69. "Newark's Booker Lures Wall Street Millions to City Few Have Seen," *Bloomberg Markets Magazine*, October 3, 2012.

70. Elizabeth Dwoskin, "As Newark Rebuilds, Help from Beyond City Limits," *New York Times*, April 26, 2008.

71. Michael Powell, "Back Home, a Mayor's Sparkle Has Begun to Dim," *New York Times*, October 24, 2011.

72. William Julius Wilson, *The Bridge Over the Racial Divide: Rising Inequality and Coalition Politics* (Berkeley: University of California Press, 2001). Edward S. Glaude Jr., *In a Shade of Blue: Pragmatism and the Politics of Black America* (Chicago: University of Chicago Press, 2007).

73. Tim Wise, *Color Blind: The Rise of Post Racial Equality and the Retreat from Racial Equity* (Ann Arbor, MI: City Lights, 2010).

74. *Meet the Press*, NBC Television, May 20, 2012.

75. Martin Kilson, A Letter from Harvard: "How to Spot a Black Trojan Horse," *Black Commentator*, no. 2 (May 8, 2002), www.blackcommentator.comharvard.html.

76. Cory Booker, interview by by Bill Moyers, PBS website, March 28, 2008.

77. New Jersey Department of Community Affairs, "Performance Audit of the City of Newark," August 27, 2009. See page 15: Item 4 under Bid, Change Order, and Other Contract Findings: "The city has adopted an Executive Order (EO) (on pay to play) as promulgated by the mayor. . . . our testing revealed numerous violations of the Executive Order."

78. Editorial, "End Waste on the Website," *Star-Ledger*, October 9, 2008.

79. David Giambusso, "Newark Mayor Cory Booker's Nonprofit Charity Remains Go-To Market Place for City Contractors," *Star-Ledger*, September 18, 2011.

80. Ibid.

81. Matt Bai, "Papa Doesn't Preach," *New York Times Magazine*, April 7, 2011.

82. Richard Ben Cramer, "Can the Best Mayor Win?" cited in Jon C. Teaford, *The Rough Road to Renaissance* (Baltimore, MD: John Hopkins University Press, 1990), 256.

9. PITY THE CHILDREN

1. Deborah Yaffe, *Other People's Children* (New Brunswick, NJ: Rutgers University Press, 2007); Joanne E. Howard, *Abbott v. Burke: An Historical Analysis of School Finance Reform in New Jersey* (Saarbrucken, Germany: VDM Verlag Dr. Muller Aktiengesellschaft, 2008).

2. New Jersey Department of Education Website, "School Expenditures in 1982, 1990, 2000, 2009," www.state.nj.us/njded.

3. Newark Board of Education website, www.nps.k12.nj.us.

4. Advocates for Children of New Jersey, Newark, New Jersey, *Kids Count, 2002–2012*, 5. Abbott Leadership Institute DVD, author's files.

6. Jean Anyon, *Ghetto Schooling: A Political Economy of Urban Education Reform* (New York: Teachers College Press, 1997).

7. Ibid., 116.

8. Quay Whitlock, interview by author, Maplewood, New Jersey, February 28, 2011, and interview with Fred Means, Monroe, New Jersey, August 19, 2008.

9. New Jersey Commission on Civil Disorders, *Report for Action*, 1968, 75.

10. Michael Lipsky and David Olsen, *Riot Commission Politics* (Madison: Institute for Research on Poverty, University of Wisconsin, 1969).

11. Robert Curvin, "The Persistent Minority" (Ph.D. diss., Princeton University, 1975).

12. Robert Dahl, *Who Governs* (New Haven, CT: Yale University Press, 1961), 150.

13. Newark Board of Education minutes, 1974–1975, New Jersey Room, Newark Public Library.

14. Means interview.

15. Eugene Campbell, interview by author, Millburn, New Jersey, June 9, 2011.

16. Daniel Gibson interview by author, Newark, New Jersey, February 27, 2012, Means interview, and Campbell interview.

17. Daniel Gibson interview, and Donaldson interview.

18. Daniel Gibson, interview, 19. Stanley Terrell, "$660,000 Salley Buyout Ratified As Newark Board Gets Resignation," *Star-Ledger*, November 5, 1985, 1

20. "Newark Schools Upheld on Race," *New York Times*, August 15, 1969. Also see Anyon, *Ghetto Schooling*, 124–126, for discussion of hiring black administrators and NTU resistance.

21. Norman Eiger, "Newark School Wars" (Ed.D. diss., Rutgers University School of Education, 1976).

22. New Jersey State Commission on Investigation website, www.state.nj.us/sci/index.shtm.

23. Ibid.

24. NTU and CASA contracts with Newark Board of Education. Copies available at Newark Board of Education.

25. Yaffe, *Other People's Children*, 16 – 18.

26. Ibid., 275.

27. Ibid., 37 – 42.

28. Ibid., 179.

29. Richard Lehne, *The Quest for Justice: The Politics of School Finance Reform* (New York: Longman Publishing, 1978), 147 – 152.

30. Margaret Goertz, "Money and Education: Where Did the 400 Million Dollars Go? The Impact of the New Jersey Public School Education Act of 1975" (Washington, DC: Education Testing Service, 1978), 2.

31. Yaffe, *Other People's Children*, 110, 145; Education Law Center website, www .edlawcenter.org.

32. Block interview.

33. Yaffe, *Other People's Children*, 98.

34. Ibid.

35. Victor DeLuca, interview by Beth Cohen by phone, August 2011. Also, Alphonso Narvaez, "Newark Schools Open with Change in Leadership," *New York Times*, September 6, 1984.

36. Marcia Brown, "All About People United For Public Schools" (presentation to Abbott Leadership Institute at Rutgers Newark, January 24, 2009); Marcia Brown, interview by author, Newark, New Jersey, April 20, 2010.

37. Marcia Brown presentation.

38. According to Carl Sharif, Adubato was not in the coalition until it became clear that the group needed the vote of Eleanor George to dismiss Superintendent Columbus Salley. Eleanor George was a member of the school board and an employee of Adubato's North Ward Center. Sharif interview.

39. Barbara Kukla, "School Board Starts Putting the Brakes on Members' Expense Accounts," *Star-Ledger*, February 4, 1985.

40. Robert J. Braun, "Officials Shocked by New Newark Teachers Contract," *Star-Ledger*, August 18, 1985.

41. Ibid.

42. Donaldson, interview, Daniel Gibson interview, December 2012; and Means interview. See also "School Official Admits Guilt in Bribery Case," *New York Times*, January 24, 1989.

43. Donaldson interview.

44. New Jersey Department of Education, Comprehensive Compliance Investigation [CCI] Report, Newark School District, vol. 1, July 1994, 3 – 4; Mary McGrath, "Battle Lines Set for Takeover of Newark Schools," *Bergen Record*, July 23, 1994. See also Kimberly J. McLarin, "New Jersey Prepares a Takeover of Newark's Desperate Schools," *New York Times*, July 23, 1994.

45. CCI Report, 5.

46. Ibid., 2.

47. Ibid., 10.

48. Rebecca Doggett, interview by author, East Orange, New Jersey, October 17, 2008.

49. Ana M. Alaya, "Newark School Chief Leaves a Daunting Mission Unfinished," *Star-Ledger*, June 20, 1999.

50. Ibid. In April 2013, Beverly Hall and thirty employees of the Atlanta Board of Education were indicted for fraud following a several-year investigation into cheating on tests. The Georgia attorney general said that a conspiracy operated involving many people who systematically changed the answers on tests after the students had completed the tests. Bail for Hall was set at $1.5 million.

51. Marion Bolden, interview by author, West Orange, New Jersey, March 1, 2011.

52. Gordon MacInnes, deputy superintendent for Abbott districts, interview by author, Millburn, New Jersey, March 3, 2011.

53. Bolden interview.

54. Kasi K. Addison, "Departing Newark School Chief Always Put Kids First," *Star-Ledger*, June 29, 2008.

55. Bolden interview.

56. I was present at the meeting at Metropolitan Baptist Church when Janey was introduced by Governor Corzine.

57. Clifford Janey, interview by author, East Newark, New Jersey, December 2, 2010.

58. Doggett interview.

59. Paul L. Tractenberg and Alan R. Sadovnik, *Governance and Urban School Improvement: Lessons for New Jersey from Nine Cities* (Institute on Education Law and Policy, Rutgers University, September 2010).

60. *Time* magazine issue of April 21, 2011, announcing 100 most influential people in the world. Winfrey wrote the essay on Newark mayor Cory Booker in which she said that Booker is a genius and his intelligence is only surpassed by his heart.

61. David Giambusso and Jessica Calefati, "Academics Say $1M Newark Reform Survey Was Inconclusive," *Star-Ledger*, December 30, 2010. Also "PENewark Outreach to Reform Newark Schools Is a Waste of Time, Money, Critics Say," *Star-Ledger*, November 12, 2010.

62. Joan Whitlow, "It's Facebook Money and Newark's Future," *Star-Ledger*, October 7, 2011.

63. Jenna Portnoy, "Cory Booker Releases Secret Emails on $100m Facebook Gift to Newark Schools," *Star-Ledger*, December 25, 2012. E-mails released per court order.

64. Ross Danis, "Finding Newark Schools Millions: Opinion," *Star-Ledger*, March 20, 2013.

65. Summary of Newark Teachers Union contract with NPS; Kelly Heyboer, "Newark Teachers Strike Historic Deal Including Bonuses for Top Educators," *Star-Ledger*, October 24, 2012; confidential interview.

66. Global Education Advisors [consultants], "Newark Public Schools: School Placement Decision Support Analysis," Newark Board of Education, February 8, 2011.

67. David Giambusso and Jessica Calefati, "Acting N.J. Education Chief Founded Consulting Firm Hired to Overhaul Failing Newark Schools," *Star-Ledger*, February 23, 2011.

68. Jessica Calefati, "Sen. Ron Rice Vows to Block Christopher Cerf's Confirmation As Next N.J. Education Chief," *Star-Ledger*, March 11, 2011.

69. Robert Curvin, "Cami Anderson Is the White Lady from Harlem," *Star-Ledger*, May 8, 2011.

70. Tractenberg and Sadovnik, *Governance and Urban School Improvement*.

71. Francis A. Campbell, Craig T. Ramey, Elizabeth Pungello, Joseph Sparling, and Shari Miller-Johnson, "Early Childhood Education: Young Adult Outcomes from the Abecedarian Project," *Applied Developmental Science* 6, no. 1 (2002): 42–47.

72. C. Theodore Pinckney, "A Case Study of State Intervention in the Newark, New Jersey Public Schools: A Contrarian Response" (Ed.D. diss., University of Sarasota, Florida, 1997).

CONCLUSION

1. Milton Honig, "Slum Elimination in Newark Urged," *New York Times*, November 13, 1957; John T. Cunningham, *Newark*, rev. ed. (Newark: New Jersey Historical Society, 1988), 307.

2. Don Dust, "A Close-Up Look at Newark," *Newark!*, 1975, 17.

3. Regional Plan Association, "New Jersey Improving," 1978, 4.

4. Ibid.

5. T. D. Allman, "Newark, 1979," *New Jersey Monthly*, January 1979.

6. Stephen Levy, "The Wanderer Gets Off at Exit 14," *New Jersey Monthly* (January 1979).

7. Richard P. Nathan and Charles F. Adams Jr., "Four Perspectives on Urban Hardship," *Political Science Quarterly* 91, no. 1 (spring 1976): 47–62.

8. Alex Plinio, interview by author, Newark, New Jersey, December 22, 2011. See also American Leadership Forum, "The Newark Collaboration Group," Fall 1991.

9. Plinio interview.

10. Corporate officials provide leadership in many ways, but it is unusual for high-level executives in Newark to directly and openly engage with the community. Arthur Ryan, a recently retired chief executive officer of Prudential Financial, was an exception. He and his wife, Pat, could be seen regularly participating in several endeavors in Newark, particularly the New Jersey Performing Arts Center and the Branch Brook Park Alliance (BBPA), for which he would show up on volunteer day in his jeans to help mulch trees. Art and his wife also made a $1 million contribution to the BBPA.

11. "James Stresses Revitalization, Boosts Goals of Collaboration," *Star-Ledger*, June 11, 1986.

12. Proposition 13 (People's Initiative to Limit Property Taxation), an amendment to the state constitution of California enacted in 1978 by means of the initiative process, affected the public's thinking about taxes throughout the nation. The proposition decreased property taxes by assessing property values at their 1975 value and restricted annual increases of real property to a percent or less. Passage of the initiative has been credited with strengthening the "taxpayer revolt" throughout the country. See Arthur O'Sullivan, Terri Sexton, and Steven M. Schifrin, *Property Taxes and Tax Revolts: The Legacy of Proposition 13* (Cambridge: Cambridge University Press, 1995).

13. "Census 2010: Gains and Losses in Congress," *New York Times*, December 21, 2010.

14. Michelle Alexander, *The New Jim Crow* (New York: The New Press, 2010), 204.

15. Newark City Budget, 2010.

16. Nelida Valentin, Executive Director of Newark Workforce Incentive Board (WIB), interview by author, Newark, New Jersey, December 27, 2011.

17. John Kania and Mark Kramer, "Collective Impact," *Stanford Social Innovation Review* 56 (Winter 2011).

18. Bayard Rustin, "From Protest to Politics," in *Black Protest Thought in the Twentieth Century*, 2nd ed., ed. August Meier, Elliott Rudwick, and Francis L Broderick (Indianapolis: Bobbs-Merrill, 1971), 452–453.

19. When Ron Rice Sr. was a member of the city council, he installed a police radio in his automobile. One day he heard notice of a police chase that was occurring in his West Ward; suddenly the police dispatcher announced that another chase was under way in the North Ward. The policemen in the West Ward then announced that they were abandoning their chase to join the chase in the North Ward. Councilman Rice complained about the incident at a council meeting, but there was no evidence that the police department began to view a police action in the West Ward as important as one in the North Ward.

Index

About the Author

ROBERT CURVIN is a Distinguished Visiting Fellow at the Edward J. Bloustein School of Planning and Public Policy at Rutgers University. He was a co-founder of the Newark-Essex Chapter of the Congress of Racial Equality (CORE), which was at the vanguard of the civil rights movement in New Jersey during the 1960s.